HBJ
LANGUAGE

4

Dorothy S. Strickland
Richard F. Abrahamson
Roger C. Farr
Nancy R. McGee
Nancy L. Roser

4

Karen S. Kutiper
Patricia Smith

HBJ
LANGUAGE

 HARCOURT BRACE JOVANOVICH, PUBLISHERS
Orlando   San Diego   Chicago   Dallas

Acknowledgments

For permission to reprint copyrighted material, grateful acknowledgment is made to the following sources:

Laura Cecil, on behalf of The James Reeves Estate: From "Shiny" in *The Wandering Moon* by James Reeves. © by James Reeves.

Clarion Books/Ticknor & Fields, a Houghton Mifflin Company: Text and illustrations from pp. 29–32 in *Fireworks, Picnics, and Flags* by James Cross Giblin. Text copyright © 1983 by James Cross Giblin. Illustrations copyright © 1983 by Ursula Arndt.

Doubleday, a division of Bantam, Doubleday, Dell Publishing Group, Inc.: *Alfalfa Hill* by Peter Parnall. Copyright © 1975 by Peter Parnall. From "Dinky" in *The Collected Poems of Theodore Roethke* by Theodore Roethke. Copyright © 1953 by Theodore Roethke. From pp. 71–72 in *Laura's Luck* by Marilyn Sachs. Copyright © 1965 by Marilyn Sachs.

GCT Inc., P.O. Box 6448, Mobile, AL 36660-0448: From "Memories" by Kimberly Freeman in *Creative Kids* Magazine, February 1988.

David R. Godine, Publisher, Inc.: From pp. 44–49 in *A Grain of Wheat* by Clyde Robert Bulla. Copyright © 1985 by Clyde Robert Bulla.

Harcourt Brace Jovanovich, Inc.: Short pronunciation key and entries from *HBJ School Dictionary.* Copyright © 1985 by Harcourt Brace Jovanovich, Inc. "Study Steps to Learn a Word" from *HBJ Spelling,* Signature Edition, Level 4 (Orange) by Thorsten Carlson and Richard Madden. Copyright © 1988, 1983 by Harcourt Brace Jovanovich, Inc.

Harper & Row, Publishers, Inc.: Text and illustrations from "The Hen and the Apple Tree" in *Fables* by Arnold Lobel. From pp. 1–5 in *Charlotte's Web* by E. B. White. Copyright 1952 by E. B. White; text copyright renewed 1980 by E. B. White.

Henry Holt and Company, Inc.: From "A Minor Bird" in *Complete Poems of Robert Frost* by Robert Frost. Copyright 1928 by Holt, Rinehart and Winston, Inc.; copyright © 1956 by Robert Frost.

Alfred A. Knopf, Inc.: From pp. 49–54 in *THE TIPI: A Center of Native American Life* by David and Charlotte Yue. Copyright © 1984 by David and Charlotte Yue.

Ray Lincoln Literary Agency, 4 Surrey Road, Melrose Park, PA 19126: From "December Leaves" in *Don't Ever Cross a Crocodile* by Kaye Starbird. Copyright © 1963 by Kaye Starbird. Published by J. B. Lippincott Company.

Samuel Menashe: "A flock of little boats" from *Collected Poems* by Samuel Menashe. Published by The National Poetry Foundation, The University of Maine, Orono, Maine, 1986.

National Wildlife Federation: From "Show-offs of the Sea" by Gerry Bishop in *Ranger Rick* Magazine, December 1987. Copyright 1987 by the National Wildlife Federation.

University Press of Hawaii: "In the ocean of the sky" by Hitomaro from *Japanese Poetry: The 'Uta',* compiled by Arthur Waley. © 1976. An East-West Center Book.

Art Acknowledgments

JoAnna Adamska: 430, 442; Ray App: 78; Meg Kelleher Aubrey: 150, 151, 404, G7; Tom Bobroski: 170; Leslie Bowman: 167, 312, 313; Suzanne Clee: 195; Roberta Collier: 108, 109, 299, G4; Bill Colrus: 180; Frank Daniel: 266; Larry Daste: 143, 155, 218; Susan David: 92, 242, 345, 348; Cathy Diefendorf: 34; Gordon P. Dunlap: 268 (bottom), 390; Don Dyen: 128 (top); George Ford: 29; Larry Frederick: 44, 216; Keith Freeman: 273, 350, 356; Bob Giuliani: 402; Linda Graves: 310; Marika Hahn: 226; Mark Hannon: 76; Todd Heckler: 139, 178, 228, 384; Erasmo Hernandez: 405; Patricia G. Hinton: 257; Mei-Ku Huang: 392; Susan Jaekel: 104, 106; Christa Kieffer: 176, 245, 246, 354; Robert Korta: 136; Mark Langeneckert: 114, 270, 271; Barbara Lanza: G6; Tom LaPadula: 32, 71; Bruce Lemerise: 212; Susan Lexa: 10, 11, 12; Richard Loehle: 36, 37, 227; Stacie Lyman: 93 (bottom); Diana Magnuson: 93 (top), 126; Susan Magurn: 220; Rebecca Merrilees: 172; Nancy Munger: 45; Michael McDermott: 134, 214; James Needham: 74; Sue Parnell: 38, 59, 72, 80, 84, 91, 112, 128 (bottom), 142, 174, 181, 224, 229, 264, 272, 346, 388, 394; Rodney Pate: 125, 308; Robert Pennell: 280–283; Steven James Petruccio: 82, 130, 132, 294, 302, 306; Ondre Pettingill: 30, 268 (top); Brian Pinkney: 304, 400; Larry Raymond: 90, 383; Keith Rocco: 40, 168; Ed Sauk: 39; Sally Schaedler: 386; Nancy Schill: 24, 240; Dan Siculan: 88; Samantha Smith: 236–239; Susan Spellman: 66; Barbara Steadman: 140, 396; Wayne Anthony Still: 162, 311, 358; Gary Torrisi: 138; Deb Troyer: 211, 340, 359; Gary Undercuffler: 86, 398, G2; Arden Von Haeger: 42; Tom Vroman: 21, 63, 116, 159, 202, 249, 291, 337, 376; Jan Wills: 222, 252, 379; Fred Windowski: 262, 263.

Cover: Tom Vroman

continued at the end of the book

Contents

1   Telling About Yourself   8

Reading ◆▶ Writing Connection

Composition Focus: Personal Narrative

Language Focus: Sentences

2 Explaining Facts

Reading ↔ Writing Connection

Composition Focus: Paragraph of Information

Language Focus: Nouns

Giving Directions

Reading ◀▶ Writing Connection

Composition Focus: How-to Paragraph

Language Focus: Verbs

4 Communicating with Others

Reading ←→ Writing Connection

Composition Focus: Friendly Letter

Language Focus: Verbs

5 Using Your Imagination

Reading ◆► Writing Connection

Composition Focus: Fable

Language Focus: Pronouns

6 Painting Pictures with Words 234

7 Persuading Others 278

Reading ◀▶ Writing Connection

Composition Focus: Persuasive Paragraph

Language Focus: Adverbs

8 Giving Information 324

Reading ◆► Writing Connection

Composition Focus: Research Report

Language Focus: More Sentences

Study Skills

Extra Practice

Writer's Handbook

Dear Student,

Suppose that on a cool fall morning you saw a gorilla riding a camel and playing a trumpet. What would you do when you got to school? You would probably tell your classmates about the strange sight, and they would listen to every word you said. Then you might write a letter to some friends about what you saw, and they might be amazed when they read it.

Your language, English, helps you to share what you see, hear, read, and write with other people. This book, HBJ Language, will help you learn to use English better.

We hope you enjoy learning more about your language.

Sincerely,
The Editors

Understanding the Writing Process

Writing a story, a poem, or a description is like following a game plan in soccer. The soccer team makes a plan before a game. Sometimes they have to change the plan a little as the game goes on. Having a plan helps them to play better and gives them a better chance of winning.

A writer also follows a plan to produce a winning piece of writing. This plan is called the **writing process.** The process has five stages:

1. Prewriting
2. Drafting
3. Responding and Revising
4. Proofreading
5. Publishing

To score a goal, a soccer player often has to move the ball backward as well as forward. In the same way, a writer may go back and forth through the stages of the writing process. The diagram shows how a writer might move through the five-stage plan.

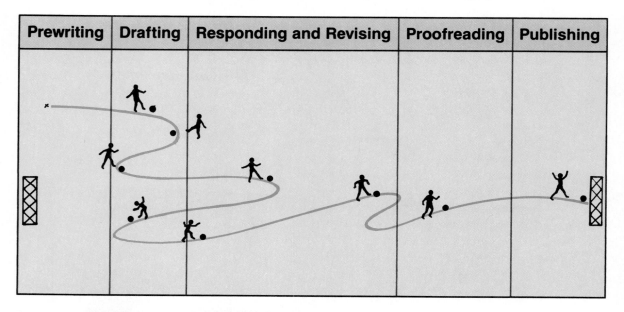

Prewriting	Drafting	Responding and Revising	Proofreading	Publishing

1 Prewriting

Sometimes the hardest part of writing is getting started. The prewriting stage of the writing process makes this easier. In the prewriting step, you

◆ think about your **audience,** or the person or persons for whom you are writing.

◆ identify your **purpose,** or reason for writing, and choose a **form** for your writing.

◆ brainstorm a list of topics to write about.

◆ choose the topic that is best for your purpose and your audience.

◆ gather and organize information about your topic.

The chart shows some different forms of writing, some audiences, and some purposes for writing.

Writing Form	Audience	Purpose
how-to paragraph	classmates	**to inform** how to make a puppet
thank-you letter	a police officer	**to express** thanks for visiting the class
story	grandparents	**to entertain** by telling about a funny event
persuasive paragraph	neighbors	**to persuade** to join a clean-up campaign

Graphic Organizers

You can use graphic organizers in the prewriting stage. A **graphic organizer** is a drawing, a chart, or an outline that helps you see and remember your ideas. It also helps you organize them and put them in order.

Cluster   Use a cluster to plan a descriptive paragraph, a poem, or a character sketch. Note your topic in the center circle. Then add details in the space around the center circle. A cluster helps you decide which details to write about.

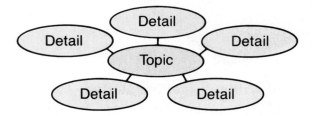

Chart   Use a chart if you are planning to write a how-to paragraph. A chart helps you put the steps in order. A chart also makes it easier to write about a chain of events.

How to _____	— Title
Materials:	— Materials
Step 1	
Step 2	
Step 3	— Steps
Step 4	
Step 5	

Time Line   Use a time line to list events in the order in which they happened. Use this graphic organizer when you write a story, a history report, or a sketch of someone's life.

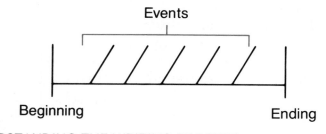

Venn Diagram   Use a Venn diagram to show what is alike and what is different about two people, places, or things. A Venn diagram is helpful when you write a paragraph of comparison and contrast.

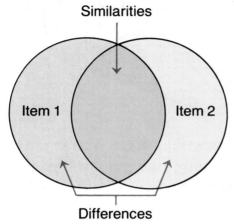

Inverted Triangle   Use an inverted triangle to help you narrow your topic. An inverted triangle can help you limit your topic when you are planning to write a research report or a persuasive paragraph.

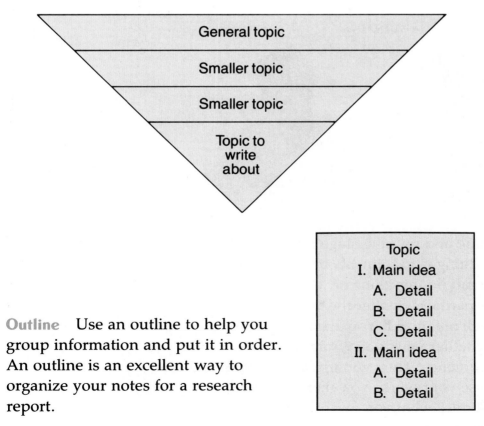

Outline   Use an outline to help you group information and put it in order. An outline is an excellent way to organize your notes for a research report.

2 Drafting

The drafting stage follows the prewriting stage. You study the notes you made of your ideas. You study your graphic organizer. Then you write a draft. At this point, you do not worry about writing carefully and correctly. Your goal is to get your ideas down on paper. As you write your draft, you may discover that you are not happy with your topic. You may want to try a new approach or to get more facts. If so, you can go back to the prewriting stage. You can do more research or work on the topic in a new way.

3 Responding and Revising

The responding and revising stage follows drafting. To respond to something is to think about it and then tell or write your ideas. You can do this alone or with a partner. You ask yourself or your partner whether the facts in your draft are complete and well organized. You ask whether the language is clear. You ask whether what you wrote satisfies your purpose and suits your audience. Then you use the answers to these questions to revise your work. You change and improve your writing so that it does what you meant it to do.

4 Proofreading

Proofreading is the polishing stage of the process. When you proofread, you look for and correct errors in grammar, spelling, capitalization, and punctuation.

5 Publishing

Publishing your writing means making it public in some way. This is the last stage of the writing process. Now you share your writing with the audience for whom you wrote it. You may choose to share it in its written form, or you may choose to share it aloud. Think about the form and the purpose of the writing as you consider how to publish it.

UNIT

1

Telling About Yourself

◆ **COMPOSITION FOCUS:**   **Personal Narrative**
◆ **LANGUAGE FOCUS:**   **Sentences**

People are like walking books. Inside each of us are thoughts and feelings like no one else's. Discovering and sharing these thoughts and feelings make our lives richer.

Talking is a way of sharing with a few people. Writing is a way of sharing with many people. Writers create personal narratives to express and share their experiences and emotions. Such a narrative might take the form of a long book or a short article.

Clyde Bulla, for example, wrote the book *A Grain of Wheat: A Writer Begins* about his own life. His purpose was to tell others about the experiences that made him a writer. He hoped that his readers might use what they read to understand their own lives better. He also hoped that they would enjoy reading about his life. In this unit you will learn how to share yourself with others through your writing.

Clyde Bulla wrote a book *to express* his thoughts and feelings about becoming a writer.

Reading with a Writer's Eye
Personal Narrative

When does someone really know what he or she wants to be in life? Clyde Bulla decided when he was very young that he would be a writer. However, no one else seemed to believe in him. In this selection from *A Grain of Wheat: A Writer Begins,* he tells how his family reacted to his decision. Notice how much you can learn about him and the other members of his family from what they say and do.

from A Grain of Wheat: A Writer Begins
by Clyde Bulla

I wanted to be a writer. I was sure of that.

"I'm going to write books," I said.

My mother said, "Castles in the air."

"What does that mean?" I asked.

"It means you're having daydreams," she said. "You'll dream of doing a lot of different things, but you probably won't do any of them. As you get older, you'll change."

I went from the second grade to the third to the fourth, and I hadn't changed. I still knew what I wanted to be.

I thought about writing and talked about it. I talked too much.

My father told me he was tired of listening to me.

"You can't be a writer," he said. "What do you know about people? What have you ever done? You don't have anything to write about."

When I thought over what he had said, it seemed to me he was right. I stopped writing. But not for long.

The city nearest us was St. Joseph, Missouri. Our newspaper came from there. In the paper I read about a contest for boys and girls—"Write the story of a grain of wheat in five hundred words or less." First prize was a hundred dollars. There were five second prizes of twenty dollars each. After that there were one hundred prizes of one dollar each.

I began to write my story. It went something like this: "I am a grain of wheat. I grew in a field where the sun shone and the rain fell."

I didn't tell anyone what I was doing. When my story was finished, I made a neat copy. I mailed it in our mailbox down the road.

Time went by. I began to look for the newspaper that would tell who had won the contest. At last it came.

There was a whole page about the contest. I saw I hadn't won the first prize. I hadn't won a second prize either. That was a disappointment. I had thought I might win one of the second prizes.

I read down the long list at the bottom of the page—the names and addresses of the boys and girls who had won the one-dollar prizes. Surely my name would be there. It *had* to be!

I read more and more slowly. Only a few names were left.

And one of them was mine! "Clyde Bulla, King City, Missouri."

"I won!" I shouted.

My mother looked at my name. "That's nice," she said.

Nice? Was that all she could say?

I started to show the paper to my father. There was something in his face that stopped me. I could see he wasn't happy that I had won a prize.

My sister Corrine was there. I could see she wasn't happy either. She was sorry for me because all I had won was a dollar.

Didn't they know it wasn't the dollar that mattered? I had written a story that was all mine. No one had helped me. I had sent it off by myself. How many other boys and girls had sent their stories? Maybe a thousand or more. But my story had won a prize, and my name was here in the paper. I was a writer. No matter what anyone else might say, I was a writer.

Respond

1. Do you feel as if you are on Clyde Bulla's side as you read his narrative? What makes you feel as you do? Does he write about an experience that many young people have? Explain.

Discuss

2. What words would you use to tell what kind of person Clyde Bulla is? What happens in his narrative to make you think of him as you do?

3. Does Clyde Bulla's mother believe in his writing? Does he tell you this outright? Explain how he reveals his mother's feelings.

Thinking As a Writer
Analyzing a Personal Narrative

Writer's Guide

A personal narrative
- is written in the first person.
- describes an experience important to the writer.
- gives details about the experience in time order.
- reveals the feelings of the people who took part.

A personal narrative describes an experience that was important to the writer. It reveals the writer's deepest thoughts and feelings about what happened.

Since a personal narrative is about the writer, it is always written in the first person, using the words *I* and *me.* Each personal narrative has a **beginning,** a **middle,** and an **ending.** You can see each part in these lines from the narrative by Clyde Bulla that you read on pages 10–12.

I wanted to be a writer. I was sure of that.

The **beginning** tells what the narrative will be about.

I thought about writing and talked about it. I talked too much.

My father told me he was tired of listening to me.

"You can't be a writer," he said. "What do you know about people? What have you ever done? You don't have anything to write about."

When I thought over what he had said, it seemed to me he was right. I stopped writing. But not for long.

The **middle** describes events that happened in time order. The words *I* and *me* show that the writer is telling about himself.

I was a writer. No matter what anyone else might say, I was a writer.

The **ending** tells what someone did, decided, or learned as a result of the events described.

Discuss

1. Tell briefly what happens in the middle passage. Name the events in the order in which they happen.
2. What does the conversation between Clyde Bulla and his father tell about each of them?
3. What happens as a result of this conversation? Where does the writer give that information?

Try Your Hand

A. Analyze a Narrative   Read the following narrative, and think about the way the author shares his or her feelings with you.

> I was writing another letter to my friend Rich in Deerfield. I told him again how much I missed my old house, my old school, and my old friends.
>
> My sister Emily burst in to ask me to swim at the pool in the park. I shook my head.
>
> My brother Sean looked in. He was tossing a soccer ball. "Forget it, Emily," said Sean. "He's going to sulk in his room all summer."
>
> They left, and I went back to my letter. "There is nothing to do in this boring place," I wrote.

1. What do you learn from the beginning of the narrative?
2. Reread the conversation. What does it tell about Sean, Emily, and the writer?
3. What does the ending tell about the writer?

B. Add Information to the Narrative
Decide how the narrative in **A** might continue. List four or five events that could happen. Number them in the order in which they would happen.

C. Write an Ending   Reread the narrative and the list of events you just made. Then write a sentence that could be used as an ending.

D. Read a Personal Narrative
Reread pages 10–12, or find another personal narrative. Read it aloud to a partner. Identify the most important information in the beginning, the middle, and the ending. Discuss what you learned about the writer's thoughts and feelings.

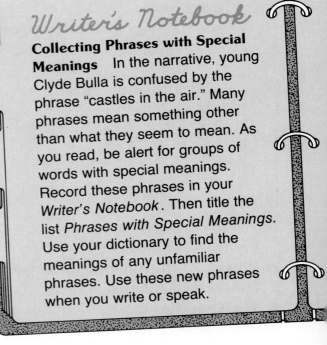

Writer's Notebook

Collecting Phrases with Special Meanings   In the narrative, young Clyde Bulla is confused by the phrase "castles in the air." Many phrases mean something other than what they seem to mean. As you read, be alert for groups of words with special meanings. Record these phrases in your *Writer's Notebook*. Then title the list *Phrases with Special Meanings.* Use your dictionary to find the meanings of any unfamiliar phrases. Use these new phrases when you write or speak.

Thinking As a Writer
Visualizing Events and Recalling Feelings

Good writers know what they are going to say before they begin to write. They get ready by picturing what they want to write about. To **visualize** something is to imagine it just as if you were watching a movie in your mind.

Before he wrote his personal narrative, Clyde Bulla may have replayed the scenes of the story in his imagination. He may have recalled the order in which the events happened. He probably remembered how each family member acted. Here is how he may have replayed one scene.

> **Writer's Guide**
>
> To create personal narratives, good writers
> - visualize events and recall feelings before they begin to write.
> - write about events and feelings in an order that makes sense.

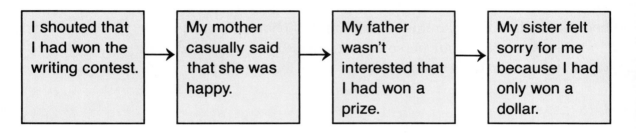

| I shouted that I had won the writing contest. | → | My mother casually said that she was happy. | → | My father wasn't interested that I had won a prize. | → | My sister felt sorry for me because I had only won a dollar. |

As you write your own personal narrative, begin by creating a "movie" in your mind of the experience you want to describe.

Discuss

1. Reread Clyde Bulla's narrative on pages 10–12. Which details describe things he recalls seeing? Which ones describe things he recalls hearing and things he recalls feeling?
2. Suppose the scene had been written by Clyde's sister. How might her memory of the experience be different?

Try Your Hand

Visualize Events   Visualize something interesting that happened to you this week. List five things that you or someone else said or did. List the events in a graphic organizer similar to the one on this page.

Developing the Writer's Craft
Using Vivid Words

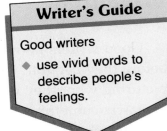

When writers create personal narratives, one of their goals is to express and describe feelings. To do this well, writers must use vivid words.

There is more than one way to make a sentence clearer and more interesting.

1. I gave a shout when I learned I had won.
2. I gave a *joyful* shout when I learned I had won.
3. I gave a *whoop* when I learned I had won.

Sentence 1 is not a very interesting sentence. Sentence 2 shows one way to make it livelier. A vivid describing word is added to make the writer's feelings clearer. Sentence 3 shows another way to make the sentence livelier. The word *shout* is replaced by the more exact word *whoop.* Your **Writer's Thesaurus** at the back of this book can help you make this second kind of change.

When you write your personal narrative, try to use vivid words to express what you and others were feeling.

Discuss

1. Look at examples 1–3. What other vivid words might the writer add or use?
2. How would each new word change what you imagine when you read the sentence?

Try Your Hand

Use Vivid Words The paragraph below does not describe the writer's feelings well. Rewrite it, adding vivid words. Make at least four changes. You may want to use your **Writer's Thesaurus.**

> Our teacher posted the list of winners' names. I went to look at it. My best friend asked if I had won a prize. I said that I had not. He looked at me. Then he wondered if there had been a mistake. The teacher told us there had not been. My friend and I walked away.

1 Prewriting
Personal Narrative

The students in Melissa's class were just getting to know one another. They decided to write personal narratives to help themselves learn more about each other. Melissa used the checklist in the **Writer's Guide** to help her plan her narrative. Look at what she did.

◆ Brainstorming and Selecting a Topic

First, Melissa brainstormed a list of possible topics to write about. Look at her list.

Next, Melissa looked at her list and crossed off topics that she did not think would be interesting to others. She also crossed off topics that were too big to say much about in one paragraph. One of her goals was to show the actions and reactions of other people. She decided to write only about experiences that included others.

Last, Melissa circled the topic she liked best. She decided that she could tell about her first experience on stage in one paragraph. She also thought that other people would enjoy reading about it.

my summer vacation
the time I got stuck by myself in the elevator
my first experience on stage
fun at the fair
me and my new dog

Discuss

1. Look at each topic that Melissa crossed off her list. Why do you think she decided against each topic?
2. Melissa crossed off the topic "my summer vacation." How might she turn that into a topic she could use?

◆ Gathering and Organizing Information

After Melissa chose her topic, she began to gather details for her narrative. She did this in two steps.

In the first step, Melissa pictured the events that had been part of her experience. She tried to remember what she and other people had said, done, and felt. She jotted down notes on a piece of paper as quickly as she could. She did not worry about writing neatly or putting details in order.

In the second step, Melissa looked over the notes she had made. She circled all the details that she thought were important enough to use in her paper. Then she used these details to make a time line. On it she noted events in the order in which they took place. The time line helped her to visualize her experience once more as she wrote.

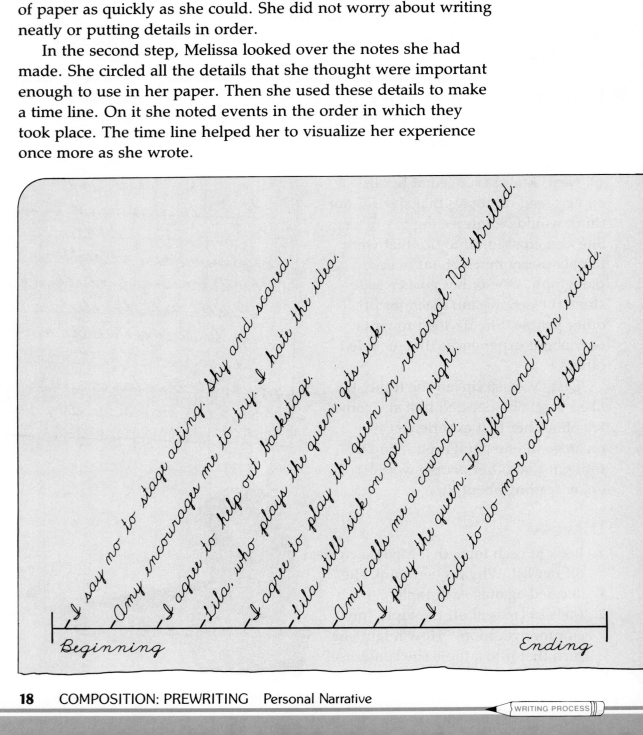

Beginning

I say no to stage acting. Shy and scared.

Amy encourages me to try. I hate the idea.

I agree to help out backstage.

Lila, who plays the queen, gets sick.

I agree to play the queen in rehearsal. Not thrilled.

Lila still sick on opening night.

Amy calls me a coward.

I play the queen. Terrified and then excited.

I decide to do more acting. Glad.

Ending

Discuss

1. In the first step, Melissa did not worry about jotting down her notes in the correct order. Why do you think she did not worry about this?
2. Melissa used only some of the notes she had jotted down. What kinds of details do you think she might have left out?
3. In the time line, Melissa made notes about what people said and did. What else did she jot down? Why do you think she wrote these notes?

Try Your Hand

Now plan a personal narrative of your own.

A. Brainstorm and Select a Topic   Brainstorm a list of possible topics. Write down some important experiences in your life. Think about each topic and about your audience.

◆ Cross out topics that will not interest your audience.
◆ Cross out topics that are too big to cover in just one paragraph.
◆ Cross out topics that are about events that do not include other people.
◆ Circle the most interesting topic left on your list. This will be the topic of your personal narrative.

B. Gather and Organize Information   When you are satisfied with your topic, decide on the details you want to include in your narrative.

◆ Visualize the experience you want to write about. Jot down everything you can recall about it. Include how you and others felt.
◆ Look over your notes. Identify the details that are most important. Think about your audience, and choose details that will interest them.
◆ Organize your notes in time order. You may want to make a time line like Melissa's.

 Save your notes and time line in your *Writer's Notebook*. You will use them when you draft your personal narrative.

Listening and Speaking
Tips on How to Tell a Story About Yourself

1. Remember that one of your goals is to express and share your experiences. Your audience will enjoy your story more if you try to connect your story with some of their experiences.
2. Remember that another goal is to keep your audience interested. Leave out details that will not appeal to your particular audience. Add details that will interest them.
3. Use exact and vivid words to make the story about yourself lively and entertaining.
4. Include the necessary details. Make sure your audience has enough information to understand how and why each event took place.
5. Leave out unimportant details that will confuse or bore your audience.
6. Tell the events in the order in which they happened. Be careful not to confuse your audience by telling the events out of order.
7. Remember that the story you tell must have an ending that makes a point and satisfies the audience. Before you begin, think of the ending you want. Then, aim for it without including unnecessary details.
8. Speak clearly and loudly. Do not speak too slowly or too quickly.

2 Drafting
Personal Narrative

Using her notes and her time line, Melissa followed the **Writer's Guide** to draft her personal narrative. Look at the way she began.

> There was no way I was going to be in the 4H Club show. Just the thought of being on stage gave me goose bumps. My friend Amy said that I would have fun if I gave it a chance. I just made a face at her.

Discuss

1. What details did Melissa give in the beginning of her paragraph?
2. Compare Melissa's draft with her time line on page 18. How did her time line help her?

Try Your Hand

Now you are ready to write a personal narrative.

A. Review Your Information Think about the details you gathered and organized in the last lesson. Decide if you want to add or leave out anything. If so, change your notes.

B. Think About Your TAP Remember that your task is to write a personal narrative. Your purpose is to express to your audience your feelings about an experience that was important to you.

C. Write Your First Draft Follow the steps in the **Writer's Guide** to write your personal narrative.

    When you write your draft, just put all your ideas on paper. Do not worry about spelling, punctuation, or grammar. You can correct the draft later.

Task: What?
Audience: Who?
Purpose: Why?

Save your first draft in your *Writer's Notebook*. You will use it when you revise your narrative.

3 Responding and Revising
Personal Narrative

Writer's Guide

Revising Checklist

☑ Read your narrative to yourself or to a partner.

☑ Think about your audience and your purpose. Add or cut information.

☑ Check to see that your narrative is organized in time order and that it contains details about what people said, did, and felt.

☑ Add vivid words, or replace dull words with colorful ones.

Melissa used the checklist in the **Writer's Guide** to revise her personal narrative. Look at what she did.

◆ Checking Information

In her narrative, Melissa found a sentence that gave unimportant information. She decided to take it out and used this mark ✄ to show the change. Then she decided that the words *at rehearsals* would make another sentence clearer. To show the addition, she used this mark ∧ .

◆ Checking Organization

Melissa decided that the next-to-last sentence was in the wrong time order. To show that it should be moved, she used this mark ◌ .

◆ Checking Language

Melissa found a dull word that she could replace with a more vivid word. She used this mark ⌃ to make her change.

I would help make the costumes. That was enough fun for me!

Then one day the girl playing Queen Iris got sick. *at rehearsals* My group needed someone to say her lines. They talked me into doing it until she got well. On opening night she was still in bed. ~~She had the flu.~~ Amy told me not to be a coward and to help save the show. The next thing I knew, I was on stage. The applause at the end was ~~neat.~~ *thrilling* To my surprise, my goose bumps vanished. Now I have decided to be an actress.

Add

Cut

Replace

Move

Discuss

1. Melissa took out the sentence telling that the girl had the flu. Why is the information unimportant?
2. Why did it make sense to move the next-to-last sentence?
3. Can you suggest any other improvements that can be made in Melissa's narrative?

Try Your Hand

Now revise your first draft.

A. Read Your First Draft   As you read your narrative, think about your audience and your purpose. Read your paragraph silently or to a partner to see if it is complete and well organized. Ask yourself or your partner the questions in the box.

Responding and Revising Strategies

✔ **Respond**
Ask yourself or your partner:

◆ Have I begun with a sentence that tells what my narrative is about?

◆ Have I described events in the order in which they took place?

◆ Have I used vivid words to describe feelings?

✔ **Revise**
Try these solutions:

◆ **Add** information that is needed.

◆ **Move** any sentences that seem to be in the wrong place.

◆ **Add** vivid words or **replace** dull words. See the **Writer's Thesaurus** at the back of the book and the **Revising Workshop** on page 24.

B. Make Your Changes   If the answer to any question in the box is *no,* try the solution. Use the **Editor's Marks** to show your changes.

C. Review Your Personal Narrative Again   Decide if there is anything else you want to revise. Keep revising your narrative until you feel it is well organized and complete.

EDITOR'S MARKS

∧ Add something.
➥ Cut something.
◯ Move something.
⋏ Replace something.

Save your revised narrative in your *Writer's Notebook*. You will use it when you proofread your narrative.

Revising Workshop
Using a Thesaurus

Good writers know their audience would lose interest if the same dull words appeared again and again. They use a thesaurus to find vivid words. A **thesaurus** lists groups of **synonyms,** words with nearly the same meanings. This entry is from the **Writer's Thesaurus** at the back of this book.

---

bright adj. Giving off a lot of light. The room is too *bright* without shades.
glowing Showing a warm color. The July sun was *glowing*.
shiny Able to reflect light. The *shiny* gold ring fit Maria perfectly.
ANTONYMS: dark, dim, dull, gloomy, gray

The synonyms for *bright* are listed in alphabetical order. Each is followed by a definition and a sentence that shows how to use the synonym correctly. At the end of the entry is a list of **antonyms,** words with the opposite meaning. These can help you write sentences in which you create a contrast.

Practice

Follow the directions. Replace the underlined words with more vivid or more exact words. Use your **Writer's Thesaurus.**

1. Write a sentence about a <u>hot</u> afternoon.
2. Write a sentence about a <u>huge</u> animal.
3. Write a sentence about a <u>funny</u> character in a story.
4. Write a sentence about a <u>brave</u> person.
5. Write a sentence in which someone <u>walks</u>.
6. Write a sentence about someone who <u>takes</u> an object.
7. Write a sentence about a <u>good</u> party.

4 Proofreading
Personal Narrative

After revising her personal narrative, Melissa used the **Writer's Guide** and the **Editor's Marks** to proofread it. Look at what she did.

Writer's Guide

Proofreading Checklist

☑ Check that every sentence begins with a capital letter.

☑ Check for errors in punctuation.

☑ Check for errors in grammar.

☑ Circle any words you think are misspelled. Find out how to spell them correctly.

⇨ For proofreading help, use the **Writer's Handbook.**

director

the director said the show would not have gone on without Queen Iris. Who would have played the queen? I was nervous when I saw everyone looking at me. Now I am glad that fear did not stop me from trying something new.

EDITOR'S MARKS

≡ Capitalize.

⊙ Add a period.

∧ Add something.

⋀ Add a comma.

ⱽⱽ Add quotation marks.

✁ Cut something.

⋀ Replace something.

∿ Transpose.

◯ Spell correctly.

⊬ Indent paragraph.

∕ Make a lowercase letter.

Discuss

1. Look at Melissa's proofread narrative. What kinds of mistakes did she make?
2. Why did Melissa circle the word *nervous*? Why do you think she did not write a new spelling above it?

Try Your Hand

Proofread Your Personal Narrative   Now use the **Writer's Guide** and the **Editor's Marks** to proofread your narrative.

 Save your corrected narrative in your *Writer's Notebook.* You will use it when you publish your narrative.

5 Publishing
Personal Narrative

Melissa made a clean copy of her personal narrative and checked it to be sure she had not left out anything. Then she and her classmates published their narratives in a bulletin board display. You can find Melissa's narrative on page 27 of the **Writer's Handbook.**

Here's how Melissa and her classmates published their narratives.

Writer's Guide

Publishing Checklist

☑ Make a clean copy of your personal narrative.

☑ Be sure that nothing has been left out.

☑ Check to see that there are no mistakes.

☑ Share your narrative in a special way.

1. They brought in photographs of themselves from home or made drawings of themselves. The students attached each photograph or drawing to a large sheet of colored paper.
2. Melissa copied her narrative neatly onto lined paper and attached it to the large sheet with her picture on it.

3. Two students made a title for the bulletin board. It was "Getting to Know One Another."

4. They stapled the completed narratives to the bulletin board.

5. When Melissa and her classmates were finished, they took turns reading the narratives aloud. Then they discussed what they learned about each other. They invited students from other classes in to see the display.

Discuss

1. What might have happened if they tried to attach their pictures after they copied their narratives?
2. What are some good rules for listening to and talking about the narratives?

Try Your Hand

Publish Your Personal Narrative Follow the checklist in the **Writer's Guide.** If possible, create a bulletin board display, or try one of these ideas for sharing your narrative.

◆ **Class Magazine** Use your narratives to create a class magazine called "Our Lives." Use photographs or drawings to illustrate it. Then make a copy for everyone in the class.
◆ **Guessing Game** Mix up the narratives and hand them out. Have each student read aloud someone else's narrative. Do not say who wrote it. Let everyone try to guess the name of the writer.

Writing in the Content Areas

Use what you learned to write about your own experiences, thoughts, and feelings. Use one of these ideas or an idea of your own.

Writer's Guide

When you write, remember the stages of the Writing Process.

◆ Prewriting
◆ Drafting
◆ Responding and Revising
◆ Proofreading
◆ Publishing

Literature

Has your life ever been changed by a book? Has one book meant more to you than any other? The book might be one you have read during the last year. It might be one you liked when you were younger. Tell what happened in the book and why the book was important to you.

Science

Each new invention has an effect on people's lives. Some inventions bring great changes, and some bring small changes. Think about things people have invented during the past two hundred years. Choose one that you are grateful for. Tell how it affects your life.

Fine Arts

Have you ever been in a play? Have you ever danced, sung, or played music for an audience? Write about what happened. Tell what you did. Tell how you felt as you performed. Would you enjoy doing it again? Why or why not?

Health

Most people know that they should eat right to be healthy. Many of us need to improve our eating habits. Think of an eating habit that you would like to improve. Tell what it is. What plan can you make to improve it?

CONNECTING
WRITING ⟷ LANGUAGE

Writers want to communicate ideas and feelings to their audiences. To hold the attention of their readers, writers must present their thoughts clearly and completely. How does this piece hold your attention?

I was five years old before I said my first real word aloud. I had never learned to speak because I could not hear other people talk. I didn't know that sounds named things. My hands were all I needed to speak to my family.

Then, one day, I tried to make friends with a new neighbor. I asked his name. Why didn't he answer? I was hurt. I ran to my mother. Imagine my surprise when I learned that there was another way to communicate! I decided that I must learn this way too. It took me quite a while to learn to use my voice. How wonderful it was when I first said hello!

◆ **Sentences in a Personal Narrative** The thoughts in the paragraphs are easy to follow because the writer uses sentences correctly. The sentences are complete. They contain all the information you need. The writer also keeps your interest by varying the kinds of sentences. As you read, notice that good writers are careful not to leave out important parts of their sentences. Notice how often they use different kinds of sentences.

◆ **Language Focus: Sentences** In the following lessons you will learn more about the different kinds of sentences.

1 Sentences

◆ **FOCUS**   A **sentence** is a group of words that expresses a complete thought.

These word groups are sentences.

1. David is writing to a pen pal.
2. Who is his pen pal?
3. His pen pal is a girl from Texas.

Some groups of words are not sentences. They do not express complete thoughts.

4. the pen pal in Mexico
5. like many of the same interests

Link to Speaking and Writing
Use complete sentences so your meaning will be clear. What other words could you add to make a sentence?

Pat
∧*Wrote a letter yesterday.*

Guided Practice

A. Tell if each word group is a *sentence* or *not a sentence*.

1. Do you enjoy writing letters?
2. A pen pal club may be for you.
3. Just ten dollars a year.
4. A pen pal magazine in the mail.
5. Many ads in the magazine.
6. Any club member can send in an ad.

B. 7.–12.   Make sentences from those word groups in **A** that are not sentences by adding words to them.

THINK AND REMEMBER
◆ Remember to use a **sentence** to express a complete thought.

Independent Practice

C. Identifying Sentences Read each group of words. Then, write *sentence* or *not a sentence.*

13. Where does Julia Lopez live?

MODEL > sentence

14. Her home is in Fort Worth, Texas.
15. Just thirty miles away from Dallas.
16. Her mother a museum guide.
17. Mrs. Lopez works in the Fort Worth Art Museum.
18. Much to see at the museum.
19. Julia thinks David would enjoy Fort Worth.
20. Invited him for a visit.
21. Can stay for two weeks.

D. Completing Sentences Choose the group of words that will make the first group a complete sentence. Then write the sentence.

22. _____ come once a month.
 a. Julia's letters **b.** Are they

MODEL > Julia's letters come once a month.

23. _____ David and his family.
 a. On a visit to Texas **b.** Julia wants to visit
24. _____ write very interesting letters.
 a. Both of them **b.** Often
25. Julia _____ .
 a. plays on a soccer team **b.** in Fort Worth
26. _____ for players of all ages.
 a. Many teams **b.** There are teams
27. Julia's team _____ .
 a. won four games **b.** last month
28. She wants _____ .
 a. yesterday **b.** a new ball

Application—Writing

Sentences About Yourself Imagine that you are the student in the picture. You are writing to a new pen pal. Write sentences that tell what you are like and what interests you have. Be sure that each group of words is a complete sentence.

2 Declarative and Interrogative Sentences

FOCUS

◆ A **declarative sentence** makes a statement.
◆ An **interrogative sentence** asks a question.

Remember that a sentence expresses a complete thought. A declarative sentence makes a statement. It begins with a capital letter and ends with a period.

1. Ashley will give her report next.

An interrogative sentence asks a question. It begins with a capital letter and ends with a question mark.

2. Can everyone see and hear her?

Link to Speaking and Writing

Sometimes you can change a declarative sentence into an interrogative sentence by changing the order of the words.

Ashley is explaining the charts?

Guided Practice

A. Tell if each sentence is *declarative* or *interrogative*.

1. What are you going to talk about?

2. My talk will be about the solar system.

3. Why did you choose that subject?

4. I watched a program about it.

5. I learned some amazing facts.

THINK AND REMEMBER

◆ Use a **declarative sentence** to make a statement. Begin it with a capital letter and end it with a period(.).

◆ Use an **interrogative sentence** to ask a question. Begin it with a capital letter and end it with a question mark(?).

Independent Practice

B. Identifying Kinds of Sentences Write if each sentence is *declarative* or *interrogative*.

6. Are you nervous, Paul?

MODEL > interrogative

7. Yes, I am a little scared.
8. It is hard to speak before the class.
9. Did you do a lot of research?
10. What is your science report about?
11. I studied bees.
12. What is that picture?
13. It shows the inside of a hive.

C. Proofreading Sentences Write each sentence so that it begins and ends correctly.

14. what did Paul learn about bees

MODEL > What did Paul learn about bees?

15. a bee is a type of insect
16. only the honeybee makes honey
17. why are some people afraid of bees
18. bees sting only when they are hurt or scared
19. during which season do you see the most bees
20. the bees store nectar to feed their young

D. Revising Sentences Change each declarative sentence into an interrogative sentence.

21. Maria is giving her science report.

MODEL > Is Maria giving her science report?

22. Maria will tell about raccoons.
23. Raccoons are good climbers.
24. Raccoons can grasp things easily.
25. The students are enjoying her report.

Application—Writing

Questions and Answers Imagine that you are the girl in the picture. You are giving a report on our solar system. Write some questions that your audience might ask. After each question, write a short answer that you might give.

3 Imperative and Exclamatory Sentences

FOCUS
◆ An **imperative sentence** makes a request or gives a command.
◆ An **exclamatory sentence** expresses strong feeling.

Not every sentence makes a statement or asks a question. An imperative sentence makes a request or gives a command. It begins with a capital letter and ends with a period.

   1. Please spin the wheel.   **2.** Move two spaces back.

An exclamatory sentence expresses strong feeling. It begins with a capital letter and ends with an exclamation point.

   3. Wow, I won a free turn!

> **Link to Speaking and Writing**
> Your voice tells listeners when you are excited. An exclamation point tells readers the same thing.

Guided Practice

A. Tell if each sentence is *imperative* or *exclamatory*.

   1. Please read the rules aloud.
   2. How easy the rules are to learn!
   3. Oops, I am in big trouble!
   4. Let Lee play first.
   5. Oh, that is a lucky spin!
   6. Do not make a bad move.

> **THINK AND REMEMBER**
> ◆ Use an **imperative sentence** to make a request or give a command. End it with a period(.).
> ◆ Use an **exclamatory sentence** to express strong feeling. End it with an exclamation point(!).
> ◆ Begin every sentence with a capital letter.

Independent Practice

B. Identifying Types of Sentences   Write if each sentence is *imperative* or *exclamatory*.

7. Come and play the new game with us.

> MODEL > imperative

8. Please teach me how to play.

9. Oh, Erin is playing, too!

10. Write movie titles on slips of paper.

11. Wow, Jenny has written six titles already!

12. You have listed such a lot of titles!

C. Proofreading Sentences   Write each sentence so that it begins and ends correctly.

13. please leave the room

> MODEL > Please leave the room.

14. hide this eraser under the desk

15. oh, I can still see it

16. try to find the eraser

17. please give me a clue

18. oh, you are getting warmer now

19. wow, Nicole almost found it

D. Writing Original Sentences   Add words to each word group to make an imperative sentence and an exclamatory sentence. Write the sentences.

20.–21. my team

> MODEL > Please be on my team. Wow, my team has good players!

22.–23. your turn	**28.–29.** on the board
24.–25. great move	**30.–31.** back to Ryan
26.–27. lucky card	**32.–33.** lost the game

Application—Writing

Board Game Sentences   The picture shows a family playing a board game. Write some sentences that might be on the playing cards. Be sure some are imperative sentences that tell the players what to do. Make the rest exclamatory sentences that tell the players good or bad news.

4 Subjects and Predicates

◆ **FOCUS**   Each sentence is made up of two parts, the subject and the predicate.

The **subject** of a sentence is the part that names whom or what the sentence is about. The **predicate** is the part that tells what the subject is or does.

1. People use special codes in many ways.

2. The code for telegraphing is the Morse code.

3. The telegraph operator waits.

Sometimes the subject can be just one word, as in sentence 1. The subject can also be made up of more than one word, as in sentences 2 and 3.

Notice that in sentences 1 and 2 the predicates contain several words. In sentence 3 the predicate is just one word.

Guided Practice

A. Tell if the underlined part of the sentence is the *subject* or the *predicate*.

1. The Morse code was invented by Samuel F. B. Morse.
2. This clever man developed the first telegraph.
3. Morse became interested in the idea in 1832.
4. Passengers on a voyage gave him valuable ideas.
5. Electricity can be sent over a wire.
6. A very excited Morse cheered.
7. He worked on the telegraph for five years.
8. Electric signals were sent over a wire.

> **THINK AND REMEMBER**
> ◆ Be sure your sentence has two parts, a subject and a predicate.

Independent Practice

B. Identifying Subjects and Predicates   Study the underlined words. Then write *subject* or *predicate*.

9. <u>Samuel F. B. Morse</u> was also a painter.

MODEL > subject

10. <u>Morse</u> earned money from teaching painting.
11. <u>All his time and money</u> went into the telegraph.
12. The telegraph <u>was first demonstrated in 1837</u>.
13. Another big demonstration <u>was planned for 1842</u>.
14. A cable <u>was laid underwater to an island</u>.

C. Choosing Subjects and Predicates   Write each sentence. Underline the subject once. Underline the predicate twice.

15. A few friends encouraged the inventor.

MODEL > <u>A few friends</u> encouraged the inventor.

16. Samuel Morse did not give up easily.

17. Congress awarded him a large sum of money.

18. A telegraph line was strung between two cities.

19. A great crowd gathered for the demonstration.

20. The inventor tapped out his message.

21. The Baltimore operator received Morse's message.

D. Writing Original Sentences   Make up a predicate to go with each subject or a subject to go with each predicate. Write your new sentences.

22. Rapid clicks

MODEL > Rapid clicks spell words.

23. takes time to learn.   26. Most people
24. An inventor   27. can carry messages.
25. My friends and I   28. uses a code.

The bridge is out.

Application—Writing and Speaking

A Story Beginning   What is happening in the pictures? Write the beginning sentences of a story about the pictures. Read your sentences to a classmate and talk about what might happen next. Be sure that each sentence has a subject and a predicate.

5 Complete and Simple Subjects

FOCUS

◆ The **complete subject** includes all the words that tell whom or what the sentence is about.

◆ The **simple subject** is the main word in the complete subject of a sentence.

Each complete sentence has a complete subject that tells whom or what the sentence is about. The key, or main, word in the complete subject is called the simple subject. The word in color is the simple subject of each sentence.

1. A gale is a strong wind.

2. A dangerous gale is coming this way.

3. A gale at sea can sink small boats.

Look at the other words that make up the complete subject in each sentence. These words tell more about the simple subject.

Gale

Storm

Hurricane

Guided Practice

A. Identify the simple subject in each sentence. The underline shows the complete subject.

1. Special signals are used to tell about weather.
2. The stations on shore fly colored flags.
3. Workers at the station listen to weather reports.
4. Fierce storms may come up suddenly at sea.
5. Not every small boat has a radio.
6. The ship's crew checks the station flags.
7. The bright banners give warnings to sailors.
8. Two red flags warn of a gale.

THINK AND REMEMBER

◆ To locate the simple subject, find the key word in the complete subject.

Independent Practice

B. Identifying Simple Subjects   Write the word that is the simple subject of each sentence.

   9. Different <u>signals</u> are used at night.

MODEL > signals

   10. Colored <u>lights</u> give weather messages.
   11. A storm <u>warning</u> is two red lights.
   12. <u>Boats out at sea</u> can see these lights.
   13. <u>Sea charts</u> show where each buoy is located.

C. Choosing Complete and Simple Subjects   Write each complete subject. Then, underline the simple subject.

   14. Other messages are sent from the shore.

MODEL > Other <u>messages</u>

   15. The first lighthouses were built long ago.
   16. Many large harbors have lighthouses.
   17. Some tall towers warn of dangerous rocks.
   18. A beam of light shines through a stormy sky.
   19. The captain of the ship knows each lighthouse.

D. Writing Original Sentences   Create a complete subject to finish each sentence. Write the sentence. Then, underline the simple subject.

   20. _____ hid the shore.

MODEL > Dense <u>fog</u> hid the shore.

   21. _____ passed the fishing boat.
   22. _____ tossed the little boat.
   23. _____ was soon full of boats.
   24. _____ steered away from the rocks.
   25. _____ can come up suddenly.

Application—Writing and Speaking

Sentences in a News Report   Imagine that you are reporting local news for a television show. You are at the Coast Guard station in the picture. Write some sentences that tell your listeners what can be seen and heard. Underline each simple subject. Then, read your sentences aloud to the class.

6 Complete and Simple Predicates

FOCUS

◆ The **complete predicate** includes all the words that tell what the subject of the sentence is or does.

◆ The **simple predicate** is the main word in the complete predicate of a sentence.

Each sentence has a complete predicate that tells what the subject is or does. The key word in the complete predicate is called the simple predicate. The word in color is the simple predicate of each sentence.

1. The Indians trade their furs for blankets.

2. Their leader uses sign language.

3. The man in front is their leader.

In sentence 1 the key word *trade* tells what the Indians do. In sentence 2 the key word *uses* tells what their leader does. Sometimes, the simple predicate may be *is, are, was,* or *were*.

Guided Practice

A. Identify the simple predicate in each sentence. The underline shows the complete predicate.

1. The Plains Indians spoke many languages.
2. Not everyone understood neighboring tribes.
3. The tribes used a language of hand movements.
4. Some movements were simple.
5. Traders traveled all over the plains.
6. Traders learned sign language, too.

THINK AND REMEMBER

◆ To locate the simple predicate, find the key word in the complete predicate of a sentence.

Independent Practice

B. Identifying Simple Predicates   Write the word that is the simple predicate of each sentence.

7. Plains Indians <u>lived</u> in villages at times.

MODEL > lived

8. The men <u>were hunters</u>.
9. The women <u>raised</u> corn, beans, and squash.
10. The hunters <u>chased the buffalo on foot</u>.
11. Then the Europeans <u>brought</u> horses to the plains.
12. Hunters easily <u>followed the buffalo</u>.

C. Choosing Complete and Simple Predicates   Write each complete predicate. Then, underline the simple predicate.

13. The Indians made everyday items into art.

MODEL > <u>made</u> everyday items into art

14. Many Plains Indians wore buffalo robes.
15. A whole buffalo hide made one robe.
16. The Indians were painters, too.
17. The warriors painted pictures on the robes.
18. Some pictures showed successful hunts.

D. Writing Original Sentences   Create a complete predicate to finish each sentence. Write the sentence. Then, underline the simple predicate.

19. The leader

MODEL > The leader <u>met</u> with the traders.

20. A painted tipi
21. Museums
22. Buffalo skins
23. Each tribe
24. Sign language
25. A feather headdress

Application—Writing

Sentences in a Letter   Imagine that you are a trader. Write some sentences that might be in a letter you are sending home to your family. Give a clear description of your meeting with some Plains Indians. Underline each simple predicate.

Building Vocabulary
Context Clues

"And that's what's happening in other parts of the country. Now here's J.J. Allen with the local news."

What kind of news is *local* news? If you read only that question, you might not know what *local* means. Sometimes, however, an entire sentence can give clues to a word's meaning.

    We watched the *local* news to find out what was happening in our area.

Think about the sentence you just read. You already know that news comes from all over the world. The last few words tell you that *local* news tells about the speaker's own area.

    Here is what to do when you come to a word you don't know. Study the words or sentences around it. Look for context clues. **Context clues** are useful nearby information. These clues can help you figure out a word's meaning.

Reading Practice

Read each sentence. Look for context clues. Then, write the correct definition of each underlined word.

1. I learned some interesting facts about zebras by watching a television <u>documentary</u> on Africa.
   a. a show that gives facts
   b. a show that makes people laugh
2. News programs should be <u>objective</u> and should not contain the speakers' own thoughts.
   a. based on things that can be proved
   b. full of ideas about what is right and wrong
3. The news program lasts only half an hour because most people would rather watch a <u>brief</u> show than a long one.
   a. quiet   b. short
4. Millions of people are interested in the news, so the evening news shows are watched by a <u>vast</u> audience.
   a. very large   b. small and special

Writing Practice

5.–8. The words below have to do with television. Choose four of the words. Write a sentence for each one. Give context clues. Make the meaning of the word clear to a reader.

commercial	sponsor	cancel
rehearse	public	replay
broadcast	script	cue

Project

Work in a group to make up some nonsense words. Choose the five you like best. Decide on a meaning for each. Then, write a sentence for each word. Give strong context clues that will help readers understand its meaning. Trade your completed sentences with another group. Write the definitions of their nonsense words as they try to do the same with yours. Compare the results.

1. When I heard the coyote howl, I <u>mollied</u> under my cot.
2. The path began to get <u>wilsy</u> as the rain came down.

Language Enrichment

Sentences

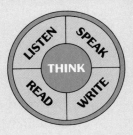

Use what you know about sentences to do these activities.

 Create a Cartoon

What do you think is happening in this cartoon? Think about what the characters could be saying. For each speech balloon, write one or more complete sentences that might make sense there. Be sure that your sentences include at least one interrogative, one imperative, and one exclamatory sentence.

When you are finished, read to your classmates what you have written. After everyone has read, discuss one another's ideas.

 Secret Messages

When you write in code, you substitute symbols or letters for whole words or letters. Work in a small group to create your own code.

Have each group member write a message to the others in the code. Include an interrogative sentence in your message. Next, have each group member write a coded answer to each message. Be sure that each group member understands all the messages.

CONNECTING
LANGUAGE ⬌ WRITING

In this unit you learned about the four types of sentences. A sentence may be declarative, interrogative, imperative, or exclamatory. A sentence must have both a subject and a predicate.

◆ **Using Sentences in Your Writing** Knowing when to use each type of sentence helps you write or tell your ideas clearly. You need to write complete sentences to express complete thoughts. Be sure to use complete sentences as you do these activities.

A World of People

Choose one of the pictures on this page. Think about what the person in the picture might say about his or her life.

Pretend you are that person. Write a paragraph about your life. You may write about something you like to do. You may describe something interesting that happened to you. Use complete sentences in your paragraph. Then, with your classmates, make a bulletin board display.

Living Words

You learned how to use context clues to figure out word meanings on the **Building Vocabulary** pages. Here's another challenging way to use this skill.

Find a newspaper article or a magazine story about an unusual person. Copy some sentences that contain difficult words. Highlight these words with a marking pen or by underlining them. Write sentences that tell what you think each word means. Then, check the words in a dictionary. Write the definitions in complete sentences. How many of your guesses were correct?

Think Back	Think Ahead
◆ What did you learn about personal narratives in this unit? What did you do to write one?	◆ How will what you learned about personal narratives help you tell about yourself? ◆ How will visualizing events and feelings help you when you want to describe how you feel?
◆ Look at the writing you did in this unit. How did complete sentences help you express ideas?	◆ What is one way that you can use complete sentences to improve your writing?

Analyzing a Personal Narrative *pages 13–14*

Read this narrative. Then follow the directions.

Never Too Old

One summer, I wanted to go to camp with my friend Anne. My mom warned, "You might be homesick."

"Oh, I'm too old for that," I said.

"You never outgrow your family," Mom replied. Finally, she said I could go.

A few days later, I boarded the bus. My mom kissed me good-bye, and I felt a funny lump in my throat. Anne and I laughed and sang all the way to camp. I didn't think about my family even once.

All week Anne and I hiked, swam, watched funny skits, and sang campfire songs. At bedtime, some girls told scary stories. We giggled and tried not to get scared. I thought about how much fun I was having. Then, when all I could hear was the crickets, that funny lump came back to my throat. I realized that Mom was right. I wasn't too old to miss my family.

1. Describe the person who wrote this narrative.
2. Tell why the short conversation at the beginning of the narrative is important.
3. Tell why time order is important in this narrative.
4. Describe the two different feelings that the writer felt while she was at camp.
5. Tell what the writer learned through this experience.

Visualizing Events and Recalling Feelings   *page 15*

Rewrite the following events in time order. For each sentence, write another sentence describing the writer's feelings about the event.

6. So, I sneaked into her room.
7. One day I decided to write a book about my sister.
8. She told me I couldn't use *her* diaries to write a book!
9. Just then my sister came in.
10. I swiped her diaries from under the bed.

Using Vivid Words   *page 16*

Replace the underlined words with more vivid words.

11. I <u>thought</u> about going to camp.
12. I <u>asked</u> my mom to let me go.
13. The skits were <u>funny</u>.
14. The stories that the girls told <u>scared</u> me.
15. <u>I was so hungry</u> that I always <u>ate</u> my food.

The Writing Process   *pages 17–27*

Write the letter of the correct response to each question.

16. Pick the best topic for a personal narrative.
    a. how I play with my baby brother
    b. why I like to write
    c. how my sisters and brothers and I planned a family party one night

17. Choose the detail that is the most important for a personal narrative.
    a. I became a reporter for the school newspaper.
    b. Jonathan said, "This pen ran out of ink."
    c. Martha Sue and Jonathan always wrote the headlines.

18. When you are revising your narrative, what is a special help you can use?
    a. an encyclopedia
    b. an atlas
    c. a thesaurus

19. As you proofread your narrative, what should you do to show the changes you need to make?
    a. Copy everything over as you go along.
    b. Use Editor's Marks.
    c. Highlight things with a yellow marker.

20. After copying your narrative, you find that you left out something. What should you do?
   a. Leave it out and go on.
   b. Write it at the end.
   c. Make another clean copy.

Sentences   *pages 30–31*

Read each group of words. Then write *sentence* or *not a sentence*.

21. All the bees in a beehive work together.
22. Has its own job to do and does it.
23. One bee on a long flight to a good nectar source.
24. That bee will use movements to tell the others where to find the flowers.
25. Then they will know exactly where they should go.
26. No scientist understands exactly how bees communicate.
27. Anybody with a sweet tooth bees makes great honey!

Declarative and Interrogative Sentences   *pages 32–33*

Write each sentence so that it begins and ends correctly.

28. did you know that you can communicate using your body
29. shaking your head is one kind of body language
30. how do you use your body to show that you are happy
31. if you move farther away from someone, you are communicating something
32. what do you mean when you hold your arms across your chest and frown
33. i think a smile is the best kind of body language

Imperative and Exclamatory Sentences   *pages 34–35*

Write each sentence so that it begins and ends correctly.

34. listen to your pet "talking" to you
35. oh, that dog has a loud bark
36. come close to the kitten so you can hear it purr
37. what a talented talking parrot Ms. Chisholm has
38. sometime, watch your pets communicate with each other
39. be sure to get a pet if you're lonely

Subjects and Predicates   *pages 36–37*

Study the underlined words. Then write *subject* or *predicate*.

40. Have you ever seen a baby watch you while you speak?
41. That baby is working very hard to understand what you are saying.
42. Most babies understand much more than they can say.
43. They learn to speak slowly, bit by bit.
44. Just a few words might be in a baby's vocabulary.
45. At two years of age, the same child might be able to say a hundred words!

Complete and Simple Subjects   *pages 38–39*

Write each complete subject. Then underline the simple subject.

46. Alexander Graham Bell worked with deaf people.
47. The study of the ear helped him to understand their problem.
48. A special plan began to form in his mind.
49. Many people had dreamed of communicating over long distances.
50. One man had invented the telegraph.
51. This man wanted to invent a device that would send voices over a wire.

Complete and Simple Predicates   *pages 40–41*

Write each complete predicate. Then underline the simple predicate.

52. Mr. Bell called his invention the telephone.
53. His faithful assistant was Mr. Watson.
54. The two men worked many long days and nights together.
55. Again and again their attempts failed.
56. Mr. Watson got discouraged.
57. The determined Mr. Bell never gave up.

Context Clues   *pages 42–43*

Read each sentence. Look for context clues. Then write the correct definition of each underlined word.

58. People have written letters to each other since history began, for <u>centuries</u>.
59. They wrote about <u>events</u> happening in their lives, just as we do today.
60. Letters are one <u>method</u> that we use to find out about history.
61. Have you read an <u>ancient</u> letter, yellowed with age?
62. Some special old letters are <u>preserved</u> in museums.

UNIT

2

Explaining Facts

◆ **COMPOSITION FOCUS:** **Paragraph of Information**
◆ **LANGUAGE FOCUS:** **Nouns**

Flip through a file drawer in a library card catalogue. What subjects catch your eye? Does Dairying, Dakota Indians, Dallas, Dams, Dance, Dark Ages, or some other subject interest you? Hundreds of books have been written on some of these subjects. The writers felt they had important information to share.

Two types of people write books that give information. In the first group are experts, such as scientists or historians. They spend their lives learning as much as they can about one field. They write books to share the results of their work.

In the second group are writers like Charlotte Yue. She and her husband, David Yue, an artist who illustrates books, are not experts in one particular field. They choose a subject that interests them, do research, and talk to experts. They learn enough to put together a book for readers like themselves who are not experts. In this unit you will read an information article by Charlotte and David Yue. Then you will learn how to write a paragraph of information about something that interests you.

Charlotte Yue and David Yue wrote a book *to inform* people about an interesting part of American history.

Reading with a Writer's Eye
Paragraph of Information

Few Americans today have ever seen a real tipi. However, a century ago, the tipi was a familiar sight on the Great Plains. Charlotte Yue and David Yue created a book called *The Tipi* because they felt that Americans should know how some of their ancestors lived. As you read this selection from their book, notice that the writer tells not only what the tipi was like but why it was built as it was.

from The Tipi: A Center of Native American Life
by Charlotte Yue and David Yue

When Indians stopped somewhere overnight, tipis were just pitched as shelters to sleep in. But when they camped in one place for any length of time, they added amenities, things to make the tipi and the camp more pleasant and comfortable to live in.

The lining, or dew cloth, looked like a curtain that went all the way around the inside of the tipi. It was tied to the lodge poles at a height of about six feet and went all the way to the floor.

The lining was an important part of the tipi. It made the lodge a more comfortable place to live. The lining served as insulation, helping to keep the lodge warm in the winter and cool in the summer.

It also improved ventilation, increasing the flow of air in the tipi and preventing the lodge from getting too smoky. As air inside the tipi was warmed by the fire, the warm air would rise and cold air would be drawn in from the outside. The cold air could come in under the cover and go up behind the lining. This flow of air would keep the fire burning well, and smoke from the fire would be drawn out the smoke hole.

The lining kept drafts and dampness away from the living quarters. It kept dew from condensing inside. And it kept any rain dripping off the poles out of the living area. The lining helped keep the lodge dry.

At night the top of the tipi would glow brightly above the lining. Without a lining, the people inside would cast their shadows on the tipi wall. But there were no shadows when the lining was in place. The lining not only ensured privacy, but it was also important for the safety of the people inside: if an enemy was nearby, shadows would be targets to aim at.

Linings were often decorated with very beautiful designs of beaded stripes, feathers, dyed hair, tassels, or buffalo dewclaws. Men sometimes painted the lining to record experiences. They would illustrate personal triumphs as hunters or warriors or stories about tribal events. The lining added to the beauty of the lodge and made each home a special place. It also added comfort, privacy, and safety to the home.

Different kinds of doors were used on tipis. They varied in their shape and decoration. A door might be a hide embellished with designs worked in beads, paint, or quills. Or it might be nothing more than an old blanket attached to the lacing pins above the doorway. (A stick could be fastened across the blanket to stretch it over the door opening.)

Some doors were made by stretching a skin between two sticks. Others were stretched on a willow frame that was bent into an oval or round shape. Some doors were made from buffalo, bear, or other animal skin with the hair left on. Hides with hair left on shed water well and would help keep the entryway dry.

Indians kept few belongings. They had to be able to pack everything they owned quickly and be able to move easily from camp to camp. But even with limited furnishings, the Indians' homes provided them with some luxury.

Furs were placed on the floors as ground cloths. Beds were pallets made of buffalo hides. These were put on the ground along the sides and back of the lodge.

Women made willow-rod backrests to provide comfortable places to sit. Peeled willow rods about as thick as pencils were strung together with sinew thread to make a mat. The top of the mat was hung from a tripod — three thin poles which were beautifully painted and carved. The mat rested against two of the poles, and the third was used to adjust the angle of the backrest so that a person could sit up straight or lean back. The lower part of the mat was wider than the top and was laid on the floor to make a seat. In winter a buffalo robe might be hung over the mat for extra warmth. These backrests were usually kept at the head of the bed.

Beautifully decorated rawhide storage boxes or envelopes, called parfleches (pär′flesh), were kept behind the beds. These were used to store food, clothing, and personal belongings. When the Indians traveled, they slung their parfleches on either side of the pack saddle, so these were often made in pairs, each pair being decorated exactly alike.

The fireplace was the center of the home, and everything was placed symmetrically around it. Furnishings and belongings were arranged to give a balanced and neat appearance to the tipi.

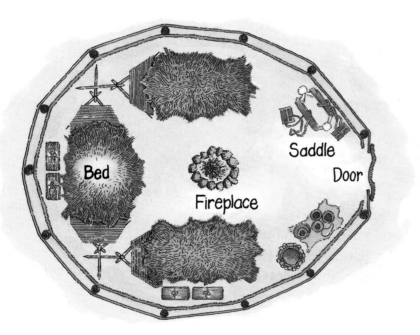

Respond

1. How much of the Yues' information is new to you? What is the most interesting new fact you learned?

Discuss

2. What explanations does the writer give for why the tipi was made as it was? How would the selection be different without this information?

3. Why do you think Charlotte Yue and David Yue wrote about the tipi?

Thinking As a Writer
Analyzing a Paragraph of Information

A paragraph of information contains facts about one topic. What the writer has to say about the topic can be summed up in one sentence that states the main idea. This is usually the first sentence of the paragraph. Good writers write about only one topic at a time.

Every paragraph of information has a **topic sentence** and **detail sentences.** The detail sentences give more facts and information related to the main idea. Details that do not keep to the topic make a paragraph difficult to understand. The first word of a paragraph is indented, or moved in. This is done to show where a new topic begins.

Different kinds of doors were used on tipis. They varied in their shape and decoration. A door might be a hide embellished with designs worked in beads, paint, or quills. Or it might be nothing more than an old blanket attached to the lacing pins above the doorway. (A stick could be fastened across the blanket to stretch it over the door opening.)

A **topic sentence** introduces the main idea. It is usually the first sentence of a paragraph.

Detail sentences give more facts about the main idea.

Discuss

1. Identify the topic of the paragraph. Then state the main idea in one sentence.
2. Look at the second sentence. What information does it add to the topic sentence?
3. What type of information do the other detail sentences add? Why are they important? Explain your answer.

Try Your Hand

A. Analyze Paragraphs   The sentence beginnings below are from pages 53, 54, and 55 of *The Tipi* selection. Find the paragraphs with these beginnings. Then write a sentence in your own words that tells the main idea of each paragraph.

◆ The lining kept drafts and dampness away. . .
◆ Women made willow-rod backrests. . .
◆ Beautifully decorated rawhide storage boxes . . .

B. Distinguish Unnecessary Detail Sentences   The following paragraph contains two detail sentences that do not tell about the main idea. Write these two sentences.

The American Indians of the midwestern prairies built earth lodges. They put up a framework of thick wooden poles. They added a skeleton of lighter rafters. Then they covered these curved rafters with willow branches. Willows and black walnut trees grew in that area. The Indians put grass, then sod, and then earth over the branches. Sometimes they tied bundles of grass over the whole house. In the Swiss countryside, you can actually see grass growing from some roofs. The thick covering made the houses snug and warm.

C. Write Topic Sentences   Think of a main idea for each of these topics. Then write a topic sentence to introduce each main idea.

a subject in school	clothing
movies	a vacation

D. Read a Paragraph of Information   Choose one of the paragraphs in *The Tipi* selection on pages 52–55, or find a paragraph of information in a book or a magazine. Then read it aloud to a partner. State the main idea in your own words. Then identify the details the writer gives about the main idea.

Writer's Notebook

Collecting Nouns with Special Meanings   In *The Tipi*, the writer introduced the reader to words like *parfleches* and *pallets*. As people study a subject, they learn the special names. As you read, record in your *Writer's Notebook* any sentences that contain special names for things. After you have looked these names up in a reference book, record their meanings. Label the list *Nouns with Special Meanings*. Try to use these new words when you write and speak.

Thinking As a Writer
Connecting Main Idea and Details

Writer's Guide

As they begin to write a paragraph of information, writers

◆ identify a main idea.

◆ gather only details that tell about the main idea.

As writers prepare to write a paragraph of information, they remind themselves that it must be about only one main idea. They choose only those details and facts that are related to the main idea. Some writers use diagrams like this to help them.

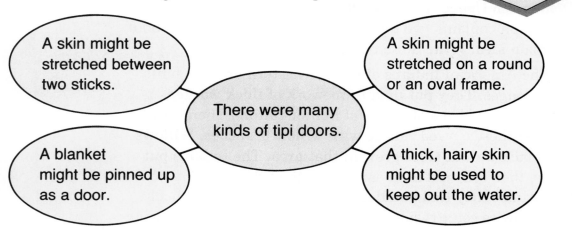

The sentence in the center circle states the main idea. Each fact in the other circles is related to the main idea.

As you write your paragraph of information, be sure to present only details that are related to the main idea.

Discuss

1. How are the facts in the outside circles related to the main idea?
2. What facts could you add to the diagram? Give your reasons.

Try Your Hand

Classify Details   Make a diagram like the one above to show which of the following details belong with the main idea.

Main Idea: The eastern Pueblo Indians built adobe homes.
Details:
Indians patted the adobe into turtle-shaped lumps.
Each town had *kivas,* special meeting chambers.
They piled up the bricks and plastered between them.
They put adobe on top of their flat roofs.

Developing the Writer's Craft
Using Exact Words

Writers whose goal is to give information must present facts clearly. To make themselves understood by their readers, writers use exact words.
Compare these two sentences.

1. If <u>someone</u> was nearby, the <u>shapes</u> inside would be <u>something</u> to aim at.
2. If <u>an enemy</u> was nearby, the <u>shadows of the people</u> inside would be <u>targets</u> to aim at.

The first sentence does not contain enough information to be understood clearly. When the writer replaces the underlined words with words that are more exact, the picture becomes clear to the reader.

When you write your paragraph of information, try to present details clearly. Use strong, exact words to help your readers see what you want them to see.

Discuss

1. Look at sentence 1 in the example above. Why are parts of it not clear? How do the changes in sentence 2 improve each part?
2. Turn to page 54 and reread the paragraph that describes the willow-rod backrests. Which nouns in this paragraph create pictures in your mind? Why are these words helpful?

Try Your Hand

Use Exact Words Choose one of the objects in the pictures. Write three sentences that tell what it looks like. Use exact words.

1 Prewriting
Paragraph of Information

Steve and his classmates decided to pretend to be historians living in the year 2200. Their plan was to publish a "history magazine" describing everyday objects used by Americans in the twentieth century, from 1901 to the year 2000. Steve used the checklist in the **Writer's Guide** to help him plan his paragraph of information. Look at what he did.

◆ Brainstorming and Selecting a Topic

First, Steve brainstormed some possible topics for his paragraph. Look at his list. He wrote down some topics he thought would be fun to write about.

Next, Steve looked at his list and crossed out objects that he could not describe easily in just one paragraph. He also crossed off objects that were not part of everyday life.

Finally, Steve circled the topic he thought would be most interesting. He chose the phonograph because he could study the record player at school. He also thought he could write about it in just one paragraph. Then Steve and his classmates compared their ideas. Some found they had chosen the same objects. These students looked at their lists again to find other topics.

the automobile
the phonograph
rockets
the typewriter
a parka
a canning factory

Discuss

1. Look at each topic that Steve crossed off his list. Why do you think he decided not to use each one?
2. Suppose Steve found that he and another student had chosen the same topic. Which other topic on his list would make a good choice? Why?

◆ Gathering and Organizing Information

After choosing his topic, Steve began to gather details for his paragraph. He studied the phonograph at school. He asked his teacher the names of some parts that he didn't know. He made notes on the information he thought he might use. He reminded himself that his task was to describe what the object looked like and what it did. Then he made a diagram to help him organize his facts.

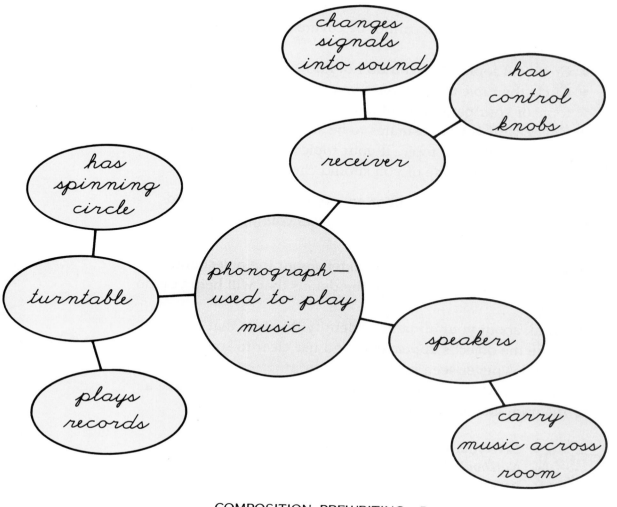

Discuss

1. What will be the main idea of Steve's paragraph?
2. Read the facts Steve wrote in the outer circles. How are they related to the main idea?
3. Notice that Steve connected some of the circles. Why did he connect these groups of facts?

Try Your Hand

Now plan a paragraph of information of your own for people of the distant future to read.

A. Brainstorm and Select a Topic   Brainstorm a list of possible topics. Include items you think it would be fun to write about. Think about each topic and the audience that will read your paragraph in the year 2200.

- ◆ Cross out topics that cannot be covered in just one paragraph.
- ◆ Cross out topics that you do not know well enough.
- ◆ Circle the topic that interests you most. This will be the topic of your paragraph of information.
- ◆ Check with your classmates to be sure you have each chosen a different topic. If your topic is the same as someone else's, one of you should choose another topic.

B. Gather and Organize Information   When you are satisfied with your topic, gather and list the facts you might use in your paragraph.

- ◆ Remember that your goal is to tell about the object and how it is used. Write down the details that will help you do that.
- ◆ Think about your audience. Identify the facts that will make the object's appearance and use clear to someone who has never seen it.
- ◆ Make a plan for your paragraph. You may want to make a diagram like Steve's to help you organize your ideas.

 Save your notes and diagram in your _Writer's Notebook_. You will use them when you draft your paragraph of information.

2 Drafting
Paragraph of Information

Using his notes and his diagram, Steve followed the **Writer's Guide** to draft his paragraph of information. Look at the way he began.

When Americans wanted to listen to music, they often used the phonograph. This electrical machine had three main parts. The turntable was a round spinning platform on a small, flat box.

Discuss

1. Look at Steve's topic sentence. What important information does it give the readers?
2. Compare Steve's beginning to his diagram on page 61. Which details hasn't he added yet?

Try Your Hand

Now you are ready to write a paragraph of information.

A. Review Your Information   Think about the information you gathered and organized in the last lesson. Decide whether you want to add or cut any details. If so, do it now.

B. Think About Your TAP   Remember that your task is to write a paragraph of information. Your purpose is to inform the readers of the future about an object they have never seen.

Task: What?
Audience: Who?
Purpose: Why?

C. Write Your First Draft   Follow the **Writer's Guide** to write your first draft.

When you write your draft, just put all your ideas on paper. Do not worry about spelling, punctuation, or grammar. You can correct the draft later.

Save your first draft in your *Writer's Notebook*. You will use it when you revise your paragraph of information.

3 Responding and Revising
Paragraph of Information

Steve used the checklist in the **Writer's Guide** to revise his paragraph of information. Look at what he did.

◆ Checking Information

Steve found a sentence that gave information that did not belong in his paragraph. He used this mark ✗ to take out the sentence. Then he realized that adding a word before *wires* would give his readers a clearer picture. To show the addition, he used this mark ∧ .

◆ Checking Organization

Steve moved the last sentence because it belongs with the facts about the receiver. To show it should be moved, he used this mark ↻ .

◆ Checking Language

In one sentence, Steve found two words that he could replace with words that are more exact. By doing so, he could make sure his readers understood him. He used this mark ‿ to make his changes.

Writer's Guide

Revising Checklist
- ☑ Read your paragraph of information to yourself or to a partner.
- ☑ Think about your audience and your purpose. Add or cut information.
- ☑ Check to see that your paragraph begins with a topic sentence.
- ☑ Check for details that do not belong, and cut them.
- ☑ Check to be sure you used exact words.

A moving turntable arm read the soundtracks in the grooves of the records. Another part of the phonograph was a box called a receiver. ~~It was nothing like a telephone receiver.~~ It turned the ^signals^ information from the turntable into ^music^ ~~sounds~~. The third part was made up of two boxes called speakers. They were connected by ^long^ wires to the receiver. They carried music to different parts of the room. Knobs on the receiver were used to adjust the sound.

Cut — Replace — Add — Move

Discuss

1. Look at the sentence that Steve thought did not belong. Was it a good idea to take it out? Explain your answer.
2. Find the two words that Steve replaced. Do these changes improve the sentence? Explain your opinion.

Try Your Hand

Now revise your first draft.

A. Read Your First Draft   As you read your paragraph of information, think about your audience and your purpose. Read your paragraph silently or to a partner to see if it is complete and well organized. Ask yourself or your partner the questions in the box.

Responding and Revising Strategies

✔ **Respond**
Ask yourself or your partner:

◆ Does my topic sentence tell the main idea of my paragraph?

◆ Do all my detail sentences give facts about the main idea? Have I kept to the topic?

◆ Do I present my information in an order that makes sense?

◆ Do I use exact words to make a clear picture for my readers?

✔ **Revise**
Try these solutions:

◆ **Replace** or **add** information to your topic sentence.

◆ **Cut** any details that do not belong. See the **Revising Workshop** on page 66.

◆ **Move** any sentences that seem to be in the wrong place.

◆ **Replace** weak words with exact, strong words.

B. Make Your Changes   If the answer to any question in the box is *no*, try the solution. Use the **Editor's Marks** to show your changes.

C. Review Your Paragraph of Information Again
Decide if there is anything else you want to revise. Keep revising your paragraph until you feel it is well organized and complete.

EDITOR'S MARKS

∧ Add something.
↗ Cut something.
◯ Move something.
∧ Replace something.

Save your revised paragraph of information in your *Writer's Notebook*. You will use it when you proofread your paragraph.

COMPOSITION: RESPONDING/REVISING   Paragraph of Information   **65**

Revising Workshop
Keeping to the Topic

Good writers stick to the point when they give information. They do not put in facts that have nothing to do with their main idea. The paragraph below has one sentence in it that does not belong.

> The microwave oven was an oven with a brain. The user could program it to cook oatmeal for exactly 2 minutes and 30 seconds. Most foods took a little longer than that to cook. Then, after exactly 2 minutes and 30 seconds, the oven shut itself off.

Did you identify the third sentence as the one that should be taken out? The main idea of the paragraph is that the microwave oven acted as if it had a brain. Since the third sentence does not make that point, it should be taken out. Reread the paragraph without that sentence to hear the way the paragraph is improved.

Practice

Here is a paragraph of information about an object we have now. The writer is taking a historical look at microwave ovens. Write the numbers of the detail sentences that do not support the main idea. Then write a sentence that tells why each does not belong.

Main Idea: A microwave oven saved the user time and work.
Details:
1. You could heat food on a plate and eat it from the same plate, so there were fewer pans to wash.
2. It shut off by itself, so that when you came back you did not find a burnt pan to clean.
3. Some vegetables, like potatoes, cooked three times as fast as they would with a different kind of oven.
4. You could overcook food by setting the timer for too long.
5. You had to remember not to use metal pans in it.
6. To heat a baby bottle, you didn't need to fill a pan with water. After removing the nipple, just put the bottle itself into the oven.

Listening and Speaking
Tips on How to Speak and Listen in a Response Group

Speaking in a Response Group

1. Begin by making sure that all group members understand that the purpose of the response group is to improve writing.
2. Take turns speaking about each other's writing. Speak clearly so that everyone can hear you. Think about what you want to say before you speak.
3. Be polite when you respond. Do not interrupt while another person is speaking.
4. Describe what you liked about the other group members' writing. Ask questions about the parts you do not understand. Make suggestions.

Listening in a Response Group

1. Listen carefully to the person speaking. Think about how the speaker's suggestions could improve your writing.
2. Wait until the speaker is finished before you respond.
3. Listen to discover ideas from other group members' writing.
4. Thank the group members for their help.

4 Proofreading
Paragraph of Information

Writer's Guide

Proofreading Checklist

☑ Look for errors in capitalization. Be sure each sentence begins with a capital letter.

☑ Check for errors in the end punctuation of sentences.

☑ Be sure that your paragraph is indented.

☑ Check for errors in grammar.

☑ Circle any words you think are misspelled. Find out how to spell them correctly.

⇨ For proofreading help, use the **Writer's Handbook.**

After revising his paragraph of information, Steve used the **Writer's Guide** and the **Editor's Marks** to proofread it. Look at what he did.

> the (reciever) *receiver* contained the control knobs. One knob turned the machine on and off⊙ Another (controlled) the (volyum) *volum* of the sound from the speakers. others were used ∧*to* (ajust) *adjust* the high and low sounds⊙

Discuss

1. Look at Steve's proofread paragraph. Why did he make each correction?

2. Why did Steve circle the word *controlled*? Why didn't he write a correction above it?

Try Your Hand

Proofread Your Paragraph of Information   Now use the **Writer's Guide** and the **Editor's Marks** to proofread your paragraph.

Save your corrected paragraph of information in your *Writer's Notebook.* You will use it when you publish your paragraph.

EDITOR'S MARKS

≡ Capitalize.

⊙ Add a period.

∧ Add something.

⋏ Add a comma.

⌄⌄ Add quotation marks.

✍ Cut something.

⌃ Replace something.

↰↱ Transpose.

◯ Spell correctly.

₮ Indent paragraph.

/ Make a lowercase letter.

WRITING PROCESS

5 Publishing
Paragraph of Information

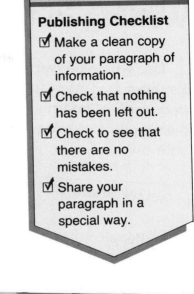

Writer's Guide

Publishing Checklist

☑ Make a clean copy of your paragraph of information.

☑ Check that nothing has been left out.

☑ Check to see that there are no mistakes.

☑ Share your paragraph in a special way.

Steve made a clean copy of his paragraph and checked it to be sure that he had not left out anything. Then he and his classmates published their paragraphs in a class magazine called *Exploring Our Past.* You can find Steve's paragraph of information on page 20 of the **Writer's Handbook.**

Here's how Steve and his classmates published their paragraphs in a class magazine.

1. First, they chose a name for their magazine. They decided who would create the magazine cover.
2. They decided how the paragraphs would be illustrated and brought in pictures or drawings of the objects they wrote about.
3. They planned the pages so that each page contained two columns. They wrote or typed each story so that it was as wide as one column.
4. They decided in what order to place the paragraphs. They pasted the paragraphs and the pictures on each page.
5. Then they numbered the pages, beginning with page 1.
6. When the pages were in order, they had them copied and stapled them together. Then they shared their magazine with their families.

Discuss

1. Why is the same plan used for all the pages?
2. What could they add to make it look like a real magazine?

Try Your Hand

Publish Your Paragraph of Information   Follow the checklist in the **Writer's Guide.** If possible, create a magazine, or try this idea for sharing information.

◆ Create a display. Bring in small models or pictures of the objects you wrote about. Use your paragraphs to identify the objects.

Writing in the Content Areas

Use what you learned to write about a person or a subject that interests you. You could write a paragraph of information or another kind of paragraph. Use one of these ideas or an idea of your own.

Writer's Guide

When you write, remember the stages of the Writing Process.

◆ Prewriting
◆ Drafting
◆ Responding and Revising
◆ Proofreading
◆ Publishing

Social Studies

People enjoy work that makes use of their talents. Ask an adult who enjoys his or her job what skills and training are needed for that job. Ask about the rewards of that kind of work. Be sure to find out why the person chose that job.

Health

List the foods served on the school lunch menu for one day. Tell why you think that group of foods was chosen. Then write a paragraph about your favorite school lunch. Tell why it is your favorite.

Physical Education

What makes a winner? Talk to a local athlete you admire. Find out how he or she became a good athlete. Find out which other athlete he or she admires. Ask what advice the athlete would give to others.

Science

Watch a nature or wildlife program on television. Take notes as you watch. Think about what you learned. Write a paragraph of information telling about the subject of the program.

CONNECTING

WRITING ⟷ LANGUAGE

A paragraph of information tells about a person, a place, or an object. The paragraph should include details that help readers understand the information. What details help you learn more about the person in this paragraph?

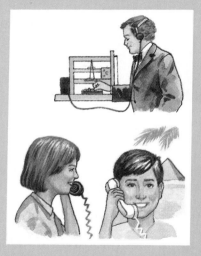

> Samuel Morse was an inventor in America who developed the first successful electric telegraph . He also invented the Morse code , which is sometimes still used to send telegrams . For years he experimented with ways to send messages . Finally, he was able to create a very useful machine that helped people communicate with friends and relatives in other parts of the country .

◆ **Nouns in a Paragraph of Information**   The highlighted words are nouns. They tell *who*, *what*, and *where*. Some nouns, like *Samuel Morse*, *America*, and *Morse code*, give exact information. Each names a particular person, place, or thing. Other nouns, like *inventor*, *country*, and *messages*, are less exact. They are useful because they refer to almost any person, place, or thing. Writers use a different spelling for nouns when the nouns refer to more than one. The *s* in *years* tells you that Samuel Morse worked on his invention for more than one year. Writers can use nouns in many ways to give readers details.

◆ **Language Focus: Nouns**   In the following lessons you will learn more about using different kinds of nouns in your writing.

1 Nouns

◆ **FOCUS** A **noun** is a word that names a person, a place, or a thing.

The words in color in these sentences are nouns.

1. Our family goes to the beach each year .

2. Matt swims in the lake after lunch .

The nouns *family* and *Matt* name persons. The nouns *beach* and *lake* name places. The nouns *year* and *lunch* name things.

> **Link to Speaking and Writing**
> Use exact nouns to paint a clear picture.
> Why is the new sentence clearer?

The ~~child~~ girl played with a ~~toy~~ sailboat.

Guided Practice

A. Identify the nouns in each sentence.

    1. Jennifer lives in a large city.
    2. Her vacations are spent in Kingsport.
    3. This town is many miles from her home.
    4. Her first trip there was ten years ago.

B. Replace the underlined words with more exact nouns.

    5. Now many visitors come to this popular place.
    6. Food is sold at a small stand.
    7. Children play on the things in the new playground.
    8. People follow trails through the woods.

> **THINK AND REMEMBER**
> ◆ Remember that a **noun** names a person, a place, or a thing.
> ◆ Use exact nouns to make clear pictures.

Independent Practice

C. Identifying Nouns   Write the nouns you find in each
sentence.

   9. Her parents rent a cabin close to the water.

MODEL parents, cabin, water

   10. Sometimes relatives come for a visit.
   11. Her uncle packs food in a big basket.
   12. A blue umbrella protects the babies from the sun.
   13. Mother spreads a tablecloth in a peaceful spot.
   14. Dad takes another piece of delicious chicken.
   15. A gull sits on a post and watches their feast.
   16. The greedy bird hopes to pick up scraps.

D. 17.–24. Classifying Nouns   Make a chart with three columns.
   Head the columns *People, Places,* and *Things.* Use the nouns in
   C. Write each noun under the correct heading. Be careful to
   put all the nouns that tell *where* in the *Places* column.

People	Places	Things
MODEL 17. parents		cabin, water

E. Revising Sentences   Replace the underlined word or words
   with a more exact noun. Write the sentence.

   25. Eric bought a thing to eat.

MODEL Eric bought a sandwich to eat.

   26. He bought it from the person at a little store.
   27. The children are playing a game.
   28. Jennifer throws a thing to Tom.
   29. It flutters to a stop at the place.
   30. Jennifer sees a flower beside the path.
   31. Then she notices the building ahead.
   32. Aunt Ellen rides a thing into the city.
   33. She wants to buy things.

Application—Writing

A Postcard   Imagine that you are at a beach. Write some
sentences that you might put on a postcard to a friend. Tell
whether you like the beach. Give your reasons. Underline the
nouns you use.

2 Singular and Plural Nouns

FOCUS

◆ A **singular noun** names one person, place, or thing.
◆ A **plural noun** names more than one person, place, or thing.

Remember that nouns are naming words. The words in color are nouns.

1. The guide talked to the students .
2. One room held many interesting displays .
3. This fox lived near the marshes .

The words *guide, room,* and *fox* are singular nouns. The words *students, displays,* and *marshes* are plural nouns. You add the letter *s* to make most singular nouns into plural nouns.

Spelling Other Plural Nouns
1. Add *es* to form the plural of nouns that end in *s, x, ch,* or *sh: glass—glasses, tax—taxes, porch—porches, ash—ashes.*
2. When a noun ends in a consonant and *y,* change the *y* to *i* and add *es: cherry—cherries.*
3. When a noun ends in a vowel and *y,* just add *s: bay—bays.*

Guided Practice

A. Tell if each noun is *singular* or *plural* .

1. faces
2. inches
3. beach
4. ways
5. walrus
6. pennies
7. eyelash
8. hoses
9. business
10. mystery
11. addresses
12. mixes

B. 13.–24. Tell how to form the plural of each singular noun in **A.**

Independent Practice

C. Identifying Nouns   Write each underlined noun. Then, write *singular* or *plural* after each one.

25. Our <u>class</u> enjoys visiting <u>museums</u>.

MODEL > class—singular, museums—plural

26. We have made three <u>trips</u> to it this <u>year</u>.
27. Two <u>buses</u> carried our <u>group</u> there.
28. We took our <u>lunches</u> in cardboard <u>boxes</u>.
29. The <u>teacher</u> told some interesting <u>facts</u>.
30. Our wilderness <u>areas</u> have changed over <u>time</u>.
31. <u>Settlers</u> came into the wild <u>country</u>.
32. They hunted the <u>animals</u> and destroyed their <u>homes</u>.
33. Only a small <u>number</u> of buffalo <u>herds</u> were left.
34. The last passenger <u>pigeon</u> died in a <u>zoo</u> in 1914.

D. Spelling Plural Nouns   Write the plural form of each noun.

35. sea

MODEL > seas

36. dress   38. mailbox   40. dish
37. tablecloth   39. city   41. patch

E. 42.–48. Writing Original Sentences   Use the plural forms of the words in **D**. Write each plural noun in a sentence.

42. seas

MODEL > I saw an exhibit about life in the seas.

Application—Writing and Speaking

A Speech   Imagine that you are a guide for a natural history museum. Write some sentences that tell your listeners about the displays. Use five or more plural nouns in your speech. Then read your speech to a classmate.

3 More Plural Nouns

◆ **FOCUS**   The plural forms of some nouns follow special rules.

Remember that most plural nouns are formed by adding *s* or *es* to singular nouns. Some nouns follow other rules.

1. One ox pulled a wagon.   Several oxen pulled the wagons.

2. The little family had one sheep .   Five sheep had died.

Notice that the spelling of *ox* changed when it became the plural noun *oxen*. The singular and plural forms of *sheep* are the same. This chart shows how some words form their plurals.

Spelling More Plural Nouns

1. The spelling is changed to form the plural of these nouns.

Singular	Plural	Singular	Plural
child	children	mouse	mice
foot	feet	ox	oxen
goose	geese	tooth	teeth
man	men	woman	women

2. The singular and the plural forms of these nouns are the same.

Singular	Plural	Singular	Plural
deer	deer	sheep	sheep
elk	elk	trout	trout
moose	moose	salmon	salmon

Guided Practice

A. Identify each underlined noun as *singular* or *plural*.

1. The <u>woman</u> carried a baby.
2. Her <u>child</u> was tired and thirsty.
3. The boy had a bad cut on one <u>foot</u>.
4. He had two tame <u>mice</u> for pets.

Independent Practice

B. Identifying Singular and Plural Nouns   Write *singular* or *plural* for each underlined noun.

5. The <u>children</u> walked beside the wagon.

MODEL ⟩ plural

6. Their <u>feet</u> were tired by the end of the day.
7. They rested at noon and fed the <u>oxen</u>.
8. A <u>sheep</u> was dragged away by wolves.
9. Each <u>man</u> went hunting for game.
10. Mr. Brewer chased a big <u>elk</u> for miles.

C. Spelling Plural Nouns   Write the plural form of the noun in parentheses ( ) in each sentence.

11. Beavers have sharp little (tooth).

MODEL ⟩ teeth

12. The (woman) talked about the animals they had seen.
13. Sometimes they spotted shy (deer) along the trail.
14. Owls came out at night to hunt (mouse).
15. Ann Brewer had seen many (moose) back in Wyoming.
16. Sarah Walsh told about herds of (elk) there.

D. 17.–26. Writing Original Sentences   Choose five singular nouns and five plural nouns from the chart on page 76. Write a sentence using each one. Give clues that make it clear whether the noun is singular or plural.

17. deer

MODEL ⟩ We saw two deer near the trail.

Application—Writing

A Journal   Imagine that you are the person in the picture. Write some sentences that might be in your journal. Tell about some adventures that helped you change and grow. Use at least five of the plural nouns you studied in this lesson. If you need help writing a journal entry, see page 26 of the **Writer's Handbook.**

4 Common and Proper Nouns

FOCUS

◆ A **common noun** names any person, place, or thing.

◆ A **proper noun** names a particular person, place, or thing.

Remember that nouns name people, places, or things. Look at the nouns in these sentences. The proper nouns begin with capital letters.

1. The woman in the picture is Claire Yien.

2. She lives in the city of Houston.

3. She works for a company called Kent Laboratories.

Notice that some proper nouns are made up of more than one word. Each important word begins with a capital letter.

Link to Speaking and Writing

You can sometimes make your writing more exact by replacing a common noun with a proper noun. Why is the new sentence better?

> Neil Armstrong
> An astronaut walked on the moon.

Guided Practice

A. Identify each word or word group as a *common noun* or a *proper noun*.

1. doctor
2. Mrs. Bethune
3. Florida
4. January
5. canyon
6. holiday
7. desert
8. person
9. Rocky Mountains
10. Statue of Liberty
11. street
12. Pluto

B. 13.–24. Replace each common noun in **A** with a proper noun.

Independent Practice

C. Identifying Common and Proper Nouns Write each underlined noun. Then, write *common* or *proper* after it.

25. A great <u>scientist</u> was born in <u>Poland</u> in 1473.

MODEL ▷ scientist—common, Poland—proper

26. <u>Copernicus</u> said the <u>planets</u> moved around the <u>sun</u>.
27. <u>Galileo Galilei</u> looked at the <u>sky</u> with a <u>telescope</u>.
28. He saw that the <u>Milky Way</u> was made up of many <u>stars</u>.
29. He also discovered four <u>moons</u> around <u>Jupiter</u>.

D. Proofreading Sentences Write each sentence correctly. Capitalize all proper nouns.

30. Astronauts train at the johnson space center.

MODEL ▷ Astronauts train at the Johnson Space Center.

31. Sally ride was born in encino, california.
32. She took classes at stanford university.
33. Then, she trained for the space program in houston.
34. She traveled into space aboard the challenger.

E. Revising Sentences Make each sentence more exact. Replace one or more common nouns in each sentence with proper nouns.

35. The man waved good-bye to the young woman.

MODEL ▷ The man waved good-bye to Sally Ride.

36. The young woman traveled to another state.
37. The plane arrived at the airport.
38. It was a weekday and a holiday.
39. She took a bus into the city.

Application—Writing

A Job Application Imagine that you are Claire Yien. You want to change your job. Write some sentences about yourself. Tell what you have done and what you want to do. Use at least five common nouns and five proper nouns.

5 Names and Titles of People

◆ **FOCUS** Each word in a person's name begins with a capital letter.

When you use proper nouns, you must be careful to write them correctly. Notice how the names on the list are written.

Each word in a name begins with a capital letter. Sometimes an initial is used in place of a person's name. An **initial** is the first letter of a name. It is written as a capital letter and followed by a period.

Notice that some names begin with titles. Titles begin with capital letters. Often titles are written as abbreviations. **Abbreviations** are short forms of words. They usually end with periods.

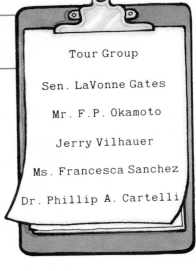

Tour Group

Sen. LaVonne Gates

Mr. F.P. Okamoto

Jerry Vilhauer

Ms. Francesca Sanchez

Dr. Phillip A. Cartelli

Common Titles			
Title	**Used for**	**Title**	**Used for**
Mr.	any man	Ms.	any woman
Mrs.	a married woman	Miss	an unmarried woman
Dr.	a doctor	Sen.	a U.S. senator
Gov.	a state governor	Capt.	a captain

Guided Practice

A. Tell how to write these names correctly.

1. dr Janice lee
2. Mr. h. i. palacios
3. ms. Gloria Molina
4. gov Edmund g. Brown
5. Sen. alice Blackwell
6. Mrs J H. cohen
7. sam s. rao
8. jorge gonzales

THINK AND REMEMBER
- ◆ Begin each part of a person's name with a capital letter.
- ◆ Begin a person's title with a capital letter.
- ◆ Use a period after an initial or an abbreviation of a title.

Independent Practice

B. Identifying Errors Write these names. Use capital letters and periods correctly.

9. ms Lillian Spielman

MODEL > Ms. Lillian Spielman

10. sen Ted Kennedy
11. capt l. p. Morelli
12. mr Kenneth Yien
13. gov robert Martinez
14. mrs M A Doherty
15. Dr Teresa j. McSwain

C. Proofreading Sentences Write each sentence. Correct the capitalization and punctuation of the names and titles.

16. The bus driver's name was mr. omar waziri.

MODEL > The bus driver's name was Mr. Omar Waziri.

17. Our guide, susan lopez, took us to the canyon.
18. I rode a mule named lulu down the path.
19. My brother michael fell off his mule.
20. ms julia armstrong took pictures of amy and me.
21. I learned the canyon's history from dr david ho.
22. francisco tomás garcés visited it in 1776.
23. Then, joseph c ives explored it in 1858.
24. The first person to sail down the river was j w powell.
25. I told these facts to mr and mrs burns.

D. Revising Sentences Write these sentences. Replace the underlined titles with abbreviations. Replace the underlined names with initials.

26. Senator Angela Noyes Fargo joined our group.

MODEL > Sen. A. N. Fargo joined our group.

27. Mister Raymond Alonzo Garcia sat in front.
28. Doctor Mary Ann Noguchi talked to my brother.
29. She introduced him to Captain Lydia Louise Pym.
30. I read about Governor John Routt.
31. We hoped to meet Senator William Armstrong.

Application—Writing

A List Finish the list of people on the sample tour. Add the names of other people. Use at least three titles and three initials. Write the names clearly and correctly so that a guide can read them easily.

6 Capitalization of Proper Nouns

◆ **FOCUS** The name of a place, a day, a month, or a holiday begins with a capital letter.

Remember that proper nouns name particular people, places, and things. Notice the proper nouns in color in these sentences.

1. The bookstore is in Denver, Colorado .

2. Thanksgiving comes on the fourth
   Thursday in November .

In sentence 1 the proper nouns name particular places. In sentence 2 the proper nouns name a particular holiday, a day of the week, and a month. Each of these kinds of words begins with a capital letter.

Remember that only the important words in a proper noun are capitalized.

3. I like to watch the fireworks on the
    Fourth of July .

Guided Practice

A. Tell how to correct these proper nouns.

1. Columbus day
2. thursday
3. evergreen Drive
4. wednesday, March 7
5. Oakland city College
6. La Fayette, georgia
7. Chinese new year
8. monday, October 13
9. Ocala, florida
10. Puerto rico
11. mother's day
12. austin, Texas

THINK AND REMEMBER
- ◆ Remember that a proper noun names a particular place, holiday, day of the week, or month.
- ◆ Capitalize the first letter of each important word in a proper noun.

Independent Practice

B. Capitalizing Proper Nouns   Write each proper noun correctly.

13. United states of America

MODEL > United States of America

14. ames, iowa
15. Memorial day
16. san Diego, california

17. wednesday, December 3
18. gulf of mexico
19. saturday, april 3

C. Proofreading Sentences   Write each sentence correctly. Add capital letters where they are needed.

20. I live in sharon, pennsylvania.

MODEL > I live in Sharon, Pennsylvania.

21. Every january I send a calendar to my aunt in hawaii.
22. I shop at the bookstore on churchill avenue.
23. Their sale is on the last saturday in december.
24. The store will be closed tomorrow for new year's day.
25. It will reopen on monday, january 2.
26. This calendar shows all the holidays in north america.
27. What a lot of special days there are in march!
28. March 15 is buzzard's day in hinckley, ohio.
29. Does my aunt know about the prince kuhio festival?

D. Writing Proper Nouns   Answer these questions in complete sentences. Be sure to capitalize all proper nouns.

30. In which state do you live?

MODEL > I live in Massachusetts.

31. When is your birthday?
32. What is your favorite holiday?
33. What is your favorite day of the week?
34. Where would you live if you could live anywhere in the world?
35. What large city do you think is the most interesting?

Application—Writing

Holiday Descriptions   Invent four holidays. Make up one for each season of the year. Write some sentences describing each holiday. Tell where, when, and how they are celebrated. Be sure to use proper nouns that name places, days, and months as well as holidays.

7 Abbreviations

◆ An **abbreviation** is a shortened form of a word.
◆ Many abbreviations begin with a capital letter and end with a period.

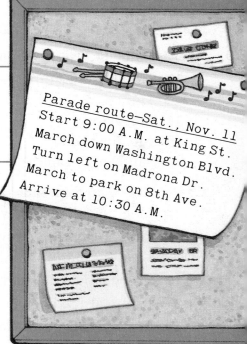

Days, months, and some parts of addresses can be abbreviated. Address and date abbreviations are used in some kinds of writing. You may use abbreviations when you take notes, make lists, write in a journal, or address an envelope. In other kinds of writing, the complete word is usually written out.

The time words *A.M.* and *P.M.* are also abbreviations. The time word *A.M.* stands for the Latin words that mean "before noon," while *P.M.* stands for the Latin words for "after noon."

Common Abbreviations					
Ave.	Avenue	Dr.	Drive	St.	Street
Blvd.	Boulevard	Rd.	Road		
Sun.	Sunday	Wed.	Wednesday	Fri.	Friday
Mon.	Monday	Thurs.	Thursday	Sat.	Saturday
Tues.	Tuesday				
Jan.	January	Apr.	April	Oct.	October
Feb.	February	Aug.	August	Nov.	November
Mar.	March	Sept.	September	Dec.	December

Guided Practice

A. Tell the abbreviations for the underlined words.

1. <u>April</u> 5, 1989
2. Graham Hill <u>Road</u>
3. <u>Thursday</u>, <u>August</u> 8
4. Hacienda <u>Drive</u>
5. Winke <u>Avenue</u>
6. <u>Tuesday</u>, <u>December</u> 6
7. Morrissey <u>Boulevard</u>
8. <u>Friday</u>, May 7

Independent Practice

B. Writing Abbreviations   Write each item. Use abbreviations for the underlined words.

9. 740 Chester <u>Avenue</u>

MODEL ▷ 740 Chester Ave.

10. <u>Sunday</u>, <u>October</u> 12
11. National <u>Boulevard</u>
12. Escalona <u>Drive</u>
13. <u>Wednesday</u>, June 8

14. Olive Springs <u>Road</u>
15. <u>Monday</u>, <u>February</u> 2
16. <u>Saturday</u>, <u>November</u> 8
17. Mission <u>Street</u>

C. Proofreading Abbreviations   Rewrite each item. Correct any errors in the abbreviations.

18. appointment on Feb 2

MODEL ▷ appointment on Feb. 2

19. 5077 Branch dr.
20. band concert on sun., aug. 8
21. meet at park at 7:00 pm.
22. 1432 Rio Del Mar blvd
23. lunch served from 11:30 AM to 2:00 PM
24. 166 Sugar Pine Rd
25. corner of Pacific Ave and Cooper St
26. Jennie's birthday on apr. 7
27. library closed Sept 5 for Labor Day
28. open Tues through Sat at 10:00 am
29. meeting changed to fri.
30. wedding in jan.
31. 981 Bellmont ave
32. puppies born on Nov 12 at 3:00 pm

Application—Writing

A Schedule   Think of an occasion for a parade in your community. Make a schedule like the one that begins this lesson. Use abbreviations for days, months, addresses, and times.

8 Singular Possessive Nouns

◆ **FOCUS** A **singular possessive noun** shows ownership by one person or thing.

Sometimes nouns tell what someone or something owns or has. Nouns that show ownership are **possessive nouns.**

1. My son's drawing is the one on the end.

2. Laura's writing shows imagination.

The word *son's* tells to whom the drawing belongs. The word *Laura's* tells whose writing is being described. Both words are singular possessive nouns. Each one contains a punctuation mark called an apostrophe ('). The letter *s* follows this mark.

Welcome to Our Open House

Our Class's Work

Link to Speaking and Writing
You can use fewer words by using the possessive form of nouns. Why is the new sentence better?

A <u>boy's</u> jacket of a boy was in the closet.

Guided Practice

A. Make each singular noun into a possessive noun.

1. Mike
2. waitress
3. pony
4. Ms. Hill
5. Rex
6. puppy

B. Use the possessive form for each word group.

7. the fur of the kitten
8. a hand of a student
9. a book belonging to Ann
10. the desk of the teacher

THINK AND REMEMBER
◆ Remember that a **possessive noun** shows ownership.
◆ Add an apostrophe and an *s* (*'s*) to a singular noun to form a possessive noun.

Independent Practice

C. Spelling Possessive Nouns   Rewrite each singular noun so that it shows ownership.

11. Sergio
MODEL > Sergio's

12. boss
13. Texas
14. Ann Clark
15. nurse

16. pitcher
17. Chris
18. lady
19. walrus

D. Revising Sentences   Write each sentence. Replace the underlined words with the possessive form.

20. The parents enjoy <u>the speech of the teacher</u>.
MODEL > The parents enjoy the teacher's speech.

21. <u>The picture belonging to Kim</u> shows an African plain and many large animals.
22. <u>The smoke of a volcano</u> rises above the plain.
23. She has painted <u>the hide of the rhinoceros</u> gray.
24. <u>The painting of Roy Sanchez</u> is of a forest.
25. A large rock shelters <u>the den of a fox</u>.
26. You can almost hear <u>the murmur of the waterfall</u>.
27. <u>The notebook belonging to Lisa</u> is full of drawings she made.
28. <u>The favorite of David</u> is on this page.
29. <u>The wings of the butterfly</u> are blue and green.
30. <u>The father of David Weiner</u> admires the drawing, too.

E. 31.–39. Writing Original Sentences   Use the possessive form of the words in C in sentences of your own.

31. Sergio
MODEL > Sergio's picture shows his cat in action.

Application—Writing

Sentences in a Letter   Imagine that you attended an open house at school. Write some sentences that might be in a note to a friend who knows the students in your class. Tell your friend what you saw at the open house. Use at least five possessive nouns in your sentences.

9 Plural Possessive Nouns

◆ **FOCUS** A **plural possessive noun** shows ownership by more than one person or thing.

Remember that singular nouns can show ownership. Plural nouns can also show ownership.

1. the nests of the birds   the birds' nests
2. the discovery of the girls   the girls' discovery

The words in color are plural possessive nouns. They show ownership by more than one person or thing. In each case just an apostrophe follows the *s* of the plural form.

Some plural nouns do not end in *s*. To make these nouns plural, add both an apostrophe and *s*.

3. the gardens of the women

   the women's gardens

Guided Practice

A. Tell how you would form the possessive of each of these plural nouns. Use just an apostrophe or an apostrophe and *s*.

1. teachers	5. monkeys	9. groups
2. canaries	6. sheep	10. geese
3. oxen	7. witches	11. mice
4. irises	8. men	12. choruses

THINK AND REMEMBER

◆ Remember that a **plural possessive noun** shows ownership by more than one person or thing.
◆ To form the possessive of a plural noun ending in *s* or *es*, add only an apostrophe.
◆ To form the possessive of a plural noun that does not end in *s*, add an apostrophe and *s*.

Independent Practice

B. Spelling Possessive Forms   Write the possessive form of each of these plural nouns.

13. boys

MODEL > boys'

14. classes	**18.** turkeys	**22.** lionesses
15. deer	**19.** girls	**23.** children
16. sisters	**20.** fishes	**24.** burros
17. teeth	**21.** bullies	**25.** dogs

C. Revising Sentences   Write each sentence. Replace the underlined words with the possessive form.

26. How pretty the patterns of snowflakes are!

MODEL > How pretty the snowflakes' patterns are!

27. The mother of the children dresses them warmly before they leave the house.

28. The cries of the birds sound sharp and sad.

29. The houses of their friends are covered with snow during the winter months.

30. Snow also covers the homes of the wild creatures.

31. Jenny spots the burrow of some deer mice.

32. Ana sees the pups of two red foxes.

33. The coats of the pups are thick and warm now.

34. The antlers of elk are shed in winter.

35. The nests of the wild geese have been long empty.

36. The noses of both girls are red with cold.

D. 37.–49. Writing Original Sentences   Use the possessive form of the words in **B** in sentences of your own.

37. boys

MODEL > The boys' glasses fogged up in the cold air.

Application—Writing and Speaking

A Description   Imagine that you are one of the children in the picture. Write some sentences that describe what you notice about spring. Share your sentences with a classmate. Talk with him or her about the images your sentences create. Try to use at least four plural possessive nouns in your sentences.

Building Vocabulary
Compound Words

The day of John's birth!
July 8, 1980

John's tenth birthday!
July 8, 1990

Suppose you did not know the meaning of the word *birthday*. You could figure it out if you knew what *birth* and *day* mean. Many words are made by putting two smaller words together. Words made like this are called **compound words.** They are written as one word.

Some compound words are easy to figure out. The meanings of *snowstorm* and *homemade* are easy to figure out.

Some compound words are more challenging. Think about the words *baseball* and *thumbtack*. The two small words do give clues, but it takes more work to figure out the meaning.

1. In <u>baseball</u>, a player hits a ball to get to a base.
2. A <u>thumbtack</u> is a tack with a broad head that can be pushed in with the thumb.

When you come to a compound word, think of what each smaller word means. Then, you can figure out the meaning of the compound word.

Reading Practice

Read the sentences. Write the compound word. Then write your own definition for it.

1. We had a wonderful, sunny weekend for our picnic.
2. I couldn't go fishing because I had lost my fishhooks.
3. I put on my swimsuit and went down to the sandy beach.
4. We built a campfire close to our tent.
5. We hung our wet clothing on a clothesline made of rope.

Writing Practice

Rewrite the following sentences. Replace the underlined words with a compound word.

6. Mom found the bean salad recipe in a <u>book for a cook</u>.
7. We spread our picnic on a <u>cloth to cover a table</u>.
8. I had two helpings of <u>sauce made from apples</u>.
9. We picked <u>berries that are blue</u>.
10. Later we rented a <u>boat to sail</u> and went out on the bay.
11. My sister stayed on the <u>shore of the sea</u>.
12. I got a little <u>burn from the sun</u> on my nose.

Project

List some compound words you find in books, magazines, and newspapers. Make a card for each word, like the one shown in the picture. Show the two small words that make up the compound word. Then, write a definition of the compound word. Finally, write a sentence with the compound word. Work with your classmates to make a bulletin board display of the words.

hall + way = hallway

A hallway is a way through a hall.
The classrooms lay along a long hallway.

Language Enrichment
Nouns

Use what you know about nouns to do these activities.

What's Wrong with This Picture?

There are many things wrong in this picture. List all the mistakes you can spot. Be sure that you use singular and plural nouns correctly. Capitalize all proper nouns.

Read five items from your list to your classmates. Listen to your classmates read their lists. Each time a new mistake is identified, add it to a list on the chalkboard. When no one has any more mistakes to add, count the mistakes the class found together. Then find out which students listed the most mistakes correctly on their own lists.

Test Your Memory

You can play this memory game with one partner or in a group. You will need a picture that shows a busy scene. Use a magazine picture if a few people play. Use a poster if a large group plays. Begin by displaying the picture for exactly one minute. Then, put it away.

Now list everything you saw in the picture. If there are two or more things of the same kind, write how many there are. Be sure to use singular and plural nouns correctly.

When everyone is finished, exchange lists. Display the picture again. Read aloud a list. Ask your classmates which items are correct. Give one point for each correctly named object. Subtract a point for each mistake. Check everyone's list. The player with the most points wins.

CONNECTING

In this unit you learned about nouns. Nouns can name any person, place, or thing, or a particular person, place, or thing. Nouns tell whether something is singular or plural. They also may show ownership.

◆ **Using Nouns in Your Writing** To write and speak well, you must be able to use nouns correctly. Exact nouns make your writing clear. They help your readers and listeners form exact pictures in their minds. Pay special attention to the nouns you use as you do these activities.

 ## Dreaming About Me

If you could be anyone in the world, who would you be? Would you be a king or a queen? Would you be an inventor or a circus clown?

Where would you live? Who would your friends be? What kinds of things would you own? Write a paragraph that answers questions like these. Let your imagination do the dreaming! Use proper nouns and singular and plural nouns so that your readers can form clear pictures.

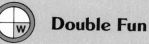 ## Double Fun

You learned about compound words on the **Building Vocabulary** pages. Here is a way to have fun with these words.

Brainstorm all the compound nouns you can think of. Then, write five sentences that have compound nouns. Try to use two or more compound nouns in each sentence. Then draw a picture to go with each sentence. Make a poster with your sentences and pictures.

This cowhand is going into the bakeshop for a cupcake.

Unit Checkup

Think Back	Think Ahead
◆ What did you learn about paragraphs of information in this unit? What did you do to write one?	◆ How will what you learned about paragraphs of information help you when you read an information book? ◆ How will connecting main ideas and details help you write?
◆ Look at the writing you did in this unit. How did nouns help you express your ideas?	◆ What is one way that you can use nouns to improve your writing?

Analyzing a Paragraph of Information   *pages 56–57*

Read this paragraph. Then answer the questions.

> Our family lives in a different type of house, a mobile home. A mobile home is built quickly in a factory. This means that it costs much less than an ordinary house. Once built, it is carried to the new owner's land. The trucks that carry mobile homes are very big. The mobile home is secured by long steel cables that run down into the ground. When these cables are pulled out, the home can be moved. That is why it is called a "mobile" home.

1. What is the main idea of the paragraph?
2. Write the sentence that does not really tell about the main idea.
3. How many facts tell about the main idea?
4. Choose one detail sentence, and tell why it is important to the paragraph.

Connecting Main Idea and Details   *page 58*

Write the sentences that would fit under the main idea of *camping*.

5. Choosing your campsite is important.   6. The mountains are beautiful.
7. Your tent should be set up first.
8. The bridge leading across the river appears wobbly.
9. The campfire is usually the center of the campsite.

Using Exact Words   *page 59*

Write more exact words for the underlined words.

10. I go into <u>a room</u> to read <u>a book</u>.
11. We go to <u>a restaurant</u> to have <u>some food</u>.
12. <u>Sometimes</u> I like to have <u>a cold drink</u>.
13. <u>The children</u> are playing <u>a game</u>.

The Writing Process   *pages 60–69*

Write the letter of the correct response to each question.

14. Which is a good way to decide what topic you should write an information paragraph about?
    a. Read books to find a topic.
    b. Choose a topic that interests you.
    c. Choose a topic that another classmate is also writing about.
15. Which topic would be best for an audience of first-graders?
    a. how a simple toy works
    b. how a factory in your town works
    c. how to drive a car
16. When revising your paragraph, how can you check to see that you have kept to the topic?
    a. Make sure you have used exact words.
    b. Decide if everything is in the proper order.
    c. Make sure that all the detail sentences tell about the main idea.

Nouns   *pages 72–73*

Write the nouns you find in each sentence.

17. My parents had a big wedding.
18. Then they lived with my grandparents for a year.
19. My sister was born early one morning.
20. Mom and Dad moved into an apartment.
21. When I came, my folks bought a big old house.

Singular and Plural Nouns   *pages 74–75*

Write each underlined noun. Then write *singular* or *plural* after each one.

22. List some <u>ways</u> you have changed since you were a <u>baby</u>.
23. How many <u>inches</u> have you grown?
24. You can cut an <u>apple</u> with a <u>knife</u> now.

25. Now you can read the <u>funnies</u> or a <u>magazine</u>.

26. You don't make a <u>mess</u> with <u>food</u> any more.

More Plural Nouns   *pages 76–77*

Write the plural form of the noun in parentheses ( ) in each sentence.

27. Men and (woman) often care for newborn babies.

28. Their (tooth) haven't broken through yet.

29. Their little squeaks might remind you of (mouse).

30. A baby's (foot) could fit in your hand.

31. But as babies become (child), just look how they grow!

Common and Proper Nouns   *pages 78–79*

Write each underlined noun. Then write *common* or *proper* after it.

32. Many <u>men</u> and <u>women</u> came to the <u>New World</u>.

33. <u>William Bradford</u> led the <u>Pilgrims</u> from <u>England</u> to <u>America</u>.

34. They crossed the <u>ocean</u> on a <u>ship</u> called the <u>Mayflower</u>.

35. They first landed at <u>Plymouth Rock</u>.

36. They even made <u>friends</u> with some of the <u>Indians</u>.

Names and Titles of People   *pages 80–81*

Write each sentence. Correct the capitalization and punctuation of the names and titles.

37. The country's first President was mr george washington.

38. Gov ronald reagan became our fortieth President.

39. mr reagan was the nation's oldest President.

40. England's prime minister is ms margaret thatcher.

41. One of the oldest senators is sen strom thurmond.

Capitalization of Proper Nouns   *pages 82–83*

Write each proper noun correctly.

42. japan

43. labor day

44. thursday, december 6

45. san antonio, texas

46. thanksgiving

47. atlantic ocean

Abbreviations *pages 84–85*

Write each item. Use abbreviations for the underlined words.

48. 1221 East Idlewild <u>Avenue</u>
49. <u>Monday</u>, August 29
50. Central <u>Street</u>
51. <u>Wednesday</u>, October 19
52. Friday, <u>October</u> 3

Singular Possessive Nouns *pages 86–87*

Write each sentence. Replace the underlined words with the possessive form.

53. Long ago <u>the job of the mailman</u> didn't exist.
54. <u>News of a battle</u> would come from a fast runner.
55. <u>The message of a king</u> came through an edict.
56. <u>The loud voice of a man</u> trumpeted the message.
57. How could <u>the letter of one person</u> be sent?

Plural Possessive Nouns *pages 88–89*

Write each sentence. Replace the underlined words with the possessive form.

58. <u>The slowness of the mails</u> disturbed some people.
59. The pony express was <u>the idea of several partners</u>.
60. Riders would hop onto the <u>backs of these ponies</u>.
61. <u>The fierce snows of blizzards</u> might blow.
62. <u>The rage of warring Indians</u> might endanger them.
63. <u>The courage of the riders</u> kept them riding on.

Compound Words *pages 90–91*

Rewrite the following sentences. Replace the underlined words with a compound word.

64. Miss Nye's <u>store to sell books</u> has expanded this year.
65. We hardly ever see a <u>man who delivers milk</u> anymore.
66. Use a <u>brush for applying paint</u> to paint that house.
67. Some people need <u>glasses for their eyes</u> to see better.
68. Does your <u>room for your class</u> look different from the one you had last year?

1-2 Cumulative Review

Declarative and Interrogative Sentences *pages 32–33*

Write each sentence so that it begins and ends correctly.

1. do you know about writing secret codes
2. you have to decide to let symbols stand for words
3. then you can write symbols into sentences
4. can you understand your own code
5. now you are ready to communicate with someone
6. you might decide to keep it to yourself
7. do you want it to be your secret
8. i enjoy trying to break new codes
9. codes have been used for years to keep secrets
10. how many symbols can you think of

Imperative and Exclamatory Sentences *pages 34–35*

Write each sentence so that it begins and ends correctly.

11. hey, I saw a great documentary about robots
12. be sure to read about them in this magazine
13. they are being used for so many tasks
14. just think of all the possibilities
15. boy, they can save our lives
16. they can even handle dangerous chemicals
17. look up "robot" in the encyclopedia
18. please let me see that photograph
19. gee, here is one that can do housecleaning
20. hey, maybe someday we'll build one

Complete and Simple Subjects *pages 38–39*

Write each complete subject. Then underline the simple subject.

21. We filmed a documentary about gardening.
22. Hardly any bugs attacked those strong plants.
23. You can pull out one of those.

24. A long, orange carrot is on the other end.
25. We filmed some close-up shots of the vegetables.
26. Those little radishes are bright and colorful.
27. Some nice, plump cucumbers are over there.
28. A great salad will come of all these vegetables!
29. Gardening is a great hobby for someone who likes to spend time outdoors.
30. You can't get fresh food like this in the stores in my neighborhood.

Complete and Simple Predicates   *pages 40–41*

Write each complete predicate. Then underline the simple predicate.

31. The telephone changed over the years.
32. Big boxes once hung on people's walls.
33. The caller spoke through a hole in the box.
34. He held a funny piece up to his ear.
35. The operator came on the line for each call.
36. A clever person invented the dial.
37. Everyone in the town had his own phone number after this.
38. Modern telephoning is even quicker.
39. The new push-button telephones operate easily and quickly.
40. Your call goes through in an instant!

Nouns   *pages 72–73*

Write the nouns you find in each sentence.

41. Television was invented about fifty years ago.
42. Some folks thought television was just a fad.
43. People didn't know what this invention meant.
44. Soon, programs were coming into homes.
45. Families watched Milton Berle and Howdy Doody.
46. Children loved their special programs.
47. Television is not as special these days.
48. People use it to amuse their pets.
49. Children watch it after school.
50. Some families keep it on all day long.

Singular and Plural Nouns   *pages 74–75*

Write each underlined noun. Then write *singular* or *plural* after each one.

51. One important <u>invention</u> is the <u>computer</u>.
52. The first computers were huge <u>machines</u>.
53. One of them could barely fit inside a big <u>room</u>.
54. But <u>scientists</u> have learned more and more.
55. Now they make computers as small as your <u>hand</u>.
56. These amazing <u>devices</u> are used all around us.
57. The <u>store</u> uses a computer at the checkout <u>counter</u>.
58. <u>Banks</u> use them to keep track of their <u>accounts</u>.
59. <u>Authors</u> even write <u>books</u> on computers.
60. What did <u>people</u> ever do without them?

Common and Proper Nouns   *pages 78–79*

Write each underlined noun. Then write *common* or *proper* after each one.

61. Long ago, no <u>books</u> were ever written for <u>children</u>.
62. A <u>man</u> named <u>John Newbery</u> wanted to change that.
63. He wrote a little book of <u>stories</u> and <u>games</u>.
64. The children of <u>England</u> loved it.
65. He is called <u>The Father of Children's Literature</u>.
66. The <u>Newbery Medal</u> is named for him.
67. <u>Randolph Caldecott</u> loved to draw <u>pictures</u>.
68. He drew <u>children</u> playing and having a good <u>time</u>.
69. Caldecott became a popular children's <u>artist</u>.
70. The <u>Caldecott Medal</u> is named for him.

Abbreviations   *pages 84–85*

Rewrite each item. Correct any errors in abbreviations.

71. dental appointment on Jan 10
72. 2918 howell branch rd
73. rock concert on sat , apr 8
74. Steve's birthday on Oct 2
75. wedding in nov
76. baby born on Mar 20 at 6:00 am
77. 189 sanford ave

78. meeting on mon at 2:00 PM
79. party at 7324 indiana st
80. lunch at restaurant on colonial dr.

Singular Possessive Nouns   *pages 86–87*

Write each sentence. Replace the underlined words with the correct possessive form.

81. The dream of Beatrix Potter was to publish a book.
82. It told about the adventure of a little rabbit.
83. She had written it for the enjoyment of a friend.
84. The name of the friend was Noel Moore.
85. The age of Noel was five.
86. Noel read the story in a letter of Beatrix.
87. The mother of Peter Rabbit gave a warning.
88. "Stay out of the garden of Mr. McGregor."
89. The curiosity of Peter got the best of him.
90. The shoes and jacket of the bunny got lost.
91. The cold of Peter made him have to go to bed.

Plural Possessive Nouns   *pages 88–89*

Write each sentence. Replace the underlined words with the possessive form.

92. The rejections of publishers didn't stop Beatrix.
93. She paid for the printing of the pages herself.
94. Relatives and friends of friends bought copies.
95. Soon, the parents of little ones all over were reading *The Tale of Peter Rabbit*.
96. Then the requests of the publishers came.
97. "Can we print the worth of several hundred dollars of your book?"
98. The popularity of her books grew and grew.
99. The joy of children increased with each one.
100. The characters in the books became familiar to children through the years.
101. Similar animals appear in the writing of some children.
102. The drawings of students often look like illustrations in Beatrix Potter's books.

UNIT

3

Giving Directions

◆ **COMPOSITION FOCUS:** How-to Paragraph
◆ **LANGUAGE FOCUS:** Verbs

Do you know how to play hide-and-seek? Do you know how to plant a window-box garden or build a model bridge? How could you find out how to do something new? You might be shown by someone else. You might also use written directions.

Many writers enjoy sharing their interests. They write books and articles that teach how to do something. If you flip through magazines or any library card catalogue, you will be surprised at how much of this type of writing there is.

Many types of people write to share what they know. Mary C. Lewis, a teacher, writes to tell other teachers about useful teaching methods she has discovered. Her student Ramona Hudson first wrote to express her feelings. Then Ramona discovered that she could write to inform other students how to take part in an activity she enjoyed. In this unit you will learn how to write a paragraph that explains how to do something.

Mary C. Lewis wrote *to inform* other teachers about a challenging classroom activity.

Ramona Hudson wrote *to inform* other students how to take part in that activity.

Reading with a Writer's Eye
How-to Paragraph

Mary C. Lewis was faced with a group of students who were bored by writing. She met the challenge by coming up with an activity that excited Ramona Hudson and her classmates. Read what each has to say about that experience. Notice that each writer has a different way of telling her audience how to go about trying the activity themselves.

Free to Write
by Mary C. Lewis

"I thought you would just give us things to write about, and it would be like school. I felt bored."

Those words were spoken by Ramona Hudson, a student with whom I have worked since she was a fourth-grader. I have been holding writing workshops at her school, Alexandre Dumas, for several years. Ramona's comment describes what she thought it would be like to use a writing log. Over a two-year period, her idea changed.

At first, Ramona was unsure and confused. She had thought of writing only as a school subject, a chore to be done. A writing log was completely new to her. She was not used to the freedom of writing about anything she wanted. Ramona expected me to tell her what to do and how to do it. Even when I explained she could write about anything, she was confused. Ramona spent the first few workshops staring at her empty notebook and wrote very little in her writing log. Clearly she needed my guidance and encouragement.

I needed to help Ramona change the way she viewed writing. More than anything else, I hoped Ramona and the other students would gain greater confidence in themselves through their writing. I knew a writing log could help them to express their ideas, thoughts, and feelings without the fear of making mistakes. If Ramona and the others would take a few risks, they could achieve this freedom. First, they had to risk being themselves while writing their logs. Then, they had to risk being creative when they put their thoughts and ideas into writing that others might read.

My next step was to use my own writing log to help Ramona. In my log, I brainstormed for ideas. The ideas were really starting points that Ramona and others might use to express their feelings. At the next workshop, I suggested these ideas. One idea, "I become happy when . . . ," must have interested Ramona because she wrote quite a bit. This is some of what she wrote that day.

> *I become happy when my grade is just the way I want it, and it is what I believe I earned. This happened one time I studied very hard for a math test and got an A.*

Now, Ramona was beginning to change the way she thought about writing. By connecting happiness to her own experiences, she was becoming more personal in her writing. First, she compared happiness with getting good grades. Later, she remembered the happiness she felt when she and another girl had fun dancing. Here is part of one log entry.

> One day a girl named Shelia came over
> to my house, and we practiced a dance.
> It was for a talent show. Boy did we
> have fun.

I was very pleased to see that writing was becoming easier for Ramona. Soon, she was busily using her writing log. Mainly, she used it to write stories or poems. This is a poem Ramona wrote after the first year.

> My Lovely Picture
>
> The wind is cloudy
> Smoky and foggy.
> The water is smooth, wavy
> And fresh.
> Let's listen to the beautiful
> Creative and different clouds
> And talk about the
> Peaceful and clear water.
> The shining and
> Gleaming sky
> Lights up and I call that
> Lovely, plain and cool.
> The earth is beautiful.

In the end, this workshop at the Alexandre Dumas School was a success. Over a two-year period, Ramona and her classmates went from being non-writers to being eager writers. Here is an example of one of Ramona's later entries. She shared it with me so that I might share it with others.

If you want to get your feelings out in some way, or to get new ideas for other writing projects, you can start your very own writing log. For instance, if you get angry, you might usually want to holler at someone. Put it on paper instead, and turn a problem into something creative. It is also possible to use your writing log to create characters for stories. For example, you can use your own life's situations to develop a character's situations.

Here is how to start your writing log. You will need paper, pencils or pens, and a safe place to keep your writing log. First, stop and think about what you want to write. Next, write the first thing that comes to mind. Then, keep writing. Don't stop until you run out of ideas. Look over your writing to see how you expressed your ideas, or to see if you want to use them for another piece. Finally, put your writing log in a safe place until you are ready to write again.

Respond

1. Whose writing interests you more, Ramona's or her teacher's? Explain your answer.

Discuss

2. Which part of Ramona's writing tells her readers how to do something? What did you learn from her directions?
3. Mary C. Lewis does not write how-to directions in the same way that Ramona does. Who are her readers? What does she want to teach them? How does she give information that will help them?

Thinking As a Writer
Analyzing a How-to Paragraph

A **how-to paragraph** tells how to do something. It may explain how to make something or how to do an activity.

Every how-to paragraph has a topic sentence and detail sentences.

Here is a how-to paragraph written by a student who wanted to share an enjoyable activity. Since this paragraph is about playing a game, the last detail sentence tells how it is won.

> Drop the Clothespins into the Bottle is an easy game to play with friends. You will need an empty plastic bottle and ten clothespins. First, place the bottle on the floor. Next, stand about six inches behind the bottle. Then, have someone hand you the clothespins, one at a time. Finally, try to drop each clothespin into the bottle without bending over. The person who gets the most clothespins in the bottle wins the game.

A **topic sentence** names the game.
The **first detail sentence** names the materials.

The **other detail sentences** tell how to play the game.

The **last detail sentence** tells how to decide who wins.

Discuss

1. What are the four parts of the how-to paragraph you just read?
2. Why did the writer list the materials before giving the directions?
3. Does the order of the game steps make sense? Give a reason for your answer.
4. Find the sentence that tells how to decide who wins. Could it be moved so that it is the third sentence? Why or why not?

Try Your Hand

A. Write Topic Sentences Read this list of activities. Choose three that you know well. Write a topic sentence for a how-to paragraph about each of the three.

softball   Chinese checkers   hide-and-seek
checkers   musical chairs   horseshoes
tag   jacks   hopscotch

B. Write Detail Sentences Reread the three topic sentences you just wrote. Now, write a detail sentence that tells what materials are needed for each of the three activities.

C. Add Missing Information This paragraph is missing two important sentences. Decide what is missing. Then, rewrite the paragraph. Add new sentences that give the missing information.

> Everyone has fun playing Penny Toss. Place the hat on the ground. Mark a spot three feet away. Give each player ten pennies. The player kneels on the mark and tries to toss the pennies into the hat. Count the pennies that land in the hat.

D. Read Directions Reread Ramona's how-to paragraph on page 107, or find another set of directions in a book or a magazine. Read the directions. Identify the sentences that name the topic, list the materials needed, and tell what to do. If the directions are for a game, find the sentence that tells how to choose the winner.

Writer's Notebook

Collecting Time-Order Words
Did you notice that when writers give game directions, they tell the order of steps without using numbers? What are some of the words used to do this in the paragraphs you have read so far? List these words in your *Writer's Notebook.* Use the heading *Words That Tell Order.* Watch for these kinds of words as you read. Add them to your list. You can use some of these words when you write about things in order.

Thinking As a Writer
Visualizing Steps in a Process

Writer's Guide

When writing a how-to paragraph, good writers

◆ make a movie in their heads of the steps in the process.

◆ write directions for the steps in the order in which they happened.

Writers can give readers good directions to follow only if they themselves can clearly imagine the steps. When writers get ready to write how-to paragraphs, the first thing they do is visualize the process. To **visualize** something is to make pictures inside your head as if you were playing a movie.

Some writers make notes or draw diagrams and then review them while they "replay" that "movie." They give the steps exactly in the order they "saw" them as they imagined the process. Here is the way one writer visualizes steps in a process.

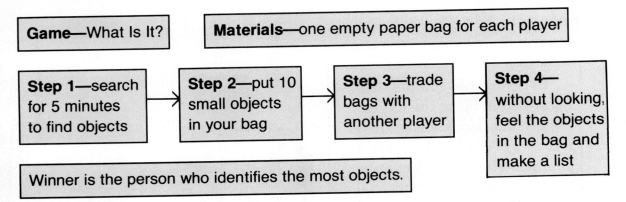

Game—What Is It?   **Materials**—one empty paper bag for each player

Step 1—search for 5 minutes to find objects → **Step 2**—put 10 small objects in your bag → **Step 3**—trade bags with another player → **Step 4**—without looking, feel the objects in the bag and make a list

Winner is the person who identifies the most objects.

Before you begin your own how-to paragraph, create a "movie" of the process from the beginning to the end.

Discuss

1. Suppose the writer had begun the diagram by describing the game. What problems might this create?
2. What does the writer do to help visualize the steps?

Try Your Hand

Visualize Events   Try to visualize the main events of the first half hour in school this morning. Then use a diagram to list these activities. Write them in the order in which they happened. Compare your list with a partner's.

Developing the Writer's Craft
Writing for an Audience and a Purpose

Good writers know that it is important to write directions clearly. If a reader misunderstands directions, he or she may not succeed in performing the activity or the process.

Writers do several things to make sure their writing is clear. They use exact words and cut unnecessary words. They realize that too many words or details can make it hard for a reader to find important information.

Naomi wrote some directions for her classmates. The first paragraph shows her first draft. It is unclear and wordy. The second paragraph shows her revision.

> Here's how to have an egg race for a lot of fun for everyone. You and all your friends will enjoy it. Give each player an egg and a spoon. Then, have the players get into a line. They should line up at the starting line. Each should take the egg and place the egg in the spoon. They shouldn't drop the eggs. Then, they should all start racing. The winner is the first player of all the players to reach the line.

> Here's how to have an egg race. Give each player an uncooked egg and a tablespoon. Then, have the players line up at the starting line. Each should place the egg in the spoon. At a signal, all should race toward the finish line. The winner is the first to reach the line with an unbroken egg.

Contrast Naomi's revision with her first draft. She added exact words to make the meaning clearer. She explained that the egg was to be *uncooked* and that the spoon was a *tablespoon*. She added the information that the players were to start *at a signal* and were to head toward *the finish line*. She also added that the winner must reach the line *with an unbroken egg*.

Naomi cut unnecessary information. She did not need to say that the game was fun. She realized that her readers would understand that they were not to drop the egg.

Naomi cut unnecessary words as well as unnecessary information. By making these cuts, she was able to make the fourth and fifth sentences into one. She also cut some useless words out of the next sentence.

Naomi wrote her directions for her fourth-grade classmates. Then, her teacher suggested that Naomi make a poster for the second-graders to teach them this game. Naomi knew that she would have to write differently for a different audience. She thought about the second-graders and how well they could read. She thought about the information that might be hard for them to understand. This is how she began her poster.

Do you want to have an EGG RACE ? Try this!

1. Give everyone one egg and one BIG spoon.
   Don't cook the eggs!

2. Draw a line on the ground.
   Start your race there.
   Draw a line far away. End your race there.

start

Naomi changed the way she wrote to suit her new audience.

When you write your how-to paragraph, be sure to use clear and simple language. Remember to write for your audience.

Discuss

1. Contrast Naomi's revised paragraph with her first draft. Recall the reason for each change. Tell how the changes improved her paragraph.
2. Look at how Naomi began the directions for her classmates and how she began them for the second-graders. In what ways are they different? How does each set of directions suit its audience?

Try Your Hand

Write for an Audience   Look back at the diagram on page 110. Write directions for the game for an audience of second-graders. Share your work with a partner. Discuss what each of you did and why you did it.

1 Prewriting
How-to Paragraph

Writer's Guide

Prewriting Checklist
- ☑ Brainstorm topics.
- ☑ Think about your audience and your purpose. Choose words your audience will understand.
- ☑ Select a topic.
- ☑ Make a movie in your mind that shows the steps.
- ☑ Write the steps in the correct order.

Chris's teacher told the class they were going to make a manual of game rules. They would share the manual with one another and with other schoolmates. Chris thought about what he could write. He used the checklist in the **Writer's Guide** as he planned his paragraph. Look at what he did.

◆ Brainstorming and Selecting a Topic

First, Chris brainstormed a list of games he enjoyed. Chris studied his list. He crossed off games that had many rules. He also crossed off games that he did not understand well enough to explain.

Then, he looked at the ideas that were left. He circled Fishing in the Dark. It seemed like a good choice because not everyone knew how to play it. Chris felt that he could explain the game easily and clearly.

baseball
~~Fishing in the Dark~~ (circled)
Scissors, Paper, Rock
~~dodge ball~~
~~Twenty Questions~~
~~soccer~~

Discuss

1. Why do you think Chris decided not to use each of the topics he crossed out?
2. Why do you think he wanted to choose a game that was not well known to everyone?

◆ Gathering and Organizing Information

Next, Chris gathered and organized information for his how-to paragraph. He created a movie in his mind of someone playing Fishing in the Dark. He began by imagining what had to be done to prepare for the game. He ended by recalling how the winner was decided when the game was over. As he imagined the game, he jotted down notes on how it was played. He tried to put the steps in the correct order.

After Chris made his notes, he reviewed them. He replayed the movie in his mind. He made corrections and added things to his notes.

Make fishing pole with spoon, string, magnet.
Cut out paper fish and add paper clips.
Blindfold player.
Give player pole.
Scatter fish on floor.
Give each player one minute to fish.
Count fish caught.   Other players take fish off line.
Winner is player who has caught the most.

WRITING PROCESS

Discuss

1. Look at how Chris marked his note *Scatter fish on the floor*. What does this mark mean? Why do you think Chris made this correction?
2. Look at the information Chris added. When did he add it? Do you think he should have added it? Explain.
3. Why is it a good idea to play the movie in your mind twice?

Try Your Hand

Now plan a how-to paragraph of your own.

A. Brainstorm and Select a Topic   Brainstorm a list of possible topics. Write down all the games you enjoy. Think about each game and about your audience.

- ◆ Cross out games that have many rules and that take a long time to explain.
- ◆ Cross out games that you do not understand well.
- ◆ Cross out games that everyone else knows well.
- ◆ Circle the most interesting game left on your list. This will be the topic of your how-to paragraph.

B. Gather and Organize Information   When you are satisfied with your topic, gather and list the information you might use in your how-to paragraph.

- ◆ Make a movie in your mind of people playing the game. Note the steps of the game in the order in which players must follow them.
- ◆ Review your notes. Replay the movie of the game in your mind. Add to your notes, or correct information in them.
- ◆ Think about your audience. Check to be sure you have noted all the information they will need to understand a game that may be new to them.

 Save your notes in your *Writer's Notebook*. You will use them when you draft your how-to paragraph.

2 Drafting
How-to Paragraph

Writer's Guide

Drafting Checklist
- ☑ Use your notes.
- ☑ Write a topic sentence that tells what the paragraph is about.
- ☑ Identify the materials.
- ☑ Describe the steps in the correct order.
- ☑ End the directions for a game by telling how it is won.
- ☑ Write a title.

Chris thought about how he could make his directions clear to his classmates. Then he used his notes and followed the checklist in the **Writer's Guide** to draft his paragraph. Look at how he began.

> Fishing in the Dark is fun for people of all ages. You will need a blindfold and a fishing pole made from a wooden spoon. It is also made from string.

Discuss

1. How and where did Chris identify the game?
2. What details did Chris give next?

Try Your Hand

Now you are ready to write a how-to paragraph.

A. Review Your Information   Think about the information you organized in the last lesson. Ask yourself whether you have left out any important steps. If so, add them.

B. Think About Your TAP   Remember that your task is to write a how-to paragraph. Your purpose is to inform your audience about how to do something.

C. Write Your First Draft   Follow the **Writer's Guide** to write your first draft.

   When you write your draft, just put all your ideas on paper. Do not worry about spelling, punctuation, or grammar. You can correct the draft later.

Task: What?
Audience: Who?
Purpose: Why?

Save your first draft in your *Writer's Notebook*. You will use it when you revise your how-to paragraph.

WRITING PROCESS

3 Responding and Revising
How-to Paragraph

Chris read over his how-to paragraph. Then, he revised it. He used the checklist in the **Writer's Guide.** Look at what he did.

Writer's Guide

Revising Checklist
- ☑ Read your how-to paragraph to yourself or to a partner.
- ☑ Think about your audience and your purpose. Add or cut information.
- ☑ Check to see that your paragraph is organized in the correct order.
- ☑ Check for sentences that can be combined.
- ☑ Make changes.

◆ Checking Information

Chris read over what he had written. He decided that the information about going around more than once was unnecessary. Look at his first draft. To show his change, Chris used this mark ⚭ .

◆ Checking Organization

Chris decided that the last sentence was not in the right order. To show that the sentence should be moved, he used this mark ⟲ .

◆ Checking Language

Chris realized that he could combine sentences to avoid using unnecessary words. He used two commas and the word *and*. He used this mark ∧ to make the change.

Replace — You will need a blindfold and a fishing pole ⟨, string, and a magnet⟩ made from a wooden spoon. It is also made from string. It is made from a magnet too. You will also need twenty paper fish with paper clips. Here's how to play. First, scatter the fish on the floor. Then, blindfold the first player. The player holds the pole over the fish and drags the magnet across the floor. The magnet picks up fish. Everyone takes a turn for one minute.

Cut — You can go around many times. The players who catch the most fish are the winners.

Move — The other players take off the fish the magnet picks up.

Discuss

1. Why did Chris think it was important to add the information that each player gets only one minute to fish?
2. How did combining sentences change the paragraph?
3. Are there other changes Chris could have made? Explain your answer.

Try Your Hand

Now revise your first draft.

A. **Read Your First Draft**   As you read your how-to paragraph, think about your audience and your purpose. Read your paragraph silently or to a partner to see if it is complete and well organized. Ask yourself or your partner the questions in the box.

Responding and Revising Strategies	
✔ **Respond** **Ask yourself or your partner:**	✔ **Revise** **Try these solutions:**
◆ Does the topic sentence tell what the paragraph is about?	◆ **Replace** your topic sentence with one that gives this information.
◆ Do I give all the information needed to follow the directions?	◆ Check your notes. **Add** any important information that you left out.
◆ Do I present the steps in the correct order?	◆ **Move** any sentences that are in the wrong place.
◆ Is my language right for my audience?	◆ Rewrite to suit your audience.
◆ Do I say what I have to say without using unnecessary words?	◆ Combine any sentences that can be made into one sentence. See the **Revising Workshop** on page 119.

B. **Make Your Changes**   If the answer to any question in the box is *no*, try the solution. Use the **Editor's Marks** to show your changes.

C. **Review Your How-to Paragraph Again**   Decide if there is anything else you want to revise. Keep revising your how-to paragraph until you feel it is well organized and complete.

EDITOR'S MARKS

∧ Add something.
✂ Cut something.
◯ Move something.
∧ Replace something.

Save your revised how-to paragraph in your *Writer's Notebook.* You will use it when you proofread your paragraph.

WRITING PROCESS

Revising Workshop
Combining Sentences with Words in a Series

Good writers are always alert for repeated words. They find ways to avoid them.

1. They made a game board. They made game pieces. They made a spinner.
2. They made a game board, game pieces, and a spinner.

In item 2, the writer used the words *They made* just once. Then the writer used words in a series to list the things that were made. A **series** is made up of three or more things that belong together. The words are placed in the sentence one after the other. Notice that commas separate items in a series. The word *and* joins the final item to the rest. Use words in a series to combine sentences that have three or more parts that belong together.

Practice

Combine each group of sentences to make one sentence. Write the new sentence.

1. You can fish this morning. You can fish this afternoon. You can fish this evening.
2. Players must be quick. Players must be clever. Players must be sneaky.
3. The player who is "It" must giggle. The player who is "It" must laugh. The player who is "It" must smile.
4. You can guess a person. You can guess a place. You can guess a thing.
5. The game is easy. The game is simple. The game is fun.
6. Shana played the game. Lien played the game. Ramon played the game.
7. They wanted prizes. They wanted awards. They wanted gifts.
8. They felt pleased. They felt happy. They felt excited.
9. All the children knew the number of players. All the children knew the rules. All the children knew how to win.

4 Proofreading
How-to Paragraph

Chris revised his how-to paragraph. Then he used the **Writer's Guide** and the **Editor's Marks** to proofread it. He checked another paragraph that he had added. Look at how he marked it.

Writer's Guide

Proofreading Checklist

- ☑ Check for errors in capitalization. Be sure to capitalize all proper nouns.
- ☑ Check for errors in punctuation. Be sure to add commas between words in a series.
- ☑ Check to see that all your paragraphs are indented.
- ☑ Check for errors in grammar.
- ☑ Circle any words you think are misspelled. Find out how to spell them correctly.
- ⇨ For proofreading help, use the **Writer's Handbook.**

Here's another way to score Fishing in the dark. write a number on each fish. Use the numbers one. five. ten. and twenty. Hang on to all the fish each player catches. Then. add up the numbers at the end of the player's turn. The total is the player's score.

Discuss

1. Look at Chris's proofread paragraph. What kinds of mistakes did he make?
2. Why did Chris capitalize the name of the game?

Try Your Hand

Proofread Your How-to Paragraph Now use the **Writer's Guide** and the **Editor's Marks** to proofread your paragraph.

EDITOR'S MARKS

- ≡ Capitalize.
- ⊙ Add a period.
- ∧ Add something.
- ⋏ Add a comma.
- ⱽⱽ Add quotation marks.
- ⌄ Cut something.
- ⋀ Replace something.
- ∼/tr Transpose.
- ◯ Spell correctly.
- ⌐ Indent paragraph.
- / Make a lowercase letter.

Save your corrected how-to paragraph in your *Writer's Notebook*. You will use it when you publish your paragraph.

WRITING PROCESS

5 Publishing
How-to Paragraph

Chris and his classmates made clean copies of their paragraphs. They acted out the steps in their minds to be sure nothing had been left out. Then they published their paragraphs in a manual of game rules. You can find Chris's how-to paragraph on page 19 of the **Writer's Handbook.**

Here's how Chris and his classmates published their manual.

Writer's Guide

Publishing Checklist

☑ Make a clean copy of your paragraph.

☑ Be sure that nothing has been left out.

☑ Check to see that there are no mistakes.

☑ Share your how-to paragraph in a special way.

1. Chris made a drawing to go with the directions he wrote.
2. He planned where the art would go on his page. He left room for the title at the top. He also left a wide margin on the left. He pasted the drawing in place. Then, he neatly wrote the directions in the space around the art, to fit into that space.

3. He met with his classmates to decide how to group the pages. They considered grouping indoor games, outdoor games, games for just a few players, and games for many players. They sorted the pages into groups and put them in order.
4. They numbered the pages, starting with 2. For page 1, they created a table of contents.

5. They used a paper punch to make holes in the pages. Then they put the pages in a binder. One or two students made a drawing and a title for the cover of the binder.

6. They looked through their binder when they were not sure how to play a game. They invited students from other classes to share it with them.

Discuss

1. How might a drawing help someone understand the directions better?
2. Why is it a good idea to organize the games into groups?

Try Your Hand

Publish Your How-to Paragraph Follow the checklist in the **Writer's Guide.** If possible, put together a manual of games, or try one of these ideas for sharing your how-to paragraph.

◆ **Bulletin Board** Make a bulletin board display about games. Post the paragraphs you have written, along with drawings and magazine photographs of people playing the games.
◆ **Pantomime** Read one of the paragraphs aloud while one or two other students mime the steps. If you need help, follow the **Tips on How to Listen to and Give Directions** on page 123.

WRITING PROCESS

Listening and Speaking
Tips on How to Listen to and Give Directions

Listening to Directions

1. Give all your attention to the speaker.

2. Think about the order in which things are to be done. Imagine yourself following the directions.

3. Ask questions if something is not clear.

4. Make notes if it is necessary.

5. Try the activity while the directions are still fresh in your mind.

Giving Directions

1. Before you speak, plan what you will say. Make notes if you need to.

2. Be sure you give the steps in sequence. Help your listeners by using time-order words.

3. Pause and check to be sure that your listeners understand. Ask if anyone needs more information.

4. If your listeners are confused, try explaining a step in a new way.

5. Whenever possible, show your listeners what to do.

Writing in the Content Areas

Use what you learned to write directions for different types of activities. You might write a paragraph or make a short booklet. Use one of these ideas or an idea of your own.

Writer's Guide

When you write, remember the stages of the Writing Process.
◆ Prewriting
◆ Drafting
◆ Responding and Revising
◆ Proofreading
◆ Publishing

Science

Science activities can be fun. Remember some that you have enjoyed. Have you learned to measure rainfall? Do you know how to raise plants from seeds or how to care for goldfish? Write directions to help others have fun using science skills.

Mathematics

Sometimes it takes several steps to solve a math problem. Think of a problem that you have solved. You might have figured out how much money you would have left after buying some items. Now tell other people what steps to take to solve the problem.

Health

Do you know what to do for an injury or an illness? You might want to work with a group to create a first-aid booklet. Tell what to do if someone has a small cut or burn. Tell what to do in an emergency. Include directions for caring for someone who is sick in bed.

Fine Arts

Have you ever created a mask or a costume for a play? Can you imagine a mask or a costume you would like to make? Think about the steps in making it. Then, write the directions. Remember to tell what materials are needed. You may want to include drawings to make the steps clearer.

CONNECTING

WRITING ⬌ LANGUAGE

People write directions for many reasons. Sometimes their purpose is to tell how to use something or put something together, or it may be to explain how to do something safely and correctly. Often the purpose is to share an interesting activity. What is the purpose of these directions?

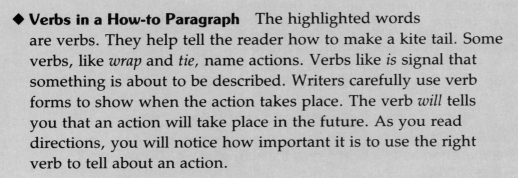

How to Make a Kite Tail

Every kite flies better with a tail. You will need bright crepe paper and string to make one. First, cut twelve strips of crepe paper. Make each strip about an inch wide and a foot long. Next, wrap the end of your string around one strip, and tie a knot around the middle of the paper. The knot will hold the paper in place. Then, tie the other strips to the string. Keep them about six inches apart. When the tail is ready, fasten it to the kite. Now your kite will not spin.

◆ **Verbs in a How-to Paragraph**   The highlighted words are verbs. They help tell the reader how to make a kite tail. Some verbs, like *wrap* and *tie*, name actions. Verbs like *is* signal that something is about to be described. Writers carefully use verb forms to show when the action takes place. The verb *will* tells you that an action will take place in the future. As you read directions, you will notice how important it is to use the right verb to tell about an action.

◆ **Language Focus: Verbs**   In the following lessons you will learn more about using different kinds of verbs in your own writing.

1 Action Verbs

◆ **FOCUS**   An **action verb** is a word that tells what the subject of a sentence does or did.

Remember that a sentence has a subject and a predicate. The main word in the predicate is the simple predicate. In each of these sentences, the simple predicate is an action verb.

1. The runner jumps over the hurdle.

2. The swimmer dives into the water.

Link to Speaking and Writing
You can use strong action verbs to paint clear and vivid pictures. Why does *flies* make a clearer picture than *goes*?

The athlete ~~goes~~ flies over the hurdle.

Guided Practice

A. Identify the action verb in each sentence.

1. The Olympic Games entertain millions of people throughout the world.
2. On opening day athletes walk into the arena.
3. Hundreds of doves rise into the air.
4. A runner comes in with a lighted torch.

B. 5.–8.   Name a vivid verb to replace each action verb in **A.**

THINK AND REMEMBER
- ◆ Remember that an **action verb** tells what the subject of a sentence does or did.
- ◆ Use strong action verbs to paint clear and vivid pictures.

Independent Practice

C. Identifying Action Verbs Write the action verb in each sentence.

  9. Billy Mills lived on a Sioux reservation.

  MODEL ▷ lived

  10. He won track awards in high school and college.
  11. After college he joined the Marines.
  12. The Marines sent him to the Olympics.
  13. Mills ran in the 10,000-meter race.
  14. Someone pushed him by accident.
  15. Mills dropped twenty yards behind.
  16. Then, at the end, he charged ahead.
  17. To everyone's surprise he finished first.
  18. This amazing runner also set a new record.

D. Revising Sentences Replace each action verb with a stronger action verb. Use the **Writer's Thesaurus**. Write the new sentences.

  19. The people walk into the auditorium.

  MODEL ▷ The people crowd into the auditorium.

  20. First, a young athlete comes into the arena.
  21. The crowd sees her.
  22. The crowd cheers loudly.

E. Using Action Verbs in Complete Predicates Create complete sentences using action verbs. Write the complete sentences. Underline the action verbs.

  23. The crowds

  MODEL ▷ The crowds clap for the athletes.

  24. The bicycle rider   **28.** Some athletes
  25. Jumpers   **29.** Swimmers
  26. A diver   **30.** Runners
  27. A relay runner   **31.** The judges

Application—Writing

Paragraph in a Letter Think of someone you know who might try out for an Olympic event. Write a paragraph that could be in a letter to the Olympic Committee. Tell the committee why that person should try out. Use strong action verbs.

2 Linking Verbs

◆ **FOCUS** A **linking verb** connects the subject of a sentence to a word or words in the predicate.

Not all verbs show action. The simple predicate in color in each of these sentences is a linking verb.

1. Isamu Noguchi `is` an artist.

2. His works `are` beautiful.

In sentence 1 the linking verb *is* connects the subject, *Isamu Noguchi*, to the words *an artist* in the predicate. In sentence 2 the linking verb *are* connects *His works* to *beautiful*. Both *is* and *are* are forms of the verb *be*. These linking verbs are all forms of *be*.

am   is   are   was   were

Guided Practice

A. Identify the linking verb in each sentence.
1. A sculptor is one kind of artist.
2. Noguchi's first teacher was Gutzon Borglum.
3. Borglum's statues were of famous people.
4. The statues are exactly like the people.
5. The work was too easy for Noguchi.
6. "I am not happy with this dull work," he said.
7. Many museums are in New York City.
8. Noguchi was often a museum visitor.
9. The works of a Paris artist were in one museum.
10. This statue is wonderful and exciting!

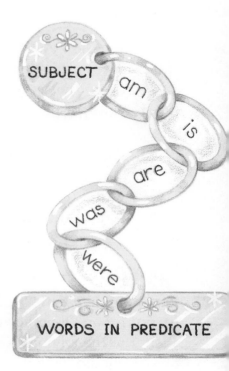

SUBJECT
am
is
are
was
were
WORDS IN PREDICATE

THINK AND REMEMBER
◆ Remember that a **linking verb** connects the subject to a word or words in the predicate.

Independent Practice

B. Identifying Linking Verbs   Write the linking verb in each sentence.

11. Many of the statues were full of energy.

MODEL > were

12. Not all of Noguchi's works are in museums.
13. His paper lanterns were beautiful.
14. One great design was for a playground.
15. The playground is in Atlanta, Georgia.
16. I am a fan of his work.

C. Recognizing Linking Verbs and Action Verbs   Write *linking verb* if the underlined word is a linking verb. Write *action verb* if it is an action verb.

17. New York City <u>was</u> his first home.

MODEL > linking verb

18. I <u>am</u> interested in Noguchi's life.
19. My parents <u>gave</u> me a book about him.
20. It <u>tells</u> about his childhood.
21. The first chapters <u>are</u> sad.
22. His early years <u>were</u> lonely ones.

D. Writing Sentences with Linking Verbs and Action Verbs   Each sentence is missing a verb. Write each sentence. Add the type of verb given in parentheses ( ).

23. Noguchi _____ the son of a poet.   (linking)

MODEL > Noguchi is the son of a poet.

24. Noguchi _____ a serious artist.   (linking)
25. However, he sometimes _____ jokes, too.   (action)
26. His "Humpty-Dumpty" _____ unusual.   (linking)
27. He _____ gardens and parks.   (action)
28. His gardens _____ all peaceful places.   (linking)

Application—Writing

A Magazine Story   Look at the picture. What does it show about the artist and his work? Imagine that you are a reporter. Write a paragraph that might be in a story about Noguchi and his art. Use at least three linking verbs.

3 Main Verbs and Helping Verbs

FOCUS
◆ The **main verb** is the most important verb in the predicate.
◆ A **helping verb** works with the main verb to tell about action.

Remember that every sentence has a predicate. In each of these sentences, the simple predicate is made up of two verbs.

1. We are enjoying the paintings.
2. She has painted many colorful pictures.
3. I have always liked watercolors.

In sentence 1 the helping verb *are* works with the main verb *enjoying*. Notice that *are* is not used as a linking verb. In sentence 2 the helping verb *has* works with the main verb *painted*. A main verb comes last in a group of verbs. Sometimes, a word that tells *when* comes between a main verb and a helping verb, as in sentence 3.

Using Main Verbs and Helping Verbs
When the main verb ends in *ing*, use *am, is, are, was,* or *were*. When the main verb ends in *ed*, use *has, have,* or *had*.

Guided Practice

A. Identify each underlined verb as a *main verb* or a *helping verb*.

1. I <u>am</u> <u>learning</u> about American art.
2. We <u>are</u> <u>studying</u> American artists in school.
3. We <u>have</u> just <u>learned</u> about Pablita Velarde.
4. I <u>had</u> <u>seen</u> her work before.
5. She <u>has</u> <u>painted</u> many pictures about the beautiful Southwest.

Independent Practice

B. Identifying Main Verbs and Helping Verbs   Make a chart with two columns. Head them *Helping Verbs* and *Main Verbs*. Write each underlined verb in the correct column.

6. Most people <u>have</u> <u>heard</u> of Geronimo.

MODEL	Helping Verbs	Main Verbs
	have	heard

7. His grandson <u>has</u> <u>made</u> a name for himself, too.
8. I <u>am</u> <u>reading</u> about this man, Alan Houser.
9. My cousins <u>have</u> <u>seen</u> his paintings in Oklahoma.
10. They <u>were</u> <u>visiting</u> an Indian museum.
11. Alice and Tom <u>have</u> <u>described</u> his work.
12. Alice <u>was</u> <u>observing</u> Pueblo artists.

C. Using Helping Verbs Correctly   Copy each sentence. Complete it with *am, is, are, have,* or *has.*

13. Our class _____ putting on an art show.

MODEL ▷ Our class is putting on an art show.

14. We all _____ created something for the show.
15. Annie _____ painted some desert pictures.
16. Paula _____ shaped some clay pots.
17. She _____ working on the last one now.
18. Two other pots _____ sitting on the shelf.
19. I _____ weaving a blanket for the show.
20. Manuela and Ben _____ making some shelves.

Application—Writing

A Journal   Imagine that you visited the museum in the picture. Write a journal entry that describes what you saw. Try to use at least four helping verbs in your sentences. If you need help writing a journal entry, see page 26 of the **Writer's Handbook.**

4 Verb Tenses

◆ **FOCUS** The **tense** of a verb tells the time of an action.

Verbs have different tenses. A verb tense may show past, present, or future time.

1. They climb the mountain. present
2. They climbed for three hours this morning. past
3. They will climb until evening. future

In sentence 1 the present-tense verb tells about something that is happening now. In sentence 2 the verb tells about something that happened in the past. It ends in *ed*. In sentence 3 the helping verb *will* tells that the verb is in the future tense.

> ## Link to Speaking
> Be sure to pronounce *ed* endings clearly. Otherwise, your listeners may not know whether you are using the past tense or the present tense.

Guided Practice

A. Identify the tense of each underlined verb as *present*, *past*, or *future*.

1. Annapurna <u>rises</u> 26,504 feet into the sky.
2. It <u>stands</u> in the country of Nepal.
3. The people <u>named</u> it "Goddess of the Harvests."
4. The Sherpa people <u>live</u> in the mountains.
5. They <u>will guide</u> the climbers up the mountain.

> ### THINK AND REMEMBER
> ◆ Use **present tense** to show action that is happening now.
> ◆ Use **past tense** to show action that happened in the past.
> ◆ Use **future tense** to show action that will happen in the future.

Independent Practice

B. Identifying Tenses Decide the tense of each underlined verb. Then write *present, past,* or *future.*

6. Arlene Blum <u>wanted</u> to climb Annapurna.

MODEL > past

7. Climbers <u>need</u> permission from Nepal's government.
8. Blum <u>waited</u> four years for permission.
9. Then, her team <u>planned</u> the trip.
10. Many questions <u>come</u> up for climbers.
11. They <u>will need</u> much equipment.
12. At last, they <u>finished</u> their planning.
13. They <u>will go</u> to Nepal in August.
14. They <u>started</u> their climb on August 23, 1978.
15. Not everyone <u>reaches</u> the top.
16. The rest of them <u>will watch</u> from the camp.
17. On October 15, four climbers <u>reached</u> the peak.

C. Using Tenses Correctly Read each sentence. Write the verb in parentheses ( ) that makes the most sense.

18. Long ago, climbers (face, faced) many hardships.

MODEL > faced

19. Climbing a mountain still (takes, took) courage.
20. My brother (is, will be) a great climber someday.
21. He recently (joins, joined) a climbing club.
22. Last year, he (climbed, will climb) Mt. Whitney.
23. Next year, he (climbs, will climb) Mt. McKinley.
24. Now, he (practices, practiced) climbing.
25. Tomorrow, he (met, will meet) with his club.
26. When I am older, I (join, will join) the club.
27. Now, I (hike, hiked) with my friends.
28. Soon, we (climb, will climb) as well as my brother.

Application—Writing and Speaking

A Speech Imagine that you are one of the climbers in the picture. You have been asked to give a speech to a climbing club about your adventure. Write a paragraph that tells what you just did, are doing, and hope to do. Use past, present, and future tenses correctly. Present your speech to the class.

5 Spelling Present-Tense Verbs

◆ **FOCUS** Some present-tense verbs change spelling to agree with the subject.

The subject and the verb of a sentence should agree. Notice the verb in each sentence.

1. Todd leads an exercise class.
2. Fifteen students take the class.

There are two forms of present-tense verbs. A **singular verb** follows a singular subject. It usually ends in *s.* In sentence 1 *leads* is a singular verb. A **plural verb** follows a plural subject. In sentence 2 *take* is a plural verb.

The singular form of most verbs is spelled by adding *s.* Sometimes, other spelling changes take place in certain verbs. This chart shows two types of spelling changes.

---

1. If a verb ends in *ss, sh, ch,* or *x,* add *es.*

address	addresses	pinch	pinches
brush	brushes	tax	taxes

2. If a verb ends in a consonant + *y,* change the *y* to *i* and then add *es.*

study	studies

Guided Practice

A. Identify the verb that correctly completes each sentence.

1. The exercise class (meet, meets) on Saturdays.
2. Todd (begin, begins) each class with warm-ups.
3. The Klein twins (bring, brings) their tape player.
4. The students (share, shares) their favorite tapes.
5. The music (make, makes) exercising more fun.

THINK AND REMEMBER

◆ Use a **singular verb** to agree with a singular subject. A singular verb ends in *s* or *es.*
◆ Use a **plural verb** to agree with a plural subject.

Independent Practice

B. Identifying Verb Forms   Write the form of the verb that correctly completes each sentence.

   6. People (exercise, exercises) for different reasons.

MODEL > exercise

   7. Caitlin (hope, hopes) to become a great athlete.
   8. Amanda (say, says) she does it for good health.
   9. Hearts (work, works) better after exercise.
  10. Exercise (build, builds) stronger muscles, too.
  11. The Klein twins (come, comes) to the class for fun.
  12. Each class (end, ends) with a race.

C. Spelling Verbs Correctly   Read each sentence. Write the present-tense form of the verb in parentheses ( ).

  13. Cathy's energy _____ everyone.   (astonish)

MODEL > astonishes

  14. Cathy never _____ a class.   (miss)
  15. The girl _____ Todd carefully.   (watch)
  16. Todd _____ his arms high over his head.   (stretch)
  17. Then, Todd _____ the students to follow him.   (ask)
  18. Cathy _____ to do every exercise perfectly.   (try)

D. Writing Original Sentences   Write two sentences using each verb in the present tense. Write one sentence using the plural form. Then write one sentence using the singular form.

  19. reach

MODEL > The students reach high. Todd reaches for the sky.

  20. press   **22.** munch   **24.** wash
  21. wax   **23.** splash   **25.** fish

Application—Writing

A Brochure   Imagine that you are an exercise instructor. You want to write a brochure for new students. Write about what you do in your classes. Use the picture to get started. Write in the present tense. Try to use at least one verb from each of these groups:

  1. *guess, pass, toss*
  2. *pitch, reach, search, touch*
  3. *dash, finish, push, rush*

6 Spelling Past-Tense Verbs

◆ **FOCUS** Some verbs change spelling when *ed* is added to form the past tense.

Many verbs form the past tense by adding *ed*. Look at the verbs in color in these sentences.

1. Inez Mexia hiked through the jungle.
2. She stopped to rest.
3. She spied an unusual plant.

Notice how the spelling of *hike, stop,* and *spy* changed when *ed* was added. This chart gives the rules for these changes.

---

1. If a verb ends in *e*, drop the *e* before adding *ed*.
    hike   *hiked*
2. If a verb has one syllable and ends with a short vowel sound and a consonant, double the final consonant before adding *ed*.
    stop   *stopped*
3. If a verb ends in a consonant and *y*, change the *y* to *i* before adding *ed*.
    spy   *spied*

Guided Practice

A. Spell the past-tense form of each verb in parentheses ( ).

1. At the age of 55, Mexia (decide) to study plants.
2. She (announce) she would go to Mexico first.
3. She (map) an interesting route for herself.
4. Later, she (explore) Alaska and South America.
5. She (study) the plants of each country.

THINK AND REMEMBER

◆ Change the spelling of some verbs before you add *ed*. You may have to drop an *e*, double a final consonant, or change a *y* to an *i*.

Independent Practice

B. Spelling Past-Tense Verbs   Read each sentence. Write the past-tense form of each verb in parentheses ( ).

   6. People (guide) her through rugged country.

MODEL ➤ guided

   7. Mexia (travel) through many wild areas.
   8. Her guides (carry) supplies, too.
   9. The expedition (canoe) down great rivers.
   10. Sometimes the canoes (glide) through smooth water.
   11. At other times, they (bob) in choppy waters.
   12. At times, Mexia got out and (wade).
   13. She (plod) for hours in the hot sun.
   14. The difficult journeys never (tire) her.

C. Proofreading Sentences   Rewrite the sentences. Spell the verbs correctly.

   15. The plants varyed in small ways.

MODEL ➤ The plants varied in small ways.

   16. Mexia noticeed every detail about a plant.
   17. She copyed them in her notebook.
   18. Then she joted down facts about each plant.
   19. She prepareed the plants to ship home.
   20. The plants were dryed carefully.
   21. They were placeed in containers.
   22. Then, they were shiped back.
   23. She planed to give plant samples to colleges.
   24. Some colleges supplyed money for the trips.
   25. Scientists admireed her careful work.

Application—Writing

Paragraph in a Letter   Imagine that you are Inez Mexia. Write a paragraph that might be in a letter to a classmate. Describe something you did that day. Try to use the past-tense forms of two verbs from each of these groups:

   1. *injure, like, note, pause, scare*
   2. *carry, cry, hurry, try, worry*
   3. *drag, slip, squat, step, trip*

Building Vocabulary
Synonyms

The mountains rose around us.

Before us ~~rose~~ *stood* the high peak of Mt. Quail.

The writer of this draft did not want to use the word *rose* twice. Instead, she chose a synonym for *rose*. A **synonym** is a word that has almost the same meaning as another word. The word *stood* is a synonym for *rose* in this sentence.

To find a synonym for a word, look in the **Writer's Thesaurus.** Many words have several synonyms. Other synonyms for *rose* are *climbed* and *wakened*. Neither of these words would have been correct in the second sentence. If you are not sure which synonym to use, check in a dictionary. The dictionary can give you the exact meaning of a word.

In these sentences, the underlined words are all synonyms for *run*. Their meanings in the sentences are shown in parentheses ( ).

1. The horses <u>gallop</u> through the woods.   (race)
2. Several rivers <u>flow</u> into the gulf.   (rush)
3. The hikes usually <u>last</u> all day.   (continue)

Think about why each word was the best to use in each sentence.

Reading Practice

Read the sentences. The words in parentheses ( )
are synonyms. Write the word that works best in
the sentence.

1. Both children and adults (joined, combined) the club.
2. All of them had (marched, hiked) on this
   trail before.
3. The sun (shone, glistened) brightly.
4. The hikers (rose, climbed) up the hillside.
5. They (took, grabbed) lunches with them.
6. They (tasted, ate) lunch in a cool part of the woods.

Writing Practice

Rewrite the following sentences. Replace the
underlined word with a synonym from the **Writer's
Thesaurus.** Be sure the synonym makes sense in the
sentence.

7. Julia and Corby <u>like</u> hiking and climbing.
8. Today they <u>begin</u> to climb Old Baldy.
9. They <u>buy</u> their lunch at the top.
10. Julia and Corby <u>slip</u> on some ice.
11. They do not <u>hurt</u> themselves.
12. Hikers should always <u>remain</u> alert.
13. Accidents can occur <u>after</u> a long day.
14. While outside, they should <u>walk</u> carefully.
15. Walkers should travel <u>together</u>.

Project

Work in a group to make up a synonym game. It
can be a board game or a card game. The players of
your game should have to match or name
synonyms. Then they should make up sentences
using these words.

Write the rules for your game. Make the articles
needed to play it. Test your game. Then give it to
another group to play.

Building Vocabulary
Antonyms

A dance rehearsal and a dance performance are very different from one another. When you write, you often want to point out differences.

1. Dancing looks <u>easy</u>, but it is <u>hard</u> work.
2. Though rehearsals can be <u>tiresome</u>, a performance is always <u>exciting</u>.

The words *easy* and *hard* are opposite in meaning. So are the words *tiresome* and *exciting*. Words with opposite meanings are called **antonyms.**

Antonyms are very useful when you want to point out differences. Often, a word has more than one antonym. You should choose the one that expresses exactly what you want to say. The **Writer's Thesaurus** can help you find antonyms.

3. Dancing looks easy, but it is <u>difficult</u>.
4. Dancing looks easy, but it is <u>tiring</u>.

How does each underlined word change the meaning of the sentence?

Reading Practice

Change the meaning of each sentence to its opposite meaning. Replace the underlined word with an antonym from the box. Write the new sentence.

together	short	least	seldom
more	always	end	after

1. The rehearsal will <u>begin</u> at 7:00.
2. They <u>never</u> come to rehearsal on time.
3. They get a pep talk <u>before</u> each rehearsal.
4. The first dance number is the <u>most</u> difficult.
5. The dancers moved <u>apart</u> as they got ready.
6. You must take <u>less</u> time when you leap.
7. After a <u>long</u> time they got the step right.
8. They <u>often</u> have to rehearse late.

Writing Practice

Rewrite each sentence. In place of the blank, write an antonym for the underlined word. Use the **Writer's Thesaurus** if you need help. You may use any antonym that makes sense.

9. The theater was <u>small</u>, but the stage was quite _____.
10. I had seen the <u>same</u> show in March but with _____ dancers.
11. Though the peasants' costumes were <u>ugly</u>, the prince's costume was _____.
12. After the prince's <u>slow</u> dance, the peasants did a _____ jig.
13. We watched the show <u>quietly</u> and clapped _____ afterward.

Project

Find two magazine pictures that show people, places, or things that are different from one another. Paste the pictures on a sheet of paper. Under the pictures list three or four pairs of word groups that describe the differences. Use antonyms in the pairs.

Then show the set of pictures to your classmates. Ask them to guess how you compared the two. Share what you wrote. Talk about the guesses that were correct.

Language Enrichment
Verbs

Use what you know about verbs to do these activities.

Cliffhangers

Work with a large group or your whole class to create a funny chain story. Together, decide who the characters of the story will be.

The first storyteller puts the characters in a hair-raising situation and stops. The student next in line tells how the characters get out of their difficulty. This storyteller then puts them in another jam and stops. Each storyteller continues the story in this way. Think up funny adventures. Use past-tense verbs to tell your story.

Winners' Circle

Make a bulletin board display with pictures of each student in the class. Leave plenty of room around each picture.

Working alone, make one small card for each of your classmates. At the top, write the student's name. Then write three sentences about him or her. In the first sentence, tell something that the student did that you admire. In the second, state something special about the student now. In the third, predict something that the student will do in the future. Make sure you use past, present, and future verb tenses correctly. Put the card near the student's picture.

When the display is complete, read the nice things your classmates wrote about you.

CONNECTING
LANGUAGE ⟷ WRITING

In this unit you learned that some verbs show action. Other verbs link subjects with words in the predicate. Verbs also tell whether the action in a sentence takes place in the present, in the past, or in the future.

◆ **Using Verbs in Your Writing** When you write, it is important to know how to use verbs. Colorful verbs make your writing more exciting. They help your audience see and feel the action. Choose your verbs carefully as you do these activities.

How Did They Ever . . . ?

The people in the picture have a silly problem to solve. Use your imagination to think of a funny solution.

Write a paragraph explaining how the problem is or was solved. You may use present-tense verbs if you pretend you are watching the action as it happens. You may use past-tense verbs to write about the events as though they have already happened. When you are finished, put your solution on a bulletin board.

Hit, Swat, and Miss

You learned about synonyms and antonyms on the **Building Vocabulary** pages. Now use them to do this activity.

Think of a verb that has both a synonym and an antonym. You may use the **Writer's Thesaurus** if you need help. Now think about how you can use all three verbs in a set of directions. Then write three sentences.

Example: run: *race*, **walk**
First, walk to first base.
Then, run to second base.
Finally, race home.

Unit Checkup

Think Back	Think Ahead
◆ What did you learn about how-to paragraphs in this unit? What did you do to write one?	◆ How will what you learned about how-to paragraphs help you when you read directions? ◆ How will visualizing steps help you explain something?
◆ Look at the writing you did in this unit. How did verbs help you express your ideas?	◆ What is one way that you can use verbs to improve your writing?

Analyzing a How-to Paragraph   *pages 108–109*
Read this paragraph. Then answer the questions that follow.

> How to Play Fictionary
>
> Have you ever played Fictionary? All you need is a dictionary and some paper and pencils for everyone. One person finds a word in the dictionary. He or she makes sure no one else knows what the word means. Then the person spells the word aloud. Everyone writes the word and what they think it means. The person with the dictionary writes the real definition. Then he or she collects all the papers and mixes them up. That person reads all the definitions, and whoever guesses the right one wins!

1. What is the game called?
2. What materials would you need to play this game?
3. What does one person do?
4. What does everybody else do?
5. How is the winner decided?

Visualizing Steps in a Process   *page 110*
Write the following steps in the correct order.

6. Everyone walks around the chairs.
7. Everyone tries to get a seat.

8. To play musical chairs, put some chairs in a circle.
9. Put on a record.
10. Someone lifts the needle from the record.

Writing for an Audience and a Purpose   *pages 111–112*
Replace the underlined words with more exact words. Make the sentences shorter and easier to understand.

11. Heat the <u>whole oven till it's hot</u>.
12. Crack <u>some</u> eggs, but put only the yolk and the white part in the mixing <u>thing</u>.
13. Put <u>some</u> sugar and one cup of <u>wet stuff</u> and <u>some</u> flour into the bowl.
14. Stir and stir until all the <u>different things that you used in your recipe</u> are mixed together extra well.
15. Put it in the oven, and let it cook <u>for a while</u>.

The Writing Process   *pages 113–122*
Write the letter of the correct response to each question.

16. What kind of game would be the best topic for a how-to paragraph?
    a. an ancient game played only by very smart people
    b. a game that makes all the players get confused
    c. a simple game that your brother made up
17. Which of the following would you use in the *materials* section?
    a. You need water balloons to play this game.
    b. The players are safe when they touch base.
    c. The one who tags the most people is the winner.
18. Which information is *not* necessary in your paragraph?
    a. Everyone should have a funny hat.
    b. The water balloon breaks when it hits someone.
    c. When you tag someone, you switch hats.
19. In what order should you write your paragraph?
    a. steps, materials, winner, name of game
    b. name of game, materials, steps, winner
    c. winner, materials, name of game, steps
20. What is the last thing you should do when composing your paragraph?
    a. Gather information.
    b. Write a title.
    c. Write a topic sentence.

Action Verbs   pages 126–127

Write the action verb in each sentence.

21. Mr. Naismith coached the men's sports teams.
22. The men had no indoor game for winter.
23. They just lifted weights over and over.
24. Some of the men complained.
25. Then Mr. Naismith invented a new game.
26. He hung a peach basket from a pole.
27. Then he gave the men a volleyball.
28. One team aims for the basket.
29. The other team gets the ball away if possible.
30. The men loved the game.
31. They named it basketball.

Linking Verbs   pages 128–129

Write the linking verb in each sentence.

32. Eric Liddell was the best runner in Scotland.
33. However, he was not sure of victory.
34. People were anxious for him.
35. "You are talented," they said.
36. The Scottish people were proud of Eric.

Main Verbs and Helping Verbs   pages 130–131

Make a chart with two columns. Head them *Helping Verbs* and
Main Verbs. Write each underlined verb in the correct column.

37. "This race is not going to be easy."
38. "I am going to do it," Eric decided.
39. "This long race is going to be hard," he said.
40. "Still, I have prepared myself as well as I can."
41. "I have done what was right," he said later.

Verb Tenses   pages 132–133

Decide the tense of each underlined verb. Then write *present, past,* or *future.*

42. Ruth wanted to work in Clark's health store.
43. Every day she watched Jason help Mr. Clark.
44. "I can do what Jason does," she said.
45. "I will show Mr. Clark what I can do."
46. "Pretty soon he will want to hire me too."

Spelling Present-Tense Verbs   *pages 134–135*

Read each sentence. Write the correct present-tense form of the verb in parentheses ( ).

47. Mrs. Wheatley (like) her new maid.
48. She (call) her Phillis.
49. Phillis's clothes (sag) on her.
50. She (hem) a new dress for Phillis.
51. For a while she (baby) Phillis.
52. Soon she (realize) that Phillis is very smart.
53. She (decide) Phillis should learn to read.

Spelling Past-Tense Verbs   *pages 136–137*

Read each sentence. Write the past-tense form of the verb in parentheses ( ).

54. One day Phillis (try) to write on the wall.
55. "What are you doing?" Mrs. Wheatley (cry).
56. "I write words from poetry books," Phillis (reply).
57. Mrs. Wheatley (plan) to teach Phillis writing.
58. Then Phillis (study) Latin.

Synonyms   *pages 138–139*

Read the sentences. The words in parentheses ( ) are synonyms. Write the word that works best in the sentence.

59. How did your room get so (confused, disorderly)?
60. We'll have to work hard to get it (purified, clean).
61. Let's (organize, classify) all the books on the shelf.
62. (Drape, Hang) all the clothes in the closet.
63. Now you can actually (see, notice) your bed again!

Antonyms   *pages 140–141*

Change the meaning of each sentence to the opposite meaning. Replace the underlined word or words with an antonym from the box. Write the sentence.

useful	change	save	always	neat

64. Pretty soon we'll have your room very <u>messy</u>.
65. Why do you <u>throw out</u> so many useless things?
66. I know you think they're <u>useless</u>, don't you?
67. You need to <u>keep</u> that attitude.
68. Then you can <u>never</u> have a neat room.

UNIT

4

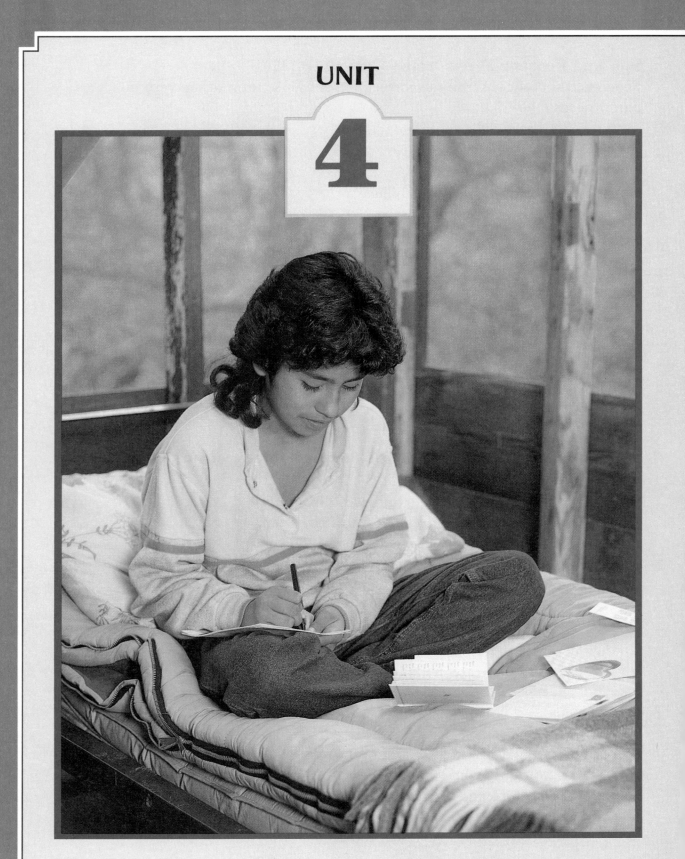

Communicating with Others

◆ **COMPOSITION FOCUS:** **Friendly Letter**
◆ **LANGUAGE FOCUS:** **Verbs**

"There is a letter for you in today's mail."

How do you feel when you hear those words? Do you feel curious, pleased, and excited, or do you have some other feeling? Sometimes getting a letter is more thrilling than getting a phone call. Also, you can look forward to sharing the letter with others.

Many people would rather write letters to their friends than telephone them. They feel they can say more in a long letter than in a short phone call. A letter might take an hour to write, but a phone call might last only five minutes.

Sooner or later, most people have to part with someone whom they care about. The separation might be a long parting from a cousin who moves to another city or a short parting from a friend who is away at summer camp. In this unit you will learn how to use a letter to stay close to a friend you want to keep.

Marilyn Sachs, a writer of children's books, created *Laura's Luck* *to entertain* and *to inform* readers.

Reading with a Writer's Eye
Friendly Letter

How can two good friends spend a summer apart and still stay close? In the book *Laura's Luck* by Marilyn Sachs, a character named Amy writes a letter to stay in touch with her friend Rosa. As you read her letter, notice that she shares her feelings.

July 11

Dear Rosa,

How are you feeling? I am feeling fine. I miss you too. The girls up here are very nice but there is nothing like the old friends. I wish you were here.

I go swimming every day and yesterday we went fishing from rowboats and I caught a fish. Nobody else caught anything, and I was so excited I nearly upset the boat. The fish was too small so we had to throw it back and we had hamburgers for supper instead of fish.

I like it here very much. Laura is having the most fun of all. She has all the luck. First she sprained her ankle and caught a cold and is still sleeping in the infirmary. They bring her her meals on a tray. Then they said when she gets better she can go to the twelve bunk even though she is only eleven.

Anyway, I like it here very much. We are going on an overnight hike next week. Do you go swimming at the pool? N.T.N.M.E.O.K.

Your friend,

P.S. That means 9 × 9 makes 81 kisses.

P.P.S. Our bunk has a pet snake named Fred. He is a rattlesnake but the ranger removed the poison so he is harmless and very affectionate. I think he likes me the best.

P.P.P.S. Did you go to the movies last Saturday? What was playing?

Respond

1. Imagine that you are Rosa. Describe your feelings after you read Amy's letter. Why does the letter bring out these feelings?

Discuss

2. In which parts of the letter does Amy share her own feelings?
3. Where and how does Amy entertain Rosa with an account of what she is doing? Why do you think Amy tells Rosa about Laura?

Thinking As a Writer
Analyzing a Friendly Letter

Writing a friendly letter is a way to share news with friends and relatives. Like the one below, a letter might be an answer to someone else's letter. A friendly letter might include an invitation for a party. Another might include a thank-you note for a gift or a favor.

Every letter has a **heading**, a **greeting**, a **body**, a **closing**, and a **signature**.

---

12 Day Street
Tampa, Florida 33612
July 14, 1990

Dear Amy,

    I seemed to hear your voice as I read your letter. I wish I could be there with you, too.

    I enjoyed your news from the camp. Have you managed to hook a big fish yet? Is Laura out of the infirmary? I wonder how she will like the twelve bunk. Her bunkmates might be very nice—or they might keep reminding her she is only eleven!

    My family went camping overnight last Saturday. Dad was very organized before the trip. He gave us each a list of things to do. Then he lined us up in the driveway and checked each list. When we finally got to the park, we had to rent a cabin to sleep in. Dad had been so worried about our forgetting something that he had left the tent behind. We had a terrific time anyway.

    Write back soon.

Your friend,
Rosa

The **heading** contains the writer's address and the date.

The **greeting** addresses the person who receives the letter.

The **body** contains information or feelings. There is often more than one paragraph in the body.

The **closing** ends the letter.

The **signature** shows who wrote the letter.

Discuss

1. How might the heading be helpful to Amy?
2. What other closings might have been used?
3. Look at the paragraphs in the body. What is the reason for each?

Try Your Hand

A. Organize a Letter   The parts of this letter are out of order. Rewrite the letter. Put the parts in order.

> January 10, 19——   Kent, Washington 98031
> Jim   Love,
> 2280 10th Street   Dear Uncle Jerry,
>   I am glad that you came to visit. I enjoyed going to the park and riding the merry-go-round. I can't wait to see you next time.

B. Write Greetings and Closings   This list shows some people to whom you might write. Write the greeting and the closing you would use for each person. You may make up names or use real names.

1. your grandmother
2. your best friend
3. a neighbor who moved away
4. a firefighter who spoke to your class

C. Write the Body of a Letter   Here are some detail sentences from the body of a letter. Put them in the order that makes the most sense. Then write them in a paragraph.

> We measured and cut the boards.
>
> We raised the deck into the tree and nailed it in place.
> On Saturday Mom and I built a deck for a tree.
> Then, we nailed the boards together on the ground.
> Next, we bought wood.
>
> First, we drew up our plans for a tree house.

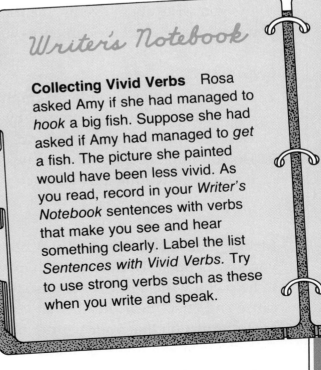

Writer's Notebook

Collecting Vivid Verbs   Rosa asked Amy if she had managed to *hook* a big fish. Suppose she had asked if Amy had managed to *get* a fish. The picture she painted would have been less vivid. As you read, record in your *Writer's Notebook* sentences with verbs that make you see and hear something clearly. Label the list *Sentences with Vivid Verbs*. Try to use strong verbs such as these when you write and speak.

D. Read a Friendly Letter   Turn to Amy's letter on page 150, or find another friendly letter. Then read the letter aloud to a partner. Identify the parts. Also, identify any parts that are missing. Discuss why the writer wrote the letter.

Thinking As a Writer
Connecting Cause and Effect

Writer's Guide

To write a friendly letter, good writers often

♦ clearly explain the **cause** that makes something happen.

♦ clearly explain the resulting **effect.**

When you describe events in a letter, you want them to make sense to your reader. You may need to show how the events are related to one another. For example, something you felt or did could have made something else happen.

Cause   Effect

I felt lonely. ——→ I wrote to my friend Amy.

In the example you just looked at, the **cause** is the first event. It makes the **effect** happen. When you write sentences that show a cause and its effect, you can put the cause first or the effect first.

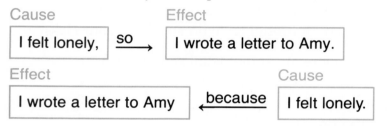

Cause

| I felt lonely, | so → |

Effect

| I wrote a letter to Amy. |

Effect

| I wrote a letter to Amy |

Cause

| ←because | I felt lonely. |

As you write about events in a friendly letter, be aware that you may need to include sentences connecting causes and effects.

Discuss

1. Look back at the second paragraph of Amy's letter on page 150. Which events were caused by something else? Describe each event in a sentence that tells why it happened.
2. Do you think you would use cause-and-effect sentences often if you were writing a friendly letter? Explain your answer.

Try Your Hand

Identify Cause and Effect   Think about something interesting you saw happen. Decide why it happened. Then use a diagram to help you write a few sentences about the event. Make each cause and effect clear. Read what you wrote to a partner. Discuss any information that your partner had trouble understanding. Talk about how it might be made clearer.

Developing the Writer's Craft
Including Details That Tell Why

When you write a letter, you tell your reader what has happened to you and to others. If you stop with that information, you are telling only half the story. To make your story interesting and complete, you must tell your reader *why* things happened.

1. When I stood up, I fell out of the boat.
2. Brenda jumped in after she saw me fall in.
3. She was scared because she thought I could not swim.
4. I came to the surface, and she was relieved.

The underlined words in each sentence tell why something happened. Without those words, a reader might not be able to figure out what was happening. Sometimes writers use words such as *when*, *after*, and *because* to signal that an explanation is coming. This tells the reader to be alert.

When you write your letter, be sure that you tell not only what happened but also why it happened.

Discuss

1. Look at Rosa's letter on page 152. Why did her father forget the tent? How would her letter be different if she had not told why this happened?
2. Read these sentences. *Lisa ran into the dining hall shouting. Soon everyone else was yelling.* What could you do to improve the sentences? Give an example of how you might change them.

Try Your Hand

Explain Why   Look at the picture. Write a short paragraph that tells what is happening in it and why.

1 Prewriting
Friendly Letter

Writer's Guide

Prewriting Checklist

☑ Think about your audience and your purpose.

☑ Brainstorm topics.

☑ Select topics that will interest your audience.

☑ Gather information.

☑ Organize the information.

Carminda decided to write to her friend Rachel, who had moved away. She knew that Rachel would enjoy a funny story about something Carminda had done or seen. She used the checklist in the **Writer's Guide** to help plan her letter. Look at what she did.

◆ Brainstorming and Selecting a Topic

First, Carminda thought about the things she had done and seen in the last few weeks. She also checked her journal to see whether she had written about anything funny. As she brainstormed, she listed her ideas.

Then, Carminda asked herself which topics would interest Rachel. She crossed out any that were about people Rachel did not know well. She decided not to write about anything that would not make an interesting story. Finally, she circled the topic that would make the most enjoyable story for Rachel.

I am invited to a party next week.

We had a funny canoe accident at day camp.

I went to the dentist.

Joel Walsh won the library reading contest.

My brother's teacher moved away.

Our new neighbors put in a vegetable garden.

Discuss

1. Why might Carminda have decided against each topic she crossed out?
2. How might each topic Carminda crossed out be turned into a different story?

◆ Gathering and Organizing Information

After Carminda had decided what to write about, she gathered information for her letter. Carminda thought about the details she wanted to include about the canoe accident. She jotted them down as she thought of them. When she had finished, she read over her notes. She crossed out the unimportant details. She identified the ending of her story. Then she made check marks next to the details that would lead up to the ending.

Mr. Goldberg is a very important program director. ✓
Mr. Goldberg got dunked, but he laughed. Ending of my story.
My little brother talked my parents into letting him go to day camp, too.
My little brother yelled because he thought he felt a fish. ✓
Julia is the oldest counselor.
Julia was paddling the canoe. ✓
My brother swam to the canoe and tried to get in. ✓
Then he tipped it over. ✓

Carminda studied her list again. Then she made a new list of the details she planned to use. This time she put them in the order in which they happened. She noted the causes of some of the events.

1. Mr. Goldberg is important director
2. Julia took him in canoe.
3. canoe passed our swim class
4. Luis got scared because he was afraid of fish.
5. He grabbed the canoe to climb out of water.
6. Canoe tipped because Luis grabbed it.
7. Mr. Goldberg got dunked!

Discuss

1. How is Carminda's second list different from her first? Why do you think she began with the fact about Mr. Goldberg?
2. Which notes suggest the causes of some events? Why is it important to describe the causes?

Try Your Hand

Now plan a friendly letter of your own.

A. Brainstorm and Select a Topic Choose someone to whom you would like to write a letter. You might pick a friend or a relative who lives in another town. Brainstorm a list of possible topics. If you have a journal or a writing log, read it over and look for ideas. Think about each topic and the person you plan to write to.

- ◆ Cross out topics that have to do with people unknown to the person you will write to.
- ◆ Cross out anything that will not make an entertaining story with a good ending.
- ◆ Circle the topic that you think your audience will enjoy the most. This will be the topic of your letter.

B. Gather and Organize Information When you are satisfied with your topic, write down everything you can think of about it. Then look over the notes you made.

- ◆ Identify the ending of your story. Then make check marks next to each event that leads up to the ending.
- ◆ Think about your audience. Add details that would interest your reader, and cross out information that is unimportant.
- ◆ Make a new list of the details that you plan to use. Put the events in the order in which they happened.
- ◆ Remember to include sentences connecting causes and effects to show how events are related.
- ◆ Check your list to be sure that you have told why important events happened. If you have not, add this information.

 Save your notes and lists in your *Writer's Notebook*. You will use them when you draft your letter.

WRITING PROCESS

2 Drafting
Friendly Letter

Carminda followed the checklist in the **Writer's Guide** to draft her letter. Look at what she did.

> 937 Shawnee Court
> Augusta, Georgia 30907
> July 18, 1990
>
> Dear Rachel,
>   I have been having a great time in day camp this summer. I have a swimming class at the lake almost every day.

Discuss

In what part of the letter does Carminda begin to tell her news? How does she begin to tell it?

Try Your Hand

Now you are ready to write a friendly letter.

A. **Review Your Information**   Look over your notes. If you left out any details, add them now.

B. **Think About Your TAP**   Remember that your task is to write a letter. Your purpose is to tell about something that happened.

C. **Write Your First Draft**   Follow the **Writer's Guide** to write your letter.
   When you write your draft, just put all your ideas on paper. Do not worry about spelling, punctuation, or grammar. You can correct the draft later.

Task: What?
Audience: Who?
Purpose: Why?

 Save your first draft in your *Writer's Notebook*. You will use it when you revise your letter.

3 Responding and Revising
Friendly Letter

Carminda used the checklist in the **Writer's Guide** to revise her letter. Look at what she did.

Writer's Guide

Revising Checklist

☑ Read your letter to yourself or to a partner.

☑ Think about your audience and your purpose. Add or cut information.

☑ Check to see that your letter is organized correctly.

☑ Check for sentences that can be combined.

◆ Checking Information

Carminda decided that the last sentence was unnecessary. She had already led up to the ending. To show her change, Carminda used this mark ✗ . Then she realized she had left out an important detail. She had not told why Luis yelled. To show the addition, she used this mark ∧ .

◆ Checking Organization

As she reread her letter, Carminda realized that a sentence was in the wrong place. To show where it should be moved, she used this mark ⌒ .

◆ Checking Language

Carminda also realized she could make two sentences into one. She crossed out the unnecessary word and used *and* to join the predicates of the sentences.

Move —

An important program director named Mr. Goldberg came to visit the camp. One of the counselors took him for a canoe ride. (The counselors showed him around.) Julia paddled him past our swimming class. I was floating on my back. Just then my little *because* he had felt a fish brush his leg. and brother Luis yelled. Then he lost his head. He grabbed the canoe. When he tried to climb on board. it tipped over. Julia and Mr. Goldberg were dunked. We were all worried then. Mr. Goldberg's head popped up. and he laughed. What a relief. ~~Some people might have been angry.~~

Add/ Replace —

Cut —

WRITING PROCESS

Discuss

1. Look at the second and third sentences in the second paragraph. Was Carminda right to change their order? Explain.
2. Look at the other changes Carminda made. How did each improve her letter?

Try Your Hand

Now revise your first draft.

A. Read Your First Draft As you read your letter, think about your audience and your purpose. Read your letter silently or to a partner to see if it is complete and well organized. Ask yourself or your partner the questions in the box.

Responding and Revising Strategies

✔ Respond
Ask yourself or your partner:

- Have I used correct letter form?

- Do I describe events in the order in which they happened?

- Does my account explain why some of the events happened?

- Check for repeated words. Have I combined sentences to avoid repeating words?

- Do I stop after I have led up to the ending?

✔ Revise
Try these solutions:

- **Add** any parts that are missing.

- **Move** information that is in the wrong place.

- **Add** sentences or groups of words that make the causes of events clear.

- **Cut** repeated words, and combine sentences. See the **Revising Workshop** on page 162.

- **Cut** sentences that add nothing.

B. Make Your Changes If the answer to any question in the box is *no,* try the solution. Use the **Editor's Marks** to show your changes.

C. Review Your Letter Again Decide if there is anything else you want to revise. Keep revising your letter until you feel it is well organized and complete.

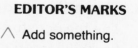

EDITOR'S MARKS

∧ Add something.
⟋ Cut something.
◯ Move something.
∧ Replace something.

Save your revised letter in your *Writer's Notebook*. You will use it when you proofread your letter.

Revising Workshop
Combining Sentences with the Same Subject

Good writers know that interesting writing makes its point and leads up to the ending of a story without repeating ideas. They use many methods to cut unnecessary words. One way is to combine sentences that have the same subject. Notice that sentences 1 and 2 have the same subject. Also, the actions in the sentences are related to one another.

1. Rachel went to day camp. 2. Rachel had a great time.
3. Rachel went to day camp and had a great time.

In sentence 3 the predicates of sentences 1 and 2 have been joined by the word *and*. In this way, one sentence can take the place of two short, choppy sentences. Be alert for subject words such as *he*, *she*, and *they*. One of these words may signal a sentence that can be combined with the one before it.

4. The campers arrived at ten.   5. They left at three.
6. The campers arrived at ten and left at three.

Practice

Combine each pair of sentences. Use the same subject. Write the new sentence.

1. Rachel loves to read plays.
   She enjoys acting in plays.
2. Ms. Ahmal teaches the music classes.
   Ms. Ahmal is in charge of the theater group.
3. The theater students put on some skits.
   The theater students did all the work themselves.
4. Rachel's group made the costumes. They painted the scenery.
5. Carlos wrote most of the skits. He directed them.
6. Alaina acted in two skits. She sang in another.
7. Kelly and Dustin sold tickets. They handed out programs.
8. Four students worked as ushers. They found seats.
9. The show lasted an hour. The show was a success.
10. Ms. Ahmal was proud. She wants to have another show.

4 Proofreading
Friendly Letter

Writer's Guide

Proofreading Checklist

☑ Check for errors in capitalization.

☑ Check for errors in punctuation. Be sure to check for commas in the heading, the greeting, and the closing of your letter.

☑ Check to see that all your paragraphs are indented.

☑ Check for errors in grammar.

☑ Circle any words you think are misspelled. Find out how to spell them correctly.

⇨ For proofreading help, use the **Writer's Handbook**.

Carminda added one more paragraph to her letter. She used the checklist in the **Writer's Guide** and the **Editor's Marks** to proofread it. Here is what she did.

There are only three more weeks of day camp left. the summer is going by quickly. I don't have enough time for everything I want do to I hope that that you are enjoying yourself this summer. let me hear from you soon.

Your Friend,
Carminda

Discuss

1. Look at the mistakes Carminda corrected in her proofread letter. Why did each need correcting?
2. Carminda corrected the closing of her letter. What mistakes do you think she checked for when she proofread the heading and the greeting?

Try Your Hand

Proofread Your Letter   Now use the **Writer's Guide** and the **Editor's Marks** to proofread your letter.

Save your corrected letter in your *Writer's Notebook*. You will use it when you publish your letter.

EDITOR'S MARKS

≡ Capitalize.
⊙ Add a period.
∧ Add something.
⋏ Add a comma.
ⱽⱽ Add quotation marks.
⤔ Cut something.
⌃ Replace something.
∼ Transpose.
◯ Spell correctly.
¶ Indent paragraph.
/ Make a lowercase letter.

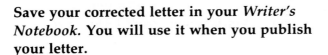

5 Publishing
Friendly Letter

Carminda copied her letter onto clean paper. She checked it over once more. She made sure that she had made no mistakes as she copied it. You can find Carminda's letter in the **Writer's Handbook.**

When Carminda finished her letter, she was ready to send it to her friend Rachel. She prepared this envelope.

Carminda Santos
937 Shawnee Court
Augusta, Georgia 30907

Rachel Liebenberg
983 King Williams Drive
Columbus, Georgia 31904

Discuss

1. Where did Carminda write her own name and address? Why is this information necessary?
2. Where did she write Rachel's name and address?

Try Your Hand

Publish Your Letter   Follow the checklist in the **Writer's Guide.** Then prepare an envelope for your own letter, using Carminda's envelope as a model. Mail your letter to your friend or your relative. You might also share your letter with the class in the following way.

◆ Make a wall display of the letters you and your classmates wrote. Place a map in the center. Mark where each letter is to be sent.

WRITING PROCESS

Listening and Speaking
Tips on How to Give and Listen to Facts and Opinions

Giving Facts and Opinions

1. First, decide on the point or ending of your topic. Review the facts. Think about the order in which you should present them. Jot down notes to help you remember the order.
2. Think about your audience. Organize your points from least important to most important.
3. When you speak, begin with a sentence that introduces your topic.
4. Speak clearly and loudly. Do not speak too slowly or too quickly. Put feeling in your voice to match your feelings about the topic.
5. Give good examples that support the facts, and give reasons for your opinions. Refer to your notes if necessary.
6. When you have made your point, stop talking. Do not add unnecessary remarks at the end.

Listening to Facts and Opinions

1. Give the speaker your full attention.
2. Listen for the difference between facts about the topic and the speaker's opinions. Opinions often begin with signal words such as *I think* or *I believe.*
3. Jot down notes about any questions you may have. You may want to ask why the speaker formed certain opinions.
4. Wait until the speaker has finished to ask your questions or to ask for information to be repeated.
5. Decide if you agree with the speaker's opinions.
6. Review the facts that you learned.

Writing in the Content Areas

Use what you learned to write about experiences that you want to share. You could write a friendly letter or tell about an event in a paragraph or two. Use one of these ideas or an idea of your own.

Writer's Guide

When you write, remember the stages of the Writing Process.
- Prewriting
- Drafting
- Responding and Revising
- Proofreading
- Publishing

Social Studies

What period in history do you find exciting? Pretend to be someone who was living during that time. Write a letter to a friend. Tell about an important event in which you took part. Include details that will make your adventure come alive.

Science

The weather each season is not the same everywhere. Choose your favorite season. Then imagine having a pen pal who lives far away. Tell your pen pal about your favorite season. Give details about how plants, animals, and the weather change.

Fine Arts

Have you enjoyed a play or a musical performance lately? Write a letter to a friend about your experience. Describe the parts that you liked best. Tell why you liked them. Would your friend have enjoyed the performance? Explain why you think so.

Literature

What is your favorite book? Ask a librarian to help you find an address for the person who wrote it. Write a letter to the author. Tell what you like about the book. Explain why the book is special to you. Then send your letter to the author.

CONNECTING

WRITING ↔ LANGUAGE

Letter-writers entertain their audiences with tales of interesting activities. A good letter-writer can make readers feel as if they have shared the writer's adventures.

6 Nuevo Drive
Miami, Florida 33156
June 16, 1990

Dear David,

You won't believe my latest adventure! I went on a camping trip with my uncle last weekend. We rented a boat and rowed it to the far side of the lake. It hit a hidden rock. We couldn't get the boat off the rock, and so we swam to a little island nearby. I was really grateful for my life jacket! We stayed there all night. In the morning, some people in a sailboat saw us, and we were safe at last. I will tell you the details when I see you next week.

Your buddy,
Manuel

◆ **Verbs in a Friendly Letter**   The highlighted words are verbs. The story is easy to follow because Manuel uses his verbs correctly. He uses *was* after *I* and *were* after *we*. He uses the correct past-tense forms of *swim* and *see*. Manuel also uses verb contractions to give his letter a lively tone. Knowing how to use verbs correctly helps letter-writers tell stories clearly.

◆ **Language Focus: Verbs**   In the following lessons you will learn about using different kinds of verbs in your own writing.

1 Agreement of Subjects and Verbs

◆ **FOCUS**　A subject and its verb should agree.

Remember that present-tense action verbs have two forms. A singular verb usually ends with *s*. It is used with a singular subject. A plural verb is used with a plural subject.

1. The trader `shows` some silver. singular
2. The Indians `show` some furs. plural

The linking verb *be* also has singular and plural forms.

3. The man `is` Jean Pointe Du Sable. singular
4. He `was` a fur trader. singular
5. The Indians `are` Potawatomi. plural
6. They `were` friendly traders. plural

This chart shows which form of *be* to use.

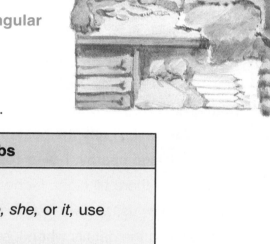

Using Subjects and Verbs
1. After the word *I*, use *am* or *was*.
2. After singular subjects and the word *he, she,* or *it*, use *is* or *was*.
3. After plural subjects and the word *we, you,* or *they*, use *are* or *were*.

Guided Practice

A. Identify which form of the verb in parentheses ( ) agrees with the subject.

1. Chicago (is, are) on the shore of Lake Michigan.
2. Nearly four million people (lives, live) there.
3. Three airports (serves, serve) the city.
4. The area (was, were) home to the Potawatomi Indians.
5. They (was, were) skilled at trapping beavers.
6. Beaver hair (was, were) the main material used in hats.

Independent Practice

B. Identifying Verb Forms   Write the verb in parentheses ( )
that agrees with the subject.

7. My name (is, are) Jean Pointe Du Sable.

MODEL ▷ is

8. I (am, are) from the city of New Orleans.
9. You (needs, need) courage to go to the wilderness.
10. It (is, are) the only life for someone like me.
11. My friends (enjoys, enjoy) nature's challenges.
12. We (is, are) not afraid of the Indians.
13. Besides, the Indians here (is, are) friendly.
14. They (brings, bring) us rich beaver furs.
15. My trading post (was, were) soon a success.
16. People (was, were) anxious to trade with me.

C. Proofreading Sentences   Rewrite these sentences. Change
the verb form to agree with the subject.

17. Du Sable were a fair and honest man.

MODEL ▷ Du Sable was a fair and honest man.

18. He were careful to give good value for the furs.
19. The traders was friends with Chief Pontiac.
20. "You is welcome in our villages," Pontiac said.
21. Du Sable said, "We respects your people."
22. "They treats us fairly," he continued.
23. Du Sable were content to live out his life there.
24. His settlement were the beginning of Chicago.

Application—Writing

A Letter   Imagine that you are Jean Pointe Du Sable. Write a
letter to a friend in New Orleans. Describe your new trading post
on Lake Michigan. Use the picture and your own imagination to
create details. Use some present-tense verbs and at least four
linking verbs in your letter. If you need help writing a friendly
letter, see pages 36–37 of the **Writer's Handbook.**

2 Irregular Verbs

◆ **FOCUS** An **irregular verb** does not end with *ed* in the past tense.

Remember that the past tense of most verbs is formed by adding *d* or *ed* to the verb. Some verbs do not add *ed* to form the past tense. Notice the verbs in color.

I swim daily.   I swam on Friday.

I have swum all week.

The verb *swim* is an example of an irregular verb. This chart shows some irregular verbs.

Irregular Verbs		
Present	**Past**	**Past with *have*, *has*, or *had***
bring(s)	brought	brought
think(s)	thought	thought
say(s)	said	said
make(s)	made	made
come(s)	came	come
become(s)	became	become
go(es)	went	gone
see(s)	saw	seen
begin(s)	began	begun
swim(s)	swam	swum

Guided Practice

A. Identify which of the verbs in parentheses ( ) is correct.

1. James Delgado had (went, gone) to old settlements.
2. Sadly, he had (saw, seen) the old sites destroyed.
3. His interest in history (begun, began) there.
4. He (went, gone) to the mayor of San Jose.
5. The mayor (think, thought) about his words.

Independent Practice

B. Identifying Correct Verb Forms   Write the verb that correctly completes each sentence.

6. Years ago, Delgado (became, become) a diver.

MODEL ▷ became

7. He had (seen, saw) old ships in museums.
8. He had (thought, think) about exploring underwater.
9. He (begun, began) to read about old shipwrecks.
10. He (swum, swam) off the California coast.
11. Delgado's team (make, made) an exciting discovery.
12. They (went, gone) onto a sunken whaling ship.
13. Treasures have (come, came) from that wreck.

C. Using Correct Verb Forms   Read each sentence. Write the correct past-tense form of the verb in parentheses ( ).

14. Carlos (become) an expert on sailing ships.

MODEL ▷ became

15. Carlos and I (make) a trip to the museum.
16. We had (come) to see a film on old ships.
17. Carlos had (see) the film before.
18. The film already had (begin) when we arrived.
19. I (think) it was interesting.
20. We (go) to look at the displays.
21. Local divers had (bring) up many of the items.
22. They had (swim) down to old wrecks in the bay.
23. Al (begin) to dive with me last summer.
24. I have (swim) underwater many times.

Application —Writing

A News Story   Imagine that you are a news reporter. Divers have taken you underwater to see an old ship. Write a news story about your underwater trip. Help your readers imagine what you saw and did. Use verbs from the chart on page 170. If you need help writing a news story, see the **Writer's Handbook**.

3 More Irregular Verbs

◆ **FOCUS**   The past tense of some irregular verbs ends with *n* or *en*.

Remember that irregular verbs are verbs that do not add *ed* to spell their past-tense forms. Some irregular verbs use *n* or *en* to form the past tense.

1. Today big planes fly across the Atlantic.
2. Markham flew across in a small plane in 1936.
3. Only a few pilots had flown across it then.

In sentence 3 the main verb ends in *n*. Sometimes the main verb ends in *en*. Study the patterns of verb forms on this chart.

Irregular Verbs		
Present	**Past**	**Past with *have*, *has*, or *had***
blow(s)	blew	blown
grow(s)	grew	grown
know(s)	knew	known
fly/flies	flew	flown
fall(s)	fell	fallen
give(s)	gave	given
ride(s)	rode	ridden
speak(s)	spoke	spoken
take(s)	took	taken
write(s)	wrote	written

Guided Practice

A. Identify which of the verbs in parentheses ( ) is correct.

1. Beryl Markham had (grown, grew) up in Africa.
2. One day she (spoke, spoken) with a pilot.
3. From that day, she (knew, known) she wanted to fly.

Independent Practice

B. Identifying Correct Verb Forms   Write the verb that correctly
completes each sentence.

  4. Before long, Markham (knew, known) how to fly.

MODEL〉 knew

  5. She had (grew, grown) to like the air.
  6. She had (given, gave) her plane a final check.
  7. She (knowed, knew) the trip might be dangerous.
  8. However, she had (taken, took) off fearlessly.
  9. Strong winds (blown, blew) the little plane.
 10. Then, her engine (give, gave) out.
 11. The plane (fell, fallen) into a swamp.
 12. Though the plane had (fell, fallen), Markham lived.
 13. She had (flew, flown) safely across the Atlantic.
 14. A fisherman (took, taken) her to a telephone.
 15. She (spoke, spoken) to the people at the airport.

C. Using Correct Verb Forms   Read each sentence. Write the
correct past-tense form of the verb in parentheses ( ).

 16. I have (take) many short plane rides.

MODEL〉 taken

 17. My uncle has (know) the pilot for years.
 18. They (grow) up in this area.
 19. He has (speak) to her often.
 20. She (ride) with us to the airport.
 21. I (give) her my book to sign then.
 22. She has (write) her name in my book.
 23. She (take) the plane up into the air.

Application—Speaking and Writing

An Interview   Imagine that you have taken an airplane trip.
Think about the details. Then work with a partner. Ask your
partner about his or her trip. Let your partner ask you about your
trip. Then write a paragraph about your partner's trip.

4 Contractions with *Not*

◆ **FOCUS**   A contraction can sometimes be formed by joining a verb with the word *not*.

A **contraction** is a shortened form of two words. Often, the word *not* is added to a helping or a linking verb to form a contraction.

1. Look, but do not touch.   **2.** Look, but don't touch.

When *not* is added, an apostrophe takes the place of the *o*. Notice that the contractions for *can* and *will* have irregular spellings.

Contractions with *Not*			
is + not = isn't		does + not = doesn't	
are + not = aren't		did + not = didn't	
was + not = wasn't		can + not = can't	
were + not = weren't		could + not = couldn't	
have + not = haven't		should + not = shouldn't	
has + not = hasn't		would + not = wouldn't	
had + not = hadn't		must + not = mustn't	
do + not = don't		will + not = won't	

Link to Speaking and Writing
Use contractions to make your speech and writing informal. Do you use contractions more often in speaking or in writing? Tell why.

I have not climbed a mountain.

Guided Practice

A. Form the contraction for each of these verbs by adding the word *not*.

1. could   **2.** was   **3.** have   **4.** will

> **THINK AND REMEMBER**
> ◆ Add *n't* to certain linking or helping verbs to form
>   **contractions.**
> ◆ Use contractions to make speech or writing informal.

Independent Practice

B. Writing Contractions   Write each verb, changing it into a
contraction with *not*.

   5. is

[MODEL] > isn't

   6. were   **7.** are   **8.** can   **9.** do

C. Using Contractions   Read each sentence. Change the
underlined verb into a contraction by adding the word *not*.
Write the contraction.

   10. We <u>did</u> see bats.

[MODEL] > didn't

   11. Our guide said that we <u>would</u> find bats there.
   12. He <u>had</u> taken us to a bat cave.
   13. There <u>are</u> many bat caves in our area.
   14. Devon and I <u>were</u> disappointed.
   15. A bat <u>is</u> an attractive creature.
   16. I <u>would</u> go out of my way to look for one.

D. Revising Sentences   Rewrite each sentence. Replace the verb
and *not* with a contraction to make the language informal.

   17. Eric could not come on the cave tour.

[MODEL] > Eric couldn't come on the cave tour.

   18. I did not want to miss it myself.
   19. I had not been inside a large cave before.
   20. There were not many people on the tour.
   21. The guide would not let us touch anything.
   22. I do not remember all the things we saw.

Application—Speaking and Writing

Rules   Imagine that you are a guide. Write a list of eight rules to
read to tourists before you take them into the cave. Use at least
four contractions. Read your rules to the class.

5 Direct Quotations and Dialogue

◆ **FOCUS** A **direct quotation** is the exact words that someone has said or written.

Writers use direct quotations when they write conversations, or story dialogue. Each time the speaker changes, the writer begins a new paragraph.

> Steve asked, "Do you like to ski?"
> "Yes!" exclaimed Leslie. "We both do."
> "My Uncle Louis taught us," added Scott.

Quotation marks are placed before and after a direct quotation. The end punctuation comes just before the ending quotation marks.

Sometimes the part of the sentence that tells who is speaking comes before the quotation. Then a comma is used before the quotation. At other times, the words of the speaker follow the quotation. Then, if a period ends the quotation, a comma is used instead of the period.

This sentence is not a direct quotation. *Scott said they liked skiing.* It does not give the exact words of the speaker.

Link to Speaking and Writing
You can make your writing more vivid by using verbs other than *said*. How does changing this verb change the meaning?

"Don't move," he said. (whispered)

Guided Practice

A. Tell if each sentence is a *direct quotation* or *not a direct quotation.*

1. Isn't skiing dangerous? asked Steve.
2. Leslie answered, Cross-country skiing is not.
3. Scott said that it is not like downhill skiing.
4. Steve wondered, How is it different?

B. **5.–8.** Tell where quotation marks are needed in **A.**

C. Identifying Direct Quotations   If the sentence needs quotation marks, write *direct quotation.* If the sentence is correct as it is, write *correct.*

   9. Uncle Louis asked, What are you going to do today?

MODEL ▷ direct quotation

  10. Scott answered, We are going to ski across the valley.

  11. His uncle said that he could not go with them.

  12. We will be all right without you, Leslie told him.

  13. Their aunt said, You cannot cross the valley alone.

D. 14.–18. Using Quotation Marks   Add quotation marks where needed in C.

MODEL ▷ 14. Uncle Louis asked, "What are you going to do today?"

E. Revising Sentences   Write each sentence. Replace *said* with a more vivid verb.

  19. "What is the matter?" said Scott.

MODEL ▷ "What is the matter?" asked Scott.

  20. Leslie said, "I hurt my ankle."

  21. "Can you walk?" said her brother.

  22. She said, "Please get Uncle Louis."

F. Proofreading Dialogue   Write each sentence. Add quotation marks, other punctuation, and capital letters where they are needed. Begin a new paragraph each time the speaker changes.

  23. Do you know where we are asked Scott. I just want to go back home Leslie wailed. Stay calm Scott ordered.

Application—Writing and Speaking

A Story Ending   Scott, the boy in the picture, is about to go for help. Write a story ending. Use dialogue correctly. Read your ending to your classmates.

Building Vocabulary
Prefixes

Preview
of
Coming Attractions

Have you ever *previewed* something? If you do not know the meaning of *preview*, you can figure it out. First look for the **base word**, the word on which it is built. The base word is *view*. There is a prefix in the word *preview*. A **prefix** is a letter or group of letters added to the beginning of a word. It changes the meaning of a word. The prefix *pre* means "before." Therefore, *preview* means "to see, or to view, something before a certain time."

If you know what a certain prefix means, you can often figure out the meaning of a new word that uses the prefix. This chart shows the meanings of some common prefixes.

Prefix	Meaning	Example
dis	opposite of	dislike
mis	incorrectly	misuse
pre	before	prepay
re	again, back	reread, replay
un	not, opposite of	unhappy, untie

Reading Practice

Read each sentence. Write the word that contains the prefix. Then write the meaning of the word.

1. The explorers distrusted their map.
2. They were worried when they misplaced their compass.
3. They unloaded everything and found an extra compass.
4. They prejudged the country before them as dangerous.
5. The explorers recrossed the same river several times.
6. They disagreed on which path to take.
7. A guide vanished and then reappeared out of the brush.
8. The group had misjudged the length of the trail.

Writing Practice

Add a prefix from the chart on page 178 to the word in parentheses ( ). Write the sentence. Be sure the new word makes sense.

9. Did Aaron (match) his socks?
10. Many people (approve) of loud music.
11. The jacket was too tight, so he (buttoned) it.
12. They (viewed) the movie last week.
13. Stephanie (spelled) five of the words.
14. Ravi (paid) the money he had borrowed from his brother.

Project

Work with a classmate. List 10 words that have prefixes. Write a sentence for each word. Then read your sentences aloud to a group of classmates. Leave out the prefixes when you read. Identify the base words. Challenge your group to name the missing prefixes.

Language Enrichment
Verbs

Use what you know about verbs to do these activities.

 A Make-Believe Adventure

Would you enjoy the adventure shown in this picture? Pretend that you are one of the people in the picture. Make notes about what happens to you.

Plan a talk for your classmates about your adventure. Make sure that all verbs agree with their subjects. After you give your talk, answer your audience's questions about what you did.

 Yesterday, Today, and Often

Make three columns on a sheet of paper, as shown below. Think of some present-tense verbs that tell about things you do almost every day. For example, each day you *eat*. Write the present-tense form of each verb in the first column. Then fill in the other two columns with the correct verb forms.

Today I	Yesterday I	I have often
eat	ate	eaten

Now have someone make a large chart on the chalkboard. Take turns listing the three verb forms and saying them aloud. See if everyone agrees with the spelling of each form.

CONNECTING
LANGUAGE ⬌ WRITING

In this unit you learned more about verbs. A verb must agree with the subject of a sentence. An irregular verb forms its past tense in unusual ways. Some verbs also can be combined with *not* to make contractions.

◆ **Using Verbs in Your Writing**   When you write, you need to know which form of a verb to use. You need to know how to spell verbs and contractions. Using correct forms helps your readers understand what is happening in your sentences. Pay special attention to the verbs you use as you do these activities.

My Animal Won't!

Think of an animal you like. Draw its picture in the middle of a sheet of paper. Write the word *not* in the center of the picture. Around the picture write some verbs that can be used in contractions with *not*. Then, draw a line from five of the verbs to *not*. Write the five contractions. Then, use these contractions to write a paragraph about your animal.

Do It Again or Before

You learned about prefixes on the **Building Vocabulary** page. Here is an activity about prefixes for you to try.

Think of a game, sport, or hobby that you enjoy. Make a list of verbs that tell about this activity. Now, try to add *re* or *pre* to some of the verbs. Use the verb and the verb with a prefix in sentences about the activity.
Example: cooking: *heated, reheated*

I heated the soup in a small pan.
Then I reheated the carrots.

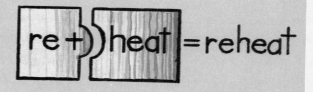

Unit Checkup

Think Back	Think Ahead
◆ What did you learn about friendly letters in this unit? What did you do to write one?	◆ How will what you learned help when you write to a friend? ◆ How will connecting cause and effect help when you perform a science experiment?
◆ Look at the writing you did in this unit. How did verbs help you express your ideas?	◆ What is one way that you can use verbs to improve your writing?

Analyzing a Friendly Letter   *pages 152–153*

Read this friendly letter. Then follow the directions.

> 144-35 Sanford Ave.
> Flushing, NY 11385
> July 17, 1990
>
> Dear Cousin Faith,
>   We had a lot of fun last week, didn't we? I'm especially glad that we went to the zoo together.
>   I remember one time when I was little. I went to the zoo, and a gate was unlocked. I didn't see the "Keep Out" sign, so I walked right in where the chimpanzees were kept. One chimpanzee almost grabbed me to play before I was found.
>   Did you have a good trip back home? I started missing you as soon as you left. I hope you can come again soon.
>   Lots of love,

1. Write the heading.
2. Write the greeting.
3. Write the closing.
4. Write your signature.
5. Write the number of paragraphs in the body.

Connecting Cause and Effect   *page 154*

Write each sentence. Underline the cause once and the effect twice.

6. Faith came to visit, so we went to the zoo.

7. I laughed and laughed when I saw the elephants.

8. After Faith left, I started to miss her.

9. Because Faith lives far away, I have to write her a letter.

10. When Faith gets my letter, she will write back to me.

Including Details That Tell *Why*   *page 155*

Add a detail to each sentence to tell why it happened. Use your imagination.

11. Faith almost fell into the flower bed.
12. Faith gave me a flower.
13. I waved my flower around wildly.
14. The dog knocked the flower out of my hand.
15. The flower got crushed.

The Writing Process   *pages 156–164*

Write the letter of the correct response to each question.

16. What should you do to think of topics when writing your friendly letter?
  a. ask someone for ideas
  b. brainstorm for ideas
  c. always write about the same thing

17. How do you decide which topics to write about in your friendly letter?
  a. tell about as many different things as you can
  b. tell things that will interest your friend
  c. tell long stories

18. You have gathered your information to tell a story. Review your notes to
  a. find what will lead up to the ending of the story.
  b. decide if you really want to write the letter.
  c. tell another story.

19. What two things belong on the right side of the page when writing your friendly letter?
  a. the heading and the closing
  b. the greeting and the body
  c. the greeting and the closing

Agreement of Subjects and Verbs   *pages 168–169*

Write the verb in parentheses ( ) that agrees with the subject.

20. Some people (likes, like) to explore caves.
21. We (calls, call) cave explorers spelunkers.
22. Spelunkers (is, are) daring people.
23. They (wears, wear) hard hats in case rocks fall.
24. Each hat (is, are) very durable.
25. A flashlight (helps, help) them see in the dark caves.
26. A spelunker (wraps, wrap) rope around himself.
27. He (lowers, lower) himself into the cave.
28. Hundreds of bats (is, are) overhead.
29. That pit (drops, drop) 400 feet.

Irregular Verbs   *pages 170–171*

Read each sentence. Write the correct past-tense form of
the verb in parentheses ( ).

30. Long ago ships (become) important.
31. People had (think) of no better way to carry things
    for long distances.
32. Sometimes sailors had (go) to the Far East.
33. They (come) back with precious cargo.
34. They (bring) spices, silks, and jewels.
35. When thieves (see) these ships, they attacked.
36. These common thieves (become) known as pirates.
37. Sometimes sailors escaped and (swim) to shore.
38. The pirates then (go) back to their own hideout.
39. They (bring) the treasure to a secret spot.
40. They (make) a treasure map.
41. They (think) they could get the treasure later.
42. But often they never (come) back.
43. People have (say) we can find pirate treasure.
44. They have (begin) to search for some.
45. Has anyone ever (become) rich from it?

More Irregular Verbs   *pages 172–173*

Read each sentence. Write the correct past-tense form of the verb in parentheses ( ).

46. Men who (fly) the first airplanes were brave.
47. They (know) that a plane might flip upside down.

48. It might have (fall) with a crash in a field.
49. A wing might have (blow) off in a storm.
50. But pilots had (grow) to love the adventure.
51. They (ride) low over the tops of trees.
52. They often (fly) low over pastures.
53. Sometimes they even (speak) to the cows!
54. People (give) these men the name "barnstormers."
55. A barnstormer (grow) very fond of his plane.
56. He (take) only a toothbrush and a razor.
57. Any passenger (take) his life in his hands.

Contractions with *Not*   *pages 174–175*

Read each sentence. Change the underlined verb into a
contraction by adding the word *not*. Write the contraction.

58. <u>Has</u> anyone heard how doughnuts were invented?
59. There was no girl who <u>was</u> crazy for Johnny Fry.
60. But he <u>could</u> stop his pony express delivery.
61. They <u>were</u> able to make him stop to visit.
62. But one girl said, "I <u>will</u> give up."
63. She <u>did</u> put any middle in the cake she made.

Direct Quotations and Dialogue   *pages 176–177*

Write each sentence. Add quotation marks, other punctuation,
and capital letters where they are needed.

64. you have to stop for this one john she said
65. i do not have any time he yelled back
66. i mustn't miss his finger she said as she tossed the cake
67. johnny fry has never seen a doughnut before she said
68. hey these finger cakes are good he said

Prefixes   *pages 178–179*

Read each sentence. Write the word that contains the prefix.
Then write the meaning of the word.

69. We asked Mr. Kelly to retell his World War II stories.
70. He had been given some predetermined orders.
71. He had misunderstood the orders, however.
72. The captain thought he had disregarded them.
73. I wonder how much of the story Grandpa left untold.

Cumulative Review

Complete and Simple Subjects   *pages 38–39*

Write each complete subject. Then underline the simple subject.

1. Airplanes were not very old in 1927.
2. No person had crossed the Atlantic Ocean alone.
3. Several brave pilots had tried.
4. None had ever been heard from again.
5. Charles Lindbergh wanted to be the first.
6. His airplane was named *The Spirit of St. Louis.*
7. Hardly any supplies were packed in his airplane.
8. Extra weight meant he would need more gas.
9. He needed all that gasoline just to get to Paris!

Complete and Simple Predicates   *pages 40–41*

Write each complete predicate. Then underline the simple predicate.

10. Five hundred people gathered for Charles's departure.
11. The brave young pilot flew away from New York.
12. His plane headed out over the ocean.
13. Newspapers and radios told about his departure.
14. Everyone wondered about his chance for success.
15. Night fell around the little plane.
16. Charles flew through a cold cloud.
17. Then, he noticed ice on the wings.
18. The young man steered his plane quickly away.

Singular Possessive Nouns   *pages 86–87*

Write each sentence. Replace the underlined words with the possessive form.

19. The pilot flew through <u>the darkness of the night</u>.
20. A sandwich stopped <u>the growls of his stomach</u>.
21. There was <u>the coast of Ireland</u>!
22. Finally, he reached Paris, <u>the capital of France</u>.
23. Thousands of people crowded <u>the roads of the airfield</u>.
24. Each person shone <u>the headlights of his car</u>.

25. The pilot heard <u>the voices of the people</u> crying, "Lindbergh! Lindbergh!"
26. Lindbergh had set a new <u>record of the world</u>.

Plural Possessive Nouns   *pages 88–89*

Write each sentence. Replace the underlined words with the possessive form.

27. <u>The adventures of flyers</u> are common nowadays.
28. Long ago <u>the existence of airplanes</u> was thought impossible.
29. Flying was still <u>the dream of many individuals</u>.
30. <u>The experiments of some inventors</u> made them think it could be done.
31. <u>The efforts of some experimenters</u> were funny.
32. Look at <u>the size of those wings</u>!
33. Did he think he could grow <u>the feathers of birds</u>?
34. Then <u>the discovery of two brothers</u> made history.

Action Verbs   *pages 126–127*

Write the action verb in each sentence.

35. The Montgolfier brothers studied hot air.
36. Hot air always rose.
37. The two men filled a bag with hot air.
38. The bag floated away!
39. Then they made a huge balloon.
40. They attached a basket underneath the balloon.
41. Nobody wanted to ride in the basket.
42. Everyone feared a disaster.
43. They used farm animals instead of people.
44. Into the basket went a rooster, a sheep, and a duck.
45. Those animals took the first balloon ride!

Linking Verbs   *pages 128–129*

Write *linking verb* if the underlined word is a linking verb. Write *action verb* if it is an action verb.

46. Later, a man <u>was</u> brave enough to ride in a balloon.
47. "Hey, this balloon ride <u>is</u> fun!"
48. The French <u>invented</u> the first piloted balloons.
49. They discovered that a balloon <u>was</u> helpful for predicting weather patterns.

50. The government <u>used</u> balloons to spy on the enemy.
51. Ballooning <u>is</u> still an enjoyable hobby today.
52. Balloons <u>are</u> useful in wartime.

Main Verbs and Helping Verbs   *pages 130–131*

Make a chart with two columns. Head the columns *Helping Verbs* and *Main Verbs*. Write each underlined verb in the correct column.

53. I <u>am</u> <u>reading</u> a book about black holes.
54. Scientists think some stars <u>have</u> <u>collapsed</u>.
55. They <u>are</u> <u>calling</u> these stars black holes.
56. Gravity there <u>is</u> <u>pulling</u> with tremendous strength.
57. What <u>is</u> <u>happening</u> at the edge of a black hole?
58. <u>Is</u> time strangely <u>twisted</u> by its force?
59. <u>Has</u> a black hole ever <u>sent</u> anyone back in time?
60. Pretend you <u>are</u> <u>planning</u> a voyage into space.
61. Scientists and writers <u>have</u> <u>created</u> new ideas.

Verb Tenses   *pages 132–133*

Write if each underlined verb is in the *past, present,* or *future* tense.

62. The invention <u>will send</u> you back in time.
63. The landscape <u>looks</u> beautiful.
64. It <u>will</u> never <u>look</u> this green to you again.
65. You now <u>see</u> knights, ladies, and peasants.
66. They <u>thought</u> your clothes looked hilarious!
67. They <u>imagined</u> your watch was alive.
68. Their talk <u>sounded</u> like a foreign language.
69. They <u>said</u> your speech was funny, too.
70. You <u>get</u> back into your spaceship.
71. Scientific achievements <u>will continue</u> in the future.

Agreement of Subjects and Verbs   *pages 168–169*

Write the verb in parentheses ( ) that agrees with the subject.

72. The black hole (throws, throw) you to the future.
73. There the people (wears, wear) many clothes.
74. That boy (has, have) special sunglasses.
75. "I protect myself from the sunlight," the boy (says, say).
76. "The ultraviolet rays (harms, harm) my skin."

Agreement of Subjects and Verbs   *pages 168–169*

Rewrite these sentences. Change the verb form to agree with the subject.

77. Once an old soldier were ready to retire.
78. He were faithful to the king for many years.
79. However, he were still very poor.
80. "Is I worth only three farthings?" he asked.
81. The soldier were very angry.
82. "That man are strong," he noticed.
83. "He pull up trees easily."
84. "Together we is capable of repaying this king!"
85. A third man were a swift runner.
86. "I has some exciting news."
87. "The king's daughter are a swift runner too."
88. "Her new husband have to outrun her."
89. "I is easily able to outrun her."

Irregular Verbs   *pages 170–171*

Write the verb in parentheses ( ) that agrees with the subject.

90. The runner (came, come) to the finish line first.
91. "Father! I won't marry him!" the girl (say, said).
92. "Good sirs, you have (seen, see) the many riches I have."
93. He (make, made) the girl and her father think they would be happy with some of them.
94. The soldier (thought, think) for a moment.
95. "You must fill the bags my friend has (bring, brought)."
96. The soldiers (gone, went) to see the treasure.
97. They (begun, began) to bring wagonloads of gold.

More Irregular Verbs   *pages 172–173*

Write the correct past-tense form of the verb in parentheses ( ).

98. The strong man (knows) he could carry more.
99. He (takes) silver, jewels, furs, and silk.
100. Finally, he had (take) all the king's treasures.
101. The king's legs (grow) weak.
102. Then he (falls) down and begged for mercy.
103. The strong man laughed as he (speak).

UNIT

5

Using Your Imagination

◆ **COMPOSITION FOCUS:** **Fable**
◆ **LANGUAGE FOCUS:** **Pronouns**

Have you ever known a hen that could say "Good morning" or a wolf that could disguise itself as a tree? You will never come across these animals in our everyday world. However, you will often meet characters like them in the fantasy worlds that are found in books.

Writers have fun inventing stories about places and characters that don't really exist. It delights them to think that their readers will also enjoy these tales.

Writers create many types of fantasy stories. Some stories are for adults, and some are for children. Some are about events that might have happened, and others are about events that are just not possible. Arnold Lobel was a writer whose stories for children are about animals that act like people. Sometimes he wrote fables, stories that not only entertain his readers but also teach lessons about life. In this unit you will learn how to write a fable with a message for your audience.

Arnold Lobel
wrote humorous
stories *to entertain*
his readers.

Reading with a Writer's Eye
Fable

Any farmer will tell you that a real hen deserves to be called "bird-brained." However, in a fantasy story anything is possible, and a hen can outwit her craftiest enemy. As you read Arnold Lobel's fable, notice that he uses humor to entertain his readers and to get his message across.

The Hen and the Apple Tree

by Arnold Lobel

One October day, a Hen looked out her window. She saw an apple tree growing in her backyard.

"Now that is odd," said the Hen. "I am certain that there was no tree standing in that spot yesterday."

"There are some of us that grow fast," said the tree.

The Hen looked at the bottom of the tree.

"I have never seen a tree," she said, "that has ten furry toes."

"There are some of us that do," said the tree. "Hen, come outside and enjoy the cool shade of my leafy branches."

The Hen looked at the top of the tree.

"I have never seen a tree," she said, "that has two long, pointed ears."

"There are some of us that have," said the tree. "Hen, come outside and eat one of my delicious apples."

"Come to think of it," said the Hen, "I have never heard a tree speak from a mouth that is full of sharp teeth."

"There are some of us that can," said the tree. "Hen, come outside and rest your back against the bark of my trunk."

"I have heard," said the Hen, "that some of you trees lose all of your leaves at this time of the year."

"Oh, yes," said the tree, "there are some of us that will." The tree began to quiver and shake. All of its leaves quickly dropped off.

The Hen was not surprised to see a large Wolf in the place where an apple tree had been standing just a moment before. She locked her shutters and slammed her window closed.

The Wolf knew that he had been outsmarted. He stormed away in a hungry rage.

———————

It is always difficult to pose as something that one is not.

Respond

1. Do you find this story humorous? If so, which parts make you smile?

Discuss

2. What lesson does this story teach? How does the writer teach this lesson? Would the story be complete if the writer had not summed up its message at the end? Explain your answer.

3. How do you know that the Hen guessed quite soon that she was talking to a Wolf? Why do you think the writer did not state this in the beginning? Why do you think the writer did not have the Hen lock her shutters and close her window right away?

Thinking As a Writer
Analyzing a Fable

A story entertains its readers. All stories have **characters,** a **setting,** and a **plot.**

A **fable** is a special kind of story, one that teaches a lesson. Often it is funny and has make-believe animals as the main characters. A fable ends with a **moral,** or a lesson.

Look at this story map for the fable "The Hen and the Apple Tree."

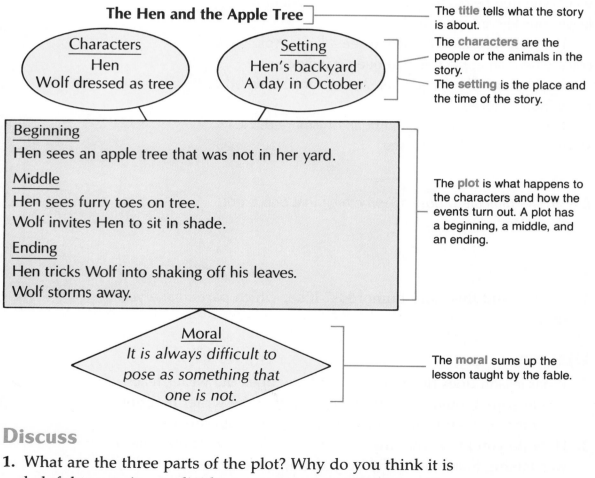

The Hen and the Apple Tree — The **title** tells what the story is about.

Characters
Hen
Wolf dressed as tree

Setting
Hen's backyard
A day in October

The **characters** are the people or the animals in the story.
The **setting** is the place and the time of the story.

Beginning
Hen sees an apple tree that was not in her yard.

Middle
Hen sees furry toes on tree.
Wolf invites Hen to sit in shade.

Ending
Hen tricks Wolf into shaking off his leaves.
Wolf storms away.

The **plot** is what happens to the characters and how the events turn out. A plot has a beginning, a middle, and an ending.

Moral
It is always difficult to pose as something that one is not.

The **moral** sums up the lesson taught by the fable.

Discuss

1. What are the three parts of the plot? Why do you think it is helpful to a writer to divide events into these three parts?
2. The list of events in the middle of the story map is not complete. What events would you add to it?

Try Your Hand

A. Identify Characters and Setting Read the following short fable. Then write who the characters are and what the setting is.

A robin and a crow agreed to have a singing contest. The robin seemed sure to win. The day before the contest, the crow's friend the raven went to the robin's tree to listen to him practice. The raven told the robin that his voice was pretty but too weak and low. The robin insisted that he could sing just as loudly as the crow. He practiced singing so loudly that he lost his voice. The next day the crow won the contest and shared the first-prize dinner of fat grubs with his friend the raven.

B. Write Morals Write a moral, or ending lesson, for the short fable you just read.

C. Write Titles Reread the short fable. Write a title for it.

D. Read a Fable Use the fable you just read, or find another fable in a book. Working with a partner or in a group, make a story map of the fable. Follow the model on page 194. Then share your work with others in your class. Explain how you identified the information to use in your map.

Writer's Notebook

Collecting Everyday Language
In the fable on pages 192 and 193, Hen begins a sentence with "Come to think of it." Story writers use informal, everyday speech in dialogue to show how people talk. Notice informal speech in stories and conversations. Record in your *Writer's Notebook* some of these expressions, along with sentences that show how they are used. Label the list *Informal Speech.* You may wish to use some of these expressions in your own informal story dialogue.

Thinking As a Writer
Evaluating Ideas to Support a Conclusion

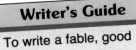

Writer's Guide

To write a fable, good writers

- choose a conclusion.
- evaluate possible events and ideas.
- select the facts that best support the conclusion.

Writers often give information through clues. They want their audience to use the clues to **draw conclusions,** or to figure out what is happening. When writers begin to plan their work, they may fill in a chart like this one. Then good writers choose for the story the idea or ideas that show, rather than tell, the conclusion.

Conclusion: It is a cold day.

Ideas that will point to the conclusion:
1. The robin longs to be indoors.
2. The robin shivers and shakes the snow off his wings. *Best!*
3. The robin stares sadly into a bakery window.

As you write your fable, think about the conclusions you want your readers to draw. Then choose your best idea to support these conclusions.

Discuss

1. The chart lists three ideas that might be used to support the conclusion. Reread the ones that were not underlined. Why are they not as good as the idea that was chosen?
2. Look at the fable on pages 192 and 193. You can draw the conclusion that the Hen is not fooled by the Wolf. What details does the writer give to support that conclusion?

Try Your Hand

Write Statements That Support Conclusions   Think about a conclusion that someone could draw about how a character in a fable is feeling. Write this conclusion as a statement. Then write three statements with clues that might help a reader draw that conclusion.

Developing the Writer's Craft
Storytelling—Dialogue and Characters

Challenging readers to use their minds keeps them reading. Good writers do not spell out facts about their characters. Instead they put in details and dialogue to give clues. These clues help their readers draw conclusions about the characters. Read this writer's description.

> The wolf hid his shaggy paws behind his back so that his long, sharp nails would not show. He tried to make his rough voice as sweet as honey. Then he asked, "Where are you going with that big basket of food, little girl?"

The details the writer gives about the wolf's appearance make it clear that the wolf is dangerous. The details about his actions reveal that he is sneaky and up to something. The dialogue helps you guess what he is thinking and planning.

When you write your fable, use details and dialogue to reveal what your characters are like and what they are thinking and feeling.

Discuss

1. Look at "The Hen and the Apple Tree" on pages 192 and 193. How does the writer use dialogue to reveal what the Hen is like?
2. Retell the fable of "The Hen and the Apple Tree." This time, put in unnecessary information. Compare this retelling to what Lobel wrote. Which would you rather read? Why?

Try Your Hand

Write Dialogue and Details   "The Hen and the Apple Tree" is a short fable. Make it longer by writing some sentences that could fit in the middle. Add details and dialogue that show what the Wolf and the Hen are like and what they are thinking.

1 Prewriting
Fable

Writer's Guide

Prewriting Checklist
- ☑ Brainstorm morals.
- ☑ Think about your audience and your purpose.
- ☑ Select a moral.
- ☑ Plan the characters and the setting.
- ☑ Plan the middle and ending of your fable.

Angela's class decided it would be fun to put together a book of original fables. Angela got ready to write her fable. She used the checklist in the **Writer's Guide** to help her plan her fable. Look at what she did.

◆ Brainstorming and Selecting an Idea

First, Angela brainstormed ideas for her fable. She decided to begin by choosing a moral that would make an interesting story.

Next, Angela thought about how to teach the moral she chose. Once again she brainstormed and listed her ideas. Then, she chose the one she thought would work best. She reminded herself that she could try other ideas on her list if her first choice did not work.

Moral: Being different is not always wrong.
Little pig feels unloved—becomes hero
Peacocks make fun of a goose's wings—wings are helpful
Elephant wants short nose—discovers uses for trunk
Baby beaver wants to climb—learns to swim

Discuss

1. Look at the ideas on Angela's list. How does each fit in with the moral she has planned?
2. Why do you think Angela circled the one idea on her list? Explain your answer.
3. What other idea would you add to the list that would teach the same moral?

WRITING PROCESS

◆ Planning and Organizing Details

Angela's next step was to plan the details of her fable. To keep everything organized, she made a story map.

Characters
a young goose
some peacocks
a bird seller

Setting
the bird seller's big cage, once upon a time

Beginning
1. Explain that the bird seller catches peacocks to sell.
2. The bird seller catches the young goose.
Middle
3. The peacocks insult the goose. ☆
4. The goose feels bad.
5. The cage is left unlocked, and the birds get out.
6. The peacocks are all caught because they have short wings.
Ending
7. The goose escapes on big, strong wings.

Moral
Being different is not always wrong.

Angela wrote her ideas on her story map. Before she wrote her plot ideas, she stopped to imagine the action. Then she made some notes on scratch paper. When she had decided what would happen, she listed the events on her story map in the order in which she planned to use them. Finally she put this mark ☆ next to one item. She used the mark to remind herself to use dialogue there.

Discuss

1. Look at Angela's story map and her notes for the beginning of her fable. Why do you think she decided the first piece of information was important?
2. Which note reminds Angela to reveal a character's feelings? Where would be a good place to show the character's feelings?
3. Find the item that Angela marked with ☆ . Why is this a good place for dialogue? Where else might Angela use dialogue?

Try Your Hand

Now plan a fable of your own.

A. Brainstorm and Select an Idea Begin by brainstorming ideas for your fable.

- ◆ First, choose a moral. Think about each idea and your audience.
- ◆ Next, brainstorm some ways to teach the moral through a story.
- ◆ Circle the one you think will work best.

B. Plan and Organize Details When you are satisfied with your story idea, plan the details you will use in your fable.

- ◆ Make a story map like Angela's to help you organize your information. Begin by identifying the characters, the setting, and the moral.
- ◆ Think about your idea for a story ending. Brainstorm events that could lead up to the ending and to the moral. You may want to note your ideas on scratch paper before you list events in order on the story map.
- ◆ Think about the conclusions you want your readers to draw. Add details that will help them draw these conclusions.
- ◆ You may make marks or notes to remind yourself to use dialogue in some parts of the story.

Save your list and story map in your *Writer's Notebook.* **You will use them when you draft your fable.**

WRITING PROCESS

2 Drafting
Fable

Angela read over her notes and her story map. She imagined the events of her story. Then she followed the checklist in the **Writer's Guide** to draft her fable. Look at how she began.

Writer's Guide

Drafting Checklist

☑ Use your list and your story map for ideas.

☑ Write a beginning in which you present the characters and the setting.

☑ Write a middle that gives the events of the plot in order. Give details that point to conclusions about the characters and their actions.

☑ Write an ending that tells how the events turn out.

☑ Sum up the fable by adding a moral.

☑ Add a title.

The Goose That Wasn't a Bird

Once there was a bird seller who trapped peacocks. She had a big cage full of them. One day she found a young wild goose in her trap and brought him home. The frightened goose was thrown into the cage.

"You can't be a bird!" exclaimed a peacock. Peacocks are very foolish creatures. "You have only a small, ugly tail. Your wings are big, clumsy things."

The little goose was very unhappy.

Then one day the bird seller left the cage door unlocked. The birds rushed out!

Discuss

1. What questions did Angela answer for the reader in the beginning of her story?
2. Study Angela's story map on page 199. How did her notes help her with this part of her story?
3. Look at her notes again. What will happen next in her story?
4. Does Angela's title fit her story? Why or why not?

Try Your Hand

Now you are ready to write a fable.

A. **Review Your Notes**   Look over the notes you made in the last lesson. If you get new ideas, add them to your notes.

B. **Think About Your TAP**   Remember that your task is to write a fable. Your purpose is to entertain your audience and to teach a lesson about life.

C. **Write Your First Draft**   Follow the **Writer's Guide** to write your fable.

* Begin by identifying your characters and your setting.
* Write about events in the order in which they take place.
* Include details and dialogue that will help your readers draw conclusions about your characters. These details should suggest what the characters are like and what they are thinking and feeling.
* At the end of your fable, add the moral.
* Last, write a title that suggests what the fable is about.

    When you write your draft, just put all your ideas on paper. Do not worry about spelling, punctuation, or grammar. You can correct the draft later.

Task: What?
Audience: Who?
Purpose: Why?

 Save your first draft in your *Writer's Notebook.* You will use it when you revise your fable.

3 Responding and Revising
Fable

Angela used the checklist in the **Writer's Guide** to revise her fable. Look at what she did.

◆ Checking Information

Angela decided to take out a sentence because she thought the information was unnecessary. To show her change, she used this mark ℒ. Then she found one sentence that was not very clear. She replaced some words in the sentence, using this mark ⋏. The change would make the sentence easier to read.

◆ Checking Organization

Angela realized that one sentence was out of order. To show that it should be moved, she used this mark ◌.

◆ Checking Language

When Angela read her fable aloud to herself, she found some wordy language. She crossed out the unnecessary words and replaced them with the word *captured*.

> **Writer's Guide**
>
> **Revising Checklist**
> - ☑ Read your fable to yourself or to a partner.
> - ☑ Think about your audience and your purpose. Add or cut information.
> - ☑ Check to see that your fable is organized correctly.
> - ☑ Check for wordy language. If you find any, use fewer words to say the same thing.

Add — "You can't be a bird!" exclaimed a ^foolish^ peacock. ~~Peacocks are very foolish creatures.~~ "You have **Cut** only a small, ugly tail. Your wings are big, clumsy things."

Replace — The little goose ^hung its head and slunk away.^ ~~was very unhappy.~~
Then one day the bird seller left the cage door unlocked. The birds rushed out! The bird seller chased them. Soon every peacock had been ^captured^ ~~made a captive.~~ (The peacocks' small
Move/ Replace — wings were not very helpful.) She did not catch the young goose, though. He spread his big, strong wings and soared into the sky. It is not always a bad thing to be different.

Discuss

1. Find the sentence in which Angela replaced some words. How does this change improve her story?
2. How do the other changes make her story better?

Try Your Hand

Now revise your first draft.

A. Read Your First Draft   As you read your fable, think about your audience and your purpose. Read your fable silently or to a partner to see if it is complete and well organized. Ask yourself or your partner the questions in the box.

Responding and Revising Strategies

✔ Respond Ask yourself or your partner:	✔ Revise Try these solutions:
◆ Do I identify the characters and the setting in the beginning?	◆ **Add** necessary information.
◆ Do I present the events in the order in which they happen?	◆ **Move** information that is in the wrong place.
◆ Do I use dialogue and details to help my readers draw conclusions?	◆ **Add** helpful dialogue and details. **Cut** details that tell too much.
◆ Is each word in my fable necessary?	◆ **Cut** unnecessary words, or **replace** them with fewer words that mean the same thing. See the **Revising Workshop** on page 205.
◆ Does my fable end with a moral?	◆ **Add** a moral.

B. Make Your Changes   If the answer to any question in the box is *no*, try the solution. Use the **Editor's Marks** to show your changes.

C. Review Your Fable Again   Decide if there is anything else you want to revise. Keep revising your fable until you feel it is well organized and complete.

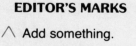

EDITOR'S MARKS

∧ Add something.
∕ Cut something.
⟲ Move something.
⋀ Replace something.

Save your revised fable in your *Writer's Notebook*. You will use it when you proofread your fable.

WRITING PROCESS

Revising Workshop
Avoiding Wordy Language

Good writers avoid wordy language. When revising their sentences, they try to say what they mean in as few words as possible. The underlined words in sentence 1 are examples of wordy language.

1. <u>Some of the</u> peacocks <u>made the attempt</u> to escape from <u>their captivity in</u> the cage.
2. <u>Some</u> peacocks <u>tried</u> to escape from the cage.

Sentence 2 shows how the writer revised sentence 1. Notice that the unnecessary words *of the* were cut. The long phrase *made the attempt* was replaced with the word *tried*. The words *their captivity in* were cut because they added nothing to the information in the sentence. The revised sentence has the same meaning as the original one, but it is much easier to read and to understand.

Practice

Rewrite each sentence. Take out the underlined words, or replace them with fewer words that mean the same thing.

1. The bird seller <u>made the discovery of</u> a goose in her trap.
2. The frightened goose trembled <u>in fear and terror</u>.
3. The bird seller took the goose home <u>to the place where she lived</u>.
4. The peacocks <u>broke into laughter</u> when they saw the goose.
5. They <u>were of the thinking</u> that the goose wasn't a bird.
6. <u>In hardly any time at all</u>, the goose doubted that it was a bird.
7. The peacocks <u>made an attempt to try</u> to escape.
8. The young goose spread its wings and flew <u>up high</u> into the sky.
9. The graceful goose looked <u>very far down upon</u> the peacocks.
10. The sorrowful peacocks <u>came to wish</u> that they had large wings.

4 Proofreading
Fable

After revising her fable, Angela used the **Writer's Guide** and the **Editor's Marks** to proofread it. She added some sentences to the middle of her fable. Look at what she did.

Writer's Guide

Proofreading Checklist

☑ Check for errors in capitalization. Be sure to capitalize the first word in a direct quotation.

☑ Check for errors in punctuation. Be sure to use quotation marks and commas correctly when you write dialogue.

☑ Check for errors in grammar.

☑ Circle any words you think are misspelled. Find out how to spell them correctly.

⇨ For proofreading help, use the **Writer's Handbook.**

¶ "Perhaps I am am a flying squirrel," said the little goose to himself. he nibbled at a nut that had rolled into the cage. He spit it out quickly. He must be not a squirrel then!

Discuss

1. Look at Angela's corrections. What was her reason for each one?
2. What other punctuation mark could be used to end the last sentence?

Try Your Hand

Proofread Your Fable   Now use the **Writer's Guide** and the **Editor's Marks** to proofread your fable.

Save your corrected fable in your *Writer's Notebook.* You will use it when you publish your fable.

EDITOR'S MARKS

☰ Capitalize.
⊙ Add a period.
∧ Add something.
⋏ Add a comma.
ⱽⱽ Add quotation marks.
⤵ Cut something.
⟋⟍ Replace something.
∿ Transpose.
◯ Spell correctly.
¶ Indent paragraph.
╱ Make a lowercase letter.

WRITING PROCESS

5 Publishing
Fable

Angela made a clean copy of her fable. She checked it to make sure she had copied it correctly and had not left out anything. Then she and her classmates published a book of their fables. You can find Angela's fable on page 29 of the **Writer's Handbook.**

Here's how Angela and her classmates published their fables.

Writer's Guide

Publishing Checklist

☑ Make a clean copy of your fable.

☑ Check to see that nothing has been left out.

☑ Check to see that there are no mistakes.

☑ Share your fable in a special way.

1. Angela had someone type her fable on an 8 $\frac{1}{2}$" by 11" piece of paper. Then, on a piece of paper the same size, she drew a picture for her fable. Together, her classmates decided how to put the fables in order. Each student's artwork faced his or her fable.

2. They numbered the pages and each art page. They made a table of contents on page 1.

3. They agreed on a title for the collection and had someone make a title page. Someone else made a cover and pasted it on the outside of a binder.

4. They used a three-hole punch to make holes on the left side of each page. They collected the pages in the binder. They presented their book to the school library so that everyone could read it.

Discuss

1. Why do you think it was a good idea for Angela and her classmates to make an art page for each story?

2. What are some interesting ways in which they might have grouped the fables in their book?

Try Your Hand

Publish Your Fable   Follow the checklist in the **Writer's Guide.** If possible, create a book of fables, or try one of these ideas for sharing your fable.

◆ Rewrite your fable as a play. Then, with a group or with a partner, perform the play for the rest of your classmates. Use the **Tips on How to Dramatize a Play** on page 209 to help you get ready.

◆ With your teacher's permission, visit a class of younger children and read your fable aloud. Stop at an exciting part, and ask your audience to guess what will happen next.

Listening and Speaking
Tips on How to Dramatize a Play

There are two ways you can present a play. You can memorize the lines and act it out, or you can read aloud from the script. Here are some hints for doing both.

1. Read the script to yourself until you know it well. Then meet with a group or with a partner and decide who will take each part. Discuss what the characters are thinking and feeling and how they would speak and act.
2. Practice reading or saying your own lines aloud when you are alone. Think about what your character feels. Make the feelings show in your voice.
3. Practice together. Listen to the others read. Give one another helpful advice on how to improve.
4. Practice your parts until you know them well and are comfortable working together.
5. Remember that it is very easy to speak too quickly and too quietly when you are nervous. When you present the play to the audience, speak slowly and clearly.
6. Remember that audiences are friendly. They want to enjoy what they see and hear. Relax and have fun with them.

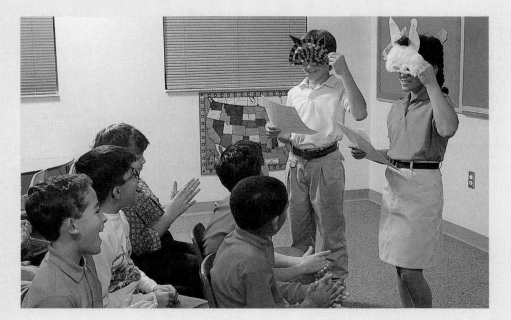

Writing in the Content Areas

Use what you learned to write another fable or a different kind of story. Try to entertain your readers. Use one of these ideas or an idea of your own.

Writer's Guide

When you write, remember the stages of the Writing Process.

◆ Prewriting
◆ Drafting
◆ Responding and Revising
◆ Proofreading
◆ Publishing

Science

The animals in fables behave more like people than like real animals. Choose an animal that you know about, or read about one that interests you. Then write a story about it. Show it acting as a real animal acts.

Literature

Fables aren't the only stories that teach lessons. Think about an experience that taught you or someone you know a lesson. Turn the experience into a story. Make up characters and details so that your story is make-believe. You may draw pictures to go with your story.

Social Studies

What would it be like to live somewhere else? Perhaps you know the answer to this question, or you could read about a different area. Think about what another place is like. Then use the place as a setting for a story about a boy or a girl your own age.

Mathematics

Word problems often appear in story form in math books. Try writing a long word problem. Entertain and puzzle your readers. Give math clues in the problem. Then ask a puzzling question at the end.

CONNECTING
WRITING ⬌ LANGUAGE

A good story holds the readers' attention. While they are reading, they feel that they are living in the time and place of the story. Think about how the writer of this fable holds your interest.

Once a very kind-hearted man owned a pet shop.

One day a farm woman came into his shop. " I am bothered by mice," she told him . " I want a cat that is good for mice."

He sighed, and then he smiled. " I have just what you want," he said. He sold her a fat, sleepy cat.

The next day the farm woman was back with the cat. She plopped it on the counter. " You told me this lazy cat is good for mice! Why, it won't even go near them !"

He smiled gently. "Isn't that good for the mice?"

Say what you mean and mean what you say.

◆ **Pronouns in a Fable**   The words highlighted are pronouns. They helped the writer tell this tale. Pronouns take the place of nouns. The pronouns helped the writer to avoid repeating words. Of course, pronouns must be used correctly if a story is to make sense. You were able to follow this story easily. The writer knew when to use *he* or *she* and whether to use *he* or *him*. You will notice that good stories sound smooth because the writers have used pronouns skillfully.

◆ **Language Focus: Pronouns**   In the following lessons you will learn more about using pronouns in your own writing.

1 Pronouns

◆ **FOCUS** A **pronoun** is a word that takes the place of a noun or nouns.

Read these sentences. The words in color are pronouns.

1. Pecos Bill wasn't afraid of anything.
2. He was the greatest cowpoke ever.
3. People tell stories about him .

In sentences 2 and 3, the singular pronouns *he* and *him* take the place of the noun *Pecos Bill*. Pronouns can be singular or plural. This chart shows some common pronouns.

Singular Pronouns	Plural Pronouns
I, you, he, she, it me, him, her	we, you, they us, them

Link to Speaking and Writing
By using pronouns, you can sometimes avoid repeating words. Why did the writer replace words in the second sentence?

The cowhands told stories about Bill. The cowhands (They) *liked the story about the cyclone and Bill.* (him)

Guided Practice

A. Identify the pronouns in each sentence.

1. Have you heard of Pecos Bill?
2. He was raised by a mother coyote.
3. She found him lost beside the trail.
4. "I will take this critter home with me," she thought.
5. The coyote pups took to him right away.

B. 6.–8. Replace the nouns in 1, 2, and 5 with pronouns.

Independent Practice

C. Identifying Pronouns   Write the pronouns in each sentence.

9. One day he was found by some cowhands.

MODEL ▷ he

10. They took him home to the ranch.
11. Now we will show you a thing or two.
12. Instead, he taught them some tricks.
13. You catch a cow the hard way!
14. I will teach you a trick with the rope.
15. Watch me toss it through the air.

D. Recognizing Nouns Replaced by Pronouns   Find the pronoun in the second sentence of each pair. Write the pronoun and the noun or nouns that it replaces.

16. Bill sold a ranch. A rich duke bought it.

MODEL ▷ it, ranch

17. The duke moved in. Bill went to welcome him.
18. The duke had a daughter. She was away at school.
19. The duke spoke to Bill. "I expect Sue home soon."
20. Sue rode a catfish. It was as big as a whale and twice as mean.
21. Bill watched the wild ride. He liked Sue's spunk.
22. Bill and Sue made a good pair. They got married.
23. Bill brought Sue two cubs. She raised the cubs.
24. The cubs were very smart. They even got voted into Congress.

Application—Speaking and Writing

A Speech   Imagine that you are Pecos Bill and you are just back from your ride on the tornado. You decide to give a speech because everyone wants to hear about your adventure. Write an entertaining speech that exaggerates what you saw and did. Underline each pronoun you use.

2 Subject Pronouns

◆ **FOCUS** A **subject pronoun** takes the place of a noun or nouns in the subject of a sentence.

Remember that a pronoun takes the place of a noun or nouns. The words in color are subject pronouns.

1. **She** must stay here.
2. **I** will not stay in Elf Land.
3. **You** cannot make me cook for all of you.

The pronouns *I, you, he, she, we, they,* and *it* can be used as subjects. Remember that *you* can be singular or plural.

The word *I* is always capitalized. When you use *I* and another noun or pronoun as subjects, you should write or say *I* last.

4. He and **I** began to argue.

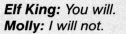

Elf King: *You will.*
Molly: *I will not.*

Guided Practice

A. Identify the subject pronoun in each sentence.

1. Fortunately, I know an old folktale.
2. We would like to hear it.
3. Then, you must listen quietly.
4. It is about a good baker.
5. She baked the most delicious meat pies.
6. They were much better than the elves' pies.
7. Now we must have Molly as our baker.
8. You must come and bake for us, Molly.
9. She laughed at the elf king.
10. Finally, he couldn't change her mind.

> **THINK AND REMEMBER**
> ◆ Use *I, you, he, she, we, they,* and *it* as subject pronouns.

Independent Practice

B. Identifying Subject Pronouns   Write the subject pronoun of each sentence.

11. We must steal Molly away.

MODEL ▷ We

12. They put a magic spell on her.

13. Instantly, she went into a deep sleep.

14. It lasted for hours.

15. Oh dear, I am not at home!

16. You are in the land of the elves.

17. She frowned at the elf king.

18. Then he smiled and bowed to her.

19. Now you must make us your meat pies.

20. I will not let you go back home.

21. He wanted Molly to stay.

C. Revising Sentences   Rewrite these sentences. Replace the underlined words with pronouns.

22. Molly was a clever woman.

MODEL ▷ She was a clever woman.

23. The elf king could not outwit her.

24. "Molly will bake for you," said Molly.

25. However, the elves had no pots and pans.

26. My people and I will bring what you need.

27. The baker asked first for her big bowl.

28. The bowl was in her kitchen at home.

29. Then messengers were sent for her spoon and flour.

30. The whisk and other things were at home also.

31. The king sent messengers to and fro all day.

32. The messengers did what they were told to do.

33. The day seemed very long to them.

Application—Writing

A Letter   Imagine that Molly is your sister. She wants to leave Elf Land. Think how she might outwit the king. Write a letter to Molly. Tell her how to get out of Elf Land. Use at least four different subject pronouns in your letter. If you need help writing a friendly letter, see pages 36–37 of the **Writer's Handbook.**

3 Object Pronouns

◆ **FOCUS** An **object pronoun** follows an action verb and words like *at, for, to,* and *with*.

Remember that pronouns can be subjects of sentences. Pronouns can also be found in the predicates of sentences. The words in color are object pronouns.

1. Bob called her .
2. No one can hear you and me .

Object pronouns can follow action verbs. The object pronouns are *me, you, him, her, it, them,* and *us*. The pronouns *you* and *it* may be used as either subject or object pronouns. Object pronouns can also follow words like *at, for, to,* and *with*.

3. Bob shouted at her .
4. Give the hat to me .

Guided Practice

A. Identify the object pronouns.

1. Bob's house had three goats in it.
2. Sue and I helped him.
3. Luis came with us.
4. Sue took a hat with her.
5. At the house the goats spotted them.
6. A goat nudged me.
7. I did not see it behind the chair.
8. Then, the other goats nudged us.
9. We avoided them as much as possible.
10. Bob told us to pet the small goat.

THINK AND REMEMBER
Use *me, you, him, her, it, us,* and *them* as object pronouns.

Independent Practice

B. Identifying Pronouns in Predicates   Write the object pronoun in each sentence.

11. "Do not leave me here with the goats," pleaded Sue.

MODEL me

    12. "We have left you in a safe place," responded Bob.

    13. The gray goat walked over to her.

    14. Sue patted it on the head.

    15. The goat moved closer to her and the hat.

    16. Bob and Luis looked at them.

C. Revising Sentences   Replace the underlined word or words with a pronoun. Write the new sentences.

17. Luis peeked over the table.

MODEL Luis peeked over it.

    18. Sue dropped her hat in front of the goat.

    19. The goat picked the hat up.

    20. "Give Sue the hat," said Sue.

    21. The goat grinned at Luis.

    22. Luis grabbed the hat.

    23. "I must join my friends," Bob said.

D. Choosing the Correct Pronoun   Read each sentence. Write one of the pronouns in parentheses ( ) to complete the sentence.

24. "(I, me) cannot hear you very well," said Sue.

MODEL I

    25. Bob brought a big broom to (she, her).

    26. "Come closer to (I, me), please," said Sue.

    27. Then, (she, her) took the broom.

    28. "Soon, (we, us) will clean up this mess," said Bob.

    29. "Then, our friends can visit (we, us)," said Luis.

    30. Politely (they, them) asked the goats to leave.

Application—Writing

A Letter   Have the goats write a letter of apology for the mess in Bob's house. Tell about some of the things they might have eaten. Make your readers laugh. Use at least four different object pronouns. If you need help writing a friendly letter, see pages 36–37 of the **Writer's Handbook.**

4 I, Me, We, Us

FOCUS

◆ *I* and *we* are subject pronouns.
◆ *Me* and *us* are object pronouns.

Notice the pronouns in color in these sentences.

1. I like to fish. Please come with me .

2. We will be home early. Save us some hooks.

3. My brother and I are busy. Don't call him or me .

I and *we* appear as subjects. *Me* and *us* follow action verbs. Notice that *I* and *me* appear last in the subject or object when these words are used with another noun or pronoun.

The words *we* and *us* can be used before nouns in a sentence.

4. We villagers were too busy to fish.

5. Mrs. Farmer chased away us children.

Guided Practice

A. Identify the pronoun in parentheses ( ) that completes each sentence correctly.

1. Grandmother tells (us, me) children a story.
2. (I, Me) will tell you about some fishermen.
3. You must listen to (I, me) quietly.
4. (We, Us) will not make a sound.
5. She told Sam and (I, me) a silly tale.
6. He and (I, me) enjoyed the story.
7. (We, Us) wanted to hear another one.
8. Grandmother told (we, us) to wait until later.

King: I count five of us.

THINK AND REMEMBER

◆ Use *I* and *we* as subject pronouns.
◆ Use *me* and *us* as object pronouns.

Independent Practice

B. Identifying the Correct Pronoun   Write the pronoun in parentheses ( ) that completes each sentence correctly.

9. My brothers and (me, I) are fishing today.

MODEL ▷ I

10. Who will come with (we, us)?

11. (I, Me) would like to come.

12. Give (I, me) a fishing pole.

13. Oh, (I, me) have no fishing pole.

14. Then (us, we) six brothers will go alone.

C. Revising Sentences   Each sentence has an incorrect pronoun. Replace the pronoun. Write the sentence.

15. Joe and me will take the boat.

MODEL ▷ Joe and I will take the boat.

16. Us will go across the river.

17. The bridge will be a good spot for I.

18. The fish will come to we.

19. My brothers and me caught many fish.

D. Using Pronouns Correctly   Read each sentence. Complete it by writing *me* or *I*.

20. _____ am ready to go home.

MODEL ▷ I

21. Are all my brothers with _____?

22. _____ will count them.

23. There are only five with _____!

24. Another brother counts my brothers and _____.

25. _____ count only five brothers too!

26. All my brothers and _____ can find only five of us!

27. Someone else must count my brothers for _____.

Application—Writing

A Journal Entry   Imagine that you meet the fishermen in the picture. After going home, you write in your journal about the silly thing that happened. Tell how you solve the brothers' problem. Use *I*, *we*, *me*, and *us* correctly. If you need help writing a journal entry, see page 26 of the **Writer's Handbook.**

5 Agreement of Subject Pronouns with Verbs

◆ **FOCUS**   A subject pronoun and its verb should agree.

Remember that the subject and the verb must agree. Notice the subject pronouns and the verbs in these sentences.

1. She holds a large apple in her mouth.

2. They hold large apples in their mouths.

Singular pronouns are followed by singular verbs. Plural pronouns and the words *I* and *you* are followed by plural verbs. This chart shows how to make pronouns and verbs agree.

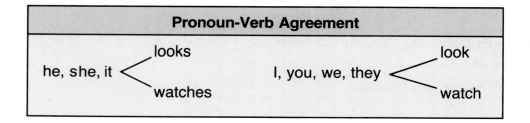

Pronoun-Verb Agreement		
he, she, it ⟨ looks / watches	I, you, we, they ⟨ look / watch	

Guided Practice

A. Identify the correct form of the verb in parentheses ( ).

1. We (admire, admires) Great Eater.
2. He (live, lives) with his sister Little One.
3. They (make, makes) a home on the island.
4. I (watch, watches) them in the contest.
5. She (hold, holds) an apple in her mouth without biting it.
6. It (appear, appears) red and juicy.
7. We (enjoy, enjoys) seeing the pigs in the contest, too.
8. I (see, sees) Great Eater sigh.
9. He (long, longs) to eat the apple instead of just holding it.
10. You (dream, dreams) of meals all the time!

Independent Practice

B. Identifying the Correct Verb   Write the verb in parentheses ( ) that completes each sentence correctly.

11. We (watch, watches) Great Eater eat the apple.

MODEL ▷ watch

12. He (break, breaks) the rules.

13. It (bring, brings) a smile to his face.

14. I (comfort, comforts) Little One.

15. She (drop, drops) her apple.

16. We (hear, hears) the contest is over.

17. They (cheer, cheers) for one of the pigs.

18. It (win, wins) the contest.

19. I (wonder, wonders) about the prize.

C. Revising Sentences   Each sentence contains a verb that does not agree with its subject. Rewrite each sentence. Replace the verb with the correct form.

20. We likes the contest.

MODEL ▷ We like the contest.

21. Now you enters the contest.

22. I holds an apple in my mouth.

23. My mouth ache after a few minutes.

24. They watches my brother and me.

25. We practices every day.

26. He hold the apple longer than I do.

27. Then, he drop it.

28. I wonders how the pig does it.

29. Now we knows the secret.

30. It have a bigger mouth!

Application—Writing

A Conversation   Write a conversation between the pig and Little One. Have the pig tell her how to hold the apple to win the contest. Use at least four different subject pronouns. Be sure the verbs agree with the subject pronouns.

6 Possessive Pronouns

◆ **FOCUS**   A **possessive pronoun** shows ownership.

A possessive pronoun takes the place of a possessive noun.

1. Jeanie's grandfather told this story.

Her grandfather told this story.

2. The children's grandfather knows many stories.

Their grandfather knows many stories.

The second sentence in each pair contains a possessive pronoun. Notice which noun each pronoun replaces.

Possessive Pronouns						
my	your	her	his	its	our	their

Guided Practice

A. Identify the possessive pronoun in each sentence.

1. Their grandfather told them a funny story.
2. Our cat did some funny things as a kitten.
3. It often chased its tail.
4. Your grandmother wondered about that kitten.
5. Her son George played with the kitten.
6. George threw the kitten his ball.
7. My kitten caught it and brought it back to him.
8. Our ball of string was also fun for the kitten.

THINK AND REMEMBER

◆ Use the possessive pronouns *my, your, her, his, its, our,* and *their* to take the place of possessive nouns.

Independent Practice

B. Identifying Possessive Pronouns Write the possessive pronoun in each sentence.

    9. My cat's name is Fluffy.

MODEL ▷ My

    10. Fluffy has many colors in its coat.

    11. Grandmother brushes her hand along the coat.

    12. George lets Fluffy climb up his arm.

    13. Then, Fluffy jumps to the top of our refrigerator.

    14. Fluffy cries its most sorrowful meow.

    15. Grandmother and George put their arms out.

    16. Fluffy misses the arms and lands on its feet.

    17. Does your cat behave like Fluffy?

    18. Many people enjoy playing with their cats.

C. Revising Sentences Rewrite each sentence. Replace the underlined words with one possessive pronoun.

    19. His and her work was done.

MODEL ▷ Their work was done.

    20. First, Fluffy jumped onto my family's and my table.

    21. Then, Fluffy jumped onto Grandmother's dresser.

    22. Fluffy looked into Grandfather's shaving mirror.

    23. The cat looked behind the mirror's stand.

    24. Fluffy did not see the stranger's paw prints.

    25. "Get out of Fluffy's house," Fluffy snarled.

    26. The stranger did not move the stranger's face from the mirror.

    27. Grandmother's and Grandfather's neighbors had two large dogs.

    28. The neighbors' dogs enjoyed teasing Fluffy.

    29. Fluffy liked to sit in Grandfather's lawn chair.

    30. The cat seemed to be thinking, "I'm safe behind Fluffy's fence."

Application—Writing

A Paragraph That Explains Pretend that Fluffy can understand you. Write a paragraph. Explain to Fluffy why the cat in the mirror in **Exercise C** above snarled back. Use at least four different possessive pronouns in your paragraph.

7 Contractions with Pronouns

◆ **FOCUS** A contraction can sometimes be formed by joining a pronoun and a verb.

A **contraction** is a shortened form of two words.

1. I am afraid of El Malo.
   I'm afraid of El Malo.
2. He has eaten everything!
   He's eaten everything!

The apostrophe takes the place of the missing letters in each contraction. This chart shows some common contractions formed with pronouns and verbs.

Contractions				
	am, is, *or* **are**	**have** *or* **has**	**had** *or* **would**	**will**
I	I'm	I've	I'd	I'll
you	you're	you've	you'd	you'll
he, she	he's, she's	he's, she's	he'd, she'd	he'll, she'll
it	it's	it's	it'd	it'll
we	we're	we've	we'd	we'll
they	they're	they've	they'd	they'll

Guided Practice

A. Identify the words each contraction stands for.

1. you'd **2.** he's **3.** she'll **4.** I'd **5.** we've **6.** you're **7.** they're **8.** it's

B. Tell how to replace the word pairs with contractions.

9. I am **10.** he has **11.** we will **12.** she is **13.** we are **14.** I will **15.** she has **16.** he will

THINK AND REMEMBER

◆ Remember that you can join some pronouns and verbs to form contractions.

Independent Practice

C. Identifying Contractions   Write the two words that each underlined contraction stands for.

17. <u>I'm</u> listening to my grandmother's story.

MODEL ▷ I am

18. <u>It's</u> about El Malo.

19. <u>He's</u> bothered us for years.

20. <u>We're</u> scared of his mean little eyes.

21. <u>They're</u> as red as hot coals.

22. Perhaps <u>we'll</u> never get rid of him.

23. "<u>You're</u> a pest," they said.

24. <u>He's</u> playing a trick on Doña Elena.

25. <u>She's</u> a kind woman with bad eyes.

26. <u>He's</u> just lain down by the road.

27. "<u>I've</u> found a little baby!" exclaims Doña Elena.

28. "<u>I'll</u> have to take it home," she adds.

D. Revising Sentences   Rewrite each sentence. Replace the underlined words with a contraction.

29. "<u>It is</u> a heavy baby," says Doña Elena.

MODEL ▷ "It's a heavy baby," says Doña Elena.

30. <u>They are</u> going into her little hut.

31. <u>She has</u> given him all her food.

32. "<u>I am</u> still hungry!" yells El Malo.

33. Now <u>he has</u> eaten the neighbor's food too.

34. They see that <u>he is</u> no baby.

35. "<u>You are</u> not welcome here," they said.

36. <u>You have</u> eaten enough for two families!

37. <u>He will</u> never go home now.

38. <u>We will</u> ask someone clever to help us.

Application—Writing

A Letter   A villager has written to you asking how to get rid of the greedy El Malo. Write an answer. Suggest a humorous plan. In your letter, use at least four different contractions made from pronouns. If you need help writing a friendly letter, see pages 36–37 of the **Writer's Handbook.**

Building Vocabulary
Homophones

Girl: My uncle writes that he just got a new herd.
Boy: Herd of what?
Girl: Herd of cows.
Boy: Why, sure I've heard of cows.

Girl: No silly! A cow herd!
Boy: What do I care if a cow heard? I haven't said anything against them.

The silly humor in this skit is based on the boy's misunderstanding of the word *herd*. It is an easy mistake to make. The words *heard* and *herd* sound exactly alike. They are homophones. **Homophones** are words that sound alike but are spelled differently and have different meanings.

When you write, you must be sure to use the correct homophone. Otherwise, your reader will be as confused as the boy in the picture. This chart shows some important homophones to learn.

your—belonging to you *you're*—a contraction of *you are*	*its*—belonging to it *it's*—a contraction of *it is*
their—belonging to them *they're*—a contraction for *they are* *there*—at that place	*too*—also *to*—toward something; for what purpose *two*—a number

Reading Practice

Read the sentences. Then decide which of the homophones in parentheses ( ) make sense. Write the correct homophones.

1. (You're, Your) going (buy, by) the Browns' house.
2. Yes, (I, eye) am. I'm going past (their, they're) door.
3. Please give this (to, two) Tony.
4. (Its, It's) a message (for, four) him.
5. I didn't (no, know) that you could write.
6. I can't, but Tom's (two, too) young to read!

Writing Practice

Each of these items contains one mistake. The wrong homophone was used. Find the mistakes and rewrite the sentences. Use the correct homophones.

7. "I have an act for you're show," said Al.
8. Then he put a tiny piano buy a mouse.
9. He set down a beautiful bird, two.
10. "Your going to love this," he said.
11. The mouse played the piano four them.
12. They herd the bird sing a lovely song.
13. "The animals are grate!" said Ted.
14. "Their not that wonderful," Al admitted.
15. "The bird doesn't know how too sing."
16. "Don't tell a sole. The mouse is a ventriloquist!"

Project

Puns are made from homophones. A **pun** is a joke in which words that sound the same but have different meanings are mixed up. The joke in the picture makes use of a pun. With a partner or group members, create jokes using homophones. Share your jokes with the class.

Boy: *Do rabbits use combs?*
Girl: *No, they use* hare *brushes!*

Language Enrichment
Pronouns

 What Is It?

One type of riddle gives you clues and then asks you to guess what it describes. Try your hand at writing one or more of these riddles. First, think of a common object or animal. Then, write several sentences about it on a card. Give good clues, but don't make it too easy to guess the answer. Use pronouns in place of the name of the object or animal. Do not write the answer on the card.

Collect the cards in a box. Then, take turns picking a riddle. Read the riddle aloud and guess the answer. If the answer is incorrect, let others in the class guess.

I have four legs.
My legs are stiff but strong.
I will not move unless
   you push me.
I am usually there when
   you eat.
What am I?

 Talk Show

Work in a group of four or five students to create a television talk show. Begin by having each group member choose a character to play. Your character can be a real person or a made-up famous person. Make notes to remind yourself of what your character is like.

Have one group member play the host. Then work together to plan what each of you will talk about. Remember to use the same pronouns as your character would.

Then put on your show before your classmates. If there is time, invite members of the audience to ask questions of the famous guests.

CONNECTING
LANGUAGE ⬄ WRITING

In this unit you learned about pronouns. Some pronouns are the subjects of sentences. Others appear after action verbs or words like *at, for, to,* and *with.* Special forms of pronouns show ownership. Some pronouns can also be joined with verbs to form contractions.

◆ **Using Pronouns in Your Writing** Knowing how to use pronouns is important to a writer. Pronouns help you keep your writing simple. They help you avoid repeating words. The right pronoun tells your audience who did what and who owned what. Pay special attention to the pronouns you use as you do these activities.

 Two by Two

You learned about homophones on the **Building Vocabulary** page. Here's a game that tests what you know.

Eleven pairs of homophones are in the drawing. List all the pairs you can find. Then choose four pairs of words. Write sentences in which you use each pair of homophones correctly.

Example: to, two
         I went TO the store TWO days ago.

Whose Is It?

Who are the people in this picture? What do you think they are doing? What might happen next?

Write a humorous story about the people in this picture. Use pronouns carefully. Draw pictures to go with your story. Then make a booklet of your story and pictures.

he'd he'll eyed hour you'll you're
I I'd heed it's their we've weed
heel eye its yule your weave
our they're we'd

5 Unit Checkup

Think Back	Think Ahead
◆ What did you learn about fables in this unit? What did you do to write one?	◆ How will what you learned about fables help when you read? ◆ How will evaluating ideas help when you want to explain something?
◆ Look at the writing you did in this unit. How did pronouns help you express your ideas?	◆ What is one way that you can use pronouns to improve your writing?

Analyzing a Fable   *pages 194–195*
Read this fable. Then answer the questions.

The Rabbit and the Pig
  Once a rabbit and a pig were arguing about who was better. The rabbit challenged the pig to jump over a ditch. The pig tried but fell into the middle of the ditch. Then the rabbit leaped but also fell short by just an inch.
  The rabbit argued that he must be better, but the pig asked a nearby horse to decide. The horse said that since both of them were in the ditch, neither one was better than the other.
  You cannot boast if you miss the mark.

1. Who are the characters?
2. What is the setting?
3. How does the fable begin?
4. How does the fable end?
5. What is the moral?

Evaluating Ideas to Support a Conclusion   *page 196*
Tell what conclusion you can draw from each sentence.

6. The pig huffed as it tried to squeeze through the hedge.
7. The rabbit whisked past all the other animals.
8. All the animals came to the horse to ask for advice.
9. No animal could jump the ditch, no matter how hard it tried.

Storytelling—Dialogue and Characters   *page 197*

Rewrite the fable "The Rabbit and the Pig," making it longer.
Answer the following questions in your new version.

10. How did the rabbit look and act?
11. What did he say?
12. How did the pig look and act?
13. What did he say?
14. What did the horse say?

The Writing Process   *pages 198–208*

Write the letter of the correct response to each question.

15. When choosing a moral to write a fable about,
    a. choose one that is important to you.
    b. write ideas that you don't understand.
    c. do not make fun of other people.
16. What are the most important parts of a fable?
    a. setting, moral, title, beginning
    b. beginning, ending, moral, title
    c. characters, setting, plot, moral
17. After you have listed all the details, the next thing you
    should do is
    a. write the story.
    b. organize the details.
    c. brainstorm ideas.
18. Which part of the fable should present the characters and the setting?
    a. the beginning
    b. the middle
    c. the ending
19. Which is the best way to tell that the rabbit was proud?
    a. The other characters said so.
    b. The rabbit was always talking about how great he was.
    c. The rabbit swelled out his chest and said, "Everyone
       knows that I'm the best jumper in the whole country."

Pronouns   *pages 212–213*

Find the pronoun in the second sentence of each pair. Write the
pronoun and the noun or nouns that it replaces.

20. Do you like cartoon characters? They are funny.
21. Bugs Bunny is clever. He outwits Elmer Fudd.

22. Daffy Duck is another character. He is jealous of Bugs.
23. Elmer has a gun. It helps him go "wabbit hunting."
24. Daffy pointed the gun at Bugs. "Shoot him now!"
25. Bugs said, "This is duck season. Don't shoot me."
26. Elmer was angry. "I thought it was wabbit season."

Subject Pronouns   *pages 214–215*
Write the subject pronoun of each sentence.

27. Do you ever watch Tweety Bird and Granny?
28. He always gets away from Sylvester the Cat.
29. She swats Sylvester with a broom.
30. They are really funny.
31. I think Tweety Bird is my favorite cartoon character.
32. We laugh and laugh at all the funny characters.

Object Pronouns   *pages 216–217*
Replace the underlined word or words with a pronoun. Write the new sentences.

33. Foghorn Leghorn bosses all the hens around.
34. A skinny hen wants Foghorn Leghorn to marry the skinny hen.
35. Her son carries a book around all the time.
36. He wears thick glasses.
37. Foghorn told the skinny hen, "I can't marry the skinny hen."
38. Foghorn said, "Your son is too smart for Foghorn."
39. "There is no future for you and me."

I, Me, We, Us   *pages 218–219*
Write the pronoun in parentheses ( ) that completes each sentence correctly.

40. Bob and (I, me) like to put on a funny play.
41. People call him and (I, me) "the two stooges."
42. (We, Us) stooges make them die laughing.
43. Sometimes Jack acts with (we, us).
44. He throws pies at Bob and (I, me).

Agreement of Subject Pronouns with Verbs   *pages 220–221*
Write the verb in parentheses ( ) that completes each sentence correctly.

45. (Has, Have) you seen any funny animal tricks?
46. We (likes, like) to watch them.

47. I (thinks, think) they are hilarious.
48. He (has, have) a dog that can talk.
49. He (asks, ask) the dog, "What covers a tree?"
50. It (answers, answer), "Bark!"

Possessive Pronouns   *pages 222–223*

Rewrite each sentence. Replace the underlined words with one possessive pronoun.

51. A man asked the farmer for <u>the farmer's</u> daughter's hand in marriage.
52. <u>The girl's</u> mind was made up against him.
53. The farmer said to the man, "Get everything ready for <u>the man's</u> wedding."
54. The man liked <u>his and the farmer's</u> plan.
55. Soon his servant asked the girl, "Where is what your father promised <u>the servant's</u> master?"
56. The girl used <u>the girl's</u> mind quickly.
57. "You mean <u>my father's and my</u> horse," she said.
58. "The horse is eating <u>the horse's</u> oats over there."

Contractions with Pronouns   *pages 224–225*

Write the two words that each underlined contraction stands for.

59. Soon the boy told the man, "<u>I've</u> brought her."
60. "<u>She's</u> supposed to go upstairs to be dressed."
61. "<u>You're</u> sure?" the boy asked in amazement.
62. "Yes, <u>I'm</u> sure!" said the man.
63. "<u>We've</u> got to get her up there to the maids."
64. The boys pushed till <u>they'd</u> gotten her upstairs.
65. "Now <u>they'll</u> dress her in the wedding finery."

Homophones   *pages 226–227*

Read the sentences. Then decide which of the homophones in parentheses ( ) makes sense. Write the correct homophones.

66. (You're, Your) the funniest boy in the class.
67. (Ewe, You) should put on a show.
68. (Their, There) could (bee, be) funny props.
69. You could bring (you're, your) hand puppets, (to, too).
70. (Its, It's) going (to, two) be a blast!

UNIT

6

Painting Pictures with Words

◆ **COMPOSITION FOCUS:** **Descriptive Paragraph**
◆ **LANGUAGE FOCUS:** **Adjectives**

Imagine yourself in the woods on an autumn day. You hear birds chirping and animals moving. Your eyes are dazzled by sunlight shining down on a clearing. Your nose is prickled by a musty smell, and the soles of your feet feel broken branches and pine cones.

Did these sentences make that moment in the woods come alive for you? When writers do this type of writing, they are not just giving information. They are also trying to share real or imaginary experiences with their audience.

Peter Parnall is one writer who is good at descriptive writing. He uses his imagination or his observation skills to find a subject. Then he thinks of ways to describe his subject that make it seem lively and real. Good descriptive writing like his makes everything fascinating to read. In this unit you will learn how to paint vivid word pictures in a descriptive paragraph.

Peter Parnall writes *to express* feelings and *to describe* experiences his readers can share.

Reading with a Writer's Eye
Description

No two people who read the words *a winter day* imagine quite the same picture. Writer Peter Parnall has his own unique view of winter to share with his readers. Read his description of the first snowfall of the year. As you read, notice that his appeal to your senses makes his view come to life in your imagination.

Alfalfa Hill
by Peter Parnall

The wind howled over Alfalfa Hill.
It ripped crisp leaves from the whipping trees
And hurled them crazily, crazily.
They crackled and scraped and nestled,
Covering the forest floor.

Warm air went and cold air came.
The robins were gone,
But the mockingbird stayed
Guarding his place in the wild rose bush.

The squirrels skittered from rock to stump
Gathering acorns, black walnuts, and tulip tree seeds.
They buried their hoards beneath the leaves
And now and then in a hollow tree.

Deer browsed on honeysuckle leaves
That still hung green in the frigid air.

Grouse leaped high for frozen clumps of dried wild grapes,
And mice raced for seed where rotten apples used to lie.

The old fat raccoon knew what was coming
And he ate and he ate, and he ate
Berries and nuts, bugs and corn,
Apples and frogs, and . . . it came . . . Whisper.

The snow.

Quiet, quiet it drifted down.
No whoosh, no sound.
No warning at all . . . Whisper.
Hour after hour it fell.

Like a world full of cotton it muffled all sound.
Deeper and deeper it whispered, whispered,
Making caves of viny honeysuckle clumps.
All night long the white blanket grew thicker and thicker.

The screech owl peered from his woody den
And stayed home from his evening hunt.

When the sun's first rays struck Alfalfa Hill
The creatures were wondering.

They were looking.

They were listening.

They did not stir.

No more rocky hedgerows wandering through the woods,
No more masses of tangled vines.
No green spruces reaching for the sky.
Now giant white mushrooms met the eye.

Ghosts, and marshmallows.
The air was still.
There were no squeaks, no chatters, no peeps or clucks.
No rustling, scratching, chewing, or caws . . .
No preening, combing, or washing one's paws.

The birds sat silently and watched their new world.

Winter.

A dangerous time for some
Whose color no longer matches the forest floor.
Beware, little mouse.
You are far from home.

Quiet is the word for winter.
Look and listen before you leap.
Find your food as fast as you can
And run home on silent feet.

Respond

1. What is your mood after reading "Alfalfa Hill"? What makes you feel this way? Would you like to share this poem with someone else? Why or why not?

Discuss

2. To which senses does this poem appeal most strongly? Give examples of words or phrases that appeal to each sense and make the writer's view come to life.

3. Contrast the first image you get of the hill with the last image. How does the writer use language to create two different images?

Thinking As a Writer
Analyzing a Descriptive Paragraph

Like a poem, a descriptive paragraph can create a vivid word picture. A descriptive paragraph describes a person, a place, an object, or an event. The paragraph should help the reader to see what is being described by giving details that appeal to the senses.

Read this writer's description of a small town in winter.

> Winter came quietly to Smithtown. From the gray, silent sky the first snowflakes fluttered like downy feathers in the still air. The rustling leaves were silenced. Snow whispered past bare tree branches and floated soundlessly into empty squirrels' nests. Soon snow had nestled softly in the hollows of fenceposts and had carpeted the hillsides in cold, white silence.

The **topic sentence** suggests what the paragraph is about and sets the mood.

Detail sentences appeal to such senses as sight and hearing. They may suggest comparisons to unlike things.

Discuss

1. How does the first sentence prepare you for the rest of the paragraph?
2. Which details appeal to your sense of sight? Which appeal to your sense of hearing?
3. In what order are the details presented in the paragraph? Would the paragraph be stronger or weaker if the writer had presented the details in a different order? Explain your answer.

Try Your Hand

A. Use Words That Appeal to the Senses   Write each sentence. Complete it with a vivid describing word that appeals to one of the senses.

  1. On a fall night there is a _____ smell in the air.
  2. I felt a _____ wind on my face.
  3. I heard the _____ call of an owl.
  4. I saw a _____ light in a window.
  5. I hurried inside to eat _____ stew.

B. Compare Unlike Things   Write each sentence. Complete it with a group of words that compares the first item to something quite different.

  6. A blue lake is like _____.
  7. A hummingbird is like _____.
  8. A lit-up city seen from above is like _____.
  9. A mushroom is like _____.
  10. A full moon is like _____.
  11. Tall buildings are like _____.
  12. The wise owl is like _____.

C. Identify and Organize Details
Imagine what someone who walked into your room at home might notice. List the details. Organize the details in the order in which they would be seen.

D. Read a Description   Turn to the description on pages 236–239, or find a descriptive paragraph in a book. Read the description aloud to a partner. Identify the vivid details and tell to which sense each appeals. Discuss the way in which the writer ordered the details.

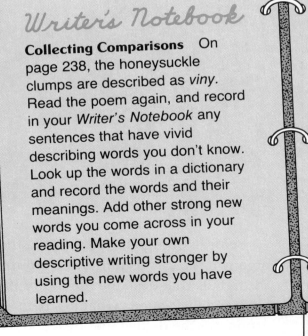

Writer's Notebook

Collecting Comparisons   On page 238, the honeysuckle clumps are described as *viny*. Read the poem again, and record in your *Writer's Notebook* any sentences that have vivid describing words you don't know. Look up the words in a dictionary and record the words and their meanings. Add other strong new words you come across in your reading. Make your own descriptive writing stronger by using the new words you have learned.

Thinking As a Writer
Observing Details

In a good description, a writer presents details in a way that makes sense to the audience. The writer tries to make readers notice things in the order they would if they were really in that place.

In a good descriptive paragraph, writers

◆ group details in a way that makes sense, such as front to back or top to bottom.

◆ Organize groups of details in a way that makes sense.

> Finally we reached the top of the hill. It was a flat, open space warmed by the sun. The tall grass rippled in the wind. Before us the path led down the sloping hillside and through the patchwork fields. In the distance was Greensboro, looking like a toy village. I turned back and saw behind me the silver ribbon of the stream winding through the woods.

Before writing this paragraph, the writer used a chart to organize the details into three groups. In the first group are the details that describe the top of the hill. In the next group are the details about what lies before the hikers. In the last group are the details that describe what is behind them.

The Top of the Hill	What Lies Before the Hikers	What Was Behind the Hikers
flat, open space tall grass	sloping hillside patchwork fields Greensboro, a toy village	winding stream woods

If the writer had mixed up these details, the readers might feel mixed up also. Instead the writer grouped and presented the details in an order that makes sense. This helps the readers see the picture clearly.

As you write a descriptive paragraph, be sure to group and organize details in a way that can be easily understood by your audience.

Discuss

1. Look over the paragraph you just read. Would it still make sense if the writer had put the groups of details in another order? Why or why not?
2. Turn to page 237 and find the section of the poem that begins "Deer browsed." Read to the end of the paragraph. In what direction does your eye travel as you imagine this scene? How would your experience be different if the writer had described the mice, then the grouse, and then the deer?
3. In the chart on this page, the writer puts the details into the groups *here*, *before*, and *behind*. What are some other ways in which you could group details according to location?

Try Your Hand

Classify Details According to Location   Find a picture of an interesting scene in a book or a magazine. List 10 or 12 of the key details in it. Group the details according to where the items are located in the picture. Give each group a heading such as "in the front" or "in the back " that suggests why the details in each group belong together. Small details may be in the front, while larger, more visible details may be placed in the back.

Developing the Writer's Craft
Using Metaphors and Similes

Good writers use comparisons to help readers see things in a new way. A writer might use a **metaphor** to compare two things that are not usually compared. This line contains a metaphor.

All night long the white blanket grew thicker and thicker.

In this line, the writer Peter Parnall suggests that the snow is a white blanket. He does not say, "The snow is like a white blanket." A metaphor suggests that one thing is something else.

A **simile** is also used to compare two things. The difference is that a simile contains the word *like* or the word *as*.

Like a world full of cotton it muffled all sound.

The writer now compares the snowy hill to a world full of cotton. The word *like* signals that a simile is being used.

When you write your descriptive paragraph, try to capture on paper a vivid word picture. Use similes and metaphors to help your readers see things in a new way.

Discuss

1. Find the section of the poem on page 238 that begins "No more rocky hedgerows." What metaphors appear in this section? What do they describe?
2. Why are metaphors and similes useful to people who are writing descriptively?

Try Your Hand

Use Metaphors and Similes   Write a sentence about each item listed. Each sentence should contain a metaphor or a simile that compares the item to something else.

1. a field   2. a bus   3. a river   4. thunder   5. the sun

Listening and Speaking
Tips on How to Listen to Poetry

Poetry is meant to be read aloud. You can enjoy it more and read it better if you pay attention to its sounds, patterns, and special features. Here are some tips to help you.

1. Listen for **rhyme.** Lines that have the same ending sounds tie a poem together. At the bottom of this page is a stanza from a poem by Kaye Starbird. Notice that it has two sets of ending rhymes. *Dish* and *swish* rhyme, and so do *noon* and *spoon.*

2. Listen for **rhythm.** Rhythm is a strong, regular beat that draws the reader onward. Read the stanza from "December Leaves" to yourself. In its third and fourth lines, every second word has a strong beat. Poems that do not rhyme are often held together by rhythm.

3. Listen for **words with the same beginning sounds.** When these words are close to one another, they create a pleasing effect. Notice that in "December Leaves" the words *night* and *noon* sound right together.

4. Listen for **sound words.** Sound words imitate sounds and make the poet's descriptions more vivid. In "December Leaves" the word *swish* really does suggest the sound of the wind stirring dry leaves.

December Leaves
by Kaye Starbird

The fallen leaves are cornflakes
That fill the lawn's wide dish,
And night and noon
The wind's a spoon
That stirs them with a swish.

5. Listen for **metaphors**. Metaphors suggest comparisons of unlike things. They can help you see things in new ways. In the following poem by Hitamaro, the writer uses metaphors to describe the sky, the moon, and the stars.

In the Ocean of the Sky
by Hitamaro
In the ocean of the sky
Wave-clouds are rising,
And the ship of the moon
Seems to be rowing along
Through a forest of stars.

Listen for metaphors suggested by other words. In the following poem, the writer does not tell what sort of flock the boats are being compared to. However, the key words *tethered* and *nibbling* help explain *flock*.

A Flock of Little Boats
by Samuel Menashe
A flock of little boats
Tethered to the shore
Drifts in still water . . .
Prows dip, nibbling.

6. Listen for **similes**. Similes also give readers new images. Here are the last lines of a poem by James Reeves. Notice that the simile brings an image to life.

Shiny
by James Reeves
But the round full moon,
So clear and white
How brightly she shines
On a winter night!
Slowly she rises,
Higher and higher,
With a cold clear light
Like ice on fire.

1 Prewriting
Descriptive Paragraph

John decided to write a description of places that could be story beginnings. John used the checklist in the **Writer's Guide** to help him plan his description. Look at what he did.

Writer's Guide

Prewriting Checklist
- ☑ Brainstorm and select a topic.
- ☑ Think about your audience and your purpose.
- ☑ List the sensory details of your topic.
- ☑ Organize the sensory details in a way that will paint a clear picture.

◆ Brainstorming and Selecting a Topic

First, John listed some places that he would enjoy describing. Then, he asked himself if he could imagine each place well enough to give good details about it. He also asked himself whether it would be easy to note details that would appeal to his readers' senses. Then, he considered whether the place would be exciting for others to read about. Finally, he circled the place he chose to describe.

on school

a country road on a dark night

inside the White House

a record store

Discuss

Look at each item John crossed out. What do you think were his reasons for crossing out each of these places?

◆ Gathering and Organizing Details

After John decided what place to write about, he made notes of the details he planned to use. He made a chart. John tried to see the place in his imagination. Then he divided the chart into three areas. Look at the chart on page 248.

The Path Under the Trees	The Path by the Open Field	The Grove Beyond the Field
darkness bumpy path cold wind	moonlight smell of alfalfa rustles in grass	a black shape a twig breaking shiny eyes

Discuss

Is making the chart a good way for John to organize details for a descriptive paragraph about a place? Explain your answer.

Try Your Hand

Now plan a descriptive paragraph of your own.

A. Brainstorm and Select a Topic   Brainstorm a list of places you might enjoy writing about.

◆ Cross out any places you don't know well.
◆ Cross out any places that will not interest your audience.
◆ Consider the places that are left. Circle the one you think will work best. This will be the topic of your paragraph.

B. Gather and Organize Details   When you are satisfied with your topic, make notes. You may want to use a chart.

◆ First, think about how you can divide the place into small areas. Give each area a name that describes it.
◆ List the details that describe each area. Remember that you want to appeal to your audience's senses.
◆ Decide which order you will describe the areas in. You might want to number the areas to remind yourself.
◆ Reread the details you noted. Think about the order in which you can present these details. You might want to number them too.

Save your notes and chart in your _Writer's Notebook._ You will use them to draft your descriptive paragraph.

WRITING PROCESS

2 Drafting
Descriptive Paragraph

John used his chart and followed the checklist in the **Writer's Guide** to draft his descriptive paragraph. Look at how he began.

> The path through the woods was like a dark tunnel. It was spooky. He knew he was on the path because the ground was hard and bumpy under his bare feet. At last he came out from under the trees. He saw a broad field lit with moonlight. He smelled freshly cut alfalfa.

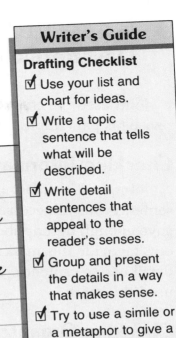

Writer's Guide

Drafting Checklist
- ☑ Use your list and chart for ideas.
- ☑ Write a topic sentence that tells what will be described.
- ☑ Write detail sentences that appeal to the reader's senses.
- ☑ Group and present the details in a way that makes sense.
- ☑ Try to use a simile or a metaphor to give a clear picture.

Discuss

1. Was John's topic sentence a good one? Explain.
2. Look at John's notes on page 248. What other details would you expect to find in this paragraph?

Try Your Hand

Now you are ready to write a descriptive paragraph.

A. Review Your Notes Look over the details you noted in the last lesson. Add more details if you need to.

B. Think About Your TAP Remember that your task is to write a descriptive paragraph. Your purpose is to express a mood that your audience can share.

C. Write Your First Draft Follow the **Writer's Guide** to write your descriptive paragraph.

When you write your draft, just put all your ideas on paper. Do not worry about spelling, punctuation, or grammar. You can correct the draft later.

 Save your first draft in your *Writer's Notebook.* You will use it when you revise your descriptive paragraph.

Task: What?
Audience: Who?
Purpose: Why?

3 Responding and Revising
Descriptive Paragraph

John used the checklist in the **Writer's Guide** to revise his paragraph. Look at what he did.

◆ Checking Information

John read his draft and decided that the second sentence was unnecessary because the first sentence gave enough description. To show he was taking it out, he made this mark ✄. Then, he added a vivid detail to one sentence. To show the addition, he used this mark ∧.

◆ Checking Organization

Next, John decided that the last two sentences were in the wrong order. To show that one sentence should be moved, he used this mark ↰.

◆ Checking Language

Finally, he found two sentences that ran together. He revised them into two separate sentences and added a period.

Cut — The path through the woods was like a dark tunnel. ~~It was spooky.~~ He knew he was on the path because the ground was hard and bumpy under his bare feet. At last, he came out from under the trees. He saw a broad field lit with moonlight. He smelled freshly **Add** — cut alfalfa. An owl hooted, small creatures rustled in the grass. Beyond the field was another grove of trees like a low black cloud. **Add** — He heard a twig snap and saw a pair of *glittering* eyes. **Move** — The path carried him near this grove.

Discuss

1. John decided that the second sentence was unnecessary. Why do you think he made this decision?
2. How did moving the last sentence improve the paragraph?

Try Your Hand

Now revise your first draft.

A. Read Your First Draft   As you read your descriptive paragraph, think about your audience and your purpose. Read your paragraph silently or to a partner to see if it is complete and well organized. Ask yourself or your partner the questions in the box.

Responding and Revising Strategies

✔ Respond
Ask yourself or your partner:

◆ Does my topic sentence identify the place and set the mood?

◆ Do my detail sentences appeal to my readers' senses?

◆ Have I grouped and ordered information in ways that make sense?

◆ Are all my sentences clear? Have I avoided run-on sentences?

✔ Revise
Try these solutions:

◆ **Add** information to your topic sentence.

◆ **Add** any details that you have left out. See the **Writer's Thesaurus** to choose words for sentences.

◆ **Move** any information that is in the wrong place.

◆ **Replace** one run-on sentence with two complete sentences. See the **Revising Workshop** on page 252.

B. Make Your Changes   If the answer to any question in the box is *no,* try the solution. Use the **Editor's Marks** to show your changes.

C. Review Your Descriptive Paragraph Again
Decide if there is anything else you want to revise. Keep revising your paragraph until you feel it is well organized and complete.

EDITOR'S MARKS

∧ Add something.
⸝ Cut something.
↻ Move something.
⟑ Replace something.

Save your revised paragraph in your *Writer's Notebook.* You will use it when you proofread your descriptive paragraph.

Revising Workshop
Avoiding Run-on Sentences

Writers want to communicate their ideas clearly. To do this, they must write correct, complete sentences that are easy to understand. One type of incorrect sentence they avoid is the run-on sentence. Sentence 1 is a run-on sentence.

1. The wind began to blow the sand swirled.   **incorrect**
2. The wind began to blow, and the sand swirled.   **correct**
3. The wind began to blow. The sand swirled.   **correct**

A run-on sentence is two sentences that have been run together. Each expresses a complete thought, but nothing separates the first thought from the second. Sentence 2 is not a run-on sentence, because the two parts are separated by the word *and* and a comma. Sentence 3 shows the easiest way to correct a run-on sentence.

Practice

Correct each of these run-on sentences by making it into two sentences.

1. I walked over the dunes my feet crunched in the packed sand.
2. The sea was a shimmering green it reminded me of silk.
3. Foam floated on the waves it was like lacy ribbons.
4. A gull swooped down I heard a loud squawk.
5. I waded into the cold sea my ankles grew numb.
6. Something tickled my calf it was a rope of coarse seaweed.
7. The fog rolled in the air smelled fishy.
8. I walked on the beach for a while I felt cold.
9. I put on my sweater it felt warm and cozy on my damp skin.
10. It was getting late we decided to leave the seashore.

4 Proofreading
Descriptive Paragraph

John added some sentences to his paragraph. Then he used the **Writer's Guide** and the **Editor's Marks** to proofread it. Look at what he did.

Writer's Guide

Proofreading Checklist
- ☑ Check for errors in capitalization.
- ☑ Check for errors in punctuation.
- ☑ Check to see that your paragraph is indented.
- ☑ Check for errors in verb tenses.
- ☑ Circle any words you think are misspelled. Find out how to spell them correctly.
- ⇨ For proofreading help, use the **Writer's Handbook.**

He heard a twig snap and saw a pair of glittering eyes. a cold wind was blowing. The trees tossed their *branches* ~~branchs~~ high. they made a sound like rushing water. The owl *hooted* hoots again.

Discuss

1. Why did John change the word *hoots* to *hooted*?
2. Look at the other corrections he made. Why did he make each one?

Try Your Hand

Proofread Your Descriptive Paragraph Now use the **Writer's Guide** and the **Editor's Marks** to proofread your paragraph.

Save your corrected descriptive paragraph in your *Writer's Notebook*. You will use it when you publish your paragraph.

EDITOR'S MARKS

- ≡ Capitalize.
- ⊙ Add a period.
- ∧ Add something.
- ⋏ Add a comma.
- ⩖⩗ Add quotation marks.
- ✂ Cut something.
- ⋀ Replace something.
- ∿ Transpose.
- ◯ Spell correctly.
- ⊬ Indent paragraph.
- / Make a lowercase letter.

COMPOSITION: PROOFREADING Descriptive Paragraph **253**

5 Publishing
Descriptive Paragraph

John made a clean copy of his paragraph and checked it to be sure he had not left out anything. Then he and his classmates published their paragraphs by making a bulletin board display. You can find John's paragraph on page 24 of the **Writer's Handbook.**

Here's how John and his classmates published their paragraphs by making a display.

Writer's Guide

Publishing Checklist

☑ Make a clean copy of your descriptive paragraph.

☑ Check to see that nothing has been left out.

☑ Check to see that there are no mistakes.

☑ Share your paragraph in a special way.

1. Each student copied his or her paragraph on the bottom of a sheet of paper. John made up a title for his that went with his story beginning. Neatly he wrote the title and his name at the top of the page.

2. Each student planned and drew a book cover to go with the paragraph and its title. The students left room for the titles and their names as they made drawings to go with their paragraphs.

3. One student listed everyone's title. Then the writers told what kind of stories their paragraphs belonged in. They used this information to plan how to group the stories in the display.

WRITING PROCESS

4. They took turns reading their paragraphs aloud.

5. They pinned the paragraphs in groups on the bulletin board so that visitors to their classroom could read them.

Discuss

1. Look at the types of stories listed on the bulletin board in step 5. Can you think of any other types you could add to this list?
2. Why is it a good idea to read the stories aloud as well as to post them on the bulletin board?

Try Your Hand

Publish Your Descriptive Paragraph   Follow the checklist in the **Writer's Guide.** If possible, create a bulletin board display, or try one of these ideas for sharing your paragraph.

◆ Trade paragraphs with a classmate. Read your classmate's paragraph aloud to the class. Then, tell what you think might happen next in a story that begins with this paragraph.

◆ Collect your paragraphs in a binder. Title the book *Wonderful and Thrilling Places to Visit*. Imagine that this is a travel guidebook, and sign up for the places that you would like to visit.

Writing in the Content Areas

Use what you learned to write descriptive paragraphs for others to enjoy. You can describe familiar sights or imaginary places and things. Use one of these ideas or an idea of your own.

Writer's Guide

When you write, remember the stages of the Writing Process.

◆ Prewriting
◆ Drafting
◆ Responding and Revising
◆ Proofreading
◆ Publishing

Science

Scientists must be good at observing and describing things. Choose a plant, a living creature, or a natural park in your community. Observe it. Make use of as many senses as you can. Record your observations in a notebook. Then describe the object as a scientist would.

Fine Arts

Music is enjoyable. It can also stir your imagination. Listen to a piece of music that you like. Does it create any pictures in your mind? Does it carry you away to another place? Tell what you can see and hear in your imagination.

Physical Education

Think about a sports activity that you like. Think about how you feel before, during, and after the activity. How do the sights and sounds around you add to your enjoyment? Describe the sport so that someone else can share your feelings about it.

Social Studies

Have you ever been to a Mexican fiesta or a Hawaiian luau? Americans have come from many different cultures. Each has contributed special ways to celebrate. Remember a special festival or a party you attended. Describe it. Tell what you heard, saw, smelled, and tasted there.

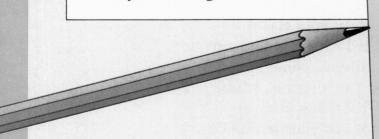

CONNECTING
WRITING ↔ LANGUAGE

Good descriptive writing excites our imaginations and stirs our senses. It makes us see what the writer sees and hear what the writer hears. Think about how this descriptive paragraph appeals to your senses.

Our shady porch is the best place to be on a hot afternoon. It is cooler there than anywhere else. I like to get a cold apple from the refrigerator and the most mysterious book I can find. Then I settle on the soft cushions of the porch swing. I feel happy as I breathe in the sweet smell of honeysuckle and hear the steady chugging of the sprinkler on the lawn. I bite into my crisp, tart apple and open my book.

◆ **Adjectives in a Descriptive Paragraph** The highlighted words are adjectives. They add vivid details to the writer's description of the shady porch. Adjectives are describing words. They give information about people, places, and things. Good writers try to choose adjectives that will give the clearest pictures to their audience. Strong, exact adjectives are often used in descriptive writing.

◆ **Language Focus: Adjectives** In the following lessons you will learn more about using different kinds of adjectives in your own writing. As you complete these lessons, you will read more about people and things that will encourage you to use your imagination.

1 Adjectives

◆ **FOCUS**   An **adjective** is a word that describes a noun or a pronoun.

Read these sentences. The words in color are adjectives.

1. All ventriloquists use puppets in shows.

2. Shari Lewis has created several fine shows.

Most adjectives tell what kind. The adjective *fine* tells what kind. Some adjectives tell how many. The adjectives *all* and *several* do this.

> **Link to Speaking and Writing**
> You can paint a vivid and more exact picture if you use adjectives carefully. How does the adjective *huge* give a clearer picture than the adjective *big?* What other adjectives might you use?

She danced with a big ^huge puppet.

Guided Practice

A. Identify the adjective that describes each underlined noun. (Do not include *a, an,* or *the.*)

1. I once watched a good <u>ventriloquist</u>.
2. He could do different <u>tricks</u> with his voice.
3. He put on an exciting <u>show</u>.
4. His mouse puppet said funny <u>things</u>.
5. He made the puppet speak in a high <u>voice</u>.
6. At the end of the show, there was loud <u>applause</u> from the audience.

B. 7.–12.   Replace each adjective you identified in **A** with a more vivid adjective. Use the **Writer's Thesaurus.**

Independent Practice

C. Identifying Adjectives   Write the adjective that describes each underlined noun.

13. Shari Lewis created several <u>programs</u>.

MODEL ▷ several

14. On some <u>shows</u> she did funny <u>tricks</u> with magic.
15. Usually her silly <u>puppets</u> added to the fun.
16. On one <u>program</u> she performed famous <u>stories</u>.
17. She won many <u>awards</u> for best <u>shows</u> for children.
18. She has also written delightful <u>books</u>.

D. Classifying Adjectives   Make two columns. Head them *How Many* and *What Kind*. Write the adjectives from each sentence in the proper column. (Do not include *a, an,* or *the*.)

19. I spent four long weeks making puppets.

MODEL ▷

How Many	What Kind
four	long

20. I have three funny puppets.
21. Pinky is a pretty pig.
22. He has bright eyes and pointy ears.
23. He does many foolish things.
24. Clara gives her two friends wise advice.

E. 25.–30. Revising Sentences   Rewrite the sentences in **D.** Replace each adjective that tells *what kind* with a vivid adjective. Use the **Writer's Thesaurus.**

25. long

MODEL ▷ I spent four lengthy weeks making puppets.

Application—Writing

A Television Review   The photograph shows Shari Lewis doing a show with puppets. Imagine that you have just seen the show. Write a paragraph that might be in a newspaper review. Use vivid adjectives to make your readers "see" this part of the show.

2 Articles

◆ **FOCUS**   The adjectives *a*, *an*, and *the* are **articles.**

Notice the words in color in these sentences. They are special adjectives called articles.

1. Bill Cosby is a comedian and an actor.

2. He is the comedian I like best.

The words *a* and *an* refer to any person, place, or thing. The word *the* refers to a specific person, place, or thing.

a	Use before singular nouns when the noun or the word before the noun begins with a consonant sound.	a comedian a funny comedian
an	Use before singular nouns when the noun or the word before the noun begins with a vowel sound.	an actor an eager actor
the	Use before a specific noun or nouns.	the shows

Guided Practice

A. Identify the correct article in each sentence.

1. Comedians have (a, an) unusual view of life.
2. They can see a joke in (a, an) bad experience.
3. Jokes make (the, a) bad experience less painful.
4. A good comedian is (a, an) honest one.
5. (The, A) audience laughs at funny stories.

> **THINK AND REMEMBER**
> ◆ Remember that the **articles** *a*, *an*, and *the* are adjectives of a special kind.

Independent Practice

B. Using Articles Correctly   Write the article that correctly completes each sentence.

6. Cosby laughed at himself as (an, the) athlete.

MODEL ▷ an

7. He joked about (an, the) experiences of his youth.
8. (The, A) listeners laughed with him, not at him.
9. His success led to (a, an) acting job.
10. He was one of (a, the) stars of the show.
11. His character was (a, an) very funny man.
12. He got (a, an) Emmy Award for his work.
13. (An, The) best actors of the year get Emmys.
14. Then, he got (a, an) hour-long show of his own.

C. Distinguishing Between Articles   Read each sentence. Write *a* or *an* to complete it.

15. I used to watch _____ funny television show.

MODEL ▷ a

16. Each character made me think of _____ friend of mine.
17. The characters always had _____ ordinary problem.
18. Often, one of them would make _____ wrong decision.
19. Then, he or she would get in _____ awful mess.
20. There was usually _____ sensible solution.

D. Writing Original Sentences   Write each noun. Put *a* or *an* before it. Write a sentence using these words. Then, write another sentence using each noun with *the*.

21. award

MODEL ▷ an award—He won an award for the show.
         The award was a great honor.

22. joke	**24.** program	**26.** laugh
23. actor	**25.** idea	**27.** hour

Application—Writing

A Plan for a Script   Imagine that you are the person who gives writers of television programs their ideas. Write a description for them that tells what will happen next in a television show. Underline each article you use.

3 Adjectives That Follow Linking Verbs

◆ **FOCUS**   An adjective that follows a linking verb can describe the subject.

Often, adjectives come before the nouns they describe. Sometimes, an adjective follows a linking verb. Then it can describe the subject of the sentence.

1. Mike draws funny cartoons.

2. His cartoons are funny .   **describes a noun**

3. They are funny .   **describes a pronoun**

Notice that an adjective after a linking verb can describe either a noun or a pronoun.

> **Link to Writing**
> Sometimes three adjectives are used to describe a noun or a pronoun. A comma is placed between the adjectives and before the word *and*.

The cartoons are simple, funny, and colorful.

Guided Practice

A. Identify the adjective that follows the linking verb. Then name the noun or pronoun it describes.

1. Mike's Woozles are ridiculous.

2. Their bodies are pink.

3. Their spots are yellow.

4. A Woozle is affectionate toward people.

5. It is cheerful from morning to night.

Independent Practice

B. Connecting Adjectives and Subjects   Write each sentence. Underline each adjective that follows the linking verb. Then draw an arrow to the noun or pronoun it describes.

6. A Woozle's habits are strange.

MODEL ▷ A Woozle's habits are <u>strange</u>.

7. For one thing, the Woozle is lazy.

8. Its burrow is messy.

9. The rubbish there is unbelievable!

10. However, Woozles are comfortable in this mess.

11. A Woozle's diet is peculiar, too.

12. To a Woozle, an old sock is tasty.

13. Fried erasers are delicious to a Woozle, too.

C. Using Adjectives   Write these sentences. Use three adjectives to complete each one.

14. A Yang-yang is _____, _____, and _____.

MODEL ▷ A Yang-yang is silly, short, and chubby.

15. Its eyes are _____, _____, and _____.
16. Its ears are _____, _____, and _____.
17. Its tail is _____, _____, and _____.
18. Its stripes are _____, _____, and _____.

Application—Listening, Speaking, Writing

A Descriptive Paragraph   Make a picture of another cartoon creature. Write a short description of it. Use adjectives following linking verbs in some sentences. Then read your description to the class. Have the class try to draw the creature as they listen to your description. If you need help writing a description, see page 24 of the **Writer's Handbook.**

4 Adjectives That Compare: with *er, est*

◆ **FOCUS** Adjectives can describe by comparing people, places, or things.

Remember that adjectives describe nouns or pronouns. Adjectives can describe by comparing two or more persons, places, or things.

1. The three theaters are small .
2. The Rio is smaller than the Republic.
3. The Grand is the smallest of all.

When two things are compared, *er* is added to many adjectives. When more than two things are compared, *est* is added. This chart shows some ways in which adjectives change their spelling.

---

1. When an adjective ends in *e*, drop the *e*.
   strange   stranger   strangest
2. When a one-syllable adjective ends in a short vowel sound and a consonant, double the last letter.
   slim   slimmer   slimmest
3. When an adjective ends in a consonant and *y*, change the *y* to *i*.
   tiny   tinier   tiniest

If the word *than* is in the sentence, use an *er* ending. If the words *of all* are in the sentence, use an *est* ending.

4. He is happier today than he was yesterday.
5. Sherry seems the happiest of all of us.

Guided Practice

A. Spell the adjectives that belong in the blanks.

1. calm, calmer, _____
2. dim, _____, dimmest
3. flat, flatter, _____
4. brave, _____, bravest
5. heavy, _____, heaviest
6. cute, cuter, _____

Independent Practice

B. Spelling Adjective Forms   Write the missing adjectives.

7. nice, nicer, _____

MODEL > nicest

8. cold, _____, coldest

9. lucky, _____, luckiest

10. hot, hotter, _____

11. zany, zanier, _____

12. large, larger, _____

13. lively, livelier,_____

14. wet, _____, wettest

15. light, lighter, _____

16. late, _____, latest

17. rough, rougher, _____

C. Writing Correct Forms   Read the sentences. Write the correct form of the adjective in parentheses ( ).

18. The Grand is the (old) theater here.

MODEL > oldest

19. The Republic is the (large) of all.

20. The Rio is much (new) than the Grand.

21. It is (roomy) than any other theater.

22. It has the (wide) aisles of all.

23. Its seats are the (cozy) I have sat in.

24. Saturday is the (busy) day at the Rio.

25. They show the (funny) movies on Saturdays.

D. 26.–36. Writing Original Sentences   Write 10 original sentences. Use each of the adjectives you listed in **B.**

26. nicest

MODEL > The Republic is the nicest theater in town.

Application—Writing

A Descriptive Paragraph   Write a paragraph that describes one of the theaters in the picture on page 264 for someone new in town. Use at least three adjectives to compare the theater to the other two theaters. If you need help writing a descriptive paragraph, see page 24 of the **Writer's Handbook.**

5 Adjectives That Compare: with *More, Most*

Kim Soon

Aaron Gome

Joy Pell

◆ **FOCUS**   *More* or *most* is used with some adjectives to make comparisons.

Many adjectives use *er* or *est* to make comparisons. However, adjectives of two or more syllables usually use the words *more* or *most* to compare people, places, or things.

1. Kim's invention is   imaginative .

2. Is Joy's invention   more   imaginative   than Kim's?

3. Aaron's invention is the   most   imaginative   of all!

When two items are compared, the word *more* is used. When more than two items are compared, the word *most* is used.

Guided Practice

A. Tell if *more* or *most* correctly completes each sentence.

1. Our class had the _____ unusual contest ever!
2. It was _____ fun than our Fall Olympics contest.
3. We drew the _____ creative inventions we could.
4. They weren't the _____ practical gadgets ever made!
5. Some ideas were _____ interesting than others.
6. Kim's dog-washer was _____ sensible than Joy's umbrella backpack.
7. Was Eric's seesaw _____ practical than Kim's dog-washer?
8. Which ideas were the _____ unusual of all?

THINK AND REMEMBER

◆ Use *more* or *most* to make comparisons with some adjectives of two or more syllables.
◆ Use *more* to compare two things.
◆ Use *most* to compare more than two things.

Independent Practice

B. Distinguishing Between Adjective Forms Read each sentence. Write *more* or *most* to complete each one.

9. Chester Greenwood created his _____ famous invention in December 1873.

MODEL ▷ most

10. No gift was _____ exciting than his new skates.
11. He was _____ eager than ever to skate on the pond.
12. The cold was the _____ unpleasant it had ever been.
13. His ears were _____ sensitive to cold than yours.
14. A scarf was _____ irritating than it was useful.
15. The _____ suitable ear covering was fur.
16. Greenwood invented the _____ effective ear protection ever—earmuffs!

C. Revising Sentences Some of the sentences have incorrect adjective forms. If the adjective form is correct, write *correct*. If it is incorrect, rewrite the sentence correctly.

17. I was most nervous about the project than Kim.

MODEL ▷ I was more nervous about the project than Kim.

18. This weekly project was the more difficult one this year.
19. Monday was the more tiring day of all!
20. Tuesday was more promising than Monday.
21. I finally settled on the more sensible idea of all.
22. I've wanted a most comfortable place to study.
23. I imagined the most efficient study chair ever.
24. It is most costly than the one I use now.
25. Which inventions are the most important to you?
26. Can you say that one invention is most valuable than another?

Application—Writing

A Letter The pictures show some entries in a contest for inventions. Imagine that you are a judge. Write a note to another judge, telling which invention should win an award and why. Use at least three adjectives that use *more* or *most* to compare. Use words like *clever, remarkable, ridiculous,* or *useful.* If you need help writing a letter, see pages 36–37 of the **Writer's Handbook.**

6 Adjectives That Compare: Special Forms

◆ **FOCUS**   Some adjectives that compare have special forms.

Notice how the adjective *good* changes in these sentences.

1. Alice knows some   good   riddles.
2. Matthew's riddles are   better   than hers.
3. Vanessa's riddles are the   best   of all.

This chart shows adjectives with special forms. Notice that the forms of *many* and *much* are the same.

One	Two	More Than Two
a *good* joke	a *better* joke	the *best* joke
a *bad* pun	a *worse* pun	the *worst* pun
a *little* fun	*less* fun	the *least* fun
many riddles	*more* riddles	the *most* riddles
much laughter	*more* laughter	the *most* laughter

Guided Practice

A. Identify which of the two forms is correct.

1. What is the (better, best) fish for a sandwich?
2. What food is (better, best) for your eyesight than carrots?
3. What kind of pine has the (more, most) needles?
4. What storm does (more, most) good than harm?
5. What is the (worse, worst) bank to keep money in?

THINK AND REMEMBER

◆ Use the special forms of *good*, *bad*, *little*, *many*, and *much* to show comparison.

Independent Practice

B. Choosing Correct Forms Write the correct form of the adjective in parentheses ( ).

   6. What is the (better, best) thing to raise in a wet climate?

MODEL ▷ best

   7. Why are spiders (best, better) at baseball than fleas?
   8. Which side of a barn gets the (less, least) sunshine?
   9. What's a (worse, worst) surprise than a worm in your apple?
   10. What animal does the (better, best) job of keeping time?

C. Writing Correct Forms Read each sentence. Write the correct form of the adjective in parentheses ( ).

   11. Eric spent the (little) time of anyone on his riddles.

MODEL ▷ least

   12. An umbrella is the (good) thing of all to raise in a wet climate.
   13. Spiders catch (many) flies than fleas do.
   14. The barn's inside gets (little) sun than its outside.
   15. Finding half a worm is the (bad) surprise of all!
   16. A watchdog does the (good) job of keeping time.

D. Creating Original Sentences Use the chart. Make up five original sentences.

Write about:	Use a form of:
17. a team	*good*
MODEL ▷ The best team is the Robins.	
18. a weather condition	*bad*
19. having fun	*much*
20. a number of people	*many*
21. a game	*good*
22. time	*little*

Application—Writing and Speaking

Riddles Write three or more riddles. Plan to ask your classmates your riddles. Use a form of *good, bad, many, much,* or *little* in each one.

Building Vocabulary
Suffixes

Remember that you learned how to change the meaning of a base word by adding a prefix to the beginning of it. You can also change the meaning of a base word by adding letters to the end. These endings are called **suffixes.**

1. The clown has a <u>cheerful</u> grin.

2. She wears a <u>bushy</u> red wig.

The suffix *ful* means "full of." In sentence 1, the underlined word *cheerful* means "full of cheer." The suffix *y* changes nouns to adjectives. It tells *what kind*. In sentence 2, *bushy* tells you that the wig is like a bush.

This chart shows some suffixes and their meanings.

Suffix	Meaning	Example
able	able to be	drinkable
er	one who	speaker
ful	full of	careful
less	without	careless
or	one who	sailor
y	"like, as"	snowy

Reading Practice

Read the sentences. Write each word that has a
suffix. Then write the meaning of that word.

1. She wears a colorful hat in her act.
2. Her clown suit is a spotless white.
3. She is the owner of a charming elephant.
4. Jumbo is a chummy creature.
5. He is also a very trainable animal.
6. The director asked her to use Jumbo in her act.
7. Jumbo does a graceful elephant dance.
8. Now the clown is training a dog to be a singer.

Writing Practice

Add a suffix from the chart on page 270 to each of
these words. Use each new word in a sentence of
your own. You may use a dictionary if you need help.

9. invent
10. wonder
11. enjoy
12. rain

13. worth
14. itch
15. farm
16. joy

17. break
18. point
19. speak
20. power

Project

Work in a small group. Brainstorm to create a list of words
with one of the suffixes shown on the chart. Put the words in
alphabetical order. Then write a definition and a sample sentence
for each. When you are finished, compare your list with the lists
of other groups who chose the same suffix. Then put all the lists
together to create a book of suffixes.

Language Enrichment
Adjectives

Use what you know about adjectives to do these activities.

Ads That Sell

Imagine that you are an advertisement writer. Your job is to make people want to buy something. You may want to sell tickets to a ball game, a trip to Hawaii, or a pair of shoes. Decide what you want to sell. Then create a magazine ad for it. Use strong adjectives. Make pictures for your ad.

When everyone is finished, place the ads around the classroom. Read them. Decide which ads make you want to buy the product.

You Be the Judge

With your classmates, brainstorm some types of interesting contests. Select the 10 or 12 everyone likes best.

Working on your own, prepare entries for at least three of these contests. For each entry, write the name of a contest at the top of a blank card. Then draw or paste on a picture of the person or thing you think should win. Below, write three or four sentences that tell why. In some of your sentences, use adjective forms that compare.

Collect each group of entries in a box. Take turns reading them aloud. After listening to all the entries in each group, vote on a winner.

1. best baseball player
2. most exciting adventure book
3. prettiest flower
4. scariest ride at the fair

CONNECTING
LANGUAGE ⟷ WRITING

In this unit you learned that adjectives describe nouns. Special forms of adjectives are used to compare two or more people, places, or things.

◆ **Using Adjectives in Your Writing**   It is important to be able to use adjectives easily when you write. Colorful adjectives make your writing lively and clear. They help your audience imagine what you are describing. Pay special attention to the adjectives you use as you do these activities.

 A Special Place

Study this picture. Imagine yourself in the scene. Think about what you might hear, smell, and feel as well as what you can see.

Write a poem about the picture. Use vivid adjectives that will stir your audience's senses. After you have finished, read what you have written to a partner.

 Way to Go

You learned about suffixes on the **Building Vocabulary** page. Here is an activity that calls for you to use them.

Brainstorm a list of adjectives that end in *ful* or *less*. Then write a brief description of what you might see and hear on your way to school. Use three or more of the adjectives from your list in your sentences.

Example: Two *gleeful* first-graders climb on the bus. They greet the *cheerful* bus driver. They see the *cloudless* sky through the window.

Think Back	Think Ahead
◆ What did you learn about descriptive paragraphs in this unit? What did you do to write one?	◆ How will what you learned about descriptive paragraphs help you when you want to describe something in a letter? ◆ How will observing details help you when you want to describe something to a classmate?
◆ Look at the writing you did in this unit. How did adjectives help you express your ideas?	◆ What is one way that you can use adjectives to improve your writing?

Analyzing a Descriptive Paragraph   *pages 240–241*
Read this paragraph. Then answer the questions.

> Truffles the Mouse gazed upon the beauty that lay before her. Down the slope of the hill she saw an old white house. A fat cat slept on the porch, breathing heavily. Its tail flicked harmlessly at the buzzing flies. Outside the big red barn, Truffles saw other mice playing and squeaking with delight. But the best sight of all was the field of corn behind the barn—standing like rows of people waving at her. The rustling sounded like whispers, inviting the little mouse to come and help herself.

1. What is the topic sentence?
2. Write some words from the paragraph that appeal to the sense of sight.
3. Write some words from the paragraph that appeal to the sense of sound.
4. List the two word pictures that compare unlike things.
5. List the three main places that are described in the paragraph.

Observing Details   *pages 242–243*

Put the following details in the order in which you would most likely see them if you were on your way home.

6. the front door of the house
7. my house from a distance
8. hot cereal in a bowl
9. flowers in front of the house
10. my dog running to greet me

Using Metaphors and Similes   *page 244*

Write a metaphor or simile comparing each set of objects.

11. fireflies, eyes
12. teeth, piano keys
13. autumn leaves, helicopters
14. fresh snow, carpet
15. a baby's hair, peach fuzz

The Writing Process   *pages 247–255*

Write the letter of the correct response to each question.

16. What should you think about as you add or delete information from your descriptive paragraph?
    a. your favorite place
    b. your audience and your purpose
    c. publishing your paragraph
17. Choose the best topic sentence for a descriptive paragraph.
    a. My paragraph is about my grandmother's house.
    b. They don't make houses like my grandmother's anymore.
    c. Where does your grandmother live?
18. Which helps make the description in a paragraph better?
    a. a good topic sentence
    b. strong describing words
    c. information given in order

Adjectives   *pages 258–259*

Write the adjective that describes each underlined noun.

19. You can make a special <u>puppet</u> of your own.
20. The most important <u>part</u> is the head.

21. Use wet <u>newspaper</u> dipped in paste.
22. Shape the paper over a small <u>ball</u> of newspaper.
23. Then, let the damp <u>head</u> dry.
24. Paint the whole <u>head</u>.
25. Then, paint on the different <u>features</u>.
26. Glue on colorful <u>yarn</u> for hair.
27. Then, make a fancy <u>costume</u>.
28. Make simple <u>hands</u> shaped like mittens.
29. Pull the bright <u>costume</u> over the head.
30. Now put on a funny <u>show</u> with your puppet!

Articles   *pages 260–261*

Write the article or articles that correctly complete each sentence.

31. Pioneer children made (a, the) toys they used.
32. (A, An) nut or (a, an) apple might make (a, an) doll's head.
33. (A, An) old corncob would make (a, an) body.
34. Corn silk could then make (an, the) doll's hair.
35. (A, The) girls made cornhusks into dresses.
36. (A, An) ordinary leaf became (a, an) apron or (a, an) amusing little hat.
37. (A, An) boy skipped stones over (a, the) creeks.
38. (A, An) large stick could become his horse.
39. (A, An) boy's knife helped him make toys.
40. He could carve (a, an) blowpipe or (a, an) whistle from a willow branch.
41. (A, An) dandelion stem became (a, an) horn.

Adjectives That Follow Linking Verbs   *pages 262–263*

Write each sentence. Underline each adjective that follows the linking verb. Then draw an arrow to the noun or pronoun it describes.

42. Two boys were eager for money.

43. Fred was glad to have a job.

44. Ed was ready for a treasure.

45. Ed's imagination was wild.

46. Soon the boys were hot and tired from digging.

47. "I am exhausted," said Fred.

48. "Maybe an invention will be useful," said Ed.

49. "Maybe we are foolish," said Fred.

50. "I am capable of inventing something," said Ed.

51. "I think it will be wonderful," said Ed.

Adjectives That Compare: with *er, est*   *pages 264–265*
Write the missing adjectives.

52. drab, _____, drabbest
53. drafty, draftier, _____
54. dark, darker, _____

55. squeaky, squeakier, _____
56. trim, trimmer, _____
57. quiet, _____, quietest

Adjectives That Compare: with *More or Most*   *pages 266–267*
Read each sentence. Write *more* or *most* to complete each one.

58. Radio programs used to be _____ popular than they are now.
59. They needed the _____ talented helpers around.
60. How could fire sound _____ realistic than it did on the radio?
61. Cellophane was the _____ efficient solution.
62. Those sound-effects people were the _____ creative ever!

Adjectives That Compare: Special Forms   *pages 268–269*
Read each sentence. Write the correct form of the adjective in parentheses ( ).

63. The moles' eyesight was the (less) developed of their senses.
64. Tanga Mouse could see (good) than the moles could.
65. "There is much (little) light here than in my home."
66. "This is the (little) light I have ever seen."
67. "My own whiskers are the (much) I can see."
68. "Worms are the (good) food we have," said Mole.
69. "Can I get some (many) seeds?" Tanga asked.
70. "Worms are the (bad) things I've ever tasted."

Suffixes   *pages 270–271*
Read the sentences. Write each word that has a suffix. Then write the meaning of that word.

71. Will that terrible disease be treatable someday?
72. Each careful scientist is studying a possible treatment.
73. Some fearless people offer to try a new medicine.
74. They hope to be helpers in research.

UNIT

Persuading Others

◆ **COMPOSITION FOCUS:** **Persuasive Paragraph**
◆ **LANGUAGE FOCUS:** **Adverbs**

"Why Americans Need More Exercise" "So You Think Another Litter Law Is Unnecessary?" Whenever you look at a book or a newspaper, you see articles with titles like these. They were written to persuade readers to do something. It might be to exercise more or vote for a law.

Writers often do persuasive writing of this type. Usually they write about events or issues in the news. They present their own opinions and then give facts to convince their audience to agree with them. Quite often they urge their readers to take action.

Sometimes this type of persuasive writing will appear in stories. Some story writers want to do more than entertain their readers. They also want to convince their audience that certain actions are right and others are wrong. When story writers do this, they present their arguments through their characters. E. B. White is one writer who has done this in a book called *Charlotte's Web*.

One reason
E. B. White wrote
Charlotte's Web
was *to persuade*
his audience to
respect life.

Reading with a Writer's Eye
Persuasion

It isn't always easy to tell right from wrong. To Fern Arable, the character in the following story, there is just no doubt at all on certain issues. She loses no time trying to convince others of her point of view. The excerpt below begins the book *Charlotte's Web,* by E. B. White. It contains a good example of a persuasive argument. Notice how the writer identifies the question, or issue, and then presents arguments that support the character's opinion.

Before Breakfast
by E.B. White

"Where's Papa going with that ax?" said Fern to her mother as they were setting the table for breakfast.

"Out to the hoghouse," replied Mrs. Arable. "Some pigs were born last night."

"I don't see why he needs an ax," continued Fern, who was only eight.

"Well," said her mother, "one of the pigs is a runt. It's very small and weak, and it will never amount to anything. So your father has decided to do away with it."

"Do *away* with it?" shrieked Fern. "You mean *kill* it? Just because it's smaller than the others?"

Mrs. Arable put a pitcher of cream on the table. "Don't yell, Fern!" she said. "Your father is right. The pig would probably die anyway."

Fern pushed a chair out of the way and ran outdoors. The grass was wet and the earth smelled of springtime. Fern's sneakers were sopping by the time she caught up with her father.

"Please don't kill it!" she said. "It's unfair."

Mr. Arable stopped walking.

"Fern," he said gently, "you will have to learn to control yourself."

"Control myself?" yelled Fern. "This is a matter of life and death, and you talk about *controlling* myself." Tears ran down her cheeks and she took hold of the ax and tried to pull it out of her father's hand.

"Fern," said Mr. Arable, "I know more about raising a litter of pigs than you do. A weakling makes trouble. Now run along!"

"But it's unfair," cried Fern. "The pig couldn't help being born small, could it? If *I* had been very small at birth, would you have killed *me*?"

Mr. Arable smiled. "Certainly not," he said, looking down at his daughter with love. "But this is different. A little girl is one thing, a little runty pig is another."

"I see no difference," replied Fern, still hanging on to the ax. "This is the most terrible case of injustice I ever heard of."

A queer look came over John Arable's face. He seemed almost ready to cry himself.

"All right," he said. "You go back to the house and I will bring the runt when I come in. I'll let you start it on a bottle, like a baby. Then you'll see what trouble a pig can be."

When Mr. Arable returned to the house half an hour later, he carried a carton under his arm. Fern was upstairs changing her sneakers. The kitchen table was set for breakfast, and the room smelled of coffee, bacon, damp plaster, and wood smoke from the stove.

"Put it on her chair!" said Mrs. Arable. Mr. Arable set the carton down at Fern's place. Then he walked to the sink and washed his hands and dried them on the roller towel.

Fern came slowly down the stairs. Her eyes were red from crying. As she approached her chair, the carton wobbled, and there was a scratching noise. Fern looked at her father. Then she lifted the lid of the carton. There, inside, looking up at her, was the newborn pig. It was a white one. The morning light shone through its ears, turning them pink.

"He's yours," said Mr. Arable. "Saved from an untimely death."

Fern couldn't take her eyes off the tiny pig. "Oh," she whispered. "Oh, *look* at him! He's absolutely perfect."

She closed the carton carefully. First she kissed her father, then she kissed her mother. Then she opened the lid again, lifted the pig out, and held it against her cheek. At this moment her brother Avery came into the room. Avery was ten.

"What's that?" he demanded. "What's Fern got?"

"She's got a guest for breakfast," said Mrs. Arable. "Wash your hands and face, Avery!"

"Let's see it!" said Avery. "You call that miserable thing a pig? That's a *fine* specimen of a pig—it's no bigger than a white rat."

"Wash up and eat your breakfast, Avery!" said his mother. "The school bus will be along in half an hour."

"Can I have a pig, too, Pop?" asked Avery.

"No, I only distribute pigs to early risers," said Mr. Arable. "Fern was up at daylight, trying to rid the world of injustice. As a result, she now has a pig. A small one, to be sure, but nevertheless a pig. It just shows what can happen if a person gets out of bed promptly. Let's eat!"

Respond

1. Does the ending of the excerpt satisfy you? Why or why not?

Discuss

2. How does the writer introduce to the reader the question, or issue, of whether or not the pig should be killed? When is this done?

3. What reasons does the writer present for and against killing the pig? What details does the writer give to show why Fern's reasons won the argument?

4. Do you agree with the reasons given by the writer? Explain your answer.

Thinking As a Writer
Analyzing a Persuasive Paragraph

The purpose of a persuasive paragraph is to persuade, or convince, readers that they should do or not do something. Writers use persuasion to state an opinion on an issue. Then they give facts and reasons to explain why they hold that opinion and why others ought to agree.

A good writer tries to change other people's opinions about an issue by influencing their thinking. Read this paragraph that a student who agreed with Fern Arable might have written.

> **Writer's Guide**
>
> A persuasive paragraph
> - tries to persuade readers to take an action.
> - identifies the issue, presents the arguments, and tells what action to take.
> - uses convincing facts and examples to support the opinion.

It is just not right to kill runt pigs. Some people claim that a runt pig will never amount to anything. How can anyone be sure? With good care and food, a pig might turn out strong and healthy. After all, our cow Daisy was a very sickly calf. Now she gives more milk than any other cow in the herd. It will not cost anything extra or be much bother to let the runt pigs live. You never know how they will turn out. So I say, "Let them live."

The **topic sentence** makes the question, or **issue,** clear.

The **detail sentences** support the writer's point of view with reasons, facts, and examples.

The **last sentence or sentences** tell the readers what action to take.

Discuss

1. What is the issue in this paragraph? How and where does the writer make it clear?
2. What action does the writer want the readers to take? Who might the audience for this paragraph be?
3. Explain the arguments the writer presents to support his or her point of view.
4. What details would you add to support the issue? Explain your answer.

Try Your Hand

A. Develop Supporting Statements   Read the following topic sentences. For each, write a reason that supports the writer's point of view.

1. Adding another month to the school year is a terrible idea.
2. A city apartment is no place to keep a dog.
3. Soccer is the best team sport.
4. Your friends can make a big difference in your life.

B. Write Topic Sentences   Write a topic sentence for a persuasive paragraph on each of these topics.

5. the restaurant you think is the best in town
6. wildlife protection
7. getting enough sleep
8. a toy that you think is dangerous or bad for children
9. recycling newspapers and magazines
10. keeping your community clean
11. a movie you shouldn't miss
12. eating balanced meals

C. Write Conclusions   Reread the topic sentences you wrote for **B**. For each, write a sentence that could end that paragraph. Tell your audience what action to take.

D. Read Persuasive Writing   Find a piece of persuasive writing in a book, a magazine, or a newspaper. Read it aloud to a partner. Identify the issue and the arguments that support the writer's point of view. Then tell whether you would take the action the writer recommends and why or why not.

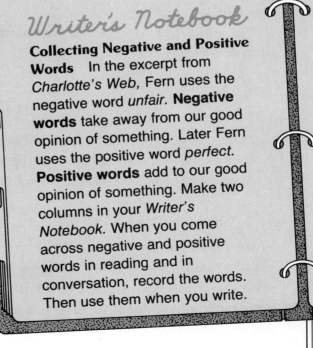

Writer's Notebook

Collecting Negative and Positive Words   In the excerpt from *Charlotte's Web*, Fern uses the negative word *unfair*. **Negative words** take away from our good opinion of something. Later Fern uses the positive word *perfect*. **Positive words** add to our good opinion of something. Make two columns in your *Writer's Notebook*. When you come across negative and positive words in reading and in conversation, record the words. Then use them when you write.

Thinking As a Writer
Classifying Fact and Opinion

Writer's Guide

In a persuasive paragraph, good writers
◆ state their opinions.
◆ present facts to support their opinions.

In a persuasive paragraph, a writer gives both opinions and facts. An **opinion** is a statement of what someone thinks or feels about a subject. It cannot be proved true or false.

1. I think that pigs make great pets.
2. Everyone should have a pig for a pet.

Writers often begin their opinions with signal words such as *I think* or *I believe*. They might also use strong positive or negative words like *great* or *horrible*. They might use words like *everyone*, *always*, *never*, or *all* in opinions. Sharp readers realize that it is rare for these kinds of statements to be always true.

Writers usually back up their opinions with facts. A **fact** is a statement that can be proved true or false.

3. Pigs keep themselves cleaner than most other farm animals.

If you check in an encyclopedia, you will find that people who have studied or raised pigs agree with that statement. Therefore, it is a fact.

As you write your persuasive paragraph, support your own opinions with facts.

Discuss

1. Reread the example paragraph on page 284. Which sentences state opinions and which state facts? How can you tell?
2. Is it likely that a persuasive paragraph will end with a statement of fact used as a supporting detail? Why or why not?

Try Your Hand

Write Facts and Opinions   Write three facts and three opinions about an animal you think makes a good pet. Mix up these sentences, and then trade them with a partner. Identify which of your partner's statements are facts and which are opinions. Then discuss how you knew the difference.

Developing the Writer's Craft
Using Examples

As you have already read, writers use facts to support their opinions. Some facts are general. **General facts** are true of many people or things. An **example** is a fact that is true either about one particular person or thing or about a small group. An example may be used to support a general fact.

1. Scientists have found pigs to be more intelligent than horses and some dogs.
2. One circus trainer was able to teach his pig Petunia 25 different tricks.

The first sentence is a general fact. It makes a true statement about most pigs. The second sentence gives an example. The example supports the general fact in the first sentence and makes the writer's argument stronger.

When you write your persuasive paragraph, use examples to support general facts. The examples will help convince your readers of the truth of the general facts.

Discuss

1. Reread the example paragraph on page 284. What example does the writer give to support his or her opinion? How is the writer's argument helped by this example?
2. Why do you think examples help convince readers that general facts are true?

Try Your Hand

Use Examples For each statement, write an example that supports it.

1. Our country is rich in history.
2. I have met some interesting people.
3. People from all nations have contributed delicious dishes to the American menu.
4. Not everything you learn in school comes from books.

1 Prewriting
Persuasive Paragraph

Writer's Guide

Prewriting Checklist

☑ Brainstorm topics.

☑ Think about your audience and your purpose.

☑ Select a topic.

☑ Gather supporting facts and examples.

☑ Organize the facts and examples.

☑ Decide which action you will recommend.

Don and his classmates decided to write persuasive paragraphs for their schoolmates. Their plan was to publish the paragraphs on posters displayed throughout the school. Don used the checklist in the **Writer's Guide** to help plan his persuasive paragraph. Look at what he did.

◆ Brainstorming and Selecting a Topic

First, Don brainstormed some topics he had opinions about. Look at his list. He wrote down his opinions as statements.

Next, Don looked over his list. He crossed out a topic that he thought everyone would agree with easily. He crossed off another topic because it would be hard to find facts about it. Then, he remembered that he had to ask his readers to take action. So he crossed off another topic that asked them only to agree with his opinion.

Finally, Don circled the most interesting topic left on his list. He decided to write about noise because he felt strongly about it. He knew that not everyone would agree with his opinion. He also knew that he could easily find information on his topic.

> Everyone should eat healthy meals.
>
> Our school song needs to be changed.
>
> My Dad is the perfect father.
>
> It would be fun to spend a year on a desert island.
>
> People should not make so much noise.
>
> Red Frost is a movie you should avoid.

Discuss

1. Look at each topic Don crossed off his list. Why do you think he decided against each one?
2. Suppose Don starts to work on his paragraph and decides he doesn't have enough information on his topic. What might he do?

◆ Gathering and Organizing Information

After choosing his topic, Don thought about the information that might go into his paragraph. He jotted down all his ideas. He talked over his ideas with his family and his friends. He made notes about some of the things they said. Then he went to the library and looked up *noise* in the encyclopedia. He found some useful facts that he jotted down on paper.

Don read over his notes and then made this list to organize his notes and put them in order of importance. He wrote the most important reason last.

My opinion: Our world is noisier than it should be.

1. Some noise can't be helped.
   Examples: transportation and building noises
2. Some noise is unnecessary.
   Examples: radios, shouting
3. Too much noise is bad for you.
   Reasons: It damages hearing and causes stress.

What I want readers to do: Cut down on noise.

Discuss

1. Why did Don divide his list into three parts? Which part will he use to write each part of his paragraph?
2. Why did Don number the items in the middle of his list?
3. Where did Don list examples? Why did he put these in his list?
4. Where did Don state on his list the action he wanted his readers to take?

Try Your Hand

Now plan a paragraph on a topic you feel strongly about.

A. **Brainstorm and Select a Topic**   Brainstorm a list of possible topics. Write down statements you feel strongly about. Think about each topic and your audience.

- ◆ Cross out topics that state opinions most people would agree with easily.
- ◆ Cross out topics that will be difficult or impossible to find information about.
- ◆ Cross out topics that ask your audience only to agree with you.
- ◆ Circle the topic that is left that you feel most strongly about. This will be the topic of your persuasive paragraph.

B. **Gather and Organize Information**   When you are satisfied with your topic, gather and list the information you might use in your paragraph.

- ◆ Jot down your thoughts on the topic.
- ◆ Add facts you learn from interviewing other people or reading. Note good examples that support general facts.
- ◆ Think about your audience. Identify the facts that will persuade them to do what you ask.
- ◆ Plan the order in which you will use your notes. You may want to make a list like Don's to help organize them. Remember to write the most important reason last.

Save your lists in your *Writer's Notebook*. You will use them when you draft your persuasive paragraph.

WRITING PROCESS

2 Drafting
Persuasive Paragraph

Don followed the checklist in the **Writer's Guide** to draft his persuasive paragraph. Look at what he did.

Writer's Guide

Drafting Checklist
- ☑ Use your lists for ideas.
- ☑ Write the topic sentence first.
- ☑ Give facts that support your opinion.
- ☑ Give examples that support facts.
- ☑ Tell your audience what action to take.

> Our world is a lot noisier and unhealthier than it needs to be. Some noises can't be helped. We have to put up with the sounds of buses, trucks, drills, and saws. After all, people have to go places and build things. We all add unnecessary noises to this uproar, however. Families in the parks play their radios loudly.

Discuss

1. Why is Don's first sentence important?
2. Which statements are backed up by examples?

Try Your Hand

Now you are ready to write your persuasive paragraph.

A. Review Your Information   Think about the information you gathered and organized in the last lesson. Is there anything you want to add or change? If so, do it now.

B. Think About Your TAP   Remember that your task is to write a persuasive paragraph. Your purpose is to persuade your audience.

C. Write Your First Draft   Follow the **Writer's Guide** to write your persuasive paragraph.
   When you write your draft, just put all your ideas on paper. Do not worry about spelling, punctuation, or grammar. You can correct the draft later.

TAP

Task: What?
Audience: Who?
Purpose: Why?

Save your first draft in your *Writer's Notebook*. You will use it when you revise your persuasive paragraph.

3 Responding and Revising
Persuasive Paragraph

Don used the checklist in the **Writer's Guide** to revise his persuasive paragraph. Look at what he did.

◆ **Checking Information**

Don discovered that he could give an example to support one of his statements. To show this change, he used this mark ∧ .

◆ **Checking Organization**

Don's next-to-the-last sentence was the one that told his audience what to do. He used this mark ⟲ to show that it should be moved to the end.

◆ **Checking Language**

Don found two sentences with the same predicate. He used this mark ∧ to combine the subjects.

Add —

Cut —

Add —

Move —

Families in the parks *and teenagers on the streets* ∧ play their radios loudly. ~~Teenagers on the streets play their radios loudly.~~ Some people shout when they could talk quietly. *Yesterday someone was shouting in the library and I couldn't study.* ∧ Scientists have found that loud noise may damage hearing. It also creates the stress that makes people cross or sick. (That's why we should do our part to cut down on the racket.) We'd all feel better and healthier in a quieter world.

Discuss

1. How did Don improve his paragraph?
2. Is there anything you would change in Don's paragraph? Explain your answer.

Try Your Hand

Now revise your first draft.

A. Read Your First Draft   As you read your persuasive paragraph, think about your audience and your purpose. Read your paragraph silently or to a partner to see if it is complete and well organized. Ask yourself or your partner the questions in the box.

Responding and Revising Strategies	
✔ **Respond** **Ask yourself or your partner:**	✔ **Revise** **Try these solutions:**
◆ Have I supported my opinions with facts and examples?	◆ **Add** facts and examples to your paragraph.
◆ Have I given all information in an order that makes sense?	◆ **Move** any sentences that seem out of place.
◆ Do my sentences contain only necessary words?	◆ Combine sentences with the same predicate. See the **Revising Workshop** on page 294.
◆ Does my paragraph end with a sentence that tells the audience what action to take?	◆ **Replace** your last sentence or **add** one that tells the audience what to do.

B. Make Your Changes   If the answer to any question in the box is *no*, try the solution. Use the **Editor's Marks** to show your changes.

C. Review Your Persuasive Paragraph Again
Decide whether there is anything else you want to revise. Keep revising your paragraph until you feel it is well organized and complete.

EDITOR'S MARKS

∧ Add something.
⤴ Cut something.
◯ Move something.
∧ Replace something.

Save your revised persuasive paragraph in your
***Writer's Notebook.* You will use it when you proofread your paragraph.**

Revising Workshop
Combining Sentences with the Same Predicate

Good writers make their points quickly and clearly. They don't waste time repeating words. Compare the sentences in the first example to the sentence in the second example.

1. Our streets <u>are</u> lined with trash. Our highways <u>are</u> lined with trash.
2. Our streets and highways <u>are</u> lined with trash.

In the first example, the two sentences have the same predicate. The information repeated in the second sentence adds nothing new to the reader's understanding. In the second example, the two sentences have been made into one. Notice that the two subjects are joined by *and* and that many words have been deleted. The information is the same, but it is given in fewer words.

When you combine sentences, you form a compound subject. Remember that a compound subject is usually followed by a plural verb form.

3. Our city council <u>says</u> the problem is serious.
   Our mayor <u>says</u> the problem is serious.
4. Our city council and mayor <u>say</u> the problem is serious.

Practice

Combine each pair of sentences to make one sentence. Write the new sentence.

1. Public beaches must be kept clean. Parks must be kept clean.
2. Rangers were not hired as garbage collectors.
   Park employees were not hired as garbage collectors.
3. Food wrappers belong in trash cans. Paper cups belong in trash cans.
4. Cans can go to recycling centers. Bottles can also go to recycling centers.
5. Two schools are holding a paper drive. A Scout troop is holding a paper drive.

4 Proofreading
Persuasive Paragraph

Don added some sentences to his paragraph. Then he used the **Writer's Guide** and the **Editor's Marks** to proofread it. Look at what he did.

some people can't enjoy themselves unless they are making a ~~loudest~~ louder rackit than anyone else. They turn their car radios all the way up. They bang doors. They yell like kindergardeners. I suppose it makes them feel important.

Discuss

1. Look at Don's proofread sentences. Why did he change the word *loudest?*
2. What are the reasons for the other changes?

Try Your Hand

Proofread Your Persuasive Paragraph Now use the **Writer's Guide** and the **Editor's Marks** to proofread your paragraph.

Save your corrected persuasive paragraph in your *Writer's Notebook.* You will use it when you publish your paragraph.

EDITOR'S MARKS

≡ Capitalize.

⊙ Add a period.

∧ Add something.

⋏ Add a comma.

ⱽⱽ Add quotation marks.

✄ Cut something.

⌇ Replace something.

⇄ Transpose.

◯ Spell correctly.

⊬ Indent paragraph.

╱ Make a lowercase letter.

5 Publishing
Persuasive Paragraph

Writer's Guide

Publishing Checklist

☑ Make a clean copy of your paragraph.

☑ Check to see that nothing has been left out.

☑ Check to see that there are no mistakes.

☑ Share your paragraph in a special way.

Don made a clean copy of his paragraph and checked it to be sure that he had not left out anything. Then he and his classmates made posters to publish their paragraphs. You can find Don's paragraph on page 23 of the **Writer's Handbook.**

Here's how Don and his classmates made posters to publish their paragraphs.

1. Don created a heading to go with what he wrote. He thought of one that would catch someone's eye.

2. He planned his poster on scratch paper. He drew a large rectangle where he wanted the text to go. He planned where he wanted to put the heading. He sketched a picture.

3. He took a large sheet of poster paper and copied his paragraph neatly in place. He added a heading and a drawing.

4. The students showed the posters to the class. They presented their arguments. They encouraged their classmates to respond.

5. With their teacher's permission, they displayed the completed posters in the school halls so that other students could react to them.

Discuss

1. Why is it a good idea to begin by making a rough sketch of your poster?
2. Why should you copy your text onto the poster before you begin drawing?

Try Your Hand

Publish Your Persuasive Paragraph Follow the checklist in the **Writer's Guide.** If possible, use your persuasive paragraph to create a poster, or you might try this idea for sharing it.

◆ Send your paragraphs to the school newspaper, or create a class newspaper to publish them.

Listening and Speaking
Tips on How to Give and Listen to an Oral Presentation

Another way you can publish your persuasive paragraph is by reading it aloud.

Giving an Oral Presentation

1. Practice reading what you wrote. You do not have to remember it word for word. You can jot down notes to help you when you speak.
2. Begin by showing any pictures or art you have.
3. Give your speech. Look at what you wrote if necessary.
4. Speak clearly and loudly. Make sure you sound convincing and interested in your subject.
5. Sum up what you said. Tell the audience what you want them to do or think.
6. Invite questions from the audience if there is time.

Listening to an Oral Presentation

1. Give the speaker your full attention.
2. Listen carefully to identify facts and the speaker's opinions.
3. Jot down notes about any questions you may want to ask. You may want to ask why the speaker formed certain opinions.
4. Wait politely until the speaker has finished to ask your questions or to ask for information to be repeated.
5. Decide if you agree with the speaker.

Writing in the Content Areas

Use what you learned to write something that persuades other people to take action. You could write a report, a review, a letter, or a paragraph. Use one of these ideas or an idea of your own.

Writer's Guide

When you write, remember the stages of the Writing Process.

◆ Prewriting
◆ Drafting
◆ Responding and Revising
◆ Proofreading
◆ Publishing

Social Studies

People have often had to decide what action to take. Imagine yourself in the past. Could you persuade someone to sail on the *Mayflower?* Choose an exciting time in history. Pretend you are living then. Write a letter to your friends. Persuade them to take a certain action.

Literature

Have you read a book in which the main character made a difficult decision? Did you agree with the decision? What happened as a result? What might have happened if the character had decided differently? Convince other people that what the character did was right or wrong.

Health

There are good reasons for every health and safety rule. Choose a rule you think is important. What would happen if someone put the rule into practice? What might happen if someone ignores the rule? Put together a strong argument for following the rule.

Physical Education

What is your favorite sports activity? Think of reasons why others would enjoy it too. Does it develop your skills and strength? Does it teach teamwork? Why is it fun? Write a paragraph that will persuade another person to try the activity.

CONNECTING

WRITING ↔ LANGUAGE

Good persuasive ~~wri~~ting is strong writing. It is meant to convince its reade~~rs~~ something. It encourages them to take action. Think ab~~out~~ ~~t~~hat the writer of this paragraph wants the readers to do.

We sho~~uld t~~ry to read more **often** . People who read **frec**~~uently~~ re~~c~~eive benefits that TV-watchers **seldom** ~~get~~. **First** , frequent readers **usually** are be~~tter re~~a~~d~~ers. The more they read, the more **word**~~s t~~h~~ey l~~earn and use. **Second** , frequent re~~aders~~ know more than others know. ~~Reading~~ s~~u~~ggests new ideas they might **never** ~~have had~~ ~~o~~therwise. **Finally** , frequent readers are ~~usually~~ **better** writers. Without **even** realizing it, ~~they be~~gin to use what they have read in their own ~~writing. T~~hey can write **down** ideas and express their ~~thoug~~hts more **clearly** . Therefore, the next time you ~~wan~~t to turn on the TV set, think about the value of ~~rea~~ding and pick up a book instead!

◆ **Adverbs in a Persuasive Paragraph** The highlighted words are adverbs. They add details to the author's argument for reading. Some adverbs, like *often* and *down*, give information about when and where something happened. Other adverbs, like *clearly*, tell how something happened. The writer of this paragraph used adverbs correctly so that the audience would not be confused. As you read persuasive writing, notice when and how writers use adverbs to help make their points.

◆ **Language Focus: Adverbs** In the following lessons you will learn more about using different kinds of adverbs in your own writing.

1 Adverbs

FOCUS
◆ An **adverb** is a word that describes a verb.
◆ Some adverbs tell *when* or *where*.

The words in color in these sentences are adverbs. They tell *when* or *where* an action takes place.

1. The climbers hike yearly . when

2. They are climbing down . where

Each adverb describes the action of the verb.

> **Link to Speaking and Writing**
> To vary your sentences, try moving adverbs to different places.

We will climb tom...

Guided Practice

A. Identify the adverbs. State if each tells *when* or *where* an action takes place.

1. Nine climbers recently met a big challenge.
2. Two of them had always been unable to hear.
3. The whole team climbed high.
4. Some had come far from their homes.
5. They flew out to Washington from many states.

B. Vary each sentence by moving the adverb.

6. We arrived in Washington yesterday.
7. Now we are meeting with our guides.
8. Usually most people climb in the summer.
9. The climb is always difficult.
10. Often we took pictures.

THINK AND REMEMBER

◆ Use an adverb to describe a verb.
◆ Remember that an adverb tells *when* or *where* an action happens.
◆ Vary your sentences by moving the adverbs.

Independent Practice

C. Identifying Adverbs   Write the adverb in each sentence. After it, write *when* or *where* to tell what the adverb describes.

11. I practiced daily for my trip.

MODEL ▷ daily—when

12. I went down to the gym.
13. Often, I exercised for long hours.
14. I had a terrific coach there.
15. I was going forward to meet this challenge.
16. Finally, the great day arrived.

D. Revising Sentences   Rewrite each sentence. Move the adverb to a different place.

17. First, I go to Oahu.

MODEL ▷ I go to Oahu first.

18. We will go to Hawaii next.
19. Mauna Loa sometimes erupts.
20. A fountain of lava may spew suddenly.

E. Completing Sentences   Write each sentence. Use an adverb that answers the question in parentheses ( ).

21. _____ I saw a snake.   (When?)

MODEL ▷ Today I saw a snake.

22. I came to a path and went _____.   (Where?)
23. I _____ grew tired.   (When?)
24. _____ I reached the lake.   (When?)

Application--Writing

A Letter   Imagine that you are one of the climbers in the picture. You have just returned home. You are typing a letter to tell a classmate about your climb. Describe what you did. Use at least three adverbs that tell *when* or *where*. If you need help writing a friendly letter, see pages 36–37 of the **Writer's Handbook**.

2 More Adverbs

◆ **FOCUS** Some adverbs tell *how*.

Read these sentences. The words in color are adverbs. Notice that they tell *how* something happened and end in *ly*.

1. The winds blew fiercely .

2. Solomon Carvalho carefully drew his map.

3. The others waited for him patiently .

Some adverbs that tell *how* do not end in *ly*.

draws well   works hard   moves fast

Link to Speaking and Writing

Use adverbs to make your sentences more vivid and exact. Why is the revised sentence better? What other adverb could you use?

He ˄*quickly* reached for his pen.

Guided Practice

A. Identify the adverb that describes the underlined verb.

1. Carvalho successfully <u>worked</u> as a painter.
2. He <u>listened</u> eagerly to plans for exploring the West.
3. He readily <u>joined</u> an 1853 expedition.
4. Slowly, Carvalho <u>made</u> maps of their route.
5. He faithfully <u>wrote</u> notes in his log.

B. Add an adverb to each sentence to make it vivid.

6. The snow fell.
7. They climbed through snowy mountains.
8. The travelers sat around their campfire.
9. They ate a stew of wild deer.
10. Then the climbers fell asleep.

Independent Practice

C. Identifying Verbs and Adverbs Write each sentence. Underline the adverb. Draw an arrow from the adverb to the verb it tells about.

11. John Frémont boldly explored the West.

MODEL ▷ John Frémont boldly explored the West.

12. People admiringly called him "Pathfinder."

13. He surveyed the Rockies independently in 1842.

14. Frémont and Kit Carson easily became friends.

15. Carson ably guided Frémont through the mountains.

16. Frémont planned new expeditions enthusiastically.

17. This explorer pushed steadily westward.

18. Gradually, he explored the West Coast.

19. He daringly led the Bear Flag Revolt.

D. Revising Sentences Rewrite the sentences. Add an adverb to each to make it more vivid.

20. The maps led them through the mountains.

MODEL ▷ The maps led them safely through the mountains.

21. The explorers went to the edge of the cliff.
22. They looked at the beautiful valley below.
23. Some deer were grazing in the valley.
24. An artist sketched the scene.

Application—Writing

A Journal Entry Imagine that you are Solomon Nunes Carvalho. You are keeping a journal. Write an entry that describes the day shown in the picture. Use at least three adverbs in your sentences. Underline each adverb you use. If you need help writing a journal entry, see page 26 of the **Writer's Handbook**.

3 Adverbs That Compare

◆ **FOCUS** Adverbs can be used to compare two or more actions.

Adverbs use different forms to compare actions. Some one-syllable adverbs add *er* to compare two actions and *est* to compare more than two actions.

1. The news of their escape traveled fast .

2. They hoped to travel faster than the news.

3. News of escapes traveled the fastest of all news.

The words *more* and *most* are used to make comparisons with adverbs ending in *ly*.

4. The runaway slaves slipped quietly into the night.

5. They moved more   quietly than cats.

6. Harriet Tubman moved the most   quietly of all.

Never use *er* and *more*. Do not use *est* and *most*.

7. Sue wrote more neatlier than Jan, but Dan wrote the most neatliest of all. incorrect

8. Sue wrote more neatly than Jan, but Dan wrote the most neatly of all. correct

Guided Practice

A. Tell which adverb forms belong in the blanks.

1. neatly, more neatly, ____
2. long, ____ , longest
3. slowly, more slowly, ____
4. gladly, ____ , most gladly
5. wide, ____ , widest
6. softly, ____ , most softly

THINK AND REMEMBER

◆ Remember that to make some one-syllable adverbs show comparison, add *er* or *est*.

◆ Remember that to make adverbs that end in *ly* show comparison, use *more* or *most*.

Independent Practice

B. Writing Adverb Forms   Write the adverbs. Fill in the missing adverb forms.

    7. fast, _____ , fastest

MODEL fast, faster, fastest

    8. sadly, more sadly,

       _____

    9. hard, _____ , hardest

    10. quickly, _____ ,
most quickly

    11. loudly, _____ ,
most loudly

    12. easily, more easily,

       _____

    13. high, _____ , highest

    14. shyly, more shyly,

       _____

    15. happily, _____ ,
most happily

C. Choosing Adverb Forms   Read each sentence. Write the correct form of the adverb in parentheses ( ).

    16. He walked the (faster, fastest) of all.

MODEL fastest

    17. No one loved freedom (deeply, more deeply) than a slave.

    18. Slaves spoke (longingly, more longingly) of life in a free state.

    19. The stories they learned the (quickly, most quickly) of all were about life in the North.

    20. Some worked (harder, hardest) than ever to buy their freedom.

    21. Others (boldly, more boldly) planned to escape.

    22. Slaves caught escaping were punished the (harshly, most harshly) of all.

    23. They traveled (fast, faster) by night than by day.

    24. Their spirits sank the (lower, lowest) when they got lost.

    25. Their hearts beat (more joyfully, most joyfully) than ever when they reached freedom.

Application—Writing and Speaking

A Story   Write a short dramatic story about the picture. Try to make your audience feel the excitement and the danger in the air. Use at least three adverbs that compare. Plan to read your story to your classmates.

4 Negatives

◆ **FOCUS**   A word that means "no" is called a **negative.**

The adverb *not* and contractions made with *not* are negatives.

1. The gorillas were   not   mean creatures.
2. Mary Jobe Akeley   wasn't   afraid of them.

Other common words are also negatives.

3.   Nobody   helped her.
4. There is   nothing   to say.
5. There is   nowhere   to work.
6. They have   no   enemies.
7. There are   none   here.
8. She   never   showed fear.

Do not use two negatives in the same sentence.

9. She hadn't no experience in Africa.   incorrect
10. She   hadn't   any experience in Africa.   correct
11. She had   no   experience in Africa.   correct

Guided Practice

A. Identify the negative in each sentence.

1. Long ago, nobody encouraged young women to explore.
2. None of Mary Jobe's friends were adventurous.
3. However, Jobe did not want to sit at home.
4. She had never seen much of the world.
5. She decided she would go nowhere unless it was interesting.

THINK AND REMEMBER
◆ Remember that a **negative** means "no" or "not."
◆ Do not use two negatives in the same sentence.

Independent Practice

B. Identifying Negatives   Write the negatives in these sentences.

6. In no time at all, Jobe and Akeley married.

MODEL > no

7. Nobody had studied gorillas in the Congo before.
8. There was nowhere that the gorillas were protected.
9. Akeley had not been there long before he died.
10. His wife would never give up on their dream.
11. Now, she did nothing but fight for wildlife.

C. Choosing Forms Correctly   Read the sentence. Write the word in parentheses ( ) that makes it correct.

12. In Africa no one (ever, never) protected wildlife.

MODEL > ever

13. People (had, hadn't) no idea species were dying.
14. Hunters didn't take (nothing, anything) but tusks.
15. The elephant meat (wasn't, was) of no value.
16. These hunters (would, wouldn't) never change.
17. Some African governments (wouldn't, would) allow no more wasteful killing.

D. Revising Sentences   Each sentence contains two negatives. Cut or replace at least one of the negatives in each sentence. Write the corrected sentence.

18. Pandas aren't safe nowhere.

MODEL > Pandas are safe nowhere. *or* Pandas aren't safe anywhere.

19. Pandas didn't have nothing to protect them.
20. No one knew nothing about them.
21. Their homes were not never preserved.
22. The Chinese government doesn't let nobody kill them.

Application—Writing

A News Story   Imagine that you are a newspaper reporter. You have just spent several days with Mary Jobe Akeley. Describe to your readers what you and she did. Tell what she is like. Use the picture and your imagination to make up details. Use at least three negatives in your news story.

5 Adverb or Adjective?

FOCUS
◆ An **adverb** describes a verb.
◆ An **adjective** describes a noun or a pronoun.

Read these sentences. The arrow shows which word the word in color describes.

1. Panning gold is hard work. adjective
2. I have worked hard here. adverb
3. I am not lucky in the gold fields. adjective
4. I luckily found a place to live. adverb

Remember to use adverbs to describe verbs. Use adjectives to describe nouns and pronouns.

Link to Speaking and Writing
You can figure out whether to use *good* or *well* if you remember that *good* is an adjective and *well* is an adverb.

He writes good *letters. He writes* well*.*

Guided Practice

A. Identify the underlined word as an *adverb* or an *adjective.*

1. low hills
2. sang cheerfully
3. noisy street
4. moved quickly
5. plays badly
6. silly joke
7. hard task
8. suddenly heard

B. Use *good* or *well* to complete each sentence.

9. I brought my _____ pan with me.
10. I hope it works _____.
11. Water in the stream was running _____.
12. _____ gold fields are not easy to find.
13. I write _____ letters about my work in the gold fields.

Independent Practice

C. Identifying Adverbs and Adjectives   Write each underlined word. Then, write *adverb* or *adjective*.

14. went <u>well</u>

MODEL ▷ well—adverb

15. go <u>far</u>

16. <u>sudden</u> storm

17. <u>carefully</u> dug

18. shouted <u>loudly</u>

19. <u>lucky</u> spot

20. <u>good</u> news

D. Choosing the Correct Form   Read these sentences. Write the word in parentheses ( ) that is correct.

21. In 1848, gold was (accidental, accidentally) found.

MODEL ▷ accidentally

22. Californians (excited, excitedly) spread the news.

23. By 1849, a (wild, wildly) gold rush was on.

24. People streamed (eager, eagerly) into the state.

25. Some came from the East in (swift, swiftly) ships.

E. Using *Good* and *Well*   Read each sentence. Write *good* or *well* to complete it.

26. With gold I could live a _____ life.

MODEL ▷ good

27. The box we built sifts out the gold _____ .

28. I got a _____ deal when I sold my nuggets in town.

29. Mr. Tracy pays _____ for pure gold.

30. I really need a _____ night's sleep.

Application—Writing

A Letter   Imagine that you are at the mining camp in the picture. Write a letter to your family. Describe your life in camp. Use adjectives and adverbs to make your writing come alive. Underline each adjective once. Underline each adverb twice. If you need help writing a letter, see the **Writer's Handbook.**

Building Vocabulary
Homographs

bow¹ [bou] To bend the head or
body in greeting and
respect.
bow² [bō] **1.** A weapon for
shooting arrows.
2. Something curved.
bow³ [bou] The forward part of
a ship.

Have you seen dictionary entries
like the ones above? There are
three entries for the word *bow*. The
numbers after the words show that
these are separate entry words. Each
has a meaning quite different from
the other meanings. Words with the
same spelling but different meanings
are called **homographs.** Notice that
the homograph *bow* is used differently
in each of these sentences.

1. The messenger must *bow* to the
king.   definition 1
2. The hunter picked up his
sturdy *bow*.   definition 2
3. The girl stood at the *bow* of the
ship.   definition 3

Notice that *bow* in sentence 2 is
not pronounced like *bow* in sentences
1 and 3. Some homographs have
different pronunciations. Always
check the pronunciations when you
look up homographs in the dictionary.

Reading Practice

Read the sentences. Then write the meaning of each underlined homograph. Use a dictionary if necessary.

1. They can <u>page</u> your parents over the loudspeaker.
2. <u>Line</u> the drawers with this pretty paper.
3. Eric swam a <u>lap</u> across the pool.
4. The tipi was made of buffalo <u>hide</u>.
5. The wheat was <u>ground</u> in a mill.

Writing Practice

Use one homograph from the box to complete each sentence. Write the sentence.

left	light	long	rest	last

6. The crew began to _____ to see land after their _____ sea voyage.
7. When the sky grew _____, a _____ rain began to fall.
8. The rain cannot _____ as long as _____ week's rain.
9. They _____ their boat on the beach and turned _____ along the shore.
10. The _____ of the tired crew stayed on the ship to _____.

Project

Below is a list of homographs that have different pronunciations. Choose five from the list. Find one definition for each pronunciation. Then write a sentence for each definition. Share your sentences with your classmates. Challenge them to define the homographs.

close	does	live	recount	tear
content	dove	minute	sewer	wind
desert	lead	present	sow	wound

A snake can slough off its old skin.
We waded into the slough to study the frogs.

Language Enrichment
Adverbs

Use what you know about adverbs to do these activities.

 Funny Punny Sayings

The students in the picture have made up puns. The pun lies in the adverb at the end of each sentence. The adverb describes how someone said something. It is a pun because it also refers to what the speaker said: the lemonade was bitter, and the draft was cool.

Try writing a pun like these. You may use any adverb that makes sense.

Put your puns on a bulletin board. Read them when you need a laugh.

 Can You See It?

Radio announcers make events come alive. Imagine that you are a radio announcer. Describe a sports event, a dance contest, a parade, or a big fire. Make the event seem vivid to your listeners. Use adverbs to tell how, when, and where the action takes place.

Present your broadcast for your classmates. Have your audience discuss whether they could picture the action.

Words Without Words

When you **pantomime,** you show an action without using words. List adverbs that you can pantomime. Then take turns with your classmates and pantomime adverbs. Have them guess the adverb you have chosen.

Girl: "The lemonade is too sour," said the child bitterly.

Boy: "You're letting a draft into the room," said the teacher coolly.

CONNECTING
LANGUAGE ⬌ WRITING

In this unit you learned that adverbs tell when, where, and how the action of verbs takes place. Special forms of adverbs can be used to compare two actions.

◆ **Using Adverbs in Your Writing** It is important to be able to use adverbs correctly. Adverbs that tell how something happens show the reader vivid action. Pay special attention to adverbs as you complete these activities.

The Same But Not the Same!

You learned about homographs on the **Building Vocabulary** page. Here's a challenging activity that calls for you to use homographs.

Study the pairs of words in the chart. The adverb in each pair is made from a homograph of the second word. The word in parentheses ( ) tells you what part of speech each word is. Choose three pairs of words from the list. For each pair, create a sentence using both words correctly. Pay attention to the words in parentheses ( ).

How Do They Do It?

Think about the actions of each person in the pictures. Think of an exact adverb that tells about each action. Then write a sentence about each picture using the adverb.

> fairly (adverb), fair (noun)
> fleetly (adverb), fleet (noun)
> kindly (adverb), kind (noun)
> lightly (adverb), light (noun)
> presently (adverb), present (noun)
> sagely (adverb), sage (noun)

Unit Checkup

Think Back	Think Ahead
◆ What did you learn about persuasive paragraphs in this unit? What did you do to write one?	◆ How will what you learned about persuasive paragraphs help you when you try to convince someone of something? ◆ How will classifying fact and opinion help you when you listen to news programs?
◆ Look at the writing you did in this unit. How did adverbs help you express your ideas?	◆ What is one way that you can use adverbs to improve your writing?

Analyzing a Persuasive Paragraph   *pages 284–285*

Read this paragraph. Then answer the questions.

> Country living is much better than city living. Country air is healthier for you. In the country there is no city smog to make your eyes tear. Country life is more natural than city life. Bright city lights do not hide the evening stars. Country life is quieter, too. Noisy neighbors do not bother you, because country neighbors are few and often live at a distance. If you try country life, the fresh air, natural surroundings, and peaceful living will make you want to stay forever.

1. What is the writer trying to persuade you to do?
2. What facts does the writer give to support his or her opinion?
3. Write the example that the writer gives for each fact.
4. In what part of the paragraph does the writer try to get you to do something?
5. Did the writer change your mind about country and city living? Why or why not?

Classifying Fact and Opinion   *page 286*

Write *fact* if the statement is a fact and *opinion* if it is an opinion.

6. Alexander the Great conquered many lands.
7. Greeks were better looking than Romans.
8. Alexander dealt kindly with the countries he conquered.
9. He was a truly great commander.
10. Alexander was young when he died.

Using Examples   *page 287*

Give an example to support each of the following statements.

11. Animals are smarter than you think.
12. December is the busiest time of the year.
13. A firefighter's job is dangerous.
14. Exercising is the best way to stay healthy.

The Writing Process   *pages 288–297*

Write the letter of the correct response to each question.

15. What do you want your persuasive paragraph to make your audience do?
    a. do what you recommend
    b. read some more on the subject
    c. write a paragraph of their own
16. When you state facts about your topic, what else should you include?
    a. your opinions about the topic
    b. facts about another topic
    c. examples to support the facts you stated
17. What should you do with unnecessary words in your paragraph?
    a. brainstorm some more
    b. think of shorter words to replace them
    c. cut them
18. Sharing your paragraph is a part of
    a. publishing.
    b. revising.
    c. proofreading.

Adverbs   *pages 300–301*

Write the adverb in each sentence. After it, write *when* or *where*.

19. Shepherds once needed helpers on the hillsides.

20. They trained wild dogs there.
21. Then they taught the dogs to return stray sheep.
22. The dogs herded the sheep nearer the camp.
23. People eventually called the dogs shepherds, too.

More Adverbs   *pages 302–303*

Write each sentence. Underline the adverb. Draw an arrow from the adverb to the verb it tells about.

24. Susan B. Anthony worked hard for women's rights.

25. Her family faithfully supported her work.

26. She continuously helped the woman suffrage movement.

27. She bravely organized women who wanted the right to vote.

28. She eagerly became a leader of the reform movement.

Adverbs That Compare   *pages 304–305*

Read each sentence. Write the correct form of the adverb in parentheses ( ).

29. On this rocky coastline, the rocks in this area jut out the (more dangerously, most dangerously).
30. The lighthouse light needed to shine (more brightly, most brightly) than the stars.
31. Of all her brothers and sisters, Abby tended the lighthouse (more cheerfully, most cheerfully).
32. Abby almost worked (harder, hardest) than her father to keep the light glowing.
33. One night a storm raged (more terribly, most terribly) than any other storm that Abby could remember.

Negatives   *pages 306–307*

Write the negatives in these sentences.

34. America has never fought a more bitter war than the War Between the States.
35. The war didn't start suddenly.
36. The South and the North were not alike.
37. Nobody could solve the differences between them.
38. Southerners and northerners couldn't understand each other.
39. They thought that nothing but separation would work.

40. No one loved the United States more than Lincoln.
41. He knew that the nation should not be split.
42. No President had ever faced such a dark time.
43. However, Lincoln didn't give up.
44. He let nothing stop him from ending the war.
45. Finally, the people weren't fighting any more.
46. However, one man wasn't glad.
47. He didn't want Lincoln to live.
48. Lincoln couldn't recover from that man's gunshot.
49. Lincoln never saw the nation become one again.

Adverb or Adjective?   *pages 308–309*
Read these sentences. Write the word in parentheses ( ) that is correct.

50. The Pilgrims wanted to worship the way they (honest, honestly) thought they should.
51. They couldn't (easy, easily) do this in England.
52. They sailed (hopeful, hopefully) to Holland.
53. From there they (eager, eagerly) sailed to America.
54. The (stormy, stormily) voyage was very difficult.
55. The (dreadful, dreadfully) winter was hard too.
56. Then the (peaceful, peacefully) Indians befriended them.
57. They (gracious, graciously) taught the Pilgrims farming methods.
58. The next fall the Pilgrims gathered a (bountiful, bountifully) harvest.
59. They (joyful, joyfully) held their Thanksgiving.
60. They (earnest, earnestly) thanked their God for his care.

Homographs   *pages 310–311*
Read the sentences. Then write the meaning of the underlined homographs. Use a dictionary if you need help.

61. The Wright brothers made a glider that was <u>light</u> enough to stay aloft.
62. Did they close their bicycle <u>firm</u> to work on the airplane?
63. Who found that penicillin could be made from <u>mold</u>?
64. The American soldiers took up <u>arms</u> against Britain.
65. With <u>grave</u> faces they aimed their guns.

1-7 Cumulative Review

Declarative, Interrogative, Imperative, and Exclamatory Sentences   *pages 32–35*

Write each sentence so that it begins and ends correctly.

1. the first American in space was Alan Shepard

2. how did he learn about rockets

3. hey, hurry up and light this candle

4. he meant that he wanted the rocket to blast off

5. what a sight that blast-off was

6. did the rocket capsule splash in the ocean

7. a helicopter hoisted up Commander Shepard

8. please lift the capsule a little higher

9. boy, that was some ride

Common and Proper Nouns   *pages 78–79*

Write each underlined noun. Then write *common* or *proper* after it.

10. Who was the first American to walk in space?
11. Mission Control in Houston set the lift-off day for Monday.
12. The rocket was called the *Gemini IV*.
13. Edward White connected an oxygen tube to his suit.
14. The astronaut floated into space and saw Earth.
15. He could even see the coast of California.
16. Then, the men landed in the ocean.
17. The landing was a success!

Singular and Plural Possessive Nouns   *pages 86–89*

Write each sentence. Replace the underlined words with the possessive form.

18. The hope of all astronauts was a space walk on the moon.
19. To be the first astronaut to go to the moon was the privilege of Neil Armstrong
20. Would the dust of the moon be too thick?
21. Scientists thought the legs of Neil Armstrong wouldn't be able to get through it.

22. However, the <u>fears of the scientists</u> were unfounded.
23. The <u>pull of gravity</u> there is less than on Earth.
24. The <u>weight of the astronauts</u> seemed less.
25. Armstrong put <u>the flag of America</u> on the moon.
26. People gave the astronauts a <u>welcome of heroes</u>.

Action and Linking Verbs   *pages 126–129*

Write *action verb* if the underlined word is an action verb. Write *linking verb* if it is a linking verb.

27. Annie Sullivan <u>was</u> almost completely blind.
28. She <u>went</u> to a place for poor people in Tewksbury.
29. Her little brother soon <u>died</u> there.
30. "Now I <u>am</u> all alone," Annie said.
31. Annie <u>loved</u> to listen to other people read books.
32. "Someday I <u>will be</u> a good reader myself."
33. One day Annie <u>heard</u> about a special school.
34. Blind people <u>learned</u> to read there.
35. "Perkins School <u>is</u> the place I will go."

Agreement of Subjects and Verbs   *pages 168–169*

Write *correct* if the underlined verb agrees with the subject. Write *not correct* if it does not.

36. Annie <u>discovers</u> a special surprise.
37. Some people <u>are</u> happy to pay her way to Perkins.
38. She <u>are</u> fifteen when she gets to Perkins.
39. She <u>has</u> to go into the first grade.
40. "Nothing else <u>matter</u> if I can learn to read."
41. Braille <u>is</u> the alphabet for blind people.
42. Annie <u>is</u> eager to study it.
43. She <u>sit</u> for hours reading Bible stories.
44. Then, some doctors <u>operates</u> on her.
45. They <u>help</u> her to see!
46. Now Annie <u>want</u> to help other blind people.

Irregular Verbs   *pages 170–171*

Write the correct past-tense form of the verb in parentheses ( ).

47. Annie (go) to meet a girl who was blind and deaf.
48. "I'll teach her the finger alphabet," she (say).

49. She (become) Helen Keller's teacher.

50. Helen (take) the doll Annie offered.

51. Annie (write) *d-o-l-l* in Helen's hand.

52. Annie (see) that Helen didn't understand.

53. Then one day Annie (give) Helen some water.

54. She (make) the sign for water over and over.

55. Suddenly she (know) that Helen understood her.

56. Annie had (begin) to teach Helen about her world.

Pronouns   *pages 212–213*

Find the pronoun or pronouns in the second sentence of each pair. Write each pronoun and the noun or nouns it replaces.

57. James Watt studied the steam from his mother's kettle. It could lift the kettle's lid.

58. James knew that steam must be powerful. "I will make that steam do something more useful."

59. James worked and experimented. Finally, he invented the steam engine.

60. Other people created the locomotive. "We will use it to carry things across the country."

61. Now steam engines are used all over the world. They provide the power for complex machinery.

Subject and Object Pronouns   *pages 214–217*

Replace the underlined words with pronouns. Write the new sentences.

62. Thomas Edison was a famous inventor.

63. Schoolwork was hard for Thomas.

64. His mother wondered about him.

65. She said, "Thomas, can't Thomas do better?"

66. Thomas looked at his mother.

67. He said, "Thomas can't concentrate."

68. The electric light bulb was one of his inventions.

69. The record player and talking pictures were also his inventions.

70. Over the years, he discovered many other uses for electricity.

Agreement of Subject Pronouns with Verbs   *pages 220–221*

Write the verb in parentheses ( ) that completes
each sentence correctly.

71. Did you (sees, see) those men?
72. They (is, are) Wilbur and Orville Wright.
73. "I (wants, want) to fly like a bird," Wilbur says.
74. They (builds, build) gliders.
75. "Now, we (creates, create) a real airplane."
76. It (has, have) a motor.
77. Finally, it (is, are) ready to try.
78. "You (cranks, crank) the motor."
79. He (climbs, climb) into the cockpit.
80. It actually (flies, fly)!

Possessive Pronouns   *pages 222–223*

Rewrite each sentence. Replace the underlined words with one
possessive pronoun.

81. Your and my land out west was once wilderness.
82. Americans called it the Americans' frontier.
83. The East Coast's towns were too full.
84. A man wanted to leave the man's crowded town.
85. He said, "I'll find land to call the man's own."
86. His wife packed his wife's important belongings.
87. The children took the children's clothes.
88. Their mother said to them, "Take the children's socks!"
89. The people brought the people's things to the wagon train.
90. The wagon's wheels creaked under the load.

Adjectives   *pages 258–259*

Write the adjective that describes each underlined noun.

91. Many large wagons traveled together for safety.
92. They formed a close circle at night.
93. The colorful wagons were used by early pioneers.
94. The wagons were usually drawn by strong teams of oxen or horses.
95. The pioneers kept a bright fire burning.
96. They feared dangerous animals.
97. They could be a fearsome threat.

98. They roamed the beautiful <u>land</u>.
99. Some tribes of American Indians lived on the open <u>plains</u>.
100. They hunted wild <u>buffalo</u>.
101. They used the fur for warm <u>clothes</u>.

Adjectives That Follow Linking Verbs   *pages 262–263*

Write each sentence. Underline the adjective that follows the linking verb. Then draw an arrow to the noun or the pronoun it describes.

102. Winters on the frontier were difficult.

103. The snow was deep in some places.

104. Supplies were scarce in the winter.

105. Sometimes a family was stuck at home for weeks.

106. Wild animals were fearsome, too.

107. Sometimes a wild animal was very hungry.

108. One was very thin.

109. The pioneers were strong.

110. They were eager for freedom in the wilderness.

Adverbs   *pages 300–303*

Write each sentence. Underline the adverbs. Draw an arrow from each adverb to the verb it tells about.

111. Young squires earnestly wanted knighthood.

112. A new knight usually went out on a quest.

113. This way he obviously proved his bravery.

114. He looked tirelessly for a brave deed.

115. He tried hard for recognition.

116. These knights' deeds eventually became legends.

117. Did the knights really kill monsters and giants?

118. It certainly seemed like it from the stories.

119. These "bards" told their stories well.

120. They told the story of Beowulf artfully.

Adverbs That Compare *pages 304–305*

Read each sentence. Write the correct form of the adverb in parentheses ( ).

121. Beowulf fought the (more bravely, most bravely) of all the warriors in the world.
122. Grendel attacked Beowulf (more fiercely, most fiercely) than he had ever been attacked before.
123. Beowulf attacked (more powerfully, most powerfully) than Grendel.
124. He hurt Grendel (more seriously, most seriously) than anyone had ever hurt him before.
125. When Grendel died, the warriors celebrated the (more happily, most happily) that they ever had.

Adverb or Adjective? *pages 308–309*

Read these sentences. Write the word in parentheses ( ) that is correct.

126. A long time ago, a king (desperate, desperately) asked for help.
127. Many knights (eager, eagerly) rode on horseback to Asia.
128. Their adventures (eventual, eventually) were called the Crusades.
129. Some of them (real, really) wanted to help.
130. Many (wild, wildly) crusaders did harm.
131. They killed many (innocent, innocently) people.
132. They brought back (odd, oddly) gifts that nobody had ever seen.
133. The new goods stirred up (great, greatly) interest in eastern trade.
134. The crusaders described the journey as a (real, really) quest.

UNIT

8

Giving Information

◆ **COMPOSITION FOCUS:** **Research Report**
◆ **LANGUAGE FOCUS:** **More Sentences**

Ancient astronomers figured out that the planets move around the sun. However, their discoveries were forgotten. For centuries most Europeans believed that the sun circled the earth. Then some new scientists found the records of the early astronomers. They added their own ideas. They published the reports. Slowly the truth came to light again.

People often write reports for the purpose of sharing knowledge. Some write descriptions of their own work and studies. They make new ideas known to the world. Other people write reports that describe the work or discoveries of others. They want to spread information to readers who might not otherwise see it.

Gerry Bishop is one writer who researches other people's work. He then writes articles for readers who may not read scientific books and magazines. In this way he helps get the information to a wide audience. In this unit you will learn about how to write a research report.

Gerry Bishop writes *to inform* the public about the natural world.

Reading with a Writer's Eye
Research Report

Most people don't even know sea slugs exist, let alone know anything about them. For this reason, just about any information in a report about sea slugs is bound to be new and entertaining. As you read this report, notice the types of facts that the writer felt would interest readers.

from Show-offs of the Sea

by Gerry Bishop

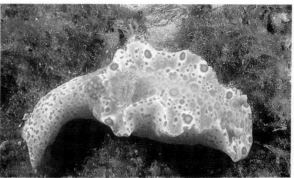

When you hear the word *slug,* what do you think of? A slimy brown blob creeping across a sidewalk? If so, then the world of sea slugs will come as a big surprise.

Slugs Here, There, Everywhere

There are over 4,000 species, or kinds, of sea slugs. They live in saltwater all over the world—from freezing polar seas to tropical coral reefs. Some sea slugs are not much bigger than a grain of sand. Others grow to the size of a football.

Sea slugs come in two basic "body styles." Some have fleshy bumps or long "fingers" all over their back. The other kind of sea slug has a circle of gills near its back end. Either kind of sea slug is sure to dazzle you with wild shapes and colors. No wonder sea slugs have been called the "butterflies of the sea."

Slugs on the Go

Some sea slugs move around by floating in the open sea and drifting with ocean currents. Others can wave the frilly sides of their body and glide through the water. But most sea slugs spend their lives creeping and crawling on the sea floor.

On the underside of a slug is a big, flat muscle called a foot. This muscle moves in tiny ripples from front to back. And as it moves, it pushes, pushes, pushes the slug slowly along.

Hiders and Stingers

When danger comes near, most sea slugs can't dash away to safety. (Only a few can swim fast.) They can't defend themselves with sharp claws or teeth. (They don't have any.) And they can't duck into a hard, safe shell, as their snail cousins can. But no problem. Sea slugs have great ways to keep from becoming someone else's dinner.

Many sea slugs just keep out of sight. They hide in the shelter of rocks or in crevices in coral reefs. They find enough food there and almost never have to come out in the open. Other sea slugs hide by copying the colors and shapes of their surroundings. The sargassum sea slug, for example, lives among sargassum plants in the Atlantic Ocean. Its color and shape match the plants almost perfectly.

Other sea slugs keep enemies away with what you could call the "yuk effect." Whenever these slugs sense danger, glands in their skin give off strong acids, stinky smells, or clouds of ink.

But some sea slugs use the trickiest defense of all. They steal their prey's weapons and use them as their own! One such trickster is the sea slug called *Glaucus*. This inch-long slug floats on the surface of the sea, nibbling on the tentacles of jellyfish. On the tentacles are stinging cells that the jellyfish use to stun their prey or to keep away most enemies.

As *Glaucus* eats, it swallows the stinging cells. (For some reason, the cells do the slug no harm.) The stingers pass through the slug's stomach and into the long "fingers" that cover its body. The stingers then move to just beneath the surface of the slug's skin and take up "battle stations." When a fish or sea bird comes along, it may try to eat the slug. But if it does, it will spit the slug out and end up with nothing but a burning, stinging mouth.

Other sea slugs gather their stingers by eating the tentacles of sea anemones. Slugs that eat stingers often have extra-bright colors that seem to say to enemies, "If you're smart, you'll stay away!" To these slugs, showing off is a way to survive.

Respond

1. Which of the writer's facts surprises or interests you the most? Explain why.

Discuss

2. What types of facts does the writer think that his readers would want to know? Is there any other type of information you feel he should have included?

3. How can you tell that the writer is writing for the general public rather than for scientists?

Thinking As a Writer
Analyzing a Research Report

A research report gives facts about something or someone. The writer has learned these facts by studying books and other materials or by talking to experts.

In a research report the writer often makes general statements about the topic. A **general statement** sums up what is usually true and does not give any details. Read the beginning of the report again.

---

from **Show-offs of the Sea**
by Gerry Bishop

When you hear the word *slug,* what do you think of? A slimy brown blob creeping across a sidewalk? If so, then the world of sea slugs will come as a big surprise.

There are over 4,000 species, or kinds, of sea slugs. They live in saltwater all over the world — from freezing polar seas to tropical coral reefs. Some sea slugs are not much bigger than a grain of sand. Others grow to the size of a football.

Sea slugs come in two basic "body styles." Some have fleshy bumps or long "fingers" all over their back. The other kind of sea slug has a circle of gills near its back end.

The **title** catches your eye.

The **opening paragraph** introduces the topic, gets your attention, and makes you want to continue reading.

The **topic sentence** of each paragraph in a research report makes a general statement about the topic. It also tells what the paragraph is about.

Detail sentences in each paragraph support the topic sentence. They contain facts that the writer learned by doing research.

Discuss

1. What does the writer do in the first paragraph to make you want to continue reading?
2. Look at the general statements made in the topic sentences of the second and third paragraphs. What facts does the writer give to support each of these statements?
3. The writer might have titled the report "Sea Slugs." Would that have been a better title? Explain your opinion.

Try Your Hand

A. Identify Detail Sentences   The following sentence is a general statement. Write each numbered sentence that supports the statement.

◆ Sea elephants are unusual creatures.
   1. The males have long trunks before their mouths.
   2. Once a year they turn bright pink when they molt.
   3. They mostly eat fish and some sea birds.
   4. They are found only in cold seas.

B. Sort Information   Write these headings.

Nesting Habits of Barn Owls   **Eating Habits of Barn Owls**

Write each sentence under the correct heading.
◆ They can eat all night long if there is enough food.
◆ They build nests in any place that gives shelter.
◆ Some have been found living in prairie dog burrows.
◆ Sometimes an owl will eat its own weight in food.
◆ They usually eat mice and gophers.
◆ They sometimes make nests of trash.

C. Write Topic Sentences   Study the two lists of sentences you just made. Imagine that you plan to use the groups to write two paragraphs about barn owls. Write a topic sentence for each group.

D. Read a Research Report   Reread the report on pages 326–328, or find another short report. Read it aloud to a partner. Identify the general statements and the details that support each one.

Writer's Notebook

Collecting Science Words   Did you understand the science words *gills* and *sargassum* in the article on sea slugs? Reread the article on pages 326–328. Record in your *Writer's Notebook* any sentences that have science words you don't know. Look up the words in a dictionary, and record their meanings. Do this with any new science words you find while doing your research. Try to use these new words when you speak and when you write your own reports.

Thinking As a Writer

Classifying Information into Categories

Writer's Guide

In a research report, good writers

- ◆ limit a topic to one category.
- ◆ group details into smaller categories.

A **category** is a common class or a group of items that have something in common. One of a writer's most valuable thinking skills is the ability to put things into categories. A writer might use this skill to find a topic to write about.

The topic "Dogs" is too broad. A good writer divides that large topic into categories and chooses one of them as a topic.

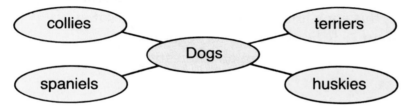

While researching a topic, a writer finds many facts about it. The writer then groups facts that are related into categories. This is one way that writers organize their facts.

Collies		
Habits	Appearance	Personality

Discuss

1. Look at the diagram. What are some other ways in which you might divide this topic into categories?
2. Look at the chart. How can sorting details into categories like these help you organize a report?

Try Your Hand

Identify Categories   Use the article on pages 326–328, or find another report. Identify the categories that the writer used to group information. Show them in a chart.

Developing the Writer's Craft
Capturing the Reader's Interest

Writers want to attract the reader's attention in the opening lines of their text. Compare these two openings.

1. The humpback whale makes a sound like singing.
2. Is that a mermaid's haunting song that sounds through the seas?

The first opening is weak because it tells almost everything the reader could want to know. The second opening is strong because it creates a mystery. It tempts the reader to find out more about this song and the creature that makes it.

The ending of a report is as important as its beginning. A good ending sums up what was written in an interesting way or refers to a main idea.

3. That's all I know about humpback whales. poor
4. Perhaps someday scientists will solve the riddle of its song. good

When you write your research report, try to capture and hold the reader's interest. Create a good opening and closing to make the report interesting.

Discuss

1. Look back at "Show-offs of the Sea" on pages 326–328. Are the opening and the closing good or poor? Explain your answer.
2. Would you begin a report with the sentence "Skunks are really interesting animals"? Explain.

Try Your Hand

Write an Opening and a Closing   Suppose you are writing a report about an unusual animal. Write an opening and a closing that you might use in your report. Then read to a partner what you have written and ask for comments.

1 Prewriting
Research Report

Mariko and her classmates at Martin Luther King Elementary School decided to put together a reference book about animals. They planned to share copies of the book with their families and friends. Mariko used the checklist in the **Writer's Guide** to help her plan her report. Look at what she did.

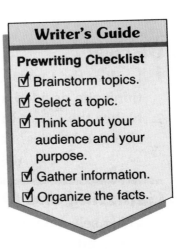

Writer's Guide

Prewriting Checklist
- ☑ Brainstorm topics.
- ☑ Select a topic.
- ☑ Think about your audience and your purpose.
- ☑ Gather information.
- ☑ Organize the facts.

◆ Brainstorming and Selecting a Topic

First, Mariko brainstormed a list of possible topics for her report. She listed animals that interested her.

When Mariko looked at her list, she realized that some topics were too broad. She crossed out the ones that could not be covered unless they were divided into smaller categories. She also crossed out topics that she thought most people already knew about.

> fish
> mud turtles
> ~~octopuses~~ (circled)
> ~~jungle animals~~
> ~~pet cats~~
> bats
> mice

Finally, she looked at the topics that were left. She decided to write about octopuses because her uncle had videotaped a fascinating television show about them. She knew that the show would be a useful source of information. She also knew she could find information in the encyclopedia. Mariko saved her list because some of her other ideas were also good. She knew that she could use one of them if her first idea did not work.

Discuss

1. Look at the topics Mariko crossed off her list. Why do you think she decided against each one?
2. Notice the topics that were not crossed off or circled. Are they also good topics? Explain your answer.

◆ Gathering and Organizing Information

After selecting their topics, Mariko and her classmates gathered information for their reports. At the library, some checked encyclopedias, and others found videotapes, wildlife magazines, and books. The students wrote the information they gathered on note cards. Look at two of Mariko's note cards.

Octopuses
What does an octopus look like?
   eight tentacles
   hard beak for breaking shells
   shiny eyes that see well
   usually small as hand
Videotape — Underwater Wonders

Octopuses
How does an octopus defend itself?
   squirts water to propel it
   hides in tiny cracks
   squirts "ink" to create fake octopus
   squirts "ink" to make dark cloud

First, Mariko wrote each question she wanted answered in her report on a note card. Then, she wrote the most important facts she found, in her own words. Finally, she wrote the source of her information.

After Mariko had gathered the information she needed, she was ready to organize her notes. She knew that each paragraph of her report should contain related facts. She sorted her note cards and put them into categories. Then she made an outline, using the information on the grouped cards.

I. Introduction
II. What an octopus looks like
    A. Eight tentacles
    B. Hard beak for breaking open shellfish
    C. Shiny eyes that see well
    D. Usually small as hand, longest 28 ft.
III. How an octopus defends itself
    A. Squirts out water to propel itself
    B. Hides in tiny cracks in rocks
    C. Squirts mucus and "ink" to create fake octopus
    D. Squirts just "ink" to make dark cloud

The outline shows how Mariko sorted her facts into categories. Notice that each part of the outline has a heading that sums up its main idea. Each heading is followed by details.

Discuss

1. Under which heading should Mariko note that an octopus has a soft, boneless body?
2. Why do you think Mariko wrote on the note card where she found her information?
3. How can Mariko use her outline to write paragraphs?

Try Your Hand

Now plan a research report of your own.

A. **Brainstorm and Select a Topic**   Brainstorm a list of possible topics. List each animal that interests you. Think about each topic and about your audience.

 ◆ Cross out topics that are too broad to write about.
 ◆ Cross out topics that you think your audience may already know about.
 ◆ Circle the most interesting topic left on your list. This will be the topic of your research report.

B. **Gather and Organize Information**   When you are satisfied with your topic, gather and list the information you might use in your research report.

 ◆ Use note cards to write the questions you want to answer in your report. Then list the facts that answer the questions on each card.
 ◆ Write the title and author of each book or magazine, or the title of any videotape you used for information.
 ◆ Think about your audience. Include information that will be new and interesting to them.
 ◆ Think about how you will put the details into categories. Also, consider how you will order the groups of information. Make an outline like Mariko's to help you organize them.

 Save your outline in your *Writer's Notebook.* You will use it when you draft your research report.

WRITING PROCESS

2 Drafting
Research Report

Mariko thought about how she could make octopuses sound interesting to her audience. Then, she used her outline and followed the **Writer's Guide** to draft her research report. Look at how she began.

> The Scary and Shy Octopus
> Have you ever seen a giant octopus? Its snaky arms would come out of the sea to crush a tiny boat. No wonder most people think of an octopus as a fierce creature. Nothing could be less true.

Discuss

What does Mariko do to capture your interest and make you want to know more?

Try Your Hand

Now you are ready to write a research report.

A. Review Your Information Think about the information you gathered and organized in the last lesson. Check your outline to be sure it is complete. If you need more details, look them up now.

B. Think About Your TAP Remember that your task is to write a research report. Your purpose is to inform your audience about the topic you have selected.

C. Write Your First Draft Follow the **Writer's Guide** to write your research report.

   When you write your draft, just put all your ideas on paper. Do not worry about spelling, punctuation, or grammar. You can correct the draft later.

Task: What?
Audience: Who?
Purpose: Why?

Save your first draft in your *Writer's Notebook*. You will use it when you revise your research report.

3 Responding and Revising
Research Report

Mariko used the checklist in the **Writer's Guide** to revise her research report. Look at what she did.

◆ Checking Information

Mariko found a sentence that needed more information. She added a detail about octopus tentacles with this mark ∧ .

◆ Checking Organization

Mariko realized that one sentence was in the wrong place. To show that the sentence should be moved, she used this mark ○ .

◆ Checking Language

Mariko realized that she could combine two sentences in her second paragraph. She used this mark ∧ to make the change. Then she decided to make her opening livelier. She used this mark ∧ to make the change.

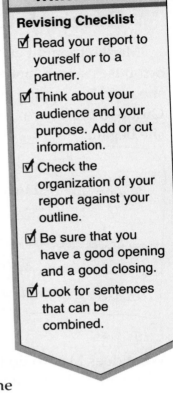

Writer's Guide

Revising Checklist
- ☑ Read your report to yourself or to a partner.
- ☑ Think about your audience and your purpose. Add or cut information.
- ☑ Check the organization of your report against your outline.
- ☑ Be sure that you have a good opening and a good closing.
- ☑ Look for sentences that can be combined.

Add — Have you ever seen a giant octopus *in an old horror movie* ? Its snaky arms would come out of the sea to crush a tiny boat. No wonder most people think of an octopus as a fierce creature. Nothing could be less true.

An octopus can't help being ugly and looking dangerous. It is made up of a fat, soft body and

Add — eight *long arms called* ∧ tentacles. ∧ Most octopuses are about as big as

Add — your hand. *but* ∧ The biggest on record was 28 feet long.

Move — It has two huge, bright eyes that see everything and a hard beak that can easily crack a crab shell.

Discuss

1. Why do you think Mariko added a detail about the tentacles?
2. Find the sentence she moved in the last paragraph. Did moving it improve her paragraph? Explain.

Try Your Hand

Now revise your first draft.

A. Read Your First Draft As you read your research report, think about your audience and your purpose. Read your report silently or to a partner to see whether it is complete and well organized. Ask yourself or your partner the questions in the box.

Responding and Revising Strategies

✔ Respond
Ask yourself or your partner:

◆ Does my opening paragraph make my audience want to read more?

◆ Is the information presented in an order that makes sense?

◆ Have all short, choppy sentences been combined with others?

◆ Does my closing end my report in an interesting way?

✔ Revise
Try these solutions:

◆ **Replace** dull sentences with livelier sentences.

◆ **Move** any sentences that are out of order.

◆ Combine two short sentences into a single sentence. See the **Revising Workshop** on page 340.

◆ **Replace** it with a more interesting one.

B. Make Your Changes If the answer to any question in the box is *no,* try the solution. Use the **Editor's Marks** to show your changes.

C. Review Your Research Report Again Decide if there is anything else you want to revise. Keep revising your report until you feel it is well organized and complete.

EDITOR'S MARKS

∧ Add something.
⤲ Cut something.
◞ Move something.
⋀ Replace something.

Save your revised research report in your *Writer's Notebook*. You will use it when you proofread your report.

Revising Workshop
Combining Two Sentences

Good writers want their sentences to sound smooth as well as to make sense. They know that one longer sentence sounds better than two short, choppy sentences. Notice the difference in how these sentences sound when they are read aloud.

1. Lizards are reptiles. Salamanders are amphibians.
2. Lizards are reptiles, and salamanders are amphibians.

In item 2, the two short sentences are joined with a comma and the word *and*. A comma and the word *but* or *or* may also be used to join sentences. Two short sentences can be joined only when the ideas in them are related. When writers join sentences like these, readers can clearly see the connection between two ideas.

Practice

Join the pairs of sentences by using the word in parentheses ( ). Write the new sentence.

1. Most lizards have legs. Some are legless. (but)
2. Gila monsters are dangerous. Their bites are poisonous. (and)
3. A frightened chuckwalla will lash its tail. It will try to bite its enemy. (or)
4. The glass snake looks like a snake. It is really a kind of lizard. (but)
5. Mud salamanders are found on the East Coast. Tree salamanders are found in the West. (and)
6. A coral snake is poisonous. A king snake is harmless. (but)
7. Many reptiles chew their food. Some swallow it whole. (but)
8. Some reptiles eat plants. Others eat animals. (and)
9. The hearing of reptiles varies. Most can hear low-pitched sounds. (but)
10. To hibernate, a reptile may burrow into the ground. It may slip into a crack between two rocks. (or)

4 Proofreading
Research Report

Mariko added some sentences to her report. Then she used the **Writer's Guide** and the **Editor's Marks** to proofread it. Look at what she did.

> ⌐ An octopus changes color easily when ⊘its⊘ *it's* excited. A relaxed octopus will ⌐shimer⌐ *shimmer* like a pale rainbow, and a frightened octopus will turn dark purple when it sees an eel. these ⌐changes color⌐ *tr* are just one more thing that make an ⌐Octopus the scary, shy, and very interesting creature that it is ⊙

Discuss

1. What corrections did Mariko make?
2. Why did Mariko add a comma?

Try Your Hand

Proofread Your Research Report Now use the **Writer's Guide** and the **Editor's Marks** to proofread your report.

Save your corrected research report in your *Writer's Notebook.* You will use it when you publish your report.

5 Publishing
Research Report

Mariko made a clean copy of her research report. She checked it carefully to be sure she had not left out anything. Then she and her classmates published their reports in an animal reference book. You can find Mariko's report on pages 34–35 of the **Writer's Handbook.**

Here's how Mariko and her classmates published their reports.

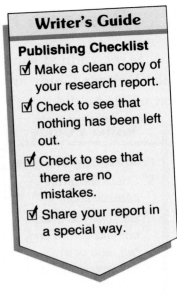

1. They planned a layout so that all the pages looked the same. They decided where the title and the art would go.

2. They drew or cut out a picture to go with each report. They made sure the picture fit the space for it on the layout. Then they copied their reports in the space left on each page. After they titled each page, they pasted each picture in place.

3. They decided how the reports would be grouped in their book. They put the reports in order and numbered the pages.

4. One student copied the pages. Each student received a full set of copies.

5. Using construction paper, each student made a front cover and a back cover for his or her book. After they made sure that the pages were in order, they stapled them together.

6. They shared their books with their families and their friends.

WRITING PROCESS

Discuss

1. Why is it a good idea to have a model layout to follow?
2. Why is it important to number the pages in step 3?

Try Your Hand

Publish Your Research Report   Follow the checklist in the **Writer's Guide.** If possible, create an animal reference book, or try this idea for sharing your report.

◆ Read your report to the class, and show pictures of the animal. Share other interesting facts you learned, and then answer any questions your classmates may have.

Listening and Speaking
Tips on How to Listen for Important Information

1. Think about the topic ahead of time. Identify questions you want answered. You may make notes of your questions.
2. Give your entire attention to the speaker. Make notes as you listen.
3. Ask politely for further explanation if you do not understand something someone says. If you do not understand something on a tape or a film, replay that section. It may make more sense the second time.
4. Listen for signals in a speaker's voice. People often make their voices louder or firmer when they give important facts. Sometimes they pause to let their audience take in important information. Sometimes they repeat their main points.
5. Notice how ideas are related to one another. Usually information is given in an organized way. If you know how the facts are organized, you will understand them and remember them more easily.

Writing in the Content Areas

Use what you learned to write about topics that you find through research. You could write a research report, a magazine article, or a paragraph. Use one of these ideas or an idea of your own.

Writer's Guide

When you write, remember the stages of the Writing Process.

- Prewriting
- Drafting
- Responding and Revising
- Proofreading
- Publishing

Physical Education

Who invented baseball? For how long have people been skiing? Choose a sports activity that interests you. Then, do research to learn about its history. Find out when it began and how it has changed. Tell facts about important events in its history.

Health

Different foods meet our bodies' needs in different ways. Read about good nutrition. Then choose one vitamin or mineral. Tell why our bodies need it. Tell which foods supply it. Explain what might happen if that vitamin or mineral were missing from someone's diet.

Fine Arts

Do you play a musical instrument? Is there one that you would like to play? Do research to learn about that instrument. Find out what is used to make it. Find out how it creates sound. Be sure to tell something about its history.

Social Studies

Choose a large city anywhere in the world. Find facts about it. Then write a guidebook for travelers. Tell them a little about the history of the city. Tell what it is like today. Be sure to include advice on which sights to see. Add any other information you think would be useful to tourists.

CONNECTING
WRITING ⬌ LANGUAGE

A well-written research report is easy to read and understand. It sticks to the main points and gives only necessary information. What types of facts are given in this report?

A Most Beautiful Moth

The luna moth has been called the most beautiful American moth. Its delicate wings are pale green and look like velvet. Its antennàe resemble two dainty feathers. Its six legs and slender body are white. The moth lays its eggs in walnut and beech trees, and the young caterpillars eat the leaves. Later the caterpillars spin their cocoons among the leaves.

◆ **Sentences in a Research Report** The long sentences highlighted have compound parts. This means that the writer put together related ideas. The writer did this to make the report sound smooth. When writers use too many short sentences, their writing may sound choppy. That is why you will often find sentences with compound parts in research reports and other works of nonfiction.

◆ **Language Focus: Sentences** In the following lessons you will learn more about using long sentences correctly in your own writing.

1 Compound Subjects

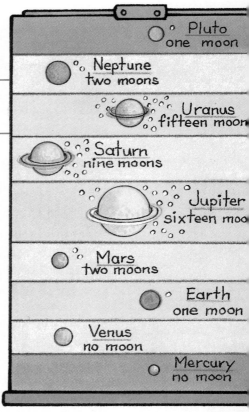

◆ **FOCUS** A **compound subject** is made up of two or more subjects joined by *and*.

Remember that the simple subject of a sentence is the key noun or pronoun in the complete subject. When a sentence has more than one simple subject, it has a compound subject.

1. Mercury and Venus have no moons.

2. An encyclopedia and a science book give facts.

Notice that the simple subjects in each sentence share the same predicate. The word *and* is usually used to join two subjects.

Guided Practice

A. Identify the two simple subjects in each sentence.

1. The sun and the stars are bright, glowing balls of very hot gases.
2. Planets and stars may look alike to our eyes.
3. The sizes and the colors of the planets in our solar system vary.
4. Saturn and Uranus both have rings.
5. Galileo and Huygens first noticed the amazing rings of Saturn.
6. Ice and particles of ice may make up these rings.
7. Dunes and rocks cover the plains of Mars.
8. Phobos and Deimos are the two moons of Mars.

THINK AND REMEMBER

◆ Remember that a sentence has a **compound subject** when it has two simple subjects that share the same predicate.
◆ Remember that two subjects are usually joined by the word *and*.

Independent Practice

B. Identifying Compound Subjects   Write the two simple subjects in each sentence.

9. The Arabs and the Egyptians named many constellations.

[MODEL]> Arabs, Egyptians

10. Ancient heroes and animals provided names.
11. A mighty hunter and a bull appear in winter.
12. A club and a lion skin are in Orion's hands.
13. A starry belt and a sword hang from his waist.
14. Hazy dust and gases form a nebula in his sword.
15. Taurus and the Bull name the same constellation.
16. The bull's horns and thin face are hard to see.

C. Completing Sentences   Complete each sentence by giving it a compound subject. You may use adjectives and articles as well as nouns. Write each sentence.

17. _____ and _____ are types of trees.

[MODEL]> Live oaks and red maples are types of trees.

18. _____ and _____ are beautiful birds.
19. _____ and _____ run faster than I do.
20. _____ and _____ appear in the sky.
21. _____ and _____ live in forests.
22. _____ and _____ are signs of spring.
23. _____ and _____ are interesting to watch.

D. Writing Original Sentences   Write sentences of your own. Use these words in the compound subjects.

24. honks, sirens

[MODEL]> Loud honks and sirens fill the air.

25. wind, rain	27. Eric, I	29. girl, dog
26. hat, coat	28. cars, buses	30. lizards, snakes

Application—Speaking and Writing

A Lecture   Imagine that you are a science teacher. Prepare a short speech to give to your class about our solar system. Use the picture to prepare your speech. You may also get facts from an encyclopedia. Write at least four sentences that have compound subjects.

2 Compound Predicates

◆ **FOCUS** A **compound predicate** is made up of two or more predicates joined by *and*.

Remember that the simple predicate of a sentence is the key verb in the complete predicate. When a sentence has more than one simple predicate, it has a compound predicate.

1. Snapping turtles `nap` and `swim` .
2. Snapping turtles `crawl` onto the beach and `lay` eggs.

Notice that the simple predicates in each sentence share the same subject. The word *and* often joins two predicates.

Guided Practice

A. Identify the two simple predicates in each sentence.

1. My family packed the car and drove south.
2. Some visitors in the park sail boats and ride trams.
3. We found a guide and joined a tour group.
4. Our group crossed a bridge and looked for wildlife.
5. The guide raised her hand and told us to listen.
6. Some birds dived and made loud splashes.
7. I watched the water and saw an alligator.
8. My father grabbed his camera and snapped a picture.

THINK AND REMEMBER
- ◆ Remember that a sentence has a **compound predicate** when it has two simple predicates that share the same subject.
- ◆ Remember that two predicates are joined by the word *and*.

Independent Practice

B. Identifying Compound Predicates   Write the two simple predicates in each sentence.

9. A black snake slithers across the path and hides.

MODEL> slithers, hides

10. An alligator heaps plants high and makes a nest.

11. Alligators hunt at night and catch garfish.

12. A spoonbill spreads its pink wings and soars high.

13. Shy panthers stay very quiet and hide from humans.

14. The gray heron catches a fish and tosses it around.

15. Storks wade through water and snap at their prey.

16. Moonflowers bloom and give a lovely scent.

C. Completing Sentences   Complete each sentence with a compound predicate. You may add other words besides verbs. Underline the simple predicates.

17. The visitors _____ and _____.

MODEL> The visitors stared and asked questions.

18. The hikers _____ and _____.

19. The birds by the pond _____ and _____.

20. The wind _____ and _____.

21. The angry tourist _____ and _____.

22. The cat _____ and _____.

23. The gardener _____ and _____.

D. Writing Original Sentences   Write original sentences. Use these verbs in compound predicates.

24. points, runs

MODEL> Maria points at the bird and runs.

25. opened, shut	**27.** dived, swam	**29.** fixed, ate
26. ran, jumped	**28.** grabs, tugs	**30.** stops, stares

Application—Writing

A Nonfiction Article   Imagine that you are writing an article about wildlife. Write a paragraph that might be in your article. Tell your readers about some of the animals' habits. You may use an encyclopedia to find ideas. Use at least four sentences with compound predicates.

3 Compound Sentences

◆ **FOCUS** A **compound sentence** is made up of two simple sentences joined by *and, or,* or *but.*

Remember that a sentence has a subject and a predicate and expresses a complete thought. A sentence that expresses one complete thought is a **simple sentence.** Sometimes two simple sentences are joined to make a compound sentence.

1. Deserts are dry places, and jungles are wet.

The word *and* often joins two short sentences. Notice that a comma appears before *and.* Sometimes the word *but* or *or* may be used to join sentences.

2. A jungle gets much rain , but a desert does not.

3. You may visit a desert , or you may go to a jungle.

> **Link to Speaking**
> In informal speech, people sometimes begin sentences with *and, but,* or *or.* Avoid doing this in formal speaking and in writing.

Guided Practice

A. Identify each sentence as a *compound sentence* or a *simple sentence.*

1. Some animals hunt at night, and others rest then.
2. Desert animals like hot temperatures.
3. A few deserts are empty, but most deserts have life.
4. Most animals hunt in the early morning and evening.
5. Desert animals rest in shady places.

Independent Practice

B. Identifying Compound Sentences If the sentence is a compound sentence, write *compound sentence*. If it is not, write *simple sentence*.

6. Jungles do not have tall trees like rain forests.

MODEL > simple sentence

7. Jungles look like hot places, but their temperatures are usually mild.
8. Plenty of sunlight reaches the ground, and plants grow everywhere.
9. You must hack a path through the thick vines.
10. Plants have fruit or blooms all year.

C. Proofreading Sentences Write the sentences. Add commas where they are needed.

11. Monkeys have tails and most apes are tailless.

MODEL > Monkeys have tails, and most apes are tailless.

12. A monkey's tail is used for balance or it may be used to grasp things.
13. Chimpanzees look like monkeys but they are really one of the four kinds of apes.
14. Monkeys vary greatly in size and the smallest monkey measures only about 6 inches in body length.
15. Chimpanzees may live in treetops or they may scamper along the ground.

Application—Writing

A Letter Imagine that you like to travel. Decide whether to go to the jungle or to the desert shown in the pictures. Write a letter to a friend. Explain your decision. Use *and*, *but*, and *or* at least once each to make compound sentences. If you need help in writing a friendly letter, see pages 36–37 of the **Writer's Handbook.**

4 Commas in Sentences

◆ **FOCUS**   Commas are used to separate words in a series.

Remember that when you write a compound sentence, you use a comma before the word that joins the sentence parts.

1. A coral reef is a busy place **,** and many fish live there.

You also use commas in a sentence to set apart words in a series. A **series** is made up of three or more words of the same type. The word *and* joins the last word to the series. You can have a series of nouns, verbs, or adjectives. Notice where the commas are in these sentences.

2. Eels **,** clams **,** and lionfish live there. **nouns**
3. The fish stopped **,** stared **,** and sped away. **verbs**
4. The lionfish was white **,** orange **,** and brown. **adjectives**

Guided Practice

A. Identify where commas belong in each sentence to separate words in a series.

1. Corals are tiny simple and beautiful creatures.
2. Colonies of corals grow form reefs and die.
3. There are feathery spiky and leafy corals.
4. Corals cannot see hear and move about.
5. Corals jellyfish and anemones live in the sea.
6. The coral used for jewelry is pink red and rose.
7. A coral reef is home to colorful unusual and interesting creatures.

THINK AND REMEMBER
◆ Use commas to set apart the words in a series.

Independent Practice

B. Adding Commas to Words in a Series   Write these sentences. Add commas to separate words in a series.

    8. A mollusk's body is soft boneless and supple.

MODEL > A mollusk's body is soft, boneless, and supple.

    9. Some common mollusks are oysters snails and squid.
  10. Mollusks are found in mountains oceans and deserts.
  11. Clams conches and oysters have shell skeletons.
  12. The shell is hard thick and firm.
  13. The shell types are plain spiraled and scalloped.
  14. A shell has an outer a middle and an inner layer.
  15. The inner layer is often pale smooth and shiny.
  16. Shells are made into buttons jewelry and pictures.
  17. Workers cut shape and polish the shells.

C. Proofreading Sentences   Write these sentences. Add commas where they are needed. Some sentences are compound sentences, and some have words in a series.

  18. My aunt taught me to dive and I enjoy it.

MODEL > My aunt taught me to dive, and I enjoy it.

  19. Divers must be cautious or they will be injured.
  20. Some reef creatures can bite sting and poison.
  21. I dived down to the reef and a new world appeared.
  22. I saw colorful towers blossoms and forests.
  23. The fish were striped spotted and checked.
  24. Some fish let me come close but others darted away.
  25. I saw a shadow and a shark sailed above me.
  26. I noticed anemones damselfish and clown fish.
  27. An anemone waved its tentacles but its prey escaped.
  28. Those tentacles trap stun and kill small creatures.

Application—Writing and Speaking

Film Narration   Imagine that you are writing the script for a television film about a coral reef. Write a brief speech for the film narrator. Tell the viewers about the creatures in the reef. You may use an encyclopedia and the pictures to get ideas. Use at least two compound sentences and two sentences with words in a series. Check your use of commas.

5 Avoiding Sentence Fragments and Run-on Sentences

◆ **FOCUS** Sentence fragments and run-on sentences are incorrect.

Remember that a complete sentence has a subject and a predicate and expresses a complete thought. A word group that does not express a complete thought is called a **sentence fragment.**

1. Are coming fast. fragment—missing subject
2. Hurricane winds. fragment—missing predicate
3. Hurricane winds are coming fast! sentence

Remember also that a compound sentence is made up of two complete sentences linked by *and,* *but,* or *or.* If the linking word and a comma are missing, the sentence is a **run-on sentence.** Run-on sentences can be corrected by adding the linking word and a comma, or by making two sentences.

4. No time is left we must hurry! run-on sentence
5. No time is left, and we must hurry! correct
6. No time is left. We must hurry! correct

Guided Practice

A. Identify each word group as a *sentence,* a *sentence fragment,* or a *run-on sentence.*

1. Is made up of powerful whirling winds.
2. Speeds of more than 74 miles per hour.
3. A hurricane has two main parts.
4. The calm center is the eye angry clouds surround it.
5. The rising waters.

B. **6.–10.** Make complete sentences of the sentence fragments and run-on sentences in **A.** You may need to add words or punctuation. Identify any sentences that are already correct.

Independent Practice

C. Identifying Errors   Read each word group. Then, write *sentence, sentence fragment,* or *run-on sentence.*

11. People stay indoors during a blizzard.

MODEL> sentence

12. A violent snowstorm.

13. Cold air moves under warm air a "cold front" is born.

14. Usually causes sudden changes in the weather.

15. A heavy snow falls fierce winds blow.

16. Can't see anything in a blizzard.

17. The winds pick up speed the temperature drops.

18. Blizzards occur most often in the Great Plains.

19. Huge banks of snow.

20. Transportation halts businesses shut down.

D. 21.–29. Revising Sentences   Rewrite the sentence fragments and the run-on sentences in **C**. Add words to make the fragments complete sentences. You may use linking words and commas to join the parts of the run-on sentences, or you may make each into two separate sentences. If a sentence is already correct, write *correct*.

21. A violent snowstorm.

MODEL> A violent snowstorm struck New England in 1978.

Application—Speaking and Writing

A Radio Play   Write a scene for a play about some people facing a hurricane. Invent any characters you need. Plan to put on your play with some classmates. Make your listeners feel the excitement. Check to be sure you did not write sentence fragments or run-on sentences.

Building Vocabulary
Borrowed Words

mesa

skunk

canyon

prairie

ravine

moose

bluff

Our language is rich and interesting. It contains many words from other languages. The words *canyon* and *mesa* come from Spanish. The words *prairie* and *ravine* were originally French words. *Bluff* is thought to come from Dutch, and the animal names *moose* and *skunk* came from American Indian words. Borrowed words are sometimes spelled and pronounced much the same as they were in the original language. The word *mesa* is the same in Spanish and in English. Other borrowed words are changed. The word *bluff* began as the Old Dutch word *blaf*.

Finding out the history of a word can be both fun and useful. Sometimes you learn something about the history of our country and the people who settled it. At the very least you will find it easier to remember the meaning of the word.

Reading Practice

Read each sentence. Study the underlined words. Items **a–e** give some sentences that tell the history of each word. Write the letter of the history that goes with each underlined word.

1. We saw an <u>alligator</u> lying on a riverbank.
2. Dan played a cheerful tune on the <u>banjo</u>.
3. They paddled their canoe down the <u>bayou</u>.
4. The waiter brought the <u>check</u> for our dinner.
5. Henry Ford was a powerful <u>tycoon</u> in the automobile industry.

a. This word is from a German word that means "bill."
b. This word is from a Spanish word that means "the lizard."
c. This word is from a Choctaw Indian word for *stream*.
d. This word is from a Japanese name for an important leader.
e. This word is from a Kimbundu (African) word that names a stringed instrument.

Writing Practice

Choose five words from this list. Look up each word in a dictionary. Write a sentence that tells what language it came from. Then write a sentence using the word as we use it today.

sleigh	okra	chow
ketchup	ukulele	pajamas
afghan	parka	kindergarten

Project

Work in a group. Create a picture dictionary of familiar objects with names that came from other languages. Brainstorm words that you think come from other languages. Check your choices in a dictionary. Then draw a picture of each correct choice. Underneath it write something about the history of the word.

Language Enrichment
Sentences

Use what you know about compound sentences and sentences with compound parts to do these activities.

Goats and trucks have horns!

Crazy Quiz Show

Divide the class into two teams for a silly quiz game. First, meet with your team. Prepare twice as many slips of paper as there are players on the other team. On each slip of paper, write a different common noun. The noun should name a person, an animal, or an object. Put all the slips from your team into a box. Then, trade boxes with the other team.

The teams take turns sending a player forward. The player draws two slips of paper from the box. He or she must use both words in the compound subject of a sentence. The sentence must make sense. The player's team gets a point for a good sentence. The whole audience decides whether a sentence should win a point.

Sentence Train

Form groups of five or six students. First, one student in each group writes a complete sentence. Then, another student in the group uses that sentence as the first sentence in a compound sentence. A third student uses the second sentence as the first sentence in a new compound sentence. Continue in this way until each student has had a turn. Finally, put your "sentence train" on a bulletin board for the rest of the class to enjoy.

CONNECTING
LANGUAGE ⬌ WRITING

In this unit you learned more about sentences. You learned about compound subjects, compound predicates, and compound sentences.

◆ **Using Sentences in Your Writing**   Knowing when to use compound parts of sentences is important. You use them so that your writing does not sound choppy. You can cut out unnecessary words and write smoother sentences. Think about using compound parts of sentences as you do these activities.

Land, Sea, and Sky

Brainstorm verbs that tell about the action in each picture. Use some of the verbs to form a compound predicate for each picture. Then, use the compound predicates in sentences about the action in each picture.

What a Menu!

You learned about words from other languages on the **Building Vocabulary** pages. Now, brainstorm all the foreign foods that you know. Make a list. You may wish to begin with *omelet*, *taco*, and *pizza*.

Choose four foods that you like from your list, and write a sentence about each of them. Two sentences should have compound subjects. Two sentences should be compound sentences.

Unit Checkup

Think Back	Think Ahead
◆ What did you learn about research reports in this unit? What did you do to write one?	◆ How will what you learned about research reports help you when you study a new subject? ◆ How will classifying information into categories help you when you study science?
◆ Look at the writing you did in this unit. How did the words *and*, *but*, and *or* help you express your ideas in sentences?	◆ What is one way that you can use the words *and*, *but*, and *or* to improve your writing?

Analyzing a Research Report   *pages 329–330*

Read these paragraphs from a research report. Then follow the directions.

A teaspoon could hold a newborn kangaroo! This tiny creature is hardly big enough to be alive. Once born, it quickly crawls into its mother's pouch and greedily drinks its mother's milk. Before long, the baby kangaroo's legs will begin to hang out of the pouch because it's growing so big.

Male kangaroos fight to decide which one will be master of a herd of females. They box each other with their front paws, and sometimes one will actually stand on his tail and kick the other with his powerful hind legs. The two will hit each other until one finally has had enough. He hops slowly away and lets the other be master of the herd.

1. Write what the first paragraph is about.
2. Write one supporting detail.
3. Write what the second paragraph is about.
4. Write one supporting detail.
5. Write an interesting title for this research report.

Classifying Information into Categories   *page 331*
Follow the directions to complete each of the following.

6. Choose a smaller category from the topic *forest creatures.*
7. List one fact you want to cover.
8. Write one detail about that fact.
9. Choose another fact you want to cover.
10. Write one detail about that fact.

Capturing the Reader's Interest   *page 332*
Analyze these openings and closings. For each one, write at least
one sentence telling why you think it is a good opening or
closing or a poor one.

11. Did you know that an ordinary cow has four stomachs?
12. As we say good-bye to the cow, she peacefully chews her
    cud.
13. My research report is about cows.
14. What animal looks like a mole with a duck's beak?
15. That's the end of my report about the duck-billed platypus.

The Writing Process   *pages 333–343*
Write the letter of the correct response to each question.

16. You have chosen to write your report on white-tailed deer.
    What is the best way to find out about them?
    a. Read books in the library.
    b. Ask your older sister.
    c. Go to the forest and look for some.
17. A book said, "Deer hold up their tails as a warning of danger."
    Which is the best note to use when gathering facts?
    a. Deer flash tails.
    b. Deer flash tails to warn others of danger.
    c. Deer hold up their tails.
18. What is the best way to prepare for a lecture on a topic that
    you are interested in?
    a. Get up early.
    b. Read several books about the subject.
    c. Think about questions you want answered.

19. Which is the first step in organizing your information?
    a. Make an outline.
    b. Write a rough draft.
    c. Sort your best research notes into categories.

Compound Subjects   *pages 346–347*

Write the two simple subjects in each sentence.

20. Rocks and cliffs on a beach hold sea animals.
21. Wind and tides send the water up the shore.
22. Some animals and plants get their food from this water.
23. Do oranges and pincushions live in the water?
24. The sea anemones and the sea urchins fit these descriptions.
25. Tiny plants and animals make these creatures open up.
26. Clams and oysters both live in shells.
27. Water and plants float into the clam's "mouth."
28. Can starfish and sand dollars be found along this beach?

Compound Predicates   *pages 348–349*

Write the two simple predicates in each sentence.

29. I sink in fresh water and float in ocean water.
30. Salt makes the difference and helps me float.
31. Salt comes from the land and goes to the ocean.
32. Water evaporates and then falls as rain or snow.
33. Then the water flows along and dissolves minerals.
34. It runs to lower and lower land and then reaches the ocean.
35. It joins the water there and evaporates again.
36. The salts stay behind and make the sea saltier.
37. Some scientists got an idea and experimented.
38. They thought and wondered what salt content could tell.
39. They figured and then discussed their results.
40. Scientists stopped this experiment and tried other things.
41. They still test and retest the accuracy of their theories.

Compound Sentences   *pages 350–351*

If the sentence is a compound sentence, write *compound sentence.*
If it is not, write *simple sentence.*

42. Not all caves are just simple tunnels.
43. Some are simple, but others twist and turn.

44. A careless explorer could get lost and die there.
45. How were caves formed?
46. Some water dissolves limestone, and this water probably formed the caves.

Commas in Sentences   *pages 352–353*

Write these sentences. Add commas where they are needed. Some sentences are compound sentences, and some have words in a series.

47. Long ago people had legends and they passed them on to us.
48. We enjoy the old stories and we like new stories that explain things too.
49. Paul Bunyan Pecos Bill and Slewfoot Sue are famous people from tall tales.
50. Some stories say that Paul Bunyan made the Grand Canyon but others say it was made by Pecos Bill.
51. The Grand Canyon is in Arizona and it is lovely.
52. Shale lava and other rocks make up the canyon.
53. The colors are red brown cream and lavender.
54. Rock formations resemble towers ruins and temples.

Avoiding Sentence Fragments and Run-on Sentences   *pages 354–355*

Read each word group. Then write *sentence, sentence fragment,* or *run-on sentence.*

55. Dolphins travel in groups.
56. They play catch and tag they help each other.
57. A shark attacks they will all attack him.
58. Dolphins will never attack people.
59. Even when the people hurt them.

Borrowed Words   *pages 356–357*

Read each sentence. Study the underlined words. Items **a** through **d** tell the history of each word. Write the letter of the history that goes with each underlined word.

60. How many <u>astronauts</u> went up in the last space shuttle?
61. Bob brought his mother a <u>bouquet</u> of daisies.
62. Look at those jagged <u>dandelion</u> leaves.
63. Do you like to eat <u>broccoli</u>?

    a. This word is from a Greek phrase meaning "sailor of the stars."
    b. This word is from an Italian word meaning "little sprout."
    c. This word is from a French word meaning "little forest."
    d. This word is from a French phrase meaning "lion's tooth."

UNIT

Comparing and Contrasting

◆ **COMPOSITION FOCUS:** **Paragraphs of Comparison and Contrast**

◆ **LANGUAGE FOCUS:** **Mechanics Wrap-up**

Look around at your classmates. Each one is different from the others. However, if you think about it, you can also name things that all of you have in common.

Some writers are fascinated by the ways in which two people, two places, or two things are alike and not alike. They feel that by analyzing the similarities and the differences, they can better understand their subjects. When they write, they share what they have learned. By showing readers likenesses and differences, they hope to make the information easier to understand.

James Cross Giblin is a writer who became interested in the American heritage. As he wrote about it, he often used comparisons and contrasts. In this unit you will learn how to write paragraphs of comparison and contrast that will help your readers understand the subject you are writing about.

James Cross Giblin wrote a book *to inform* his readers about the ways in which American culture has changed and the ways in which it has stayed the same.

Reading with a Writer's Eye
Comparison and Contrast

America has changed and grown amazingly since 1776. Even our flag was transformed as our country grew. In this excerpt from *Fireworks, Picnics, and Flags,* James Cross Giblin explains how and why our nation's flag turned into the Stars and Stripes. Notice that the details the writer gives about historic events help you remember and understand what happened and why it happened.

from Fireworks, Picnics, and Flags
by James Cross Giblin

From dawn to dusk on the Fourth of July, the American flag flies from homes and public buildings.

Today the flag has seven red stripes and six white ones, and fifty white stars on a blue square. The thirteen stripes stand for the thirteen original colonies, and the stars represent the fifty states. The design and colors of the flag have inspired many nicknames. Some people call it the Stars and Stripes, others the Star-Spangled Banner, and others simply the Red, White, and Blue.

Because the flag is so familiar, we may think it has always been the same. But before the Revolution, there was no single American flag. Each colony, and many military regiments, had their own flags or banners, just as each state has its own flag today. These colonial flags featured many different emblems. On one was a rifleman, on another a beaver, and on another a coiled rattlesnake. They carried slogans such as "Liberty or Death," "Conquer or Die," and "Don't Tread on Me!"

Our first national flag was raised on a hill near Boston on January 4, 1776, by troops serving under General George Washington. It was called the Grand Union flag and had thirteen red and white stripes. But instead of stars it displayed the crosses of Saint Andrew and Saint George, the symbols of Great Britain. For in January 1776, America was still officially tied to Britain.

After the Declaration of Independence, the American people wanted to have a purely American flag. The Second Continental Congress adopted a design for one on June 14, 1777, the day we now celebrate as Flag Day. The congressional resolution stated "That the flag of the United States be 13 stripes, alternately red and white, and that the Union be 13 stars, white in a blue field, representing a new constellation."

For a long time, people believed that Betsy Ross, an upholsterer and flagmaker in Philadelphia, made the first of the new American flags. Her grandson claimed that George Washington himself had given her the assignment. But Washington was off fighting the British in New Jersey at the time he was supposed to have called on Betsy Ross. What is probably true is that she was one of several Philadelphia flagmakers who made examples of the new flag in 1777.

Congress also passed a resolution that each time a new state was added to the Union, a new star and a new stripe would be added to the flag.

DON'T TREAD ON ME

AN APPEAL TO HEAVEN

GRAND UNION FLAG

FLAG, adopted June 14, 1777

After Vermont joined the Union in 1791 and
Kentucky in 1792, the flag had fifteen stars and
fifteen stripes. This was the flag that Francis Scott
Key saw flying over Fort McHenry, Maryland,
during the War of 1812—the flag that inspired him
to write "The Star-Spangled Banner."

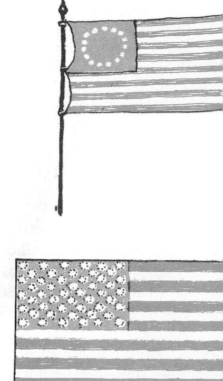

After the War of 1812 ended in 1814, many new
states wanted to join the Union. Congress realized
that if both a new star and a new stripe were added
for each state, the flag would become too large. So
in 1818 it decided that the flag would always have
just thirteen stripes, but that a star would still be
added for each new state. The addition of the star
would take place on the Fourth of July following
the state's admission into the Union.

By 1912, when Arizona and New Mexico
entered the Union, the flag had forty-eight stars.
The number remained the same until 1959, when
Alaska became a state. That Fourth of July, just
after midnight, a flag with forty-nine stars was
raised for the first time over Fort McHenry in
Maryland.

A year later, on July 4, 1960, a new flag with
fifty stars was hoisted over Fort McHenry at
12:01 A.M. This flag marked Hawaii's entry into
the Union, and it is the one we salute today.

Respond

1. How much of the information in this selection was new to
   you? Which new information was the most interesting to you?

Discuss

2. What details does the writer give to explain why changes were
   made to the flag?
3. The writer also gives details about historic events that do not
   explain why the flag was changed. Identify some of these
   details. Was it a good idea for the writer to include them?
   Explain your answer.

Thinking As a Writer
Analyzing Paragraphs of Comparison and Contrast

Paragraphs of comparison point out what is alike about two subjects. When writers **compare** two subjects, they tell how the two are alike. This is a paragraph of comparison.

In some ways the Grand Union flag was like our flag today. Running across it were thirteen stripes that stood for the original thirteen colonies. Like today's flag, it had a box with a design in the upper left-hand corner. The same red, white, and blue colors were used.

The **topic sentence** makes it clear that this paragraph will tell how the two subjects are alike.

Detail sentences support the topic sentence. They identify features that are common to both subjects. Signal words such as *like* and *same* call attention to details that are alike.

Paragraphs of contrast point out what is different about two subjects. When writers **contrast** two subjects, they tell how each is different from the other. This is a paragraph of contrast.

However, that first national flag was also quite different from the flag we call Old Glory. The box on the first flag contained all three colors rather than just blue and white. Also, instead of white stars on a blue field, the upper box contained the crosses of Saint Andrew and Saint George, the symbols of Great Britain.

The **topic sentence** makes it clear that this paragraph will tell how the two subjects are different.

Detail sentences tell what is different about the subjects. Signal words such as *rather* and *instead* alert readers to the contrasts.

The subjects that are compared and contrasted should be alike in some way. It makes sense to compare two flags or a state flag and a state seal. It does not make much sense to compare a flag and a song.

Discuss

1. What details does the writer give to support the claim that the flags had something in common? What details support the statement that the flags were unlike one another?

2. The writer created one paragraph to show how the flags were alike and a separate paragraph to tell how they were different. Why was this a good way to organize the information?

Try Your Hand

A. Identify Signal Words   The underlined words in these sentences are signal words. Make a chart with the headings *Paragraph of Comparison* and *Paragraph of Contrast.* Under each heading, write the signal words that you might find in that kind of paragraph.

1. <u>Both</u> holidays are celebrated with feasts.
2. One comes in the summer, <u>but</u> the other comes in the fall.
3. The two Presidents' birthdays that we celebrate come in the <u>same</u> month.
4. <u>Unlike</u> Independence Day, Arbor Day is a state holiday.
5. Most communities celebrate Thanksgiving quietly <u>instead</u>.

B. Use Signal Words   Look at the chart you just made. Choose two signal words from each column. Then write four sentences that compare and contrast two subjects.

C. Read Paragraphs of Comparison and Contrast   Reread the selection on pages 366–368, or find another selection that contains paragraphs of comparison and contrast. Read aloud to a partner the sentences that compare and contrast. Identify the subjects being compared, and tell how you recognized the sentences of comparison and contrast.

Writer's Notebook

Collecting Antonyms   When writers contrast two subjects, they often use antonyms such as *faded* and *bright.* As you read books and listen to people speak, be alert for antonyms. Record in your *Writer's Notebook* the sentences that contain these antonyms. Look up the words in the dictionary and record their exact meanings too. Try to use these antonyms when you contrast two subjects.

Thinking As a Writer
Evaluating for Comparison and Contrast

Writer's Guide

To plan paragraphs of comparison and contrast, good writers

- evaluate details.
- classify details with common features in categories.

When writers plan paragraphs of comparison and contrast, they begin by evaluating the details they might use. They sort the details into three categories: things true of only one subject, things true of only the other subject, and things true of both subjects. This diagram shows the categories.

Things True of Only the White House	Things True of Both Places	Things True of Only the Capitol Building
home and offices of President	huge white buildings in Washington, D.C., among oldest buildings there	lawmakers' offices and meeting rooms
132 rooms, 5 open to tourists		540 rooms, many open to public
boxy with flat roof		has huge white dome

As you plan your own paragraphs of comparison and contrast, begin by evaluating the details you will use and sorting them into categories like the ones in the diagram.

Discuss

Look at the diagram. Which details will the writer use in the paragraph of comparison? Which details will be used in the paragraph of contrast?

Try Your Hand

Evaluate and Classify Details   Think about two objects, such as a canoe and a ship, or a car and a truck. Identify how they are alike in some ways and how they are different in others. Then create your own diagram to record what you identified.

Developing the Writer's Craft
Using Formal and Informal Language

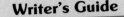

Writer's Guide

Good writers
◆ use formal language
  to give information.

Writers make sure that their language fits the type of writing they are doing. For most types of writing, they use formal language. **Formal language** is the correct English found in books and in articles. For friendly letters and story dialogue, writers may use informal language. **Informal language** is the language of everyday speech. Notice the difference in these sentences.

1. They've done lots of work on the Capitol.   Informal
2. They have done a great deal of work on the Capitol.   Formal

In formal writing, writers do not use contractions or informal expressions. The first sentence is informal because it contains both the contraction *They've* and the expression *lots of*.

When you write your paragraphs of comparison and contrast, make sure that the type of language you use fits your writing.

Discuss

1. Think about the selection on pages 366–368. Why do you think the writer chose to use formal rather than informal language? Explain your answer.
2. This sentence uses informal language.
   Is it okay to tour the Capitol Building alone?
   Rewrite it using formal language.

Try Your Hand

Using Formal Language   Rewrite each sentence. Replace any informal language with formal language. If you need help use your **Writer's Thesaurus.**
1. We've visited the Capitol Building.
2. We saw a lot of neat statues in the Capitol.
3. We hung around the Senate wing for ages.

1 Prewriting
Paragraphs of Comparison and Contrast

The students in Tom's class at Mar Vista Elementary School decided to put together for visitors a travel guide about their town. They used the checklist in the **Writer's Guide** to help them plan their paragraphs. Look at what they did.

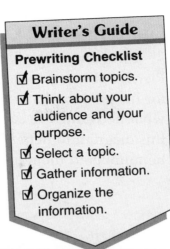

Writer's Guide

Prewriting Checklist
- ☑ Brainstorm topics.
- ☑ Think about your audience and your purpose.
- ☑ Select a topic.
- ☑ Gather information.
- ☑ Organize the information.

◆ Brainstorming and Selecting a Topic

First, the students brainstormed a list of possible topics for their paragraphs. They decided to work in groups and have each student in the group decide on a different topic.

They listed all the places they could think of that might be interesting to compare and contrast. Look at the first four items on their list.

The students studied the ideas on their list. They discussed which ideas would not work well. They crossed out the names of places that would not be interesting to visitors. They also crossed off the names of places that did not have enough in common with one another. Finally, each student chose one of the topics.

Andrea's house and Paul's house
~~*the Old Wharf and Pier 9*~~
the town plaza and Ridgeway Park
the natural history museum and the art museum

Discuss

1. Look at the topics crossed off the list. Why do you think each of them was crossed off?
2. Study the topics left on the list. Does it make sense to compare the items in each pair? Why or why not?

◆ Gathering and Organizing Information

Tom, one of the students, chose the topic "the Old Wharf and Pier 9." His next task was to gather and organize the information for his paragraphs of comparison and contrast. He thought about what he wanted to say about these two places. Then he made this diagram to help him record and organize his notes. Finally he numbered them in the order he planned to use them.

True about Old Wharf:

1. dock still used
2. fishing fleet leaves at dawn
3. deserted in afternoon

True about Both Places:

3. wooden wharves
1. built at same time
2. once used as fishing boat docks

True about Pier 9:

1. tourist attraction
4. deserted in morning
2. only harbor cruise boats dock there
3. souvenir shops and restaurants

Discuss

1. Why did Tom divide his diagram into these three categories?
2. Why do you think Tom put numbers before the details?

Try Your Hand

Now plan your paragraphs of comparison and contrast.

A. Brainstorm and Select a Topic Brainstorm a list of possible topics. Identify some interesting places in your community. Think about each topic and the audience for your travel guide.

   ◆ Cross out names of places that will not interest visitors.
   ◆ Cross out names of places that you do not know about.
   ◆ Cross out names of places that have little in common.
   ◆ Circle the topic that will be most interesting.

B. Gather and Organize Information   When you are satisfied with your topic, gather and organize the information to use in your paragraphs of comparison and contrast.

- ◆ Think about your audience. Identify the details that will help them see how the two places are alike yet different.
- ◆ Evaluate the details. Decide which will help you make a comparison and which will help you point out a contrast. Make a diagram like Tom's.

 Save your notes and diagram in your *Writer's Notebook*. You will use them when you draft your paragraphs of comparison and contrast.

Listening and Speaking
Tips on How to Have a Group Discussion

You may want to work in groups to discuss topics and ideas for paragraphs of comparison and contrast. These tips may be helpful.

1. Choose a group leader. The leader will keep order and make sure that people take turns speaking.
2. Choose someone to record the group's ideas and decisions.
3. State the problem to be solved or the task to be done. Be sure everyone agrees on what needs to be done.
4. Brainstorm ideas or solutions. Take turns. Speak clearly. Listen carefully while others speak.
5. Discuss the ideas. Give reasons why a solution will or will not work. Try to agree on the best ideas or solutions. If everyone does not agree, take a vote.
6. Make sure that someone has written down all the ideas or solutions.
7. Assign a different job to each group member. Be sure to consider what each person likes to do when you do this.

2 Drafting
Paragraphs of Comparison and Contrast

Tom followed the **Writer's Guide** to draft his paragraphs. Look at how he began.

> The Old Wharf and Pier 9 are alike in a few ways. Both were built in the early 1900's. Today, both wharves still stretch out into the green harbor. For a long time they were used as docks for fishing boats.
>
> However, the Old Wharf and Pier 9 do not look very much alike.

Writer's Guide

Drafting Checklist

☑ Use your notes and diagram for ideas.

☑ In a paragraph of comparison,

◆ Write a topic sentence stating that the places are alike.

◆ Write detail sentences to support the topic sentence.

☑ In a paragraph of contrast,

◆ Write a topic sentence stating that the places are different.

◆ Write detail sentences that describe the differences.

Discuss

What details support Tom's first topic sentence?

Try Your Hand

Now you are ready to draft your paragraphs.

A. Review Your Information Think about the information you gathered and organized. Gather more information if you need it.

B. Think About Your TAP Remember that your task is to write paragraphs of comparison and contrast. Your purpose is to inform your audience about the two places you have selected.

C. Write Your First Draft Follow the **Writer's Guide** to write your paragraphs of comparison and contrast.

When you write your draft, just put all your ideas on paper. Do not worry about spelling, punctuation, or grammar. You can correct the draft later.

Task: What?
Audience: Who?
Purpose: Why?

 Save your first draft in your *Writer's Notebook*. You will use it when you revise your paragraphs of comparison and contrast.

3 Responding and Revising
Paragraphs of Comparison and Contrast

Tom used the checklist in the **Writer's Guide** to revise his paragraphs. Look at what he did.

◆ Checking Information

Tom read his draft again. He decided to add a detail to a sentence in the first paragraph to paint a clearer picture. He used this mark ∧.

◆ Checking Organization

Tom decided that the last sentence in the first paragraph was out of order. To show that the sentence should be moved, he used this mark ◯.

◆ Checking Language

Tom found that two words were too informal. He replaced them with the word *greatly*.

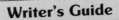

Writer's Guide

Revising Checklist

☑ Read your paragraphs to yourself or to a partner.

☑ Think about your audience and your purpose. Add or cut information.

☑ Check to see that you have stated the comparison and the contrast.

☑ Check to see that your paragraphs are organized correctly.

☑ Check to see that you used formal language.

Add
Move

The Old Wharf and Pier 9 are alike in a few ways. Both were built in the early 1900's. Today, both long-wooden wharves still stretch out into the green harbor. For a long time they were used as docks for fishing boats.

However, the Old Wharf and Pier 9 do not look very much alike. The Old Wharf is still used by the fishing fleet. At dawn it is a lively place as the fishers put their boats to sea. By late morning it is deserted, except for a few lazy gulls. Pier 9, on

Replace

the other hand has changed *greatly* a bunch.

Discuss

1. How did moving a sentence improve Tom's first paragraph?
2. How did the other changes Tom made improve his writing?

Try Your Hand

Now revise your first draft.

A. Read Your First Draft As you read your paragraphs, think about your audience and your purpose. Read your paragraphs silently or to a partner to see if they are complete and well organized. Ask yourself or your partner the questions in the box.

Responding and Revising Strategies	
✔ **Respond** **Ask yourself or your partner:**	✔ **Revise** **Try these solutions:**
◆ Does each topic sentence tell what each paragraph is about?	◆ **Add** information or **replace** your topic sentences.
◆ Does my first paragraph tell how the two places are alike?	◆ **Cut** or **move** any information that does not belong.
◆ Does my second paragraph describe how the two places are different from one another?	◆ **Add** any information that is missing.
◆ Is my language formal?	◆ **Replace** informal language with formal language.
◆ Did I use strong describing words to paint a clear picture?	◆ **Add** describing words to dull sentences. See the **Revising Workshop** on page 379.

B. Make Your Changes If the answer to any question in the box is *no*, try the solution. Use the **Editor's Marks** to show your changes.

C. Review Your Paragraphs of Comparison and Contrast Again Decide if there is anything else you want to revise. Keep revising your paragraphs until you feel they are well organized and complete.

> **EDITOR'S MARKS**
>
> ∧ Add something.
> ✗ Cut something.
> ◡ Move something.
> ∧ Replace something.

**Save your revised paragraphs in your *Writer's Notebook.*
You will use them when you proofread your paragraphs.**

Revising Workshop
Adding Describing Words to Sentences

Good writers choose the right describing words to create clear, strong pictures. Read and compare these sentences.

1. A seagull landed on the dock.
2. A <u>sleek</u> seagull landed on the <u>bustling</u> dock.
3. A <u>skinny</u> seagull landed on the <u>lonely</u> dock.
4. A <u>scrawny</u> seagull landed on the <u>lonely</u> dock.

Sentence 1 does not suggest much to the reader's imagination. In sentence 2, two describing words are added to make descriptions come to life. In sentence 3, two different describing words give the sentence a new meaning. Sentences 3 and 4 paint pictures that are alike, but not the same. The writer used a thesaurus to find the exact word to describe the seagull.

You can use your **Writer's Thesaurus** to replace dull words with vivid words that give a clear picture.

---

lonely *adj.* Feeling alone. Thoughts of my lost pet make me lonely.
alone Without anyone near. Mrs. Long lives *alone* in that big house.

homesick Unhappy because of longing for home. Lindsey was so busy at her grandparents' house that she was not *homesick* at all.
lonesome Feeling alone. Playing by myself makes me *lonesome*.

Practice

Write each sentence. Replace the underlined words with vivid and exact describing words. Use your **Writer's Thesaurus.**

1. The bay was a <u>good</u> place on a <u>hot</u> afternoon.
2. <u>Thin</u> clouds drifted across the <u>bright</u> sky.
3. A <u>mighty</u> wind swept over the <u>old</u> dock.
4. A <u>brave</u> dog barked at a <u>huge</u> crab.
5. Holding a <u>red</u> kite, a <u>happy</u> boy raced down the dunes.

4 Proofreading
Paragraphs of Comparison and Contrast

After revising their paragraphs, Tom and his classmates used the **Writer's Guide** and the **Editor's Marks** to proofread their work. Look at what Tom did to one of his paragraphs.

Writer's Guide

Proofreading Checklist

☑ Check for errors in capitalization.

☑ Check for errors in punctuation.

☑ Check to see that all your paragraphs are indented.

☑ Check your grammar. Check for correct subject-verb agreement.

☑ Circle any words you think are misspelled. Find out how to spell them correctly.

⇨ For proofreading help, use the **Writer's Handbook.**

only the Harbor cruise boat dock there now. In the morning it is as still as a ghost town. By noon its souvenier shops and fish restaurants are crowded with chattering tourists. It is a bustling place then.

EDITOR'S MARKS

≡ Capitalize.

⊙ Add a period.

∧ Add something.

⋏ Add a comma.

ⱽⱽ Add quotation marks.

_ Cut something.

⋀ Replace something.

↔ Transpose.

◯ Spell correctly.

⊤⊤ Indent paragraph.

／ Make a lowercase letter.

Discuss

1. What kinds of mistakes did Tom correct?
2. Why did Tom capitalize the first letter of *only?*

Try Your Hand

Proofread Your Paragraphs of Comparison and Contrast Now use the **Writer's Guide** and the **Editor's Marks** to proofread your paragraphs.

Save your corrected paragraphs in your *Writer's Notebook.* **You will use them when you publish your paragraphs.**

WRITING PROCESS

5 Publishing
Paragraphs of Comparison and Contrast

The students made clean copies of their paragraphs. They checked their work to be sure they had not left out anything. Then they published their paragraphs in a travel guide. You can find Tom's paragraphs in the **Writer's Handbook.**

Here is how Tom and his classmates made a travel guide.

1. After each student finished the layout of his or her travel guide page, copies were made.
2. They decided on an order for the finished pages, drew a cover, and stapled the pages together.
3. Then they asked permission to place some copies of the travel guide in their town library.

Discuss

1. Why should each page have the same layout?
2. Why is the town library a good place to put the travel guide?

Try Your Hand

Publish Your Paragraphs of Comparison and Contrast Follow the checklist in the **Writer's Guide.** If possible, create a travel guide, or try this idea for sharing your paragraphs.

◆ Read your paragraphs aloud to the class. Share drawings you have made or photographs you have taken. Invite your audience to ask you questions or to discuss your work.

Writing in the Content Areas

Use what you learned to write paragraphs of comparison and contrast about people, places, and things that interest you. You could write a magazine article or a newspaper article. Use one of these ideas or an idea of your own.

Writer's Guide

When you write, remember the stages of the Writing Process.

- ◆ Prewriting
- ◆ Drafting
- ◆ Responding and Revising
- ◆ Proofreading
- ◆ Publishing

Science

Living creatures are grouped in families. Read about two different animals that belong to the same family. Then compare and contrast them with one another. Consider how they look and where they live. Tell how their habits are alike yet different.

Mathematics

Pick two objects that have something in common. For example, you might choose two chairs or two tables. Count the parts. Figure out the difference between the numbers of parts or pieces they have. Then write a report. Compare and contrast the two objects.

Physical Education

Choose two sports activities that you enjoy. What do they have in common? How are they different? Consider how many people are needed and when the sport is played. You may want to make a diagram to go with your writing.

Fine Arts

Ask a librarian to help you find a book of paintings or photographs. Find two paintings or two photographs that have something in common. Then notice how they are different. Do they have the same subjects? Are the colors dark or bright? Compare and contrast the two works of art.

CONNECTING
WRITING ⬌ LANGUAGE

When writers compare and contrast two subjects, they organize and present their ideas carefully. They want their readers to follow their ideas easily. How are the writer's ideas organized in these paragraphs of comparison and contrast?

My grandfather and my grandmother are alike in some important ways. Both are cheerful, hardworking, honest people.

However, they are different in some other ways. My grandfather is tall, quiet, and slow. When Grandfather tackles a project, he says, "Anything worth doing is worth doing well." On the other hand, my grandmother is short, talkative, and energetic. She takes on five projects at once. She laughs and asks, "Isn't it better to do something badly than not to do it at all?"

◆ **Mechanics in Paragraphs of Comparison and Contrast**   These ideas were presented clearly. The writer paid careful attention to using correct punctuation and capitalization. Presenting information correctly helps the reader as much as organizing it well does. As you read, think about how difficult it would be if the writer did not capitalize and punctuate correctly.

◆ **Language Focus: Mechanics Wrap-up**   In the following lessons you will learn more about using correct punctuation and capitalization in your own writing.

1 Capitalization and End Punctuation of Sentences

◆ **FOCUS**   A sentence begins with a capital letter and ends with a punctuation mark.

Remember that there are four types of sentences.

1. **I** ndians were the first Americans **.**
    declarative

2. **T** ell me what you know about American Indians **.**   imperative

3. **D** id Columbus name them Indians **?**
    interrogative

4. **W** hat a mistake that was **!**   exclamatory

A declarative sentence and an imperative sentence end with a period. An interrogative sentence ends with a question mark. An exclamatory sentence ends with an exclamation point. The first word of any sentence begins with a capital letter.

A system of writing invented by Sequoya, a Cherokee Indian.

Guided Practice

A. Identify the punctuation mark needed in each sentence.

1. Read what this book says about some of the first American Indians
2. They may have come from Asia over 20,000 years ago
3. How long ago that was
4. How did they get to North America
5. They may have crossed a land bridge across the Bering Strait

---

THINK AND REMEMBER
- ◆ End a declarative sentence and an imperative sentence with a period. End an interrogative sentence with a question mark. End an exclamatory sentence with an exclamation point.
- ◆ Begin every sentence with a capital letter.

Independent Practice

B. Using Correct End Punctuation Write each sentence. Add the correct end punctuation.

6. Imagine the life of some Indian children

MODEL ▷ Imagine the life of some Indian children.

7. Some children lived with many relatives
8. How close and warm those big families must have been
9. Did everyone share the work
10. What fun it was to live with so many cousins
11. How were the children raised
12. They were praised for good behavior
13. Treat other people with respect
14. What other values did the children learn

C. Proofreading Sentences Write each sentence. Add capital letters and end punctuation.

15. look at those clouds

MODEL ▷ Look at those clouds.

16. do most people today respect nature
17. the early Indians were in harmony with nature
18. what beauty we have around us
19. always respect the land and living things
20. why did the Indians know so much about nature
21. their lives sometimes changed with the seasons
22. some tribes needed to prepare for cold weather
23. can you think of some things they needed to do
24. look at the wild things and learn from them
25. how much there is to learn
26. do you know the first signs of winter

Application—Writing

A Book Introduction Imagine that you are writing a book about the history of the American Indians. Write an opening paragraph that tells your readers about some of the things Indians have done. Use what you already know about Indians for ideas. In your paragraph use each type of sentence at least once. Be sure to begin and end each sentence correctly.

2 Commas Within Sentences

◆ **FOCUS** A **comma** separates parts of a sentence and helps make the meaning clear.

Remember that commas are used to separate the parts of compound sentences and to set apart words in a series.

1. Most Hispanic Americans have Spanish ancestors , but some have Portuguese ancestors. **compound sentence**

2. Mexico , Puerto Rico , and Chile have Hispanic cultures. **words in a series**

Commas are used to signal pauses in other places, too. The answer to a question or a remark may begin with *yes, no,* or *well.* A comma follows each of these opening words.

3. Yes , my mother's family is Hispanic.

4. No , they did not come directly from Spain.

5. Well , they lived in Mexico for five generations.

Commas are also used to set off the names of people who are spoken to in a sentence.

6. Gabriel , tell us about your family.

7. Please give me your attention , class!

Guided Practice

A. Tell where you would add commas to these sentences.

1. Amanda can you name some Spanish colonies?
2. The Spanish settled Florida Texas and California.
3. Well I know they settled much of South America.
4. No not every country was a colony of Spain.
5. Spain claimed Argentina but Portugal claimed Brazil.
6. How did the Spanish change the colonies Arnoldo?
7. The Spanish brought sheep pigs and cattle here.
8. The Spanish brought the first horses here and the Plains Indians became expert riders.

Independent Practice

B. Using Commas   Write *correct* if commas are used correctly. Write *incorrect* if commas are missing.

9. Emily, tell us about your heritage.

MODEL > correct

10. Yes my father's family came from the Philippines.
11. Europeans Asians and Americans have settled there.
12. My father speaks English, Spanish, and Pilipino.
13. I can speak Pilipino but I never learned Spanish.
14. My grandfather tells interesting stories Ms. Tang.

C. Proofreading Sentences   Each sentence needs a comma. Write the sentence and add the comma where it belongs.

15. Well let Gabriel speak first.

MODEL > Well, let Gabriel speak first.

16. Gabriel do you call yourself a Mexican American?
17. Yes I am an American with Mexican ancestors.
18. My grandparents left Mexico and they moved to Texas.
19. What part did the Mexican settlers play here Emily?
20. They taught settlers from the east how to irrigate land brand cattle, and tame horses.
21. Yes they also taught miners how to mine gold.

Application—Writing and Speaking

Dialogue   The students in the picture are writing a play about Hispanic culture. Write ten sentences of dialogue for them. Use the picture and your own experiences. Write a compound sentence, a sentence with words in a series, a sentence in which someone is addressed by name, and a sentence that begins with *yes*, *no*, or *well*. Be sure to use commas correctly.

3 Capitalization of Proper Nouns and the Pronoun *I*

◆ **FOCUS** A proper noun and the pronoun *I* are always capitalized.

Remember that a proper noun names a particular person, place, or thing. The name of a person, a street, a city, a state, a day, a month, and a holiday are all proper nouns. A common noun names any person, place, or thing.

1. Is B randon your brother?

2. My favorite city is H onolulu.

3. The last day of the week is S aturday.

4. The hottest month is A ugust.

Many proper nouns are made up of more than one word. Each important word begins with a capital letter. The words *of* and *the* are not important words.

5. They live in W ichita F alls.

6. We went to the F iesta of F ive F lags.

The pronoun *I* is always capitalized, wherever it appears in a sentence.

7. Jose and I are going to a festival.

Guided Practice

A. Identify the words that should be capitalized.

1. nation	4. lake tahoe	7. boy scouts of america
2. aunt eva	5. my uncle	8. sassafras mountain
3. desert	6. marta gomez	9. pennsylvania turnpike

> **THINK AND REMEMBER**
> ◆ Capitalize each important word in a proper noun.
> ◆ Capitalize the pronoun *I.*

Independent Practice

B. Capitalizing Proper Nouns   If the noun is written correctly, write *correct*. If it is not, rewrite it correctly.

10. monday

Monday

11. new year's day	**16.** freddy burr	**21.** festival of roses
12. plain	**17.** dade county fair	**22.** weekday
13. teacher	**18.** holiday	**23.** union pacific railroad
14. texas	**19.** state	**24.** golden gate bridge
15. silver city	**20.** railroad station	**25.** pet frog

C. Proofreading Sentences   Write these sentences. Add capital letters where they are needed.

26. Grandfather was born near loch ness.

Grandfather was born near Loch Ness.

27. Each summer my family and i go to a festival.

28. The festival is called the highland games.

29. It comes after the fourth of july.

30. It is held in the mountains of north carolina.

31. Our home is in gary, west virginia.

32. We drive down the blue ridge parkway to get there.

33. We stay with my aunt in the town of linville.

34. The festival is held high on grandfather mountain.

35. Families from scotland started the festival.

36. My grandfather's name is robert duncan.

37. He came from a city called inverness.

38. The festival lasts from thursday to sunday.

39. My father and uncle robert march in a parade.

40. Then, I watch anne stewart try to win a dance contest.

41. Someday i hope to enter a dance contest.

42. I would like to enter a dance contest in new york city.

Application—Writing

A Postcard   Imagine that you went to the festival advertised on the poster or some other festival. Write a postcard to a friend that tells what you saw and did. Use at least six proper nouns. Be sure to capitalize each one correctly.

4 Abbreviations

◆ **FOCUS** Most abbreviations begin with a capital letter and are followed by a period.

Remember that an abbreviation is a short way to write a word. Review this chart of abbreviations.

Date Words That Are Abbreviated					
Jan.	January	Oct.	October	Tues.	Tuesday
Feb.	February	Nov.	November	Wed.	Wednesday
Mar.	March	Dec.	December	Thurs.	Thursday
Apr.	April			Fri.	Friday
Aug.	August	Sun.	Sunday	Sat.	Saturday
Sept.	September	Mon.	Monday		

Parts of Addresses That Are Abbreviated					
St.	Street	Rd.	Road	Blvd.	Boulevard
Ave.	Avenue	Dr.	Drive	Ln.	Lane

Remember that an initial is a letter that stands for a person's first name or middle name. An initial is capitalized and is followed by a period. Titles of people are often abbreviated.

Mr. L. P. Grossman   Ms. G. H. Day

Guided Practice

A. Tell how to rewrite these items using abbreviations and initials. Use the chart on page 80 for more help.

1. Wednesday
2. Mister Mark Gale
3. 423 Grant Street
4. February
5. Doctor Janice Kraal
6. 34 Hickory Corner Road
7. Captain Francis Hugo Furtado
8. Thursday, October 8

THINK AND REMEMBER

◆ Begin an abbreviation with a capital letter and end it with a period.
◆ Capitalize an initial and follow it with a period.

Dad—
Mr. Klein says the meeting or Aug. 23 will be at 1775 Lobel Dr. inste of on Elm St.

Independent Practice

B. Writing Abbreviations Rewrite the following items. Use abbreviations or initials whenever possible.

9. Thursday

MODEL > Thurs.

10. 234 Railroad Avenue
11. Doctor Greg McHolm
12. Captain Kevin Tsukushi
13. November
14. 23 Pepperwood Lane

15. Governor Miriam Ferguson
16. 4930 Soquel Drive
17. Monday, March 7
18. Mister Scott Aebi
19. Senator Mark Hatfield

C. Writing Abbreviations Correctly Write each item. Use capital letters and periods correctly.

20. dec.

MODEL > Dec.

21. sen Matsunaga
22. 2532 9th ave
23. sept 8
24. 180 Ocean blvd
25. fri.

26. mrs h r Moorthy
27. sat.
28. 8025 Lilac dr
29. ms Fran Lucia
30. gov Rafael Colon

D. Proofreading Abbreviations Each item contains a spelling error. Write each abbreviation correctly.

31. Febr. 8

MODEL > Feb. 8

32. Weds.
33. Sent. R. Graham
34. 111 Stender Blv.
35. Dtr. J. G. Pho
36. 127 Happy Valley Lne

37. 18 Elgin Str.
38. Sep. 3
39. Mstr. Woody Oyung
40. Mz. H. B. Lirette
41. 18 Sequoia Av.

Application—Writing, Listening, Speaking

Phone Messages Work with a partner to practice taking phone messages. First, make notes about two different phone messages you plan to give. Note details about places and dates. Then meet with your partner. Take turns holding phone conversations in which one of you gives information to the other to write down. Use abbreviations.

5 Letters

◆ **FOCUS** The five parts of a friendly letter follow rules of capitalization and punctuation.

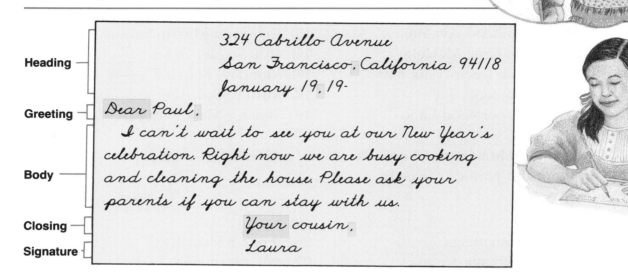

Heading

324 Cabrillo Avenue
San Francisco, California 94118
January 19, 19-

Greeting

Dear Paul,

Body

I can't wait to see you at our New Year's celebration. Right now we are busy cooking and cleaning the house. Please ask your parents if you can stay with us.

Closing

Your cousin,

Signature

Laura

This chart gives guidelines for using capitalization and punctuation in a letter.

Part of Letter	Capitalize	Use a Comma
Heading	street, city, state, month	between the city and the state, between the day and the year
Greeting	first word, proper noun	after the last word
Closing	first word	after the last word

Notice also that there is always a space between the state name and the ZIP code.

Guided Practice

A. Tell where capital letters and commas are needed in these parts of a letter.

1. 245 jacaranda drive
2. january 3 1990
3. dear lisa
4. dear grandmother
5. hilo hawaii
6. your nephew

Independent Practice

B. Writing the Parts of a Letter Rewrite these parts of a letter. Add capital letters and commas where they are needed.

7. yours truly

MODEL ▷ Yours truly,

8. october 12 1492
9. 194 peony lane
10. 310 west 89th st.
11. January 8 1990
12. 303 woodrow ave.

13. dear Uncle John
14. troy iowa 52592
15. with love
16. New York city NY 10003
17. your friend

C. Proofreading a Letter Rewrite this letter. Add capital letters and commas where they are needed.

> 1405 85th avenue
> oakland california 94621
> april 9 19– –

dear justin

    I hope you are happy in your new school. Our whole class misses you. We are having the International Fair on May 18–19. i am working on the Vietnam display. can you come to visit us that weekend?

>   your buddy
>   Cara Dat

Application—Writing

A Letter Imagine that you are Paul, a cousin of the girl in the picture. Write a letter to a pen pal. Describe your New Year's celebration. Use the picture for ideas.

6 Envelopes

◆ **FOCUS** The return address and the receiver's address on an envelope follow rules of capitalization and punctuation.

The **return address** on an envelope is the name and address of the person sending the letter. A letter that cannot be delivered will be returned to this address. The **receiver's address** is the name and address of the person who is to receive the letter.

As in a letter, all proper nouns and abbreviations are capitalized. Notice that the state names *Indiana* and *California* are not spelled out. A postal abbreviation is used instead. This special abbreviation is written with two capital letters and no period. The chart on page 395 shows all the postal abbreviations.

Stamp

Return Address

Mr. and Mrs. H. Soo
110 Holly Dr.
Evansville, IN 47712

Receiver's Address

Laura Soo
324 Cabrillo Ave.
San Francisco, CA 94118

Guided Practice

A. Tell where capital letters, commas, and periods are needed. Change the state names into postal abbreviations. Check the chart on page 395.

1. tony kohout
2. omaha nebraska 68135
3. 888 pinecrest ave
4. 121 sunset ln
5. baytown texas 77520
6. mr max ludwig

THINK AND REMEMBER

◆ Capitalize all proper nouns in envelope addresses.
◆ Use a comma between the city and the state names. Leave a space between the state and the ZIP code.
◆ Use a postal abbreviation for the state name.

Independent Practice

B. Writing the Parts of an Envelope Address   Rewrite these parts of an envelope address correctly. Add capital letters, commas, and periods. Change state names to postal abbreviations.

7. dover massachusetts 02030

MODEL ⟩ Dover, MA 02030

8. york maine 03909
9. 22 apple ln
10. 726 kessler blvd
11. ms teresa gomez
12. macon georgia 31211

13. carlin nevada 89822
14. 8222 cedar dr
15. troy new york 12180
16. mr quang pham
17. boise idaho 83706

C. Proofreading an Envelope   Copy this envelope, correcting the mistakes in punctuation and capitalization. Change the state names to postal abbreviations.

michael giannini
738 lunar dr
alta utah 84092

mr carl sullivan
5551 hickory ln
waco texas 76711

Application—Writing

Addressing Envelopes   Think of three people whom you would like to invite to a party. Find out their addresses. On a sheet of paper, draw three rectangles. Address an envelope to each of these people.

7 Outlines

◆ **FOCUS** An outline follows rules of capitalization and punctuation.

My Family History
I. Mom's family
  A. Great-grandparents come from Prague in 1922
  B. Grandfather Antonin Machotka born in 1924
  C. Antonin and Jane Kopal marry in 1946
  D. Mother, Antoinette, born in 1952 in Philadelphia
II. Dad's family
  A. Grandfather Abe Levine born in Poland in 1928
  B. Grandfather's family comes to U.S. in 1935
  C. Abe and Sarah Segal marry in 1951
  D. My father, David, born in 1953 in Boston

An outline has a **title** that tells what it is about. Each important word in the title is capitalized. The title is centered.

The outline shows two main topics that will be covered in a report. A **main topic** tells the main idea of a large part of the report. A Roman numeral and a period identify each main topic.

Subtopics are listed under each main topic. The **subtopics** are notes about facts that support each main topic. Each subtopic is indented and follows a capital letter and a period. The first word of each topic and each subtopic begins with a capital letter.

Guided Practice

A. Tell how to correct the mistakes in this outline.
  our Polish-American heritage

  1 role played by Poles in early American history
  a polish craftsworkers came to Jamestown in 1609
  b C. Pulaski fought in American Revolution
  2 contributions made by modern Polish Americans
  a olympic gold medals won by Stella Walsh
  b children's books written by Maurice Sendak

Independent Practice

B. Proofreading an Outline   Rewrite this outline. Correct mistakes in punctuation, capitalization, and outline form.

my family heritage
I   my father's family
a   grandmother Anne born in 1932
b   Anne marries William Bruce in 1953
c. my father, John, born in 1955 in Hartford
2. my mother's family
d. in 1928 grandmother Susan born
e. Susan marries James Smith in 1948
f. my mom, Annette, born in 1954 in Trenton

C. Making an Outline   Make an outline. Use these main topics and subtopics. Give the outline a title.

Main Topics
My family after I was born
My family before I was born
Subtopics
my parents met at the University of Chicago
my mother and father married in Chicago
we moved to Detroit just after I was born
my sister was born in Detroit

Application—Writing

An Outline   The boy in the picture has collected notes for a family history. Interview your family to get facts for your own family history. Arrange your notes in outline form. Punctuate and capitalize your outline correctly.

8 Titles

◆ **FOCUS** The title of a written work follows rules of capitalization and punctuation.

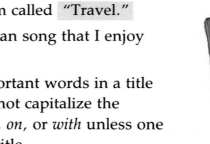

The titles of works are marked in special ways. Titles are either underlined or enclosed in quotation marks. Underline the titles of books, magazines, and newspapers.

1. The Iron Moonhunter is the name of an interesting book.
2. Have you heard of a magazine called Ebony ?
3. Several years ago she worked on a newspaper called The Globe .

Put quotation marks around the titles of shorter works, such as stories, poems, and songs.

4. I read an Indian story called "The Wishing Chair."
5. Stevenson wrote a poem called "Travel."
6. "My Boat" is a Hawaiian song that I enjoy very much.

The first word and all important words in a title begin with capital letters. Do not capitalize the words *a, an, the, and, or, in, of, on,* or *with* unless one of these is the first word of a title.

Guided Practice

A. The word in parentheses ( ) tells what kind of work each title names. Tell if each title should be marked with *underlining* or *quotation marks.*

1. Little Bear (a story)
2. Hispanic (a magazine)
3. Foreign Lands (a poem)
4. The Holland Reporter (a newspaper)
5. Carlota (a book)
6. Cielito Lindo (a song)
7. Nazar the Brave (a story)
8. The Two Uncles of Pablo (a book)

Independent Practice

B. Punctuating Titles   Write these titles correctly. Use underlining or quotation marks.

9. Zum Gali Gali (story)

MODEL "Zum Gali Gali"

10. What Then, Raman? (book)
11. Sir Patrick Spens (poem)
12. The Firebird (story)
13. Charlotte's Web (book)
14. The Ash Grove (song)
15. Pacific Citizen (newspaper)
16. Espen Cinderlad (story)
17. Alfalfa Hill (poem)

C. Proofreading Sentences   Write these sentences. Mark the titles correctly. Add capital letters where they are needed.

18. My favorite book is once upon a totem.

MODEL My favorite book is Once Upon a Totem.

19. Isn't sarasponda a Dutch song?

20. The Scottish song the campbells are coming is lively.

21. the moment of wonder is a book of Oriental poetry.

22. late snowflakes is a poem in that book.

23. nuestro was one of the first Hispanic magazines.

24. the five chinese brothers is a book about a family that thinks one brother is missing on a fishing trip.

25. In 1896 an Italian newspaper called the echo was started.

Application—Writing

Titles   Imagine that you are working on a bulletin board display for the library. Write the title of at least one story, one poem, one book, one song, and one newspaper or magazine for the display. You may work with a partner or ask a librarian for ideas. Mark and capitalize the titles.

9 Direct Quotations and Dialogue

◆ **FOCUS** A direct quotation follows rules of capitalization and punctuation.

Read these sentences. The words in color are direct quotations.

1. Mr. Miller said, "We have family roots in Africa."
2. Marcus exclaimed, "I know!"
3. "When did they come here?" asked Carrie.
4. "Our family arrived in 1800," said Dad.

Here are guidelines for writing direct quotations.

---

1. Put quotation marks before and after a quotation.
2. Capitalize the first word of the quotation.
3. When some words come before the quotation, put a comma between these words and the first quotation mark. (Study sentences 1–2.)
4. When some words come after the quotation, use a comma, a question mark, or an exclamation point to separate the quotation from the rest of the sentence. The comma takes the place of a period. (Study sentences 3–4.)
5. Always put the end mark for the quotation before the last quotation mark.
6. When you write dialogue for a story, indent and begin a new paragraph for each new speaker.

Guided Practice

A. Tell where the quotation marks belong.

1. Where are our ancestors from? asked Marcus.
2. Dad told them, My family came from Nigeria.
3. I know where that is! exclaimed Marcus.
4. Carrie said, It is on the west coast of Africa.
5. Mom's family is from Ghana, explained Dad.

Independent Practice

B. Using Quotation Marks   Write each sentence. Add quotation marks where they are needed.

6. Dad asked, How important is storytelling?

MODEL ⟩ Dad asked, "How important is storytelling?"

7. I'm not sure, replied Marcus.

8. Dad said, Storytelling is an art.

9. Of course it is! exclaimed Carrie.

10. We read African folk tales in school, she added.

C. Writing Quotations   Write each sentence. Add capital letters and punctuation where they are needed.

11. "I wonder how old those tales are" said Marcus.

MODEL ⟩ "I wonder how old those tales are," said Marcus.

12. "why do people tell folk tales" asked Dad

13. Carrie replied "they tell them for fun"

14. Marcus asked "don't folk tales teach lessons"

15. "some show what is right and wrong" Dad said

16. Carrie laughed "you tell us that directly"

D. Proofreading a Story   Rewrite this conversation. Make a new paragraph for each new speaker. Add punctuation.

Lola begged Tell us a story, Grandmother. We want a long story exclaimed her brother Tor. Well, what story do you want asked Grandmother. I like the stories about the clever spider answered Lola thoughtfully.

Application—Writing and Speaking

A Story   Imagine that you are a writer who creates stories. Write a short tale that is fun to read and teaches a lesson. Use dialogue. Be sure to punctuate and capitalize the dialogue correctly. Read your completed story to your classmates. If you need help in writing a story, see page 28 of the **Writer's Handbook.**

Building Vocabulary
Idioms

The experiment just didn't pan out. I think we have to try something new.

The two pictures show people who hoped that something would "pan out." The miner hoped to wash rocks out of his pan and find heavy gold on the bottom. The scientists hoped an experiment would produce the results they wanted.

The expression *pan out* is an idiom. An **idiom** is a group of words that has a special meaning when used together. Our language contains many idioms. Most idioms are used only in informal language.

1. The bakery was a gold mine for the Chung family.

2. If we continue with the experiment, I am sure we will hit pay dirt.

In idioms, words do not mean what they seem to mean. In sentence 1, the bakery did not turn into a real gold mine. Instead, it became a good source of income. In sentence 2, the speaker was not planning to dig to find gold or silver. The speaker was hoping to get good results.

You can find an idiom defined in a dictionary. You can look up *gold mine* and *pay dirt* to find the meanings of the idioms in the sentences above.

Reading Practice

Read the sentences. Study the underlined idioms. Then write the letter of the sentence that correctly defines the idiom.

1. The miner worked very hard until he just <u>ran out of steam</u>.
   a. He lost all his energy.
   b. He had no more steam to power his steam engine.
2. He wondered if he should go home or keep on mining. He just <u>didn't know which way to turn</u>.
   a. He wasn't sure what to do next.
   b. He got lost and couldn't find his way home.
3. He couldn't decide whether to go or to stay. His plans were <u>up in the air</u>.
   a. He planned to take an airplane home.
   b. His plans were uncertain.
4. Then he <u>got a break</u>. His pick struck a vein of gold.
   a. He broke his leg.
   b. He had good luck.
5. He grinned when he saw it. He was <u>on top of the world</u>.
   a. He was mining near the North Pole.
   b. He was very happy.

Writing Practice

Rewrite the sentences. Use formal language. Replace the underlined idioms with words that say the same thing.

6. When everyone got mad at Heather, she <u>played it cool</u>.
7. I didn't get home until after dinner. I knew I would be <u>in hot water</u>.
8. Brittany thought about hiding the vase she had broken. Then she decided to go to her mom and <u>face the music</u>.
9. Vanessa's brother pestered her until she told him to <u>go fly a kite</u>.

Project

Work with a group. Collect idioms from books, magazines, and newspapers. Use them to make a collage. Make a card for each idiom. Then write a sentence with the idiom. Tell what it means. Try to guess how the idiom got started.

Language Enrichment
Mechanics

Use what you know about punctuation and capitalization to do these activities.

 Mapping Your Neighborhood

Make a map of the neighborhood near the school, the library, the playground, or someplace else. Write in the names of the streets. Then draw boxes on each block that stand for businesses and public buildings. Inside each box write the name of the building and its address. A phone book can help you spell business names and check addresses. Use abbreviations when you can. When you finish, you and your classmates can put together an atlas, a book of maps.

Taking Dictation

Find a short paragraph that contains more than one type of end punctuation. It may contain dialogue too. Then meet with a partner. Take turns dictating to one another.

Here's what to do when you dictate. First, read the paragraph at a normal speed while your partner listens. Make your voice show the different kinds of sentences. Then, read the paragraph slowly while your partner writes. Spell any words that are hard for your partner. Repeat words if you are asked to. When you are finished, compare what your partner wrote with the original paragraph. Notice whether punctuation and capitalization are correct.

CONNECTING

LANGUAGE ↔ WRITING

In this unit you learned about punctuation and capitalization. You know that you use a period, an exclamation point, or a question mark to end a sentence. You use a comma to signal a pause. You also learned rules for using capital letters and certain punctuation marks in addresses, abbreviations, titles, and direct quotations.

◆ **Using Punctuation and Capitalization in Your Writing** It is important to use punctuation and capital letters correctly when you write. They help your reader to understand your ideas. Pay special attention to capital letters and punctuation as you do these activities.

Old and New

This family left a small village in Europe to come to the United States. What were their thoughts? Write a story about this family. Use your imagination to create names for them. Make up details about their lives. Use dialogue in your story. Check your capitalization and punctuation. Read your story to a classmate.

"You're Not Kidding!"

You learned about idioms on the **Building Vocabulary** pages. Now try this entertaining activity with idioms.

List some idioms. Use the idioms on your list to write a short dialogue. Be sure to punctuate direct quotations correctly. Then draw a picture to go along with one of your idioms.

Example: "Did you get up on the wrong side of the bed?" asked Linda.
"No," answered John. "I feel like a million dollars."

Think Back	Think Ahead
◆ What did you learn about paragraphs of comparison and contrast in this unit? What did you do to write one?	◆ How will what you learned about paragraphs of comparison and contrast help you when you want to help someone else see the differences between two things?
	◆ How will evaluating to compare and contrast help you when you have to make a choice between two things?
◆ Look at the writing you did in this unit. How did capitalization and punctuation help you express your ideas?	◆ What is one way that you can use capitalization and punctuation to improve your writing?

Analyzing Paragraphs of Comparison and Contrast *pages 369–370*

Read these paragraphs. Then follow the directions.

> If you saw my father and grandfather from the back, you would never be able to tell the difference. They are the same height and weight. They have the same hair color. They even walk the same way. My father's face shows what my grandfather's used to look like. My grandfather's face shows what my father's will look like in the future.
>
> However, the two men's personalities are completely different. My father and I do science experiments and share a stamp collection. We enjoy reading and figuring things out. My grandfather and I wrestle, play basketball, and ride go-carts. He is teaching me boxing. My grandfather is always going somewhere or doing something exciting.

1. What is the writer comparing and contrasting?
2. Name two ways the two subjects are alike.
3. Name one way each is father different.

Evaluating for Comparison and Contrast   *page 371*

List two subjects in each of the following categories. Name one way your two subjects are alike and one way they are different.

4. toys
5. places to eat
6. places to go sightseeing

Using Formal and Informal Language   *page 372*

Rewrite each sentence, changing informal language to formal language.

7. Well, my little brother is just about like every other little boy around here.
8. He's getting to where he can almost tie his shoes by himself.
9. Every once in a while a bunch of other guys comes over.

The Writing Process   *pages 373–381*

Write the letter of the correct answer for each question.

10. What should you do after you have brainstormed a list of topics for your paragraphs?
   a. Choose the best topic.
   b. Start writing your paragraphs.
   c. Start organizing information.
11. When you write your paragraphs of comparison and contrast, which paragraph should you write first?
   a. how the two subjects are different
   b. how one subject is chosen
   c. how the two subjects are alike
12. What do you write after the first topic sentence?
   a. the second topic sentence
   b. the title
   c. detail sentences to support it

Capitalization and End Punctuation of Sentences   *pages 384–385*

Write each sentence. Add capital letters and end punctuation.

13. how beautiful our American flag is
14. how can we honor it
15. salute the flag when it passes in a parade

16. civilians put their hands over their hearts

17. military personnel salute in the usual way

Commas Within Sentences   *pages 386–387*

Write *correct* if commas are used correctly. Write *incorrect* if commas are missing.

18. Tim, tell us about the history of flags.

19. Well flags were first used long ago.

20. Captains in Egypt Greece, and Persia used them.

21. Flags were squares, rectangles and triangles.

22. They even made "swallow-tail" flags Mrs. Lee.

23. Yes, flags certainly have a long history.

Capitalization of Proper Nouns and the Pronoun *I*   *pages 388–389*

If the noun is written correctly, write *correct*. If it is not, rewrite it correctly.

24. Katherine Joy Davis

25. sister

26. Newspaper

27. festival

28. eugene McCarthy

29. christmas

Abbreviations   *pages 390–391*

Rewrite the following items. Use abbreviations or initials whenever possible.

30. 656 Shady Lane

31. Hampton Boulevard

32. Doctor Vi Ann Clough

33. 200 Perry Avenue

34. February 29, 1960

35. Mister Frederick A. Pirate

Letters   *pages 392–393*

Rewrite these parts of a letter. Add capital letters and commas that are needed.

36. sincerely yours

37. with loads of love

38. dear ruth

39. tuscaloosa alabama 37401

40. 138 trent drive

41. december 7 1942

Envelopes   *pages 394–395*

Rewrite these parts of an envelope address. Add capital letters and commas where they are needed. Change state names to postal abbreviations.

42. cantonment florida 32733

43. greensboro north carolina 27408

44. governor jim hunt

45. elkton maryland 21921

46. rushford new york 14777

47. 2813 zephyr road

48. augusta georgia 30904

49. omaha nebraska 88123

Outlines *pages 396–397*

50.–56. Make an outline. Use these main topics and subtopics. Give the outline a title.

Main Topics
my English ancestors
my Indian ancestors

Subtopics
my great-grandfather was a Sioux Indian
one of my ancestors came from England
my English ancestor married an English woman
my great-grandmother was a Cherokee Indian

Titles *pages 398–399*

Write these titles correctly. Use underlining or quotation marks.

57. God Bless America (song)
58. Jack and Jill (magazine)
59. Hats Off! (poem)
60. And Now Miguel? (book)
61. The New Colossus (poem)
62. Weekly Reader (newspaper)

Direct Quotations and Dialogue *pages 400–401*

Write each sentence. Add quotation marks where they are needed.

63. Jan asked, How did the Liberty Bell get cracked?
64. The colonists wanted a big bell, Mom explained.
65. Dad said, They had a bell made in England.
66. But that one cracked when they rang it, he added.
67. Paul said, Then some people made another bell.

Idioms *pages 402–403*

Read the sentences. Study the underlined idioms. Then write the letter of the sentence that correctly defines the idiom.

68. Even though Rick was angry at the other boys, he decided he wouldn't make any waves.
    a. He wouldn't say hello to any of them any more.
    b. He wouldn't do anything about the situation.

69. Antonio was walking on air after he got his first paycheck.
    a. He was very happy.
    b. He bought some jet-propelled shoes with the money.

70. I worked around the clock to finish my project.
    a. I put a big clock in the middle of the room.
    b. I worked every hour of the day.

Cumulative Review

Complete and Simple Subjects   *pages 38–39*

Write each complete subject. Then underline the simple subject.

1. William Shakespeare is a very popular writer.
2. This famous man lived and worked in England.
3. Many people read and study his work today.
4. His great plays are still being performed.
5. A famous Shakespeare play is *Romeo and Juliet.*
6. Those two people loved each other deeply.
7. Their families were fighting a bitter battle.
8. The two young people could not be together.
9. This play has a very sad ending.
10. Other plays by Shakespeare are funny.

Complete and Simple Predicates   *pages 40–41*

Write each complete predicate. Underline the simple predicate.

11. Shakespeare acted in plays as a young man.
12. He wrote his own plays soon.
13. Actors performed the plays at the Globe Theater.
14. The stage had a balcony.
15. Juliet called to Romeo from this balcony.
16. Rich people sat in the covered balconies.
17. They stayed dry there even when it rained.
18. Poor people sat in the open yard.
19. They ignored the rain.
20. They enjoyed seeing the plays too much.

Singular and Plural Nouns   *pages 74–77*

Write each underlined noun. Then write *singular* or *plural* after each.

21. The main <u>waterway</u> in London was its huge <u>river</u>.
22. Its first <u>bridge</u> took 33 <u>years</u> to build.
23. Roaring <u>waves</u> rushed under the stone <u>arches</u>.
24. A brave <u>person</u> would enjoy riding the <u>currents</u>.
25. A <u>boat</u> could be steered through the <u>arch</u>.

26. <u>Workers</u> needed to repair the <u>structure</u> often.
27. <u>Children</u> sang about <u>London Bridge</u> falling down.

Singular and Plural Possessive Nouns *pages 86–89*
Write the possessive form of each noun or noun phrase.

28. Pilgrims
29. American Indians
30. sailors
31. ships
32. colonies
33. Founding Fathers
34. immigrants
35. land
36. home
37. countries

38. brother
39. sister
40. child
41. Americans
42. continents
43. England
44. Mexicans
45. Spain
46. South America
47. Asia

Main Verbs and Helping Verbs *pages 130–131*
Make a chart with two columns. Head them *Helping Verbs* and
Main Verbs. Write each underlined word in the correct column.

48. The Statue of Liberty <u>was</u> <u>given</u> to us by France.
49. Both countries <u>were</u> <u>longing</u> for liberty for all.
50. It <u>was</u> <u>dedicated</u> by President Grover Cleveland in 1886.
51. Frederic Bartholdi <u>had</u> <u>been</u> the sculptor.
52. He <u>was</u> <u>standing</u> inside the torch.
53. "I <u>have</u> <u>worked</u> on this statue for 20 years."
54. "She <u>has</u> <u>represented</u> friendship to me."
55. "She <u>is</u> <u>raising</u> her torch up high."
56. "Her crown's rays <u>are</u> <u>radiating</u> to all the world."

Verb Tenses *pages 132–133*
Decide which tense each underlined verb is. Then write *present,*
past, or *future.*

57. Finally, they <u>lit</u> Miss Liberty's torch.
58. "I <u>am</u> disappointed!" Bartholdi exclaimed.
59. "Her torch <u>sends</u> out only a gleam."
60. "It <u>looks</u> like a glowworm."
61. "We <u>will fix</u> it right away," said the President.
62. Workers <u>installed</u> hundreds of lights.

63. "The torch now <u>will be</u> much brighter."
64. Miss Liberty <u>had</u> her hundredth birthday in 1986.
65. She <u>received</u> a new torch of copper and gold.
66. This light <u>will shine</u> far out across the sea.
67. It <u>will say</u> to immigrants, "Liberty!"

Agreement of Subjects and Verbs   *pages 168–169*
Write the verb in parentheses ( ) that agrees with the subject.

68. The Americans (fights, fight) the British.
69. Francis Scott Key (is, are) in the war.
70. He (wants, want) to go aboard the British ship.
71. A friend of his (is, are) being held there.
72. He (holds, hold) out the white truce flag.
73. The British (lets, let) Francis aboard.
74. Then, he (discovers, discover) a British plan.
75. They (is, are) going to attack an American fort!

Irregular Verbs   *pages 170–171*
Read each sentence. Write the correct past-tense form of the verb in parentheses ( ).

76. The ship (begin) to fire rockets at the fort.
77. Then one rocket (fly) over the fort and exploded.
78. Francis (see) the American flag still there.
79. He (know) the fort had not surrendered.
80. In the morning, he (begin) to peer out again.
81. "Is the flag still there?" he (say).
82. The flag (grow) tattered and torn.
83. It still (blow) in the wind!
84. "The fort has not been conquered!" he (think).
85. Then he (write) a song.
86. He (give) it the name "The Star-Spangled Banner."
87. This song later (become) our national anthem.

Subject and Object Pronouns   *pages 214–217*
Replace the underlined words with pronouns. Write the new sentences.

88. Where did <u>you and I</u> get our first American flag?
89. An old story has come down to <u>you and me</u>.

90. President Washington went to Betsy Ross.
91. He said, "Can Betsy sew a flag for Washington?"
92. Betsy got her needle and thread out.
93. Soon Betsy gave the flag to Washington.
94. "The red, white, and blue stand for blood, purity, and loyalty."
95. "Betsy used stars for the colonies," she said.
96. Washington thanked Betsy.
97. "We will always remember Betsy," he told her.

Possessive Pronouns   *pages 222–223*

Rewrite each sentence. Replace the underlined words with one possessive pronoun.

98. An old story says that Chief Powhatan asked the prisoner, "What is the prisoner's name?"
99. The man answered, "The man's name is John Smith."
100. Someone said, "Take John Smith's life."
101. In the story Pocahontas crept out of Pocahontas's tent.
102. She told Chief Powhatan, "No, Chief Powhatan cannot do that!"
103. Chief Powhatan let the tribes' prisoner go.
104. The chief helped the colonists' colony of Jamestown.
105. Jamestown's most famous woman was Pocahontas.
106. John Smith may have said, "John Smith's wish is to introduce Pocahontas to the king."

Adjectives   *pages 258–259*

Write the adjective that describes each underlined noun.

107. John Chapman is also a famous American.
108. He used his special plants to heal people.
109. People were chopping down many trees.
110. They made good use of them.
111. However, they were not replacing the missing trees.
112. John thought about the distant future.
113. He wanted enough trees to be there later.
114. He believed in planting more seeds.
115. People soon gave him a new name.
116. They called this helpful man "Johnny Appleseed."

Adjectives That Compare: with *er, est*   *pages 264–265*
Write the missing adjectives.

117. big, bigger, _____
118. odd, odder, _____
119. moldy, _____ , moldiest
120. trim, trimmer, _____
121. firm, _____ , firmest
122. soggy, soggier _____
123. grand, grander, _____
124. huge, huger, _____
125. great, _____ , greatest
126. new, _____ , newest

127. late, later, _____
128. close, _____ , closest
129. red, redder, _____
130. noisy, _____ , noisiest
131. sweet, _____ , sweetest
132. pretty, prettier, _____
133. safe, safer, _____
134. sad, _____ , saddest
135. happy, _____ , happiest
136. long, _____ , longest

Adverbs   *pages 300–301*
Write each sentence. Underline the adverb once. Underline the verb it tells about twice.

137. Immigrants bravely left their homelands for America.
138. The people arrived early for the trip.
139. They really wanted a new life in a new land.
140. The immigrants crowded nervously onto the boat.
141. The boat moved slowly across the ocean.
142. Storms often struck at sea.
143. The waves splashed wildly against the sides of the boat.
144. The people huddled together in fear of the storm.
145. The sailors calmed the passengers continually.
146. Finally, the wind stopped howling.
147. The immigrants truly hoped there would be no more storms.
148. They cheered joyfully when they saw New York Harbor.

Adverbs That Compare   *pages 304–305*
Write the adverbs. Fill in the missing adverb forms.

149. easily, ____ , most easily
150. gently, more gently, ____
151. wisely, ____ , most wisely
152. bravely, more bravely, ____

153. suddenly, more suddenly, ____
154. carefully, more carefully, ____

Adverb or Adjective?   *pages 308–309*

Write *adverb* or *adjective* for each underlined word.

155. loved nature <u>deeply</u>
156. left <u>suddenly</u>
157. fought <u>bravely</u>
158. <u>big</u> ship
159. <u>long</u> trip
160. <u>new</u> country
161. <u>eventually</u> arrived
162. <u>huge</u> crowds
163. <u>much</u> money
164. yelled <u>eagerly</u>

165. <u>soon</u> bought
166. <u>complete</u> happiness
167. <u>difficult</u> job
168. worked <u>hard</u>
169. <u>beautiful</u> songs
170. waited <u>hopefully</u>
171. watched <u>longingly</u>
172. <u>quickly</u> learned
173. <u>finally</u> slept
174. rested <u>peacefully</u>

Compound Subjects   *pages 346–347*

Write the two simple subjects in each sentence.

175. Sunshine and blue skies will make our picnic a success.
176. Snow and ice covered the roads.
177. The sunrise and the sunset are beautiful to see.
178. Thunder and lightning scared the animals.
179. The wind and the rain kept everyone inside at lunchtime.
180. The moon and the stars are very bright tonight.
181. Mars and Venus can be seen on the horizon.
182. Stars and planets are fun to see through a telescope.

Compound Predicates   *pages 348–349*

Write the two simple predicates in each sentence.

183. The horse stood quietly and pawed at the ground.
184. Jim waved his arms and yelled to the lifeguard.
185. Terri dialed the number and waited.
186. Josh mixed the batter and poured some into the pan.
187. The doctor smiled and patted my shoulder.
188. We talked and laughed about the talent show.
189. Patricia walked and ran to arrive at the meeting on time.

STUDY SKILLS

Contents

1 Using a Dictionary

A **dictionary** is a book that gives the spellings, pronunciations, and meanings of words. The words in a dictionary are listed in **alphabetical order.** To **alphabetize** words, you arrange them by letter from *A* to *Z*. These words are alphabetized by their first letters.

airplane   center   flagpole   independent   question

When you want to alphabetize words that begin with the same letter, you must look at the second letter of each word. Sometimes the second letters are also the same. Then you must look at the third letters. To alphabetize the words in the groups below, it was necessary to look at the underlined letters.

c<u>a</u>st	c<u>e</u>nter	c<u>h</u>ase	c<u>l</u>asp	c<u>u</u>e
go<u>a</u>l	go<u>b</u>ble	go<u>l</u>den	go<u>o</u>se	go<u>u</u>rd
sen<u>a</u>te	sen<u>d</u>	sen<u>i</u>or	sen<u>s</u>e	sen<u>t</u>ry

Practice

A. List the words in each group in alphabetical order. In some cases, you will have to alphabetize by looking at the second letter.

1. view, wait, voice, uproar
   MODEL ▷ uproar, view, voice, wait
2. bloom, beach, base, bitter
3. vote, melt, regret, over
4. enjoy, edit, early, elect
5. relay, crane, jam, even
6. nickel, never, name, nod
7. only, over, none, mark
8. ache, anchor, each, odd
9. handle, hose, hush, heavy
10. rumor, sweet, pry, raise
11. pig, potato, plus, page
12. joke, ice, jewel, host
13. invite, idea, igloo, item

B. List the words in each group in alphabetical order. Alphabetize to the third or fourth letters.

14. grand, grace, grateful
    MODEL ▷ grace, grand, grateful
15. moose, moment, money
16. juice, jungle, jump
17. stormy, stolen, stove
18. reason, ready, reach
19. finish, final, finger
20. navy, Navajo, navigate
21. beam, beast, beady
22. waste, wavy, walrus
23. shark, shadow, shape
24. dairy, danger, darken
25. tramp, treat, trail

2 Finding Words in a Dictionary

How can you find a word quickly in the dictionary? First, imagine the alphabet and the dictionary divided into these three parts.

abcde	fghijklmnop	qrstuvwxyz
(front)	(middle)	(back)

Identify the group in which the beginning letter of the word belongs. This will tell you whether to open the dictionary near the front, the middle, or the back. Then turn the pages forward or backward until you have found the pages with words that begin with that letter.

Each word listed in the dictionary is called an **entry word. Guide words** at the top of each page help you find the entry word you want. The guide word at the top left shows which is the first entry word on that page. The guide word at the top right shows which is the last entry word on the page. All the other entry words on the page appear in alphabetical order between these guide words.

---

emigrate   emporium

em·i·grate [em′ə·grāt′] *v.* **em·i·grat·ed,**
  em·i·grat·ing To move from one country
  or section of a country to settle in
  another: to *emigrate* from Italy to the
  U.S. — **em′·i·gra′tion** *n.*

em·pa·thy [em′pə·thē] *n.* The capacity to
  share another person's feelings or
  thoughts.
em·per·or [em′pər·ər] *n.* A person who
  reigns over an empire or has the title of
  ruler of an empire.

Practice

A. Decide in which part of the dictionary each word will appear. Write *front, middle,* or *back.*

1. medal
   MODEL > middle
2. brief
3. date

4. whisk
5. silence
6. palace
7. grace

8. ripe
9. destiny
10. reveal
11. value

12. play
13. gopher
14. motion
15. yield

B. Write the word or words in each group that would be found on a page with the guide words *hoax* and *hollow.*

16. home, hold, holly
    MODEL > hold
17. honor, hogwash, hobby
18. hobo, hoop, horn
19. hourly, holder, hoe
20. hostage, hominy, hobble
21. horizon, hoist, hood

22. help, hurt, hoe
23. housing, hot, hog
24. hock, hoard, holdup
25. hockey, horse, holiday
26. hoarse, honey, hole
27. hodgepodge, hook, hogan

STUDY SKILLS

3 Using a Dictionary Entry

In a dictionary, each entry word is followed by a **definition** that explains what the word means. If a word has only one meaning, only one definition is given. For words that have more than one meaning, a numbered definition is given for each meaning. Some definitions are followed by **example sentences,** which show how each definition is used.

> **bor·der** [bôr′dər]   1. *n.* A margin or edge.   2. *v.* To put a border on: to *border* a handkerchief.   3. *n.* The boundary line dividing one country or state from another.   4. *v.* To lie along the border of; bound: The park *borders* the lake.

Sometimes there will be two or more entries for what seems to be the same word. Each entry word will be followed by a number. This tells you that these words are **homographs.** Though they are spelled in the same way, their meanings are completely different.

> **boot**[1] [boot]   1. *n.* A covering, usually of leather, for the foot and part of the leg.   2. *v.* To put boots on.   3. *v.* To kick.   4. *n.* A kick.   5. *n.* A thick patch on the inside of an automobile tire.
> **boot**[2] [boot] *n.* To benefit or avail: seldom used today.

Practice

A. Notice how *border* is used in each of these sentences. Then study the definitions of *border*. Write the number of the definition that applies to each sentence.

   1. A row of elms *borders* the property.

MODEL▷ 4

   2. The Ohio River *borders* Kentucky.
   3. The dancer's skirt had a red *border*.
   4. The tourists crossed the *border* into Mexico.
   5. He *bordered* the walk with yellow tulips.

B. Look up each word in your dictionary. If you find entry words followed by numbers, write *homograph*. If not, write *no homograph*.

   6. boot

MODEL▷ homograph   **9.** record   **12.** use   **15.** wind
   7. blow   **10.** pain   **13.** heap   **16.** graze
   8. date   **11.** talk   **14.** content   **17.** clean

4 Using a Dictionary for Syllabication and Parts of Speech

Besides showing how to spell a word, a dictionary shows how to divide it into syllables. A **syllable** is a word part with only one vowel sound. Sometimes dots are used to show the syllable breaks in entry words.

> **dew·claw** [d(y)o͞o′klô′] *n.* A toe or hoof that does not reach the ground on the foot of some mammals.
> **dew·drop** [d(y)o͞o′drop′] *n.* A drop of dew.

This information about syllable breaks is useful. First, it helps you pronounce words correctly. Second, if you are writing and are nearly at the end of a line, the syllable break shows you where you may divide the word.

A dictionary also indicates the part of speech of each word. In the definitions above, the letter *n.* stands for the word *noun*. This means that both entry words are used as nouns. A list of abbreviations for the parts of speech usually appears at the beginning of a dictionary. It may look like this.

n.	noun	*adj.*	adjective	*conj.*	conjunction
pron.	pronoun	*adv.*	adverb	*interj.*	interjection
v.	verb	*prep.*	preposition		

Practice

A. Look up each word in your dictionary. If it is correctly broken into syllables, write *correct*. If it is not, rewrite it correctly.

1. left·ov·er
MODEL ▷ left·o·ver
2. paj·a·mas
3. cho·co·late
4. en·gin·eer

5. trump·et
6. sat·el·lite
7. dia·ry
8. dis·cord

9. mag·ne·tic
10. de·ter·mine
11. ri·val·ry
12. se·cre·ta·ry

B. Look up these words in your dictionary. Write each one's part of speech.

13. seethe
MODEL ▷ verb
14. derrick
15. pearly

16. rough
17. limpid
18. amply

19. serenity
20. prophesy
21. flutist

5 Using a Dictionary for Pronunciation

A dictionary entry does more than show you how to write and use a word. It tells you how to pronounce, or say, it. A **pronunciation respelling** enclosed in brackets [ ] follows each entry word.

---

min·ute¹ [min'it] *n.*   **1** The 60th part of an hour; 60 seconds.   **2** A very brief time; moment.
mi·nute² [mī·n(y)ōot'] *adj.*   **1** Tiny.   **2** Very careful and precise in small details.

The pronunciation respelling is divided into syllables. Marks are used to separate the syllable in the respelling. Most consonants stand for the consonant sounds you know. A **pronunciation key** helps you to read the other combinations of letters and marks. It lists each combination and the sound it stands for. A pronunciation key is usually found on every other page of a dictionary.

a	add	i	it	ōō	took	oi	oil
ā	ace	ī	ice	ōō	pool	ou	pout
â	care	o	odd	u	up	ng	ring
ä	palm	ō	open	û	burn	th	thin
e	end	ô	order	yōō	fuse	th	this
ē	equal					zh	vision

$$ə = \begin{cases} \text{a in } above & \text{e in } sicken & \text{i in } possible \\ \text{o in } melon & \text{u in } circus \end{cases}$$

Practice

Use the key to figure out each pronunciation. Then write the word that matches it. After each word, write the number of syllables it has.

1. mīr   mirror   mire   mare

MODEL ▷ mire 1

2. thûr'ō   threw   thorough   though
3. fōōl   fuel   fall   full
4. mān   main   man   mean
5. pīn   pine   pin   pen
6. stā'shən   stashes   starches   station
7. boks   box   books   backs
8. bēst   best   beats   beast
9. hōp'ing   hoping   hopping   happening
10. tā'lər   taller   teller   tailor
11. shok   shook   shock   shack
12. chōz   chews   chose   choice
13. klōs   clothes   claws   close

6 Using the Parts of a Book

Many books contain useful facts. Certain pages at the beginning of a book can give you information about its contents and arrangement.

The **title page** gives the title of the book and the name of its author. It also tells the name of the publishing company and the city in which it is located.

The **table of contents** usually follows the title page. This section lists the units or chapters in the book and the page on which each one begins. By reading the chapter or unit titles, you can form a general idea of the contents of the book. The list of page numbers makes it easy to find the material you want.

The World of the North American Indian

by Laura Emily Janowitz

Eucalyptus Press, Inc.
Berkeley, California

Title Page

CONTENTS

Table of Contents

Practice

A. Study the title page and the table of contents. Write the answers to these questions.

   1. What is the title of the book?

MODEL > The World of the North American Indian

   2. Who wrote the book?

   3. Who published the book?

   4. Where was it published?

   5. What is the number of the chapter about the Southeastern tribes? On what page does it begin?

   6. Which chapter gives information on the Papago Indians of the Arizona pueblos?

   7. On which page would you begin looking for material on the tribes of the Canadian woodlands?

   8. Do you think this book has information about the Indians who lived in Mexico? Give a reason for your answer.

   9. Study the chapter titles. How did the writer organize the information in the book?

  10. On which page does the index begin?

B. Use the title page and the table of contents of this book to answer these questions.

  11. What is the title of this book?

MODEL > HBJ Language

  12. Who are the authors of this book?

  13. Who published this book?

  14. How many units does this book have?

  15. On which page does a lesson on negatives begin?

  16. In which unit is the research report taught?

  17. In which unit would you find the definition for *noun*?

  18. Which two units contain lessons on verbs?

  19. What is the title of Unit 6?

  20. Which unit has the title "Using Your Imagination?"

  21. What is the last part of the book listed in the table of contents?

7 Using an Index

An index often appears at the back of a book that gives information. An **index** is a list of the topics in a book and the pages on which they can be found. The topics are listed in alphabetical order so that readers can find them quickly. Sometimes a topic may be very general. Then **subtopics** are listed below it. These subtopics help readers find specific information.

Practice

Use the index to answer these questions.

1. Which of the topics have subtopics listed under them?
   MODEL> clothing, corn crops
2. On which page of the book can you find information about Chief Cochise?
3. On which page can you find information about the Aztec Indians' corn crops?
4. Suppose you were doing research about Chief Crazy Horse. Would this book be helpful to you? Tell why or why not.
5. Suppose you were doing research on pottery by the Hopi Indians. What topics would you look for in other sections of this index?
6. How is an index different from a table of contents?

STUDY SKILLS

8 Using the Card Catalogue

Every library keeps a file of the books it owns. This file is called a **card catalogue.** A card catalogue tells library users what books the library owns and where they can be found. Sometimes the card catalogue is found on a computer. Most often it is made up of cards kept in drawers. On the outside of each drawer are guide letters. These letters tell the first letter of the headings on the cards inside. The cards are filed in alphabetical order.

There are three types of cards in a card catalogue. The **author card** shows the author's last name first. The **title card** shows the book title first. This card is alphabetized according to the first important word in the title. The **subject card** shows the subject of the book first.

970.1 J	**Janowitz, Laura Emily** The world of the north american indian / Laura Emily Janowitz. Berkeley: Eucalyptus Press, 1987. 234 pp.: ill.	**author card**

970.1 J	**INDIANS** Janowitz, Laura Emily The world of the north american indian / Laura Emily Janowitz. Berkeley: Eucalyptus Press, 1987. 234 pp.: ill. 1. Indians I. Title Library of Congress	**subject card**

970.1 J	**The World of the North American Indian** Janowitz, Laura Emily The world of the north american indian / Laura Emily Janowitz. Berkeley: Eucalyptus Press, 1987. 234 pp.: ill.	**title card**

Practice

Use the catalogue cards to answer these questions.

1. To find this author card in the card catalogue, what letter should you look for on the drawer?

MODEL⟩ J

2. To search for the title card, what letter should you look for?
3. Under what subject is the book listed?
4. What type of card would you check to find out whether this author has written other books?
5. What type of card would you look under to find a book called *Native Americans*?
6. How is a subject card helpful to library users?

9 Using the Library

Each type of book in a library has its own section. One large area contains fiction books. **Fiction** books are stories that are all or partly imaginary. These are arranged on the shelves in alphabetical order according to the author's last name.

In another area are nonfiction books. **Nonfiction** books give facts about real people, things, events, and ideas. These books are grouped together by subject.

A **biography** is a certain type of nonfiction book. It tells about the life of a real person. Libraries often have special areas just for biographies. These books are arranged in alphabetical order according to the last name of the subject.

Libraries also have a reference section for nonfiction books that cannot be checked out. **Reference** books include encyclopedias, dictionaries, and atlases.

Practice

Read the list of books. Write *fiction, nonfiction, biography,* or *reference* to tell where each can be found in a library. Write *nonfiction* only if a book is not in the biography or reference area. The words in parentheses ( ) can help you decide this.

1. *Amos Fortune, Freeman* (the true story of an ex-slave)
   MODEL ▷ biography
2. *Secret of the Emerald Star* (a mystery story)
3. *Webster's Third Dictionary*
4. *The Cricket in Times Square* (a story about talking animal friends)
5. *Abe Lincoln Grows Up* (an account of Lincoln's early life)
6. *101 Science Experiments* (how to do experiments)
7. *The Art of the Eskimo* (facts about Eskimo arts)
8. *A Wrinkle in Time* (a space travel fantasy)
9. *World Book Encyclopedia*
10. *The Land and People of New Zealand* (a travel book)
11. *Cornelia* (the true story of a Civil War nurse)
12. *Atlas of American History*
13. *The Life and Letters of Lewis Carroll*
14. *A Wrinkle in Time* (a science fiction story)
15. *Cooking Metric Is Fun* (a cookbook)

10 Using Reference Books

Reference books are collections of facts. A **dictionary** is a book that gives facts about words. It shows how to spell and pronounce words and lists all their meanings. Some dictionaries list only words that involve one subject area. For example, you might see a dictionary of music or of science.

An **encyclopedia** is a set of books that contains information about people, places, things, events, and ideas. An encyclopedia article gives the most important facts and many interesting details about a topic. An article can be a few paragraphs long or many pages long.

An **atlas** is a book of maps. A world atlas contains maps for every part of the globe. Other atlases may contain maps for only certain regions. Many contain special maps that show climate and land forms.

An **almanac** contains information on many topics. Because it is printed every year, it is always up-to-date. Almanacs provide facts on current events, famous people, and the products of the nation's factories and farms. Almanacs also include information on topics of interest such as music, theater, and popular movies.

Practice

Decide which reference book you would use to answer each of these questions. Write *dictionary, encyclopedia, atlas,* or *almanac.*

1. What large cities lie on the St. Lawrence River?
   `MODEL` ▷ atlas
2. Which spelling is correct: *suceed* or *succeed*?
3. What countries are Peru's neighbors?
4. What is Shirley Chisholm known for?
5. What were the first airplanes like?
6. What is the cash value of this year's corn crop in Indiana?
7. Do you pronounce the *t* in *often*?
8. Should I use *further* or *farther* in my sentence?
9. What did dinosaurs eat?
10. What bay is near Houston?
11. What movie made the most money last year?
12. How much rain fell in Connecticut last year?
13. What causes hurricanes?
14. What is the pronunciation of *content* in the sentence *What is the silver content of this ore?*
15. How high is Mount Whitney?

11 Using an Encyclopedia

Most encyclopedias are made up of many books, which are called **volumes.**
The letters on the edge, or **spine,** of each volume show the beginning letters of
subjects included in that volume. The letters are in alphabetical order.

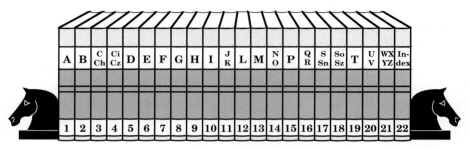

In the pages of the encyclopedia, the topics are covered in alphabetical order
too. To read about Mexico, for example, you would open the volume with *M* on
its spine. To find information on Sweden, you would use the volume labeled
So–Sz.

When you search for a topic, first decide which is the most important word,
or **key word,** in the topic. If you are looking up a famous person, the person's
last name would be the key word. Suppose you want facts about the history of
steamships. In this case *steamships*, not *history*, is the key word to use in your
search.

Practice

A. Use the encyclopedia set pictured. To find each topic, decide which volume
you need. Write the volume number.

1. guitar
   MODEL > 8
2. New England
3. lilac
4. Ethel Waters
5. computer

6. robots
7. architecture
8. Hawaii
9. kites
10. skywriting
11. sea lion

B. Write the key word you would use to look up information about each of
these topics.

12. Dr. Elizabeth Blackwell, a pioneer doctor
    MODEL > Blackwell
13. the Battle of the Alamo
14. the moons of the planet Jupiter
15. the voyages of Christopher Columbus
16. soccer, the national game of Peru
17. Brazil's annual rainfall

STUDY SKILLS

12 Using Guide Words in an Encyclopedia

Each article in an encyclopedia is called an **entry** and begins with an **entry word** that names the topic.

SNAKE ————————————————— entry word
A snake is an animal that has a long body covered with scales. Snakes have backbones but no legs. They belong to a group of animals called *reptiles*, which also includes lizards, turtles, and alligators.

Hunting for an entry word is like hunting for a word in a dictionary. To help you, an encyclopedia has a guide word at the top of each page. The one on the left page identifies the first entry word on the page. The one on the right page identifies the last entry word on that page.

SIBELIUS ————————————————— guide word

SIBELIUS, JEAN
Jean Sibelius was a composer from Finland. Symphonies are among his most important works.

Practice

A. You want to look up the entry word *minstrel*. Below are some pairs of guide words in an *M* volume. Write whether you would turn *back* or *forward* in the volume, or *look on that page.*

1. MISSISSIPPI RIVER   MISSOULA
MODEL ⟩back
2. MINNOW   MINORCA   **4.** MINUET   MIRA
3. MIRAGE   MIRROR   **5.** MINOTAUR   MINT

B. Look in an encyclopedia in your school or public library. Write the answers to these questions.

6. Look up *lentil.* Write the number of the volume in which you found this entry.
7. Write the guide words that appeared at the tops of the pages on which you found *lentil.*
8. Imagine that you are a famous person. Find the page on which your name would appear. Write the guide words that would help someone find the page with your name.

STUDY SKILLS

13 Taking Notes

Notes are the written records you make to help you remember things. You may take notes to remind you of facts.

The best way to take notes is to write them on cards. You make a separate card for each main idea. Then you add related facts to the card as you find them. Cards help you to organize your facts. You can lay out the cards in the order you will use them to write your outline.

The student who took the notes below used a question to identify the main idea. As he wrote, he **paraphrased** the information, or put the author's ideas into his own words. He also recorded the source of the information—the name of the book, its author, and the page number.

BRIDGES

What is a beam bridge?
    oldest type of nonmoving bridge
    like a board over a stream
    rests on supports on each bank
    may rest on supports in the water over long distances

<u>To Get to the Other Side</u> by Stella Hutchinson, p. 140

Tips for Taking Notes
1. Record the source of your information.
2. Sum up the main idea of each card in a heading. Use a question.
3. Record the most important facts and details.
4. Put the author's ideas into your own words. Write in phrases.

Practice

Read this paragraph. Write notes that answer the question "What is a suspension bridge?" Use the example note card as a model.

To *suspend* is to hang, so a suspension bridge is a hanging bridge. To build a modern suspension bridge, workers first put up a tall tower on or near each bank. Next, they string heavy metal cables between the towers. They fasten shorter cables to these. The short cables hang down. Then the workers attach the framework of the bridge floor to the ends of the cables. When the bridge is done, the roadway is like a long swing that hangs from its heavy cables overhead.

14 Skimming

When you need to find something quickly in a book, you skim its pages. **Skimming** is a method of reading to note the subject and its divisions.

Tips for Skimming
1. First, read quickly to identify the general subject of the material.
2. Notice how the subject is divided into parts. Sometimes section headings give you clues to this. Identifying the parts will help you understand the key ideas of the material.
3. Check the topic sentence of each paragraph. Use it to predict the contents of the paragraph and to see whether it will be helpful to you.

Practice

Read each question, and then skim the paragraphs to find the answer. Write the answer.

A Problem for Bridge Builders

In 1847 a difficult problem brought the Niagara River Bridge project to a halt. Engineers had designed a suspension bridge to carry trains across the deep canyon. However, they hadn't figured out how to get the heavy cable across. No boat could carry it over those raging waters. A reward was offered to anyone who solved the problem.

A Clever Solution

A thirteen-year-old boy named Homan Walsh claimed the reward. He flew a kite from one side of the canyon to the other. Workers on the other shore caught the kite. As they pulled it over, a heavier piece of twine was tied to the end of the kite string. Then heavier and heavier pieces of twine and rope were tied on. The cable itself was tied to the last and heaviest rope.

---

1. What are the paragraphs about?
MODEL ▷ a difficult problem on the Niagara River Bridge project
2. How is the information in them divided?
3. What might you skim the first paragraph to learn?
4. What might you skim the second paragraph to learn?
5. What is the most important fact that the second paragraph gives about the solution?

15 Scanning

Scanning is another method of reading quickly. When you scan, you do not read every word. You look through the passage for key words that have to do with your subject. For example, suppose you are searching for information on forest animals. If you are scanning an article on forests, you may look for the names of some of the forest's creatures. *Raccoon, bear, fox,* and *wolf* may be the key words that tell you when you have found your information. Only then should you stop to read more closely.

Practice

Read each question and scan the paragraph below. Then write the answers to the questions.

Niagara Falls

Niagara Falls is really two waterfalls on the Niagara River. This wide river carries water toward Lake Ontario from all the other Great Lakes. It narrows as it enters a deep canyon. Then it divides into two branches as it reaches Goat Island. The smaller branch drops over a rocky ledge and forms the American Falls near our shore. The larger branch becomes the great Horseshoe Falls between the island and the Canadian shore. Horseshoe Falls carries most of the water and is more spectacular. It is 158 feet high and about 2,600 feet across at its widest point.

---

1. What is the topic of the paragraph?
   MODEL ▷ Niagara Falls
2. You want to find names of the two waterfalls that make up Niagara Falls. What key word might you scan for? (Hint: What one word might be in the proper nouns that name them both?)
3. What are the names of the two waterfalls?
4. You want to find out which waterfall is nearer the Canadian shore. What key word or words would you scan for?
5. What is the waterfall nearer the Canadian shore called? Did you find this information in the beginning, middle, or ending of the paragraph?
6. You are looking for facts that tell sizes. What words or symbols should you scan for in the text?

16 Summarizing

Summarizing is a way of stating facts briefly. When you summarize, you give only the most important information. A **summary,** or short report, can be written or given aloud.

When you write a summary of something you have read, paraphrase the writer's ideas rather than copy them word for word. Note only main ideas and important details.

Look at the text below and then at the student's summary. Even though the passage is very brief, the student's work has made it shorter by using only the most important points.

> Much of the Niagara River is a smooth waterway for ships traveling between Lake Erie and Lake Ontario. No ship, however, can travel over the falls and through the rapids. So Canada built the Welland Canal to provide a shipping route around this dangerous stretch of water.

> Ships traveling from Lake Erie to Lake Ontario avoid Niagara Falls by taking Canada's Welland Canal.

Practice

Read each paragraph. Then write a one-sentence summary like the one in the example.

1. To get a duck's view of the falls, you can take a trip on the *Maid of the Mist*. Hundreds of tourists a day ride this small steamer through the choppy waters at the base of the falls.

   MODEL ▷ A small steamer carries tourists close to the bottom of the falls.

2. The best way to protect beautiful areas is to turn them into government parklands. New York State was the first to establish a park by the falls in 1885. In 1886 Canada established Queen Victoria Park. Now many acres of parkland surround Niagara Falls.

3. Niagara's water power is shared equally by Americans and Canadians. Its mighty flow turns the generators of many electric power plants on both sides of the river. Many factories have sprung up on both shores to take advantage of this source of energy.

17 Writing a Book Report

When you write a **book report,** you tell what the book is about. You also tell why someone might enjoy it. Here is a book report written by a fourth-grade student.

STUDY SKILLS

In the Year of the Boar and Jackie Robinson, — title
by Bette Bao Lord is a wonderful book. — author
Something interesting is always happening
to Shirley Temple Wong, the main character. — main character
Her first big adventure is her move from
China to Brooklyn, New York, in 1947. — time and place of story
    When Shirley begins school in America, she
knows only a few words of English. At first
all her efforts to stop being lonely fail. Then
a playground fight has an unexpected result.
Some new friendships and her love of — main idea of book
baseball help her to change and grow. They
also lead to a meeting with one of her
greatest heroes.
    This book will help everyone understand
what it is like to be different and lonely — why someone else might enjoy it
in a new land.

Follow these tips when you write a book report.

Tips for Writing a Book Report
1. In your first sentence, give the title of the book and the name of the author.
2. Next, tell whom or what the book is about. If it is a made-up story, tell a little about the main characters. Tell where and when the story takes place too.
3. Sum up the main idea of the book. Write some details, but do not tell what happens at the end.
4. Tell why someone else might like the book. Give your opinion of the book.

Practice

Write the answers to these questions.

1. What sentence in the model report identifies the main character? Who is the main character?

MODEL > the second one; Shirley Temple Wong

2. What is the title of the book?
3. Who is the author of the book?
4. What is the setting of the book?
5. The report writer does not tell exactly what happened because of the playground fight. Why not?
6. Why does the report writer recommend the book?
7. What are the parts of a book report?
8. In which part of a book report does the writer give a summary of the book?
9. In which part of a book report does the writer give an opinion?
10. Is an opinion necessary in a book report? Explain your answer.

18 Studying for a Test

Do you feel sure of yourself or nervous when you take a test? You can feel more confident if you follow these tips to get ready.

Tips for Studying for a Test
1. Listen carefully in class. Take notes on important facts to remember. Review your notes after school to be sure they are clear.
2. Ask questions about anything you do not understand.
3. Set aside enough study time every day for each subject.
4. Before you sit down to study, make sure you have all the books and materials you need.
5. Study in a quiet place with a good reading light.
6. Think about what you read. Try to find ways that the material you are learning applies to your own life. Ask yourself how you can use science or mathematics information.
7. Take short rest breaks when you are tired.
8. After you close your books, identify the most important things you learned. Make notes to remind yourself of key ideas.

Practice

Below are descriptions of students studying for a Friday history test. Read each one and write *good study habit* or *poor study habit*. If you write *poor study habit*, tell what the student should do instead.

1. Melissa puts off studying until Thursday night.
   MODEL▷ poor study habit; she should have studied each night
2. Kevin was out sick on Tuesday. He stays after class on Wednesday to ask the teacher what he missed.
3. Benjamin flops down on the living room floor, turns on the TV, and opens his books.
4. Tyler isn't really sure why the Boston Tea Party happened. He decides not to worry about it. He just memorizes the date and goes on reading.
5. Dominica's little sisters are being noisy. She packs up her books and goes to study in another room.
6. Lizzie decides to review all the material in the hour before her dance class. She keeps glancing at the clock and wondering whether Amy will be in class.

19 Taking Tests

The best way to do well on a test is to study for it. What can you do, though, if the test hasn't been announced and you haven't studied? These tips may help you as you work through the test.

Tips for Taking Tests
1. Listen closely while the teacher gives directions. If the directions are written, read them all the way through before you begin. Ask questions if you do not understand something.
2. If the test items are printed, scan the entire test before you begin. Estimate the time each part will take. Think about how much time you have, and plan how you will use it.
3. Answer all the easier questions first. Skip over and leave space for the harder questions. Go back and answer them after you finish the items you can answer quickly. This way you won't run out of time before answering the questions you are sure of.
4. Work quietly without disturbing those around you.
5. For some tests, you must mark boxes on an answer sheet. Check often to be sure the number of the box matches the number of the question.
6. If you finish before the test time is up, go back and read over your answers. You may want to change or add to them.

Practice

Ms. Allen's class has a half hour to take an English test. They begin at 1:30 P.M. Write *good habit* if the student is practicing a good test-taking habit. Write *poor habit* if the student is practicing a poor test-taking habit. Tell what each student practicing a poor habit should have done.

1. Jan answers the easiest questions first.
   MODEL ▷ good habit
2. Jeremy can't remember whether Ms. Allen said to underline the adjectives or the adverbs. He guesses and begins underlining adverbs.
3. Jenny is about to ask Amy whether they are to stop at the end of Part 1 or to go on to Part 2. She raises her hand and asks Ms. Allen instead.
4. Ben gets stuck on the second question in Part 1. He works on it a long time. He never finishes the test.
5. Lian finishes at 1:53. She begins drawing on scratch paper while she waits for the rest of the class to finish.
6. Luis decides that Part 1 contains the hardest questions. He skips to Part 2 and works on it first.

20 Using Bar Graphs

Some information is easier to understand if it is shown in a graph rather than summed up in a paragraph.

A **bar graph** illustrates items that are measured or counted. Look at the bar graph below. Its title tells the kind of information it contains. On the left is a list of things that have been counted. Across the top are the numbers to which the list refers. To read the graph, follow each bar with your finger until the bar ends. Then read the number above it for your answer.

Kinds of Hawks Seen While Bird-Watching: June 1990										
	1	2	3	4	5	6	7	8	9	10
Cooper's hawk	▬									
Pigeon hawk	▬▬▬▬▬▬▬									
Red-tailed hawk	▬▬▬▬▬									
Sparrow hawk	▬▬▬▬▬▬▬▬									

Practice

A. Use the graph to help you write the answers to these questions.

1. Which type of bird did the bird watcher see the least?
   MODEL▷ the Cooper's hawk
2. Which type of bird did she see the most? How many did she see?
3. Did she see more pigeon hawks or more red-tailed hawks? How many of each did she see?
4. How many more sparrow hawks than red-tailed hawks did she see?
5. How many sightings altogether did she record?
6. How many more red-tailed hawks did she see than Cooper's hawks?

B. Use the following information to make a graph like the one above. Remember to give your graph a title.

During October 1990, Melissa saw five turkey vultures, two prairie falcons, and six marsh hawks.

21 Using Tables

A **table** presents facts about a related group of items. It allows us to compare information about the items easily. Study the table below. Its title tells what kind of information is in it. The names listed in the left column tell what items are being compared. The headings across the top tell in what ways the items are being compared.

How to Tell Our Local Hawks Apart				
	Usual length	**Tail and wings**	**Flying pattern**	**Call**
Cooper's hawk	15-1/2″	long tail; short, rounded wings	beats quickly and then glides	15–20 cackles
Red-tailed hawk	18″	wide, fanned tail; wide, rounded wings	soars, circles prey, and dives steeply	high, weak scream
Pigeon hawk	12″	narrow-tipped tail; long, pointed wings	makes choppy beats and sometimes soars	"bik-bik-bik"

Reading the table is easy. Suppose you want to know what the call of a Cooper's hawk is. Find *Cooper's hawk* on the left. Move your finger across that row to the right. Stop in the column headed *Call*. The words in the box give the information you want.

Practice

Use the information in the table to write the answers to these questions.

1. Which hawk is the largest?
   MODEL ▷ the red-tailed hawk
2. Which hawk is the smallest? What is its size?
3. Suppose you see a hawk circle and dive steeply. Is it a pigeon hawk? Explain.
4. If you hear "bik-bik-bik," which hawk have you heard?
5. You think you see a Cooper's hawk. What tail and wing shape should you look for to make sure?

22 Using Maps

A **map** is a drawing that shows what a place would look like from above. It may show the whole world or just a single room. The map below is of a maze. In a maze, paths turn this way and that between high bushes. It is a challenge to find your way through one.

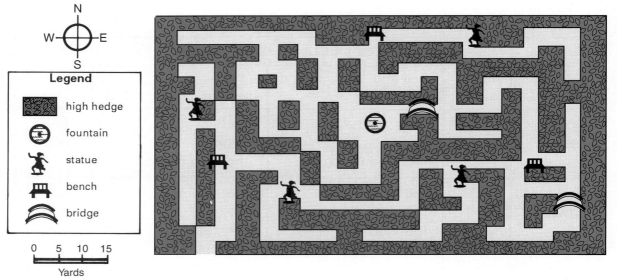

To help you use maps, map makers give you certain information. A **direction symbol,** or **compass rose,** shows which way *north, south, east,* and *west* lie on the map. A **legend** lists and explains all the symbols on the map. A **distance scale** allows you to measure the distance between places on the map. Use a ruler to measure along a route you might take. Then use the distance scale and your math skills to figure out how far apart two places are.

Practice

A. Study the map of the maze. Then write the answers to these questions.

1. Find the bridge closest to the fountain. Is it east or west of the fountain?

MODEL ▷ east of the fountain

2. How far is the bridge in item 1 from the fountain?

3. There is only one way in and out of the maze. If you were at the bench nearest the entrance, in which direction would you go to get out?

4. About how far is it from the bench to the exit?

5. Find another bench in the north part of the map. If you were walking from it to the nearest statue, in which direction would you be going?

B. Find the entrance into the maze. With your finger, trace different routes until you find the fastest one to the fountain. Write directions that tell how to get there. Use the words *north, south, east,* and *west* instead of *left* and *right*.

23 Taking Telephone Messages

The telephone is one of the fastest ways for one person to get an important message to another. If the message can't be given directly, however, a third person must see that it gets through. That is why you should know how to take phone messages clearly and completely.

Tips for Taking Telephone Messages

1. Don't depend on your memory. Write the message on a sheet of paper.
2. Ask the caller to spell or repeat anything you don't understand.
3. Write clearly. Read the message back to the caller to be sure it is correct.
4. Be sure the message contains these points.
   - the name of the person who gets the message
   - the name of the caller
   - the time and the reason for the call
   - the phone number of the caller
5. Sign the message with your name.

Practice

Take a message from each of these callers. Make up a time and sign your name to each message.

1. This is Jim at Rudy's Garage. Is your father home? Well, please tell him I've figured out the problem with the tractor, but I want to talk to him before I start work on it. Have him call me at 555–9001.

   MODEL ▷ 6:00 P.M. Tuesday

   Dad, Jim at Rudy's Garage called. He's figured out tractor problem. He wants to talk with you before he starts work. Call him at 555–9001. Rose

2. Hello, this is Janice Banks at the library. I am still holding the book Mr. Lehman asked for. Tell him to call me before eight o'clock at 555–2895. If he doesn't, I have to put the book back on the shelf.

3. Is your mother home? This is her cousin Rosa. I'm in town staying at my friend Julia's house until Friday. The number here is 555–6754. No, it's 555-6745. Tell her I'd like to see her tomorrow.

4. May I speak to Sashi? This is Anna. Oh. Please tell her that the meeting time has been changed. Tell her to call Mrs. Rosen for the new schedule. I think I have the number. Yes, it's 555–0328.

24 Completing Forms

Everyone has to fill out a form now and then. Forms are used when you apply for a job, enter a contest, join a club, or order something from a catalogue. If you make a mistake, the form will not say what you want it to. It is important to know how to fill out forms correctly.

Tips for Completing Forms

1. Read the whole form before you begin to write.
2. Be alert for directions that tell you to use pencil or pen.
3. Check carefully to see where you should write. The line on which your name should appear, for example, may not be right next to the word *Name.* Instead, it may be below or above it.
4. Be alert for directions that tell you to print instead of write. Always print or write neatly.
5. Give all the information you are asked for. When you are finished, look over the form to be sure you have completed it correctly.
6. Turn the form over to see if there are questions on both sides.

Practice

This is a copy of an entry form for a reading club. Make one like it on another sheet of paper and fill it out. Follow the tips.

Please print.

Name _____
      (last)   (first)

Address _____
         (number and street)

_____
    (city)   (state)   (ZIP code)

Name of School _____

Grade ____ Teacher's Name _____

Reading Goal _____
          (How many books will you read a month?)

Favorite Kind of Book _____

Favorite Books You Have Read _____

_____

EXTRA PRACTICE

Contents

1 Sentences *pages 30–31*

A. Identifying Sentences   Read each group of words. Then write *sentence* or *not a sentence*.

   1. We have a book fair every year.
[MODEL] > sentence
     2. The book fair is very crowded.
     3. The fair in the cafeteria.
     4. Students walk around the room.
     5. Many kinds of books.
     6. Posters are for sale.
     7. Books on tables and shelves.
     8. A woman at a table.
     9. She writes books for children.
   10. The table has a pile of books.
   11. She writes her name inside each book.

B. Completing Sentences   Choose the group of words in parentheses ( ) that will make a complete sentence.

   12. (Our class, At school) writes stories.
[MODEL] > Our class
   13. (The students, Today) made a class book.
   14. The book (has many stories, about an adventure).
   15. (One story, Tells) is about an adventure in space.
   16. Two astronauts (zoom into space, in a rocket).
   17. (A rocket, Propelled) takes the astronauts away.
   18. They (visit a planet, to a strange place).
   19. Another story (in the book, tells about a boy).
   20. The boy (travels back in time, on a ship).
   21. This story (is imaginary, before the end).
   22. The writers (read their book, on a shelf).

C. Writing Sentences   Add words to each group of words to make a complete sentence. Write each sentence.

   23. _____ is writing a play.
[MODEL] > Our class is writing a play.
   24. The play _____.
   25. _____ will act out the play.
   26. The actors _____.
   27. Many costumes _____.
   28. _____ will paint scenery.

EXTRA PRACTICE

2 Declarative and Interrogative Sentences

pages 32–33

A. Identifying Declarative and Interrogative Sentences   Write *declarative* or *interrogative* to identify each sentence.

   1. How can a person communicate?
MODEL ⟩ interrogative
   2. There are many forms of communication.
   3. Speech is a very common form of communication.
   4. Have people always been able to express themselves?
   5. Cave people painted pictures on their walls.
   6. In ancient Rome runners carried mail.
   7. Paper was invented in 105 A.D.
   8. Does the printing press print on paper?
   9. Telegraphs allowed information to travel quickly.
  10. Are television and radio used to communicate?
  11. Can a person talk to someone without speaking?

B. Correcting Declarative and Interrogative Sentences   Add capital letters and end punctuation. Write each sentence.

  12. sign language is used by deaf people
MODEL ⟩ Sign language is used by deaf people.
  13. a deaf person fingerspells the alphabet
  14. what is the sign for *dog*
  15. the first American deaf school was in Connecticut
  16. how can a hearing person learn sign language
  17. blind people use Braille to write and read
  18. a man named Louis Braille developed the code
  19. how is Braille written
  20. small raised dots on paper symbolize letters
  21. what raises the dots on paper
  22. metal plates are used to raise the dots

C. Writing Declarative and Interrogative Sentences   Write a declarative and an interrogative sentence for each item.

  23. flags
MODEL ⟩ Flags are used to send messages.
      Can two flags be used together?

24. code	**27.** alphabet	**30.** pictures
25. signals	**28.** signs	**31.** newspapers
26. telephone	**29.** music	**32.** lights

EXTRA PRACTICE

3 Imperative and Exclamatory Sentences
pages 34–35

A. Identifying Imperative and Exclamatory Sentences Write *imperative* or *exclamatory* to identify each sentence.

1. Look into the camera.
MODEL > imperative
2. Please follow the directions.
3. Meet your teacher in the studio in 10 minutes.
4. Wait for me.
5. What a great time we're going to have!
6. Listen to the photographer.
7. This will be our best class picture ever!
8. The photographer has so many cameras!
9. Sit in the first row.
10. These lights are very bright!
11. Get ready to have your picture taken.

B. Correcting Imperative and Exclamatory Sentences Add capital letters and the correct end punctuation. Write each sentence.

12. take me to the camera store
MODEL > Take me to the camera store.
13. help me find flashbulbs
14. do not forget to buy more film
15. what an amazing new camera that is
16. that camera is really tiny
17. let me look at it
18. what great photographs it takes
19. teach me how to use it
20. be sure the camera is steady

C. Writing Imperative and Exclamatory Sentences Add words to each group of words to make the kind of sentence shown in parentheses ( ). Write each sentence.

21. my new camera (exclamatory)
MODEL > How easy my new camera is to use!
22. these photographs (imperative)
23. some film (exclamatory)
24. dropped the camera (exclamatory)
25. at the photographer (imperative)

4 Subjects and Predicates *pages 36–37*

A. Identifying Subjects and Predicates Read each sentence. Write *subject* or *predicate* for the underlined words.

1. Emily <u>found a book about horses</u>.

MODEL ▷ predicate

2. <u>Our class</u> is going to the new public library.
3. The huge building <u>stands six stories tall</u>.
4. <u>Thousands of books</u> can be found in the library.
5. <u>Many different magazines</u> are in one room.
6. One room <u>displays globes and maps</u>.
7. Another section <u>contains videocassettes</u>.
8. Different sets of encyclopedias <u>fill the shelves</u>.
9. <u>The large reading room</u> has comfortable chairs.
10. Long tables <u>are arranged in four rows</u>.
11. <u>A bulletin board</u> displays a schedule of activities.

B. Choosing Subjects and Predicates Write each sentence. Underline the subject of each sentence once. Underline the predicate twice.

12. Our school library contains many books.

MODEL ▷ <u>Our school library</u> <u>contains many books</u>.

13. Some students are working in the library.
14. Their class project is a research report.
15. The librarian answers the students' questions.
16. Joe looks in the card catalogue.
17. The drawers are filled with hundreds of cards.
18. A library worker helps Joe.
19. The bookshelves are filled with books.
20. Amy looks for a book about whales.

C. Writing Sentences Add a subject or a predicate to each group of words. Write the sentences.

21. _____ belongs to a book club.

MODEL ▷ That girl belongs to a book club.

22. This new book _____.
23. _____ is reading a magazine.
24. _____ is a place to find books.
25. This story _____.

5 Complete and Simple Subjects *pages 38–39*

A. Identifying Simple Subjects   The complete subject in each
sentence is underlined. Write the simple subject.

   1. The white snow is very deep.
MODEL > snow
   2. The winter sky is full of clouds.
   3. A cold wind blows through the trees.
   4. Some happy children play in the snow.
   5. The shouts of friends echo across the park.
   6. Many sleds are being pulled up a hill.
   7. The crowded hill is filled with children.
   8. Each excited sledder waits to take a turn.
   9. The thrilling ride is over too soon.
   10. Large fluffy snowflakes begin to fall.
   11. The children's jackets are covered with snow.

B. Choosing Simple Subjects   Complete each sentence with a
simple subject from the **Word Box**. Use each simple subject
only once. Write the simple subject.

   12. The bright _____ went behind a cloud.
MODEL > sun
   13. Dark _____ gathered in the sky.
   14. A strong _____ scattered the leaves.
   15. The _____ of barking dogs was heard.
   16. Large _____ fell to the ground.
   17. The sudden _____ frightened the animals.
   18. Many little _____ flew away.
   19. Bright _____ lit up the sky.
   20. Loud _____ rumbled in the distance.
   21. The soggy _____ was full of puddles.
   22. A colorful _____ appeared after the storm.

WORD BOX
sun
storm
sound
ground
birds
raindrops
clouds
breeze
rainbow
thunder
lightning

C. Writing Sentences   Write a sentence for each complete
subject. Then underline the simple subject.

   23. the weather report
MODEL > The weather report is in the newspaper.
   24. rainy nights   **26.** winter days
   25. warm winds   **27.** one hot afternoon

EXTRA PRACTICE

6 Complete and Simple Predicates *pages 40–41*

A. **Identifying Simple Predicates**   The complete predicate in each sentence is underlined. Write the simple predicate.

  1. We <u>share our ideas in school</u>.
  MODEL ▷ share
  2. Ms. Kelly <u>asks a question</u>.
  3. She <u>looks at the class</u>.
  4. Many students <u>raise their hands</u>.
  5. Anna <u>gives an answer</u>.
  6. Jon <u>disagrees with her</u>.
  7. They <u>talk about the answer</u>.
  8. Other classmates <u>give their opinions</u>.
  9. The teacher <u>writes on the chalkboard</u>.
  10. Some pupils <u>discuss the assignment</u>.
  11. They <u>copy the teacher's directions</u>.

B. **Choosing Complete and Simple Predicates**   Write the complete predicate in each sentence. Then underline the simple predicate.

  12. The students wrote a report.
  MODEL ▷ <u>wrote</u> a report
  13. Groups of students prepared their material.
  14. They chose the topics for their reports.
  15. They went to the library next.
  16. Some looked for information in the card catalogue.
  17. Others worked in the reference room.
  18. They found many sets of encyclopedias there.
  19. Many students read magazine articles.
  20. They took notes on the facts.
  21. They gathered lots of material.
  22. The groups talked about their projects then.

C. **Writing Sentences**   Add a complete predicate to make each group of words a complete sentence. Then underline the simple predicate.

  23. Andy's report _____.
  MODEL ▷ Andy's report <u>tells</u> about dinosaurs.
  24. Our teacher _____.
  25. Some students _____.
  26. This poster _____.
  27. One report _____.
  28. The classroom _____.
  29. A bulletin board _____.

UNIT 2 1 Nouns *pages 72–73*

A. Identifying Nouns Write the nouns in each sentence.

1. There are many hairs on your head.
MODEL > hairs, head

2. Hair keeps heat inside your body.
3. It protects the skin on your scalp.
4. Hair is made of three layers of cells.
5. Its length increases every day.
6. You won't see a change in your mirror right away.
7. Each hair grows at a very slow rate.
8. Wash it with a mild shampoo and warm water.
9. Use a brush or a comb daily.
10. You can change the style of your hair.
11. Some people put a part on one side.

B. Classifying Nouns Write *person, place,* or *thing* for each underlined noun.

12. Wander into a garden on a nice day.
MODEL > garden—place, day—thing

13. With a friend, look for a caterpillar.
14. This creature is found all over the world.
15. It is the offspring of a butterfly.
16. This is the first stage of its life.
17. A tiny egg is laid by the mother.
18. After the youngster hatches, it will eat plants.
19. Soon, the insect will change into another form.
20. One day it builds a cocoon in a safe area.
21. The butterfly shows off the beauty of its wings.
22. The change will amaze you and your neighbors!

C. Writing Sentences with Nouns Write a sentence using each pair of nouns.

23. bones, body
MODEL > Your body contains many bones.

24. muscles, skeleton
25. legs, knee
26. hand, fingers
27. toes, foot
28. height, inches

29. shoulders, neck
30. arms, elbow
31. mouth, teeth
32. nose, throat
33. eyes, ears

2 Singular and Plural Nouns *pages 74–75*

A. Identifying Singular and Plural Nouns Write each underlined noun. Then write *singular* or *plural* after each one.

1. <u>Foxes</u> are about the size of small dogs.

MODEL ▷ Foxes—plural

2. These animals live on almost every <u>continent</u>.
3. Their <u>babies</u> are called kits.
4. Foxes may eat birds such as <u>turkeys</u>.
5. Their <u>diet</u> also includes different grasses.
6. Some foxes eat leaves from <u>bushes</u>.
7. They may also eat <u>bunches</u> of fruit.
8. A young fox gets food from its <u>parents</u>.
9. It will hunt later at <u>night</u>.
10. Foxes may change <u>color</u> as they grow older.
11. Foxes are about sixteen inches tall as <u>adults</u>.

B. Choosing Singular or Plural Nouns Write the form of the noun in parentheses ( ) that correctly completes each sentence.

12. Seeds are like tiny (box, boxes).

MODEL ▷ boxes

13. Each seed has a small (plant, plants) inside it.
14. Many (day, days) of warm weather help a seed grow.
15. Before too long, some (sprout, sprouts) appear.
16. All (flower, flowers) and fruits come from seeds.
17. A (daisy, daisies) produces its own seeds.
18. An apple and a (peach, peaches) do also.
19. Many (oil, oils) come from plant seeds.
20. Some leaves are used to make (brush, brushes).
21. A (package, packages) of seeds grows many flowers.

C. Writing Sentences with Plural Nouns Write a sentence using the plural form of each noun.

22. bush

MODEL ▷ The bushes are in bloom.

23. watch	27. tax	31. way
24. valley	28. flash	32. memory
25. berry	29. beach	33. eyelash
26. family	30. branch	34. gas

UNIT 2　3 More Plural Nouns *pages 76–77*

A. Identifying Plural Nouns　Write the plural noun in each sentence.

1. We watched a program about wild geese.
MODEL> geese
2. Another show explained about oxen.
3. It also showed some baby deer.
4. I liked the way children took care of them.
5. Some women explained how a deer grows.
6. They described a deer's teeth and what it eats.
7. A deer runs fast on its hooved feet.
8. Large moose are in the deer family.
9. So are reindeer, which live in the far north.
10. They are also called caribou.
11. Elk are in this family too.

B. Using Plural Nouns　Complete each sentence with the plural form of the noun in parentheses ( ).

12. One show was about _____. (sheep)
MODEL> sheep
13. These animals are as gentle as _____. (child)
14. How much do you know about big _____? (ox)
15. Some _____ use oxen to plow their fields. (man)
16. Farmers wear loose _____ in the hot sun. (trousers)
17. Some farmers may dress in short _____. (pants)
18. The farmers chase _____ from their crops. (mouse)
19. They stand on their _____ for a long time. (foot)

C. Writing Sentences with Plural Nouns　Write a sentence using the plural form of each noun.

20. goose
MODEL> Geese migrate in the winter.

21. foot	27. deer
22. tooth	28. man
23. woman	29. child
24. sheep	30. mouse
25. pants	31. moose
26. elk	32. salmon

4 Common and Proper Nouns *pages 78–79*

A. Identifying Common and Proper Nouns   Write *common* or *proper* for each underlined noun.

1. Some <u>tadpoles</u> become frogs.
> MODEL common
2. Frogs and toads do not live in <u>Antarctica</u>.
3. Tadpoles hatch from eggs and look like <u>fish</u>.
4. Bullfrogs and green frogs live in <u>America</u>.
5. After eight weeks, tadpoles grow hind <u>legs</u>.
6. Soon after, tadpoles lose their <u>tails</u>.
7. The horned frog lives in <u>Argentina</u>.
8. Frogs live in <u>ponds</u> and eat beetles.
9. Certain kinds of frogs live in <u>Europe</u>.
10. Adult frogs breathe through <u>lungs</u>.
11. Some frogs live in <u>South America</u>.

B. Correcting Proper Nouns   Add capital letters to each proper noun. Write the proper nouns correctly.

12. I went to a famous zoo in new york city.
> MODEL New York City
13. I saw baby kangaroos from australia.
14. Kangaroos also live in tasmania.
15. They come from new guinea, too.
16. These are islands in the pacific ocean.
17. I also saw giant pandas from china.
18. The pandas were loaned by a zoo in beijing.
19. Pandas are also in a zoo in washington, d.c.
20. Giant pandas have their babies in january.
21. Few pandas have been born in the united states.

C. Writing Sentences with Common and Proper Nouns
Complete the sentences with the common and proper nouns in parentheses ( ). Add a capital letter to each proper noun. Write the sentences.

22. Husky _____ live in _____. (pups, alaska)
> MODEL Husky pups live in Alaska.
23. Grown-up _____ work for _____. (huskies, eskimos)
24. Dogs called _____ are from _____. (terriers, england)
25. Is that _____ from _____? (poodle, france)
26. A dog from _____ is the _____. (wales, corgi)

5 Names and Titles of People *pages 80–81*

A. **Writing Names, Titles, and Initials**   Write the complete name of each person correctly. Add capital letters and periods where they are needed. Include all titles and initials.

1. One famous American is sen glenn of Ohio.
MODEL ⟩ Sen. Glenn
2. john h glenn was an astronaut.
3. susan b anthony fought for women's rights.
4. mrs eleanor roosevelt worked for human rights.
5. Her husband was once gov roosevelt of New York.
6. Later he became President franklin d roosevelt.
7. dr charles r drew was a famous physician.
8. sandra d o'Connor is on the Supreme Court.

B. **Correcting Names, Titles, and Initials**   Add capital letters and periods where they are needed. Write each sentence.

9. capt charles a lindbergh was a pilot.
MODEL ⟩ Capt. Charles A. Lindbergh was a pilot.
10. robert e peary reached the North Pole.
11. He went with mr matthew a henson in 1909.
12. dr frederick a cook also explored this area.
13. clara h barton started the American Red Cross.
14. Have you heard of ms madeleine m kunin?
15. She became gov kunin of Vermont.
16. sen hubert h humphrey was a Vice President.

C. **Writing Sentences Using Names, Titles, and Initials**   Replace the underlined titles of people with abbreviations. Replace the underlined names with initials. Write each sentence.

17. <u>Senator Bill</u> Bradley was a basketball star.
MODEL ⟩ Sen. B. Bradley was a basketball star.
18. <u>Doctor Jonas</u> E. Salk found a vaccine for polio.
19. <u>Mister Thomas</u> Edison was an inventor.
20. <u>Governor Ella</u> Grasso was the first woman to be elected governor.
21. <u>Senator Margaret Chase</u> Smith is from Maine.

6 Capitalization of Proper Nouns *pages 82–83*

A. Identifying Proper Nouns   Write each proper noun. Be sure to capitalize it.

1. The state of texas is growing and changing.
MODEL Texas
2. Few places in the united states are growing as rapidly.
3. The port of houston is fifty miles from the gulf of mexico.
4. Other deep ports are located in galveston and corpus christi.
5. The Gulf Intracoastal Waterway runs from brownsville to orange.
6. The state of texas is also a leader in aviation.
7. The largest airports serve dallas, fort worth, and houston.
8. These airports are very busy around christmas and labor day.
9. In december or january dallas is a busy place!

B. Using Proper Nouns   Add a proper noun to complete each sentence. Be sure to capitalize it. Write each proper noun.

10. We decided to visit the city of _____ during our vacation.
MODEL Dallas
11. Our friends visited _____ during the _____ holiday.
12. They visited the _____ and the _____, great landmarks in that city.
13. They thought they would rather go during the _____ holiday on their next visit.
14. Landmarks like _____ and _____ were too crowded.
15. When they got their tickets at the _____ airport, they couldn't believe the city had grown to be that large!
16. Tourists from _____ and _____ flocked to their destinations.

C. Writing Sentences with Proper Nouns   Replace each underlined proper noun with a suitable proper noun that can take its place. Be sure to capitalize the noun. Write each sentence.

17. Houston is a beautiful place to spend Memorial Day.
MODEL Chicago is a beautiful place to spend Labor Day.
18. On Thursday we bought our tickets at the Fort Worth airport.
19. My sister bought her tickets last May to attend Houston's celebration.
20. She saw the parade last year and wanted to attend again during Christmas vacation.
21. This year she will leave on Monday and arrive in Houston on Wednesday.

EXTRA PRACTICE

7 Abbreviations *pages 84–85*

A. Writing Abbreviations   Write the abbreviated form of each word.

1. Sunday
MODEL > Sun.

2. Avenue	12. Road
3. August	13. before noon
4. Thursday	14. September
5. Friday	15. Wednesday
6. afternoon	16. Boulevard
7. October	17. Tuesday
8. February	18. Saturday
9. March	19. January
10. November	20. Monday
11. Street	21. December

B. Using Abbreviations   Complete each sentence, using the correct form of the abbreviated word.

22. When I began gymnastics last Jan., I had no idea I would see so much change in myself.
MODEL > January

23. We have been attending competitions in Sept. and Oct.
24. Most of the meets have occurred on Sat. or Sun.
25. Last Nov., however, we had a competition on a Wed.
26. I learned the rings in Oct. and the pommel horse in Nov.
27. I enjoy working with the horizontal bars in the P.M.
28. My friend Ed has been using the parallel bars since Aug.

C. Writing Abbreviations   Each sentence contains an error in an abbreviation. Write each sentence and abbreviation correctly.

29. The men's gymnastics competition began in the a.m.
MODEL > The men's gymnastics competition began in the A.M.

30. The teams have been practicing since last janu.
31. They were ready to win the championship that they lost in dec.
32. On wen. morning both teams were ready to face the competition.
33. Since the pommel horse was added in augu., our team has improved.

8 Singular Possessive Nouns *pages 86–87*

A. Identifying Singular Possessive Nouns Write the singular possessive form of each noun.

1. student

MODEL ▷ student's

2. plant
3. parent
4. tree
5. girl
6. woman
7. baby
8. kitten

9. classmate
10. friend
11. sister
12. teacher
13. man
14. flower
15. week

16. brother
17. child
18. bird
19. infant
20. youngster
21. country
22. boy

B. Using Singular Possessive Nouns Complete each sentence with the singular possessive form of the noun in parentheses ( ).

23. Skin is the (body) biggest organ.

MODEL ▷ body's

24. A (person) skin measures over 20 square feet.
25. Your (skin) weight is over five pounds.
26. It protects you from the (sun) rays.
27. This (organ) lifespan is only a few weeks.
28. A (human) skin replaces itself.
29. An (animal) skin is thicker than yours.
30. A (snake) skin is dry and scaly.

C. Writing Sentences with Singular Possessive Nouns Write each sentence in another way. Change the underlined words to include a singular possessive noun form.

31. The ears of a human are remarkable.

MODEL ▷ A human's ears are remarkable.

32. The job of the outer ear is to pick up sound waves.
33. The vibrations of a wave reach the inner ear.
34. The roar of an airplane can be heard easily.
35. Your ears can also hear the whisper of a friend.
36. Your ears hear the notes of a song.
37. The balance of a person is controlled by the ears.

EXTRA PRACTICE

9 Plural Possessive Nouns *pages 88–89*

A. Spelling Plural Possessive Nouns Write the plural possessive form of each noun.

1. girl

MODEL > girls'

2. boys	**7.** dogs	**12.** teams
3. players	**8.** sisters	**13.** stores
4. writers	**9.** ships	**14.** songs
5. cousins	**10.** words	**15.** singers
6. poets	**11.** families	**16.** stories

B. Using Plural Possessive Nouns Complete each sentence with the plural possessive form of the noun in parentheses ( ).

17. (Countries) climates may differ.

MODEL > Countries'

18. Near the equator, many (nations) weather is hot.

19. Near the Poles, (residents) lives are affected by extreme cold.

20. (Arizonans) umbrellas don't get much use.

21. (Alaskans) clothes must be warm.

22. (Deserts) temperatures are not always hot.

23. Most (places) moist air will hold heat in.

24. Many (areas) weather changes quickly.

25. Some (places) residents need heavy and light clothing.

26. The (seasons) changes happen suddenly.

C. Writing Sentences with Plural Possessive Nouns Write each sentence in another way. Change the underlined words to include a plural possessive noun form.

27. The lifespans of animals differ.

MODEL > Animals' lifespans differ.

28. The lives of mammals are fairly long.

29. In general, the lives of humans last about 80 years.

30. The years of elephants are often more than 70.

31. The ages of giant tortoises can reach 150!

32. The lives of worms last 5 to 10 years.

EXTRA PRACTICE

1 Action Verbs *pages 126–127*

A. Identifying Action Verbs   Write the action verb in each sentence.

1. Columbus discovered America.
   MODEL▷ discovered
2. Robert E. Peary explored the Arctic.
3. He reached the North Pole in 1909.
4. Ferdinand Magellan traveled around the world.
5. He sailed for the kings of Portugal and Spain.
6. Ponce de León once journeyed with Columbus.
7. Later he searched for the Fountain of Youth.
8. He never located that wonderful place.
9. He mapped the coasts of Florida.
10. Leif Ericson led many Norse expeditions.
11. He lived in Greenland.

B. Finding Action Verbs in Predicates   The complete predicate in each sentence is underlined. Write the action verb.

12. Explorers arrive at new places.
    MODEL▷ arrive
13. They seek out new territories.
14. Explorers once took voyages in sailing ships.
15. They explored new areas on horseback or on foot.
16. Today's explorers follow a different route.
17. Some hike up the world's highest mountains.
18. Edmund Hillary climbed Mt. Everest.
19. Modern explorers move beyond land.
20. They now voyage far into space.
21. Neil Armstrong walked on the moon.
22. Other explorers go to the bottom of the sea.

C. Writing Sentences with Action Verbs   Complete each sentence with an action verb. Write the sentence.

23. Early fliers _____ like explorers.
    MODEL▷ Early fliers acted like explorers.
24. Amelia Earhart _____ across the Atlantic.
25. No woman _____ this by herself before.
26. Beryl Markham _____ many solo flights also.
27. In 1927 Charles Lindbergh _____ the first nonstop solo flight across the Atlantic.
28. He _____ in Paris as a hero.

EXTRA PRACTICE

2 Linking Verbs *pages 128–129*

A. **Identifying Linking Verbs**   Write the linking verb in each sentence.

1. Thomas Edison was an inventor.
MODEL > was

2. I am grateful for his inventions.
3. Electric light bulbs are terrific things!
4. The record player is another important invention of Edison's.
5. Alexander Graham Bell and Guglielmo Marconi were inventors.
6. Alexander Graham Bell is known for the telephone.
7. People were happy about this great new device.
8. The radio was invented by Guglielmo Marconi.
9. I am a user of all these wonderful objects.
10. Television was the invention of many people.
11. Television sets are popular all over the world.

B. **Classifying Verbs**   Write *linking verb* or *action verb* for each underlined verb.

12. George Eastman is famous.
MODEL > linking verb

13. He introduced roll film in the 1880's.
14. He was the man who invented a well-known camera.
15. Some inventions make life easier.
16. The vacuum cleaner is an invention like that.
17. People first used automatic clothes washers around 1939.
18. Washers are helpful in saving people much work.
19. Whoever designed paper towels had a good idea.
20. They clean messy spills.

C. **Writing Sentences with Linking Verbs**   Complete each sentence with a linking verb. Use *am, is, are, was,* or *were.* Write the sentence.

21. What _____ the best invention ever?
MODEL > What was the best invention ever?

22. I _____ sure it is hard to decide.
23. It _____ probably something helpful for people.
24. There _____ many unique inventions before 1988.
25. Some _____ inventions that make work easier.
26. Everyone _____ happy to escape today's tough chores.
27. I _____ a user of many household inventions.
28. I _____ lucky that there are so many choices.

EXTRA PRACTICE

3 Main Verbs and Helping Verbs *pages 130–131*

EXTRA PRACTICE

A. Identifying Main Verbs and Helping Verbs Write *main* or *helping* for each underlined verb.

1. <u>Have</u> you ever <u>noticed</u> how cold a cave is?

MODEL ▷ have—helping, noticed—main

2. Carol is <u>exploring</u> some caves.
3. She <u>was walking</u> in them yesterday.
4. I am <u>hoping</u> to join her on her walk.
5. I <u>had learned</u> cave exploring from her.
6. We are <u>photographing</u> the beautiful rocks.
7. Carol and I are <u>helping</u> others to explore.
8. They <u>have enjoyed</u> learning about caves.
9. For millions of years water <u>has carved</u> out the rocks.
10. We are <u>seeing</u> things that began long ago.
11. Water and time <u>have created</u> art from the rocks.

B. Choosing Helping Verbs Write the helping verb in parentheses ( ) that completes each sentence correctly.

12. People (are, have) studying caves.

MODEL ▷ are

13. Cave explorers (were, have) learned a lot.
14. Scientists (were, have) discovered many caves.
15. I (am, had) thinking of hiking today.
16. Some say that caves (was, were) formed by rain.
17. Prehistoric people (have, were) lived in caves.
18. Caves (was, had) sheltered them very well.
19. People (had, are) now going into caves for fun.
20. We (are, was) climbing down a ladder.
21. They (is, have) seen different animals.
22. Part of the fun (has, is) ducking from the bats!

C. Writing Sentences with Helping Verbs Complete each sentence with a helping verb. Use *am, is, are, have,* or *has.* Write the sentence.

23. The cave explorer _____ carrying lanterns.

MODEL ▷ The cave explorer is carrying lanterns.

24. I _____ wearing a protective helmet.
25. She _____ explored this area before.
26. A bat _____ flying over there.
27. People _____ searched for hidden springs before.
28. They _____ searching for caverns also.

UNIT 3   4 Verb Tenses *pages 132–133*

A. Identifying Verb Tenses   Decide the tense of each underlined verb. Then write *present, past,* or *future.*

1. Yoshiro <u>plays</u> the piano.

MODEL present

2. Today he <u>practiced</u> a new piece.
3. He <u>will rehearse</u> it in the concert hall.
4. Yoshiro <u>feels</u> the music in his fingers.
5. He <u>believes</u> he must practice daily.
6. He <u>will increase</u> his playing time each day.
7. Yoshiro always <u>wanted</u> to be a musician.
8. He <u>worked</u> hard at his music lessons.
9. Yoshiro <u>fills</u> a room with magnificent sounds.
10. This young man <u>will share</u> his talent always.

B. Using Verb Tenses Correctly   Complete each sentence with the verb and the tense given in parentheses ( ). Write the verb.

11. Wendy _____ the harp. (like—present)

MODEL likes

12. She _____ how to play at school. (learn—past)
13. Wendy _____ on her harp daily. (practice—past)
14. She _____ a concert next week. (give—future)
15. She _____ hearing harp music. (enjoy—present)
16. Her teacher _____ a solo piece. (record—past)
17. The students _____ carefully. (listen—past)
18. They _____ to hear the song again. (want—past)
19. Wendy _____ for her family also. (play—future)
20. She _____ confidence in herself. (gain—past)

C. Writing Sentences with Verbs in Different Tenses   Write two sentences. Use the tenses of the verb given.

21. rehearse—past, future

MODEL The band rehearsed for two hours.
        Tomorrow they will rehearse longer.

22. perform—present, past
23. conduct—past, future
24. listen—future, present
25. compose—present, past
26. sing—present, future
27. play—past, present

Identifying the Correct Spelling of Verbs   In each pair, write the verb that has the correct ending added to it.

1. copys, copies
MODEL > copies

2. studys, studies
3. holds, holdes
4. spys, spies
5. hurries, hurrys
6. beges, begs
7. frys, fries
8. crushs, crushes
9. flys, flies
10. buys, buies
11. trys, tries

12. plaies, plays
13. crys, cries
14. dries, drys
15. marrys, marries
16. waxes, waxs
17. carries, carrys
18. makes, makees
19. presses, presss
20. applies, applys
21. catchs, catches

B. Choosing Verbs   Write the verb in parentheses ( ) that is spelled correctly.

22. An owl (cries, crys) out in the night.
MODEL > cries

23. A frightened mouse (scurrys, scurries) for cover.
24. Our leader (carrys, carries) the lantern.
25. Leading the way, he never (varys, varies) his pace.
26. He (spies, spys) another group of explorers nearby.
27. One member (dries, drys) his socks near a fire.
28. He (worrys, worries) about keeping warm.
29. Another (applys, applies) insect repellent.
30. The group (studys, studies) to earn merit badges.
31. This (occupys, occupies) much of their time.
32. Our leader (enjoys, enjoies) his role.

C. Writing Sentences with Verbs   Add the ending in parentheses ( ) to the underlined verb in each sentence. Write the sentences.

33. The group play during the lunch break. (s)
MODEL > The group plays during the lunch break.

34. The heat of the day worry no one. (ies)
35. One camper enjoy the cool shade instead. (s)
36. Another carry firewood to the area. (ies)
37. He fry a hamburger for his lunch. (ies)

6 Spelling Past-Tense Verbs *pages 136–137*

A. Identifying the Correct Spelling of Verbs   In each pair, write the verb that has the correct past-tense ending added to it.

    1. shop, shopped

MODEL ▷ shopped

2. try, tried	**12.** buried, bury
3. faced, face	**13.** clip, clipped
4. plan, planned	**14.** saved, save
5. trot, trotted	**15.** worried, worry
6. moved, move	**16.** rub, rubbed
7. erase, erased	**17.** married, marry
8. fried, fry	**18.** code, coded
9. use, used	**19.** skid, skidded
10. flapped, flap	**20.** dried, dry
11. pat, patted	**21.** store, stored

B. Choosing Verbs   Write the verb in parentheses ( ) that is spelled correctly.

    22. We (carried, carryed) backpacks.

MODEL ▷ carried

    23. The hikers (hurryed, hurried) up that hill!
    24. Water had (driped, dripped) down the rocks.
    25. One hiker (sliped, slipped) on a slick rock.
    26. He (dried, dryed) himself off and walked on.
    27. The group (stopped, stoped) for a rest.
    28. Then one girl (spyed, spied) some mosquitoes.
    29. Someone else (cryed, cried) for the bug spray.
    30. Sure enough, the mosquitoes (arrivved, arrived).
    31. The hikers (swated, swatted) at them.
    32. Later they (jokeed, joked) about the adventure.

C. Writing Sentences with Verbs   Add the ending in parentheses ( ) to the underlined verb in each sentence. Write the sentences.

    33. The hike was better than we had <u>hope</u>. (ed)

MODEL ▷ The hike was better than we had hoped.

    34. We <u>snap</u> many photographs. (ed)
    35. Even a beetle <u>pose</u> for us! (ed)
    36. The insect <u>scurry</u> along the ground. (ied)
    37. The group <u>note</u> the plants on the trail. (ed)
    38. Everyone <u>try</u> hard to identify them all. (ied)

1 Agreement of Subjects and Verbs *pages 168–169*

A. Identifying Subjects and Verbs That Agree   Write *correct* if the underlined verb agrees with its subject. Write *incorrect* if it does not.

   1. They <u>rides</u> in hot-air balloons.

MODEL▷ incorrect

   2. The balloon <u>rises</u> up in the air.
   3. A large basket <u>are</u> part of the equipment.
   4. People <u>travels</u> in this basket.
   5. The balloon <u>lifts</u> off the ground.
   6. The travelers <u>are</u> over the countryside!
   7. I <u>is</u> afraid to ride the wind.
   8. The trip <u>excite</u> the passengers.
   9. Everyone <u>was</u> up so high.
  10. People <u>look</u> down at the ground.
  11. Then the balloon <u>land</u> in a field.

B. Choosing Verbs That Agree with Their Subjects   Write the verb in parentheses ( ) that agrees with the subject.

  12. The pilot (fly, flies) the plane.

MODEL▷ flies

  13. She (is, are) way up in the air.
  14. She (steer, steers) the aircraft carefully.
  15. Pilots (checks, check) their instrument panels.
  16. She (sees, see) how fast she is moving.
  17. Some hills (is, are) in the distance.
  18. The plane (climb, climbs) higher.
  19. Now the pilot (is, are) not afraid to soar.
  20. The plane (glide, glides) over a lake.
  21. Tiny boats (is, are) on the lake.
  22. The wind (push, pushes) the plane along.

C. Writing Verbs That Agree with Their Subjects   Complete each sentence with the correct form of the verb in parentheses ( ). Write each sentence.

  23. A hang glider (soar) with one wing.

MODEL▷ A hang glider soars with one wing.

  24. Pilots (be) beneath this large wing.
  25. They (wear) a harness around their waists.

UNIT 4 2 Irregular Verbs *pages 170–171*

A. Identifying Irregular Verbs   Write the verb in each sentence.

1. The woman went on the high wire.

MODEL ▷ went

2. Her partners saw her.
3. They began their own walk across.
4. The acrobats become daring.
5. They bring their legs up very high.
6. The crowd became very quiet.
7. No one made a sound.
8. No one has seen such a thrilling act before.
9. The acrobats have brought thrills to the people.

B. Identifying Correct Verb Forms   Write the verb in parentheses ( ) that completes each sentence correctly.

10. The trapeze artists (gone, go) up.

MODEL ▷ go

11. They have (began, begun) their performance.
12. They have (came, come) gracefully through the air.
13. They (think, has thought) about what they do.
14. They have (brought, bring) thrills to the circus.
15. They (becomes, became) circus stars for adventure.
16. They (says, say) they are unafraid of heights.
17. I have (seen, saw) them before.
18. We (went, gone) to the circus twice last year.
19. Each time we have (came, come) away amazed.

C. Writing Sentences with Irregular Verbs   Complete each sentence with the correct past-tense form of the verb in parentheses ( ). Write each sentence.

20. The trainer has (go) into the tigers' cage.

MODEL ▷ The trainer has gone into the tigers' cage.

21. People have (begin) to worry.
22. They had (see) the fierce tigers.
23. He has (make) the tigers obey him.
24. The trainer's bravery has (bring) the crowd to its feet.

3 More Irregular Verbs *pages 172–173*

A. Listing Forms of Irregular Verbs Write the past-tense form and the past with *have*, *has*, or *had* for each verb.

1. grow
MODEL > grew, grown

2. know   **5.** ride   **8.** fall
3. fly   **6.** speak   **9.** give
4. blow   **7.** take   **10.** write

B. Choosing Irregular Verbs Write the verb in parentheses ( ) that completes each sentence correctly.

11. Horsemen (ridden, rode) the broncos.
MODEL > rode
12. Even experts have (fell, fallen) off horses.
13. The young rider (took, taken) the reins.
14. She (blown, blew) out a deep breath.
15. The bronco (given, gave) her quite a bounce!
16. She has (flown, flew) out of the saddle.
17. An older rider (knew, known) how to stay on.
18. She (rode, ridden) for eight seconds.
19. Reporters (wrote, written) about the event.
20. The rider (spoke, spoken) of horses with love.
21. She had (grown, grew) fond of them in childhood.

C. Writing Sentences with Irregular Verbs Complete each sentence with the correct past-tense form of the verb in parentheses ( ). Write each sentence.

22. The rodeo has (grow) very popular.
MODEL > The rodeo has grown very popular.
23. The fans have (know) rodeos are fun.
24. Some rodeo stars have (ride) bulls.
25. A few (take) a chance on bucking broncos.
26. Riders (give) crowds their money's worth.
27. Fans had (speak) about the excitement.
28. They pity a rider who has (fall).
29. A rider can't join until he or she has (grow).

4 Contractions with *Not* pages 174–175

A. Writing Contractions   Write the contraction for these words.

1. is not
MODEL > isn't

2. are not	**7.** did not	**12.** had not
3. was not	**8.** cannot	**13.** do not
4. were not	**9.** could not	**14.** must not
5. have not	**10.** should not	**15.** will not
6. has not	**11.** would not	**16.** is not

B. Using Contractions   Write the contraction that can be made from the underlined words in each sentence.

17. Animal lovers <u>will not</u> hurt animals.
MODEL > won't
18. They go on safaris but <u>do not</u> harm the animals.
19. They photograph animals they <u>could not</u> see in zoos.
20. An adventurer <u>does not</u> mind the jungle.
21. He or she <u>has not</u> been bothered by the heat.
22. People on safari <u>have not</u> forgotten bug spray!
23. They <u>would not</u> have missed this adventure.
24. They <u>did not</u> know how exciting it would be.
25. You <u>are not</u> sorry when you see an animal in person.
26. It <u>is not</u> every day you meet a giraffe.
27. They <u>had not</u> been so close to nature before.
28. If you go, you <u>must not</u> bother the animals.
29. They <u>will not</u> always come close to you.
30. You <u>should not</u> get too close to some animals.
31. They <u>were not</u> trained to be with people.
32. The lion <u>was not</u> ready to be a house pet.

C. Writing Sentences with Contractions   Make each sentence less formal. Use a contraction in place of some words. Write each sentence.

33. The trip through the jungle was not easy.
MODEL > The trip through the jungle wasn't easy.
34. The explorers could not cut through the trees.
35. They were not sure there was enough water.
36. The hot sun does not stop beating down.
37. They will not explore without a guide anymore.
38. The explorers cannot find a cool place.

EXTRA PRACTICE

A. Identifying Direct Quotations   None of these sentences has quotation marks. If you think the sentence should be punctuated as a direct quotation, write it correctly. If you think it is correct as it is, write *correct*.

1. Why are you frowning, Ramon? asked his grandmother.
   MODEL > "Why are you frowning, Ramon?" asked his grandmother.
2. Ramon answered, My homework is giving me problems.
3. Tell me about it, suggested Grandmother.
4. He said that he had to write a true adventure story.
5. That sounds like fun! she exclaimed.
6. I suppose it could be, he said in a dull voice.
7. What is the problem? she asked.
8. He explained that he didn't know what to write about.
9. She told him that she had spent a year in a jungle.

B. Punctuating Direct Quotations   Write each sentence. Add punctuation, quotation marks, and capital letters where they are needed.

10. the jungle was in the Yucatan explained Grandmother
    MODEL > "The jungle was in the Yucatan," explained Grandmother.
11. Ramon asked what is the Yucatan
12. she said the Yucatan is an area in southern Mexico
13. ancient Indians built great cities there she added
14. why did you go there Ramon asked
15. i wanted to learn about their art she answered
16. grandmother continued i hiked in to see old ruins
17. she said I climbed a lot of pyramids

C. Writing Direct Quotations   Add speaker words to these sentences to make them direct quotations. Try to use verbs other than *said*. Be sure to punctuate correctly. Write the sentences.

18. Who were the Maya?
    MODEL > "Who were the Maya?" asked Maria.
19. They were the Indians of Middle America.
20. The Maya built great stone buildings and pyramids.
21. What happened to them?
22. Their culture ended about a thousand years ago.
23. Why were they forgotten for a long time?

UNIT 5 1 Pronouns *pages 212–213*

A. Identifying Pronouns Write the pronoun in each sentence.

1. Bob made her laugh.
MODEL ▷ her
2. He has a good sense of humor.
3. She enjoys good jokes.
4. Some of them are corny.
5. I groaned at some of the jokes.
6. Bob told us a funny story.
7. We all laughed a lot.
8. Then Bob pointed to me.
9. "Now you tell a joke," Bob said.
10. What do they call a lion's hairdresser?
11. People call him a mane man.

B. Choosing Pronouns Write the pronoun in parentheses ( ) that completes each sentence correctly.

12. (We, Us) need a good laugh.
MODEL ▷ We
13. Tell (we, us) some jokes.
14. (I, Me) have seen the Milky Way.
15. (It, They) is where butter flies.
16. (Us, We) saw some rocking chairs.
17. (They, Them) dance to rock music!
18. What does an egg say when (him, he) laughs?
19. (He, Him) laughs, "Yolk, yolk."
20. What did the hen say to (him, he) at the party?
21. Will (us, you) dance chick to chick?
22. Army ants are after (me, I)!
23. Are army uncles with (them, they)?

C. Writing Sentences with Pronouns Replace each underlined word or words with a pronoun. Write each sentence.

24. You and I like riddles.
MODEL ▷ We like riddles.
25. Tell a riddle to Wendy and me.
26. What does Tom call a book with cat products?
27. He calls this book a catalogue!
28. Why do potatoes see so well?
29. Potatoes have eyes.

2 Subject Pronouns *pages 214–215*

A. Identifying Subject Pronouns Write the subject pronoun in each sentence.

　1. I like fruit jokes.
MODEL > I
　2. They are so silly!
　3. You know a lot of these jokes.
　4. We love the one about the electric plum.
　5. It is purple and goes "buzz, buzz."
　6. He told me that joke.
　7. I told you about the four-door grape.
　8. It is purple and goes "slam, slam, slam, slam."

B. Using Subject Pronouns Choose a pronoun from the **Word Box** to complete each sentence correctly. Write the pronoun.

　9. _____ know a good fruit joke.
MODEL > We
　10. Do _____ know what is round and has four wheels?
　11. ____ say it is an orange on a skateboard.
　12. Next _____ ask what is green and has four keyholes.
　13. ____ is a four-room watermelon.
　14. _____ told me about ballpoint bananas.
　15. _____ are yellow and go "click, click."
　16. ____ know a vegetable joke.
　17. _____ asks what is green and has light bulbs.
　18. _____ answers, "Electric celery."
　19. ____ brightens up any salad!

WORD BOX
we
I
she
it
he
they
you

C. Writing Sentences with Subject Pronouns Replace the underlined words in each sentence with a subject pronoun. Write each sentence.

　20. He and she tell jokes all the time.
MODEL > They tell jokes all the time.
　21. Bob asks, "What's orange and warm?"
　22. Sandra answers, "A carrot wearing a coat."
　23. That joke is silly!
　24. Fruit jokes are not enjoyed by everyone.
　25. Sandra does not like them at all.
　26. Her brother Joe likes them, though.
　27. Joe told someone a vegetable joke.

EXTRA PRACTICE

3 Object Pronouns *pages 216–217*

A. Identifying Object Pronouns   Write the object pronoun in each sentence.

1. Mom drove Diane and me to the circus.

MODEL > me

2. Two clowns entertained us.
3. One clown pushed him down.
4. The other clown splashed her.
5. The show was great, and the audience liked it.
6. The ringmaster asked us to clap.
7. The crowd applauded them.
8. Mom let me buy a program.
9. "Please take it," Mom said to Carol.
10. "Mom will drive you home," Carol told Diane.

B. Using Object Pronouns   Replace the underlined word or words with an object pronoun. Write each sentence.

11. The clown got into a little car.

MODEL > The clown got into it.

12. Many other clowns followed the male clown.
13. More clowns followed those clowns.
14. There seemed to be no more room in the car.
15. Along came a lady, and a clown put the lady in.
16. The act had you and me rolling in the aisles.
17. "Ann, I'll take Ann here again," Dad said to me.

C. Writing Sentences with Object Pronouns   Add an object pronoun to each sentence. Write each sentence.

18. A clown threw a pie at _____.

MODEL > A clown threw a pie at him.

19. The other clown yelled, "I'll get _____!"
20. He ran around chasing _____.
21. The audience cheered _____ on.
22. One clown said, "Give _____ that flower."
23. A spray of water came out of _____.
24. It sprayed _____ right in the face.
25. This made _____ laugh.

A. Identifying the Correct Pronoun   Write the correct sentence in each pair.

1. I watch a funny television show.
   Me watch a funny television show.
   `MODEL` > I watch a funny television show.
2. My family and I see it every week.
   My family and me see it every week.
3. The star of the show makes we laugh.
   The star of the show makes us laugh.
4. We never saw anyone act so funny.
   Us never saw anyone act so funny.
5. I laughed when she imitated a chicken.
   Me laughed when she imitated a chicken.
6. We won't forget the time her hair turned green.
   Us won't forget the time her hair turned green.

B. Choosing Pronouns   Write the pronoun in parentheses ( ) that completes each sentence correctly.

7. (We, Us) think she is the funniest woman.
   `MODEL` > We
8. (Me, I) can't forget the pail that got stuck on her foot.
9. Give (me, I) reruns of this show any time.
10. (Me, I) remember when she played a kangaroo.
11. If only she could have seen (us, we) laugh!
12. (I, Me) think her show should be on every night.
13. (We, Us) should thank her for her show.
14. She helps (we, us) feel great.

C. Writing Sentences with *I, Me, We, Us*   Complete each sentence with *I, me, we,* or *us*. Use the words in parentheses ( ) to help you choose the correct pronoun. Write each sentence.

15. _____ watch another funny show.   (you and your friends)
    `MODEL` > We watch another funny show.
16. This show keeps _____ home on Friday evenings.   (you and your friends)
17. _____ like the characters.   (you and your friends)
18. _____ think the dog is funny, too.   (you)
19. The characters make _____ want to be their friend.   (you)
20. _____ never miss the show.   (you and your friends)
21. _____ would like to meet the star of the show.   (you)

5 Agreement of Subject Pronouns with Verbs

pages 220–221

A. Identifying Agreement of Subject Pronouns and Verbs   Write *correct* if the underlined verb in each sentence agrees with the subject pronoun. Write *incorrect* if it does not.

1. He <u>tell</u> jokes.
> MODEL   incorrect

2. It <u>takes</u> courage to tell jokes in front of people.
3. They <u>does</u> not always laugh.
4. It <u>mean</u> the jokes are not funny.
5. He <u>needs</u> new ones.
6. We <u>know</u> better jokes.
7. You <u>has</u> to think of funny things.
8. I <u>write</u> funny stories.
9. I <u>tries</u> them out in front of my friend.
10. She <u>listens</u> carefully to them.
11. They <u>sound</u> good to her.

B. Choosing Verbs That Agree with Subject Pronouns   Write the form of the verb in parentheses ( ) that completes each sentence correctly.

12. I (see, sees) a comedian in a theater.
> MODEL   see

13. I (laughs, laugh) loudly.
14. It (is, are) hard to hear while I'm laughing.
15. He (tell, tells) about a restaurant.
16. I (see, sees) flies in this dining room!
17. They (is, are) in my soup!

C. Writing Verbs That Agree with Subject Pronouns   Complete each sentence with the correct present-tense form of the verb in parentheses ( ). Write each sentence.

18. He (tell) a story about his aunt.
> MODEL   He tells a story about his aunt.

19. She (drive) to a car dealer.
20. She (buy) snow tires.
21. They (melt).
22. Do you (know) about wood stoves?
23. I (think) a stove made of wood will burn.
24. We (visit) dentists.
25. They (put) in gold fillings.
26. They (make) our mouths rich.

6 Possessive Pronouns *pages 222–223*

A. Identifying Possessive Pronouns Write the possessive pronoun in each sentence.

1. Here is my list of silly facts.
MODEL > my
2. Your dog will not learn math in the month of July.
3. Goats take their kids to the movies on Tuesdays.
4. No girl ever carpets her bird's cage.
5. I read my newspaper only when I wear purple socks.
6. Llamas never send postcards to our house.
7. Every boy wants an anteater in his room.
8. A cat licks its paws only on summer vacation.

B. Choosing Possessive Pronouns Write the possessive pronoun in parentheses ( ) that completes each sentence correctly.

9. Books never turn (their, its) own pages.
MODEL > their
10. Many Martians do (her, their) laundry every day.
11. A man will forget to tie (his, her) shoes today.
12. Somewhere a girl will put (its, her) feet in mud.
13. Will you ask (your, its) pet to answer the telephone?
14. A telephone likes to dial (its, her) own area code.
15. I always wear slippers with (my, its) best outfit.
16. Do roses grow thorns just to hurt (its, our) fingers?

C. Writing Sentences with Possessive Pronouns Replace the underlined words in each sentence with a possessive pronoun. Write each sentence.

17. Robots visit <u>robots'</u> dentists twice a year.
MODEL > Robots visit their dentists twice a year.
18. A pencil can sharpen <u>a pencil's</u> own point.
19. Bears will listen to <u>the bears'</u> records.
20. Those peaches may shave off <u>peaches'</u> own fuzz.
21. A girl may walk <u>a girl's</u> mouse on a leash today.
22. A boy can wear <u>a boy's</u> socks on his ears.
23. <u>Your and my</u> moon is made of green cheese.

EXTRA PRACTICE

UNIT 5   7 Contractions with Pronouns *pages 224–225*

A. Identifying Contractions with Pronouns   Write the contraction in each sentence. Then write the two words that each contraction stands for.

1. I've seen a funny commercial.
MODEL > I've—I have
2. Maybe you've seen it too.
3. It's for a soup company.
4. It shows vegetables you'll never see in the store.
5. They're all dancing and singing.
6. They've got fancy costumes and funny wigs.
7. We've all sung the jingle.
8. A woman says she'd eat the soup all day long.
9. She'll have to buy a lot of soup.
10. It'd be fun to open a can right now.
11. You'd jump if peas just popped out and sang.

B. Using Contractions with Pronouns   Write a contraction to replace the underlined words in each sentence.

12. It is fun to watch commercials.
MODEL > It's
13. Sometimes they are better than the shows.
14. You are going to remember funny ads.
15. I will bet that many people know jingles.
16. I am sure they sometimes forget the products!
17. We will always love the dancing cows.
18. It is hard not to smile at them.
19. I would like to meet a talking sandwich.
20. I have never spoken to food.

C. Writing Sentences Using Contractions with Pronouns   Rewrite each sentence, using a contraction.

21. He is mopping the floor.
MODEL > He's mopping the floor.
22. You would think the man would be happy.
23. You will see that the man is very unhappy.
24. It will be hard to cheer him up.
25. He has got a dull and dirty floor.
26. He had better buy Fine Shine floor polish.
27. Then he will see himself in his floor.

UNIT 6   1 Adjectives *pages 258–259*

A. Identifying Adjectives   Write the adjective that describes the underlined noun in each sentence.

1. The little <u>elephant</u> flew away.

MODEL ▷ little

2. Its big <u>ears</u> flapped in the wind.
3. The gentle <u>breeze</u> carried it along.
4. A tiny <u>bird</u> spoke to the elephant.
5. There would be a great <u>party</u> at its house.
6. All the friendly <u>animals</u> would be there.
7. The happy <u>elephant</u> agreed to come.
8. It saw a spotted <u>fawn</u> near a cloud.
9. The elephant told the pretty <u>deer</u> about the party.
10. The two <u>friends</u> decided to go together.
11. They floated across the wooden <u>bridge</u>.

B. Classifying Adjectives   Write the adjective in each sentence. Then write whether it describes *how many* or *what kind*.

12. Four flowers sang a song.

MODEL ▷ Four—how many

13. A small bush joined in.
14. Then three trees harmonized with the group.
15. Soon a chorus of pretty voices was heard.
16. Along came one fox to lead the orchestra.
17. Six leaves danced in time to the music.
18. Blades of tall grass swayed in the wind.
19. Some cute chipmunks clapped their paws.
20. The red rose tried to hide.
21. It wanted the loud noise to end.
22. Ten dandelions told the rose not to fuss.

C. Writing Sentences with Adjectives   Add an adjective to each sentence. Write each sentence.

23. The _____ children followed the rainbow.

MODEL ▷ The excited children followed the rainbow.

24. The _____ colors lit up the sky.
25. At the end was a _____ pot of gold.
26. A _____ man guarded the pot.
27. He gave each child _____ gold coins.
28. The _____ children thanked him and skipped home.

2 Articles *pages 260–261*

A. Identifying Articles   Write the article that describes the underlined noun in each sentence.

   1. Tell me a <u>story</u>.

`MODEL` a

   2. It's about a <u>rabbit</u> that can talk.
   3. The <u>bunny</u> and its friends leave their homes.
   4. They meet an <u>owl</u> on their way.
   5. Soon a <u>monkey</u> joins them.
   6. The <u>people</u> who see them think they are funny.
   7. An <u>ostrich</u> packs its suitcase and comes along.
   8. A <u>crowd</u> gathers to watch this strange group.
   9. They rest at an <u>inn</u> one night.
  10. They tell the <u>guests</u> stories.
  11. They build a <u>house</u> and live happily ever after.

B. Choosing Articles   Write the article in parentheses ( ) that completes each sentence correctly.

  12. Have you ever heard (a, an) dog talk?

`MODEL` a

  13. (A, An) animal has interesting things to say.
  14. You can have (a, an) real chat.
  15. Did you ever see (an, a) ape read books?
  16. Animal stories are (an, the) ones apes like best.
  17. Did you ever hear (an, the) fish sing?
  18. Your goldfish probably has (a, an) good voice.
  19. When have you heard (an, a) eagle speak French?

C. Writing Sentences with Articles   Complete each sentence with *a* or *an*. Write each sentence correctly.

  20. The tree threw _____ apple at Dorothy.

`MODEL` The tree threw an apple at Dorothy.

  21. _____ cloud decided not to rain anymore.
  22. Two forks danced on _____ table.
  23. _____ elf came home with me.
  24. A character stepped out of _____ book and spoke.
  25. Maria goes to school in _____ spaceship.
  26. There is _____ elephant in Tanya's dancing class.
  27. _____ envelope stamped itself.
  28. The woman walked out of _____ painting.

3 Adjectives That Follow Linking Verbs
pages 262–263

A. Identifying Adjectives Write the adjective that follows the linking verb in each sentence.

1. That drawing is funny.

MODEL ▷ funny

2. Some things in it are silly.
3. The bark of a tree is red.
4. Its leaves are blue.

5. In the drawing it is sunny.
6. The sun is green.
7. An elephant is orange.

B. Connecting Adjectives and Subjects Write each sentence. Underline the adjective that follows the linking verb in each. Then draw an arrow to the noun or pronoun it describes.

8. This zoo is unusual!

MODEL ▷ This zoo is <u>unusual</u>!

9. Visitors to this zoo are amazed.

10. The seals in that pool are pink.

11. They are funny.

12. At this zoo the lions are purple.

13. Some giraffes are short.

14. The monkeys in that tree are sad.

15. One of the leopards is sick.

16. Its spots are green.

17. The grass over there is silver.

18. Two tigers are red.

C. Writing Sentences with Adjectives Add an adjective to each sentence. Write each sentence.

19. The two children are _____.

MODEL ▷ The two children are happy.

20. The butterflies are _____.
21. One of them is _____.
22. The boy and the girl are _____.
23. The butterflies have a home that is _____.
24. In the butterflies' house it is _____.
25. Soon the children are _____.

EXTRA PRACTICE

UNIT 6   4 Adjectives That Compare: with *er, est*
pages 264–265

A. Writing Adjectives That Compare   Write the form of each adjective that compares two things and more than two things.

1. funny

MODEL ▷ funnier, funniest

2. hot	**7.** sad	**12.** juicy
3. wise	**8.** shiny	**13.** wet
4. brave	**9.** glad	**14.** fine
5. happy	**10.** nice	**15.** red
6. strong	**11.** curly	**16.** tiny

B. Choosing Adjectives That Compare   Write the form of the adjective in parentheses ( ) that completes each sentence correctly.

17. The mouse is (bigger, biggest) than the cheese.

MODEL ▷ bigger

18. The bushes are (wider, widest) than the flowers.

19. These trees are the (taller, tallest) of all.

20. The bear is (fatter, fattest) than the snake.

21. That cloud is (whiter, whitest) than snow.

22. Grass has the (greener, greenest) color of all.

23. The sky is much (bluer, bluest) than the sea.

24. Rocks are (heavier, heaviest) than pebbles.

25. The ladybug is (thinner, thinnest) than the frog.

26. This orange is (juicier, juiciest) than that apple.

27. Peaches have the (fuzzier, fuzziest) skin of all.

C. Writing Sentences with Adjectives That Compare   Complete each sentence with the correct form of the adjective in parentheses ( ). Write each sentence.

28. Billy is (tall) than Bobby.

MODEL ▷ Billy is taller than Bobby.

29. Billy's head is (high) than the trees.

30. His planet is the (large) in the galaxy.

31. Its water is the (pure) in the universe.

32. Billy and Bobby are (silly) than the other boys in the class.

33. They are also the (kind) boys around.

34. Their mother is the (smart) woman anywhere.

35. Her spaceship is (fast) than anyone's.

36. No one on her planet is (friendly) than she.

UNIT 6 **5 Adjectives That Compare: with *More, Most***
pages 266–267

A. Writing Adjectives That Compare Write the form of each adjective that compares two things and more than two things.

1. wonderful
   MODEL ▷ more wonderful, most wonderful

2. beautiful
3. interesting
4. curious
5. helpful
6. precious

7. fascinating
8. comfortable
9. disappointed
10. difficult
11. boring

12. valuable
13. expensive
14. careful
15. necessary
16. generous

B. Choosing Adjectives Write *more* or *most* to complete each sentence correctly.

17. That dog is the _____ amazing animal of all.
    MODEL ▷ most

18. It is _____ famous than any other dog.
19. It is the _____ popular animal TV star of all time.
20. Its tricks are the _____ fabulous I've ever seen.
21. Nothing is _____ incredible than a talking dog.
22. It is the _____ unbelievable thing of all.
23. For this dog, speaking is _____ important than barking!

C. Writing Sentences with Adjectives That Compare
Complete each sentence with the correct form of the adjective in parentheses ( ). Write each sentence.

24. His story was the (remarkable) of all.
    MODEL ▷ His story was the most remarkable of all.

25. He was the (colorful) storyteller I ever heard.
26. He climbed the world's (tremendous) tree.
27. (astounding) than that, he did it backwards!
28. This was not the (astonishing) act of all.
29. He thought walking to the moon was (exciting) than anything else he had done.
30. He told the (entertaining) story of all.
31. We were (delighted) by that story than by any other.
32. It was the (thrilling) story in the world.
33. What is (daring) than walking to the moon?
34. Even (outstanding) is doing it barefoot.

6 Adjectives That Compare: Special Forms
pages 268–269

A. Identifying Adjectives That Compare   Write the adjective that describes the underlined noun in each sentence.

1. That is the best <u>story</u> I ever read.
[MODEL] best

2. It gave me more <u>thrills</u> than any other story.
3. I liked the good <u>characters</u>, who were unicorns.
4. They did many <u>things</u> to help people in trouble.
5. These people got little <u>help</u> from anyone else.
6. The unicorns got into much <u>mischief</u>.
7. They had the most <u>fun</u> playing with the children.
8. The worst <u>creatures</u> in the story were the trolls.
9. Everyone had a better <u>life</u> when the trolls ran away.
10. Bad <u>times</u> were gone forever.

B. Choosing Adjectives That Compare   Write the form of the adjective in parentheses ( ) that completes each sentence correctly.

11. Her story is (better, best) than mine.
[MODEL] better

12. It has (many, more) excitement than mine.
13. Her story was the (best, good) in the whole school.
14. Even the (worst, bad) character of all is fun to read about.
15. There are (many, most) elves in her story.
16. My story has (less, least) humor than hers.

C. Writing Sentences with Adjectives That Compare   Complete each sentence with the correct form of the adjective in parentheses ( ). Write each sentence.

17. Ed had the (much) fun of all.
[MODEL] Ed had the most fun of all.

18. Of the two of us, he had (much) excitement.
19. He had the (good) luck of anyone.
20. What could be (good) than walking into a story?
21. Ed had (little) to do than the other characters.
22. They had (much) words to say than he.
23. The main character was (bad) than the rest.
24. The (bad) part of all was having to leave the story.

UNIT 7 1 Adverbs *pages 300–301*

A. Identifying Adverbs Write the adverb in each sentence. Then write whether it tells *when* or *where*.

1. James runs three miles daily.
   MODEL> daily—when
2. Even in bad weather James runs outside.
3. If necessary he runs late.
4. He is running today.
5. James takes long strides forward.
6. He always stays in shape.
7. Tomorrow he will run in a big marathon.
8. All the marathon runners will race downtown.
9. James has raced in a marathon before.

B. Using Adverbs Move the adverb in each sentence to a different place. Write each sentence.

10. The weather was stormy yesterday.
    MODEL> Yesterday the weather was stormy.
11. The rain came pouring down here.
12. Today the sky was clear.
13. The weather might be good for racing tomorrow.
14. The runners are hoping for dry streets there.
15. Lately the weather has been poor.
16. Many spectators often come out to see the runners.
17. The streets are immediately lined with people.
18. Nearby television cameras are set up.

C. Writing Adverbs To each sentence add an adverb that answers the question in parentheses ( ). Then write each sentence.

19. _____ the sky turned dark. (when)
    MODEL> Suddenly the sky turned dark.
20. _____ the lightning flashed. (when)
21. _____ came the crash of thunder. (where)
22. Rain poured _____ the runners looked. (where)
23. Many spectators rushed to shelters _____. (where)
24. Some runners _____ dropped out. (when)
25. James continued to dash _____. (where)
26. He _____ had wanted to run in the marathon. (when)
27. Nothing was going to stop him _____. (when)

EXTRA PRACTICE

A. Identifying Adverbs   Write the adverb that tells more about the underlined verb in each sentence.

1. Columbus carefully <u>planned</u> his voyage.

MODEL ▷ carefully

2. He <u>looked</u> thoughtfully over his maps.
3. He <u>knew</u> exactly how he would go.
4. Ferdinand and Isabella <u>encouraged</u> him completely.
5. They gladly <u>gave</u> him money and ships.
6. They heartily <u>hoped</u> Columbus would find new lands.
7. They <u>waited</u> expectantly in Spain.
8. Columbus and his men bravely <u>began</u> their journey.
9. Columbus finally <u>landed</u> in the New World.
10. He thought he really <u>had arrived</u> in India.
11. He actually <u>had reached</u> America.

B. Connecting Verbs and Adverbs   Write each sentence. Underline the adverb in each. Then draw an arrow from each adverb to the verb it tells about.

12. The sailors cried loudly.

MODEL ▷ The sailors cried <u>loudly</u>.

13. They peered excitedly into the distance.

14. Suddenly they saw land.

15. Columbus speedily sailed toward it.

16. He searched anxiously for a place to land.

17. Eventually he spotted a good location.

18. He and his men happily stepped onto the shore.

C. Writing Sentences with Adverbs   Add an adverb to each sentence to make it more vivid. Write each sentence.

19. The ship sailed _____ across the sea.

MODEL ▷ The ship sailed quickly across the sea.

20. The men rowed _____.
21. The ocean rocked the ship _____.
22. When the men saw land, they shouted _____.
23. They _____ prepared to leave the ship.
24. They looked around _____.

3 Adverbs That Compare *pages 304–305*

A. Writing Adverbs That Compare Write the form of each adverb that compares two actions and more than two actions. Use *more* and *most*.

1. quietly

MODEL ⟩ more quietly, most quietly

2. quickly	6. loudly	10. gently
3. eagerly	7. sadly	11. shyly
4. seriously	8. rapidly	12. softly
5. nervously	9. slowly	13. fairly

B. Using Adverbs That Compare Write *more* or *most* to complete each sentence correctly.

14. Sue learned to swim _____ quickly than Ann.

MODEL ⟩ more

15. Of all the students, Sue took to the water _____ easily.
16. Then Ann practiced her strokes _____ carefully.
17. She swam _____ frequently than she had before.
18. Ann moved through the water _____ confidently.
19. Of all the campers, Ann came to class _____ willingly.
20. Soon Ann approached deep water _____ comfortably.
21. Out of the whole group, Ann is _____ likely to become a champion.
22. Ann is facing the race _____ calmly than the others.

C. Writing Sentences with Adverbs That Compare Complete each sentence with the correct form of the adverb in parentheses ( ). Write each sentence.

23. Ann swims (fast) of all the campers.

MODEL ⟩ Ann swims fastest of all the campers.

24. She moves (smoothly) than the other swimmers.
25. Of all the fans, Ann's parents smile (proudly).
26. They arrived (early) than anyone else.
27. They cheered (loud) than all the other fans.
28. Once Ann might have finished (late) than the rest of her team.
29. Now Ann wins (often) than not.
30. She glides through water (naturally) than a fish!

4 Negatives *pages 306–307*

A. Identifying Negatives   Write the negative in each sentence.

1. Sally Ride was not afraid.

MODEL > not

2. She never feared going into space.

3. Dr. Ride knew an astronaut's work wasn't easy.

4. No American woman had ever been in space.

5. None had been selected before her.

6. Nothing was going to stop Sally Ride.

7. She knew she wouldn't fail.

8. She didn't miss her chance.

9. Weren't we all proud of her?

B. Correcting Double Negatives   Each sentence has two negatives. Rewrite each sentence correctly.

10. There weren't no female astronauts before.

MODEL > There weren't any female astronauts before.
OR
There were no female astronauts before.

11. Hadn't no American woman wanted to become one?

12. Nobody nowhere thought women would go into space.

13. NASA couldn't pick no better person than Dr. Ride.

14. She wouldn't do nothing wrong.

15. Nobody can't tell girls to stop dreaming about being astronauts.

16. Students shouldn't never stop studying science.

17. Sally Ride didn't never stop.

18. Doesn't nobody know she is a scientist?

C. Writing Sentences with Negatives   Answer each question with a sentence that uses a negative.

19. Have you ever walked on the moon?

MODEL > I have never walked on the moon.

20. Do you think humans will live on Venus someday?

21. Have you ever touched a star?

22. Do you think plants can live on the moon?

23. Do you believe the sun will burn out someday?

24. Have you ever been inside a spaceship?

25. In the future will people build houses on Mars?

26. Have you ever visited another planet?

UNIT 7   5 Adverb or Adjective? *pages 308–309*

A. Identifying Adjectives and Adverbs   Write *adjective* if the underlined word in each sentence is an adjective. Write *adverb* if it is an adverb.

1. Kay Cottee worked <u>hard</u>.
MODEL adverb
2. She broke an <u>exciting</u> record.
3. She was the <u>first</u> woman to break a sailing record.
4. Kay Cottee sailed <u>nonstop</u> around the world.
5. She sailed <u>alone</u> many thousands of miles.
6. No woman had done these things <u>before</u>.
7. She finished her journey in <u>early</u> June 1988.
8. The 189-day trip must have been <u>lonely</u> for her.
9. Ten thousand fans had waited <u>expectantly</u> for Kay.
10. She landed to <u>wild</u> cheering in Australia.
11. Kay Cottee had <u>never</u> given up.

B. Using *Good* and *Well* Correctly   Write *good* or *well* to complete each sentence correctly.

12. The pilots flew (good, well).
MODEL well
13. They were in a (good, well) plane.
14. It performed (well, good) for them.
15. The around-the-world trip was going (good, well).
16. Both pilots were in a (good, well) mood.
17. Sometimes the weather was not (well, good).
18. Still the pilots stayed (well, good) on course.

C. Writing Sentences with Adjectives or Adverbs   Complete each sentence with the correct word in parentheses ( ). Write the sentence.

19. One author travels by train (glad, gladly).
MODEL One author travels by train gladly.
20. He rides trains (constant, constantly).
21. He writes (eager, eagerly) about his trips.
22. He meets many (different, differently) people.
23. Some countries have (wonderful, wonderfully) trains.
24. In other places the trains run (poor, poorly).
25. It must be (great, greatly) to see the world.
26. People (true, truly) want to learn about each other.

EXTRA PRACTICE

1 Compound Subjects *pages 346–347*

A. Identifying Compound Subjects   Write the two simple subjects in each sentence.

 1. Ships and boats travel the oceans.
MODEL > ships, boats
 2. The hull and the mast are two parts of a sailboat.
 3. Winds and currents help a ship to sail.
 4. Officers and crew sail the vessels.
 5. Explorers and traders use ships to travel.
 6. Passengers and cargo are carried on them.
 7. Radar and radio signals help the sailors to travel.

B. Writing Compound Subjects   Write each sentence. Underline the compound subject in each.

 8. Wind and water pushed the sailboat along.
MODEL > Wind and water pushed the sailboat along.
 9. Breezes and waves gently rocked the boats.
10. Sailboats and canoes shared the water.
11. Sails and oars moved the boats.
12. Laughter and cheers filled the air.
13. Swimmers and boaters enjoyed the day.
14. Parents and children played together.
15. Sunshine and warmth made everything perfect.

C. Joining Sentences to Form Compound Subjects   Combine each pair of sentences to make one sentence with a compound subject.

16. The rowboat raced across the lake.
    The canoe raced across the lake.
MODEL > The rowboat and the canoe raced across the lake.
17. The man rowed quickly.
    The woman rowed quickly.
18. The current carried the boats forward.
    The oars carried the boats forward.
19. The clouds floated in the blue sky.
    The birds floated in the blue sky.
20. The waves gently rocked the boat.
    The wind gently rocked the boat.

UNIT 8   2 Compound Predicates *pages 348–349*

A. Identifying Compound Predicates   Write the two simple predicates in each sentence.

1. The seal dived into the water and swam away.
[MODEL] dived, swam
2. It popped up and gobbled the fish.
3. The people laughed and clapped.
4. The seal balanced a ball and waved its flippers.
5. It barked and waddled along the ground.
6. The zookeeper talked to the seal and fed it fish.
7. Another seal came and pushed the first one.
8. They played in the pool and splashed each other.

B. Writing Compound Predicates   Write each sentence. Underline the compound predicate in each.

9. We saw a monkey and watched it.
[MODEL] We <u>saw</u> a monkey and <u>watched</u> it.
10. It showed its teeth and made a funny face.
11. Then it climbed a tree and swung from a branch.
12. The monkey peeled a banana and quickly ate it.
13. Then it leaped and jumped among the branches.
14. People observed and photographed the monkey.
15. The monkey came down and played with its mother.

C. Joining Sentences to Form Compound Predicates   Combine each pair of sentences to make one sentence with a compound predicate. Write the sentence.

16. A koala climbed a tree.
    A koala ate leaves.
[MODEL] A koala climbed a tree and ate leaves.
17. The koala clung to the branch.
    The koala looked for more food.
18. A koala lives in Australia.
    A koala carries its baby in a pouch.
19. It drinks no water.
    It eats only one kind of leaf.
20. This animal is cuddly.
    This animal looks like a teddy bear.

3 Compound Sentences *pages 350–351*

A. Identifying Compound Sentences   Write *compound* if the sentence is a compound sentence. Write *simple* if it is not.

1. Penguins cannot fly, but they are good swimmers.
MODEL > compound

2. Penguins live in the coldest parts of the world.
3. Layers of fat keep them warm in cold water.
4. Penguins have short tails, and their feet are webbed.
5. They can walk upright, but they do bellyflops in the snow.
6. Penguins have strong bills and short necks.
7. Penguins eat fish, and they live in colonies.
8. Penguins live in Antarctica or on nearby islands.
9. The emperor penguin is the largest type.

B. Forming Compound Sentences   Join each pair of simple sentences. Use the word in parentheses ( ) to connect them. Add commas where they belong. Write the sentences.

10. Snow fell last night. It covered the city.   (and)
MODEL > Snow fell last night, and it covered the city.

11. Everything was white. Everything was clean.   (and)
12. The cars looked pretty. They were stuck.   (but)
13. Children came out. They brought their sleds.   (and)
14. Skiers loved the snow. They tried the slopes.   (and)
15. People made snowballs. They built snowmen.   (or)
16. At first the snow was soft. It soon hardened.   (but)

C. Writing Compound Sentences   Form a compound sentence from each pair of simple sentences. Use the words *and, but,* or *or* to join the sentences. Remember to use commas correctly. Write the sentences.

17. Joe enjoys skiing. He also likes skating.
MODEL > Joe enjoys skiing, and he also likes skating.

18. He ice-skates. He makes figures on the ice.
19. He skis downhill. He dislikes very steep slopes.
20. He might ride on a sled. He might go in a sleigh.
21. Joe likes winter. He likes the crunch of snow.
22. He likes ice fishing. He does not do it often.

4 Commas in Sentences *pages 352–353*

A. **Identifying Correct Usage of Commas in a Series**   Write *correct* for each sentence that uses commas correctly. Write *incorrect* for each sentence that does not.

  1. The air is cool, dry, and crisp.
  MODEL ▷ correct
  2. The autumn weather makes me feel peppy, happy, and fine.
  3. The clouds are white puffy and large.
  4. The wind is gentle mild and pleasant.
  5. Leaves are falling, swirling, and covering the ground.
  6. The leaves are brown, red, and yellow.
  7. Later the air may become cold, biting and unpleasant.
  8. Rain will fall on houses, trees and people.

B. **Using Commas Correctly**   Write each sentence correctly. Add commas where they are needed.

  9. Dad raked the leaves and the children put them into bags.
  MODEL ▷ Dad raked the leaves, and the children put them into bags.
  10. Now the bags are full and they will be tied up.
  11. Dad and the children will pick them up and they will carry the bags to the front of the house.
  12. More leaves fall and they collect beneath the trees.
  13. The children rake them but they soon pile up again.
  14. The children walk in the piles and they listen to the crunch of the leaves.

C. **Writing Sentences Using Commas in a Series**   Add words to complete each sentence. Write each sentence. Add commas where they are needed.

  15. The sky is _____ _____ and _____.
  MODEL ▷ The sky is blue, clear, and bright.
  16. The sun is _____ _____ and _____.
  17. Children are _____ _____ and _____.
  18. _____ _____ and _____ grass feels good under their feet.
  19. The trees in the orchard are full of _____ _____ and _____.
  20. The playground has _____ _____ and _____.
  21. The day is _____ _____ and _____.

EXTRA PRACTICE

5 Avoiding Sentence Fragments and Run-on Sentences *pages 354–355*

A. Identifying Sentence Errors   Write *sentence, sentence fragment,* or *run-on sentence* for each group of words.

1. Ran down the beach.
MODEL> sentence fragment
2. We walked along the water's edge.
3. Searched for shells.
4. Picked them up.
5. We filled our pails with different shells.
6. We ran into the waves they slapped at our faces.
7. We jumped through them.
8. Crashed over our heads.
9. We were completely wet no one minded.

B. Correcting Sentence Fragments   Add words to each sentence fragment to make it a complete sentence. Write each sentence.

10. Made a sand castle.
MODEL> The children made a sand castle.
11. Had many towers.
12. Filled the moats.
13. Shoveled sand into pails.
14. Came and looked.
15. Picked up shovels.
16. Footprints in the sand.
17. Washed everything away.
18. Many sand sculptures.

C. Correcting Run-on Sentences   Correct each run-on sentence. You may use linking words and commas to join parts of the run-on sentences, or you may make each into two separate sentences. Write the sentences correctly.

19. The ocean is salty it helps you float.
MODEL> The ocean is salty. It helps you float.
OR
The ocean is salty, and it helps you float.
20. Ocean salt came from the land it is a mineral.
21. Salt is in rocks it is found in soil also.
22. Rain falls to the earth some goes into the ground.
23. Rainwater washes over rocks it goes along the earth.
24. Rivers go into oceans salt is carried along.
25. Salt goes into oceans it stays there.

1 Capitalization and End Punctuation of Sentences *pages 384–385*

A. Identifying Kinds of Sentences   Write whether each sentence is *declarative*, *imperative*, *interrogative*, or *exclamatory*. Then write the kind of punctuation mark that is needed in each sentence.

1. The Pilgrims landed in 1620
   MODEL ▷ declarative—period
2. Do you know what country the Pilgrims sailed from
3. Look this up in an encyclopedia
4. What a long, terrible journey they had
5. Do you know where the Pilgrims first landed
6. They first landed at Provincetown, Massachusetts
7. Then they sailed down to Plymouth
8. How interesting that is
9. Check the facts for yourself

B. Capitalizing and Punctuating Sentences Correctly   Write each sentence correctly. Add capital letters and end punctuation.

10. how did the first settlers arrive in America
   MODEL ▷ How did the first settlers arrive in America?
11. the first settlers arrived by ship
12. how uncomfortable their living conditions were
13. there was little water or decent food
14. would you have liked to travel in those days
15. the settlers didn't know what they would find
16. were they sorry they had left their homeland
17. try going on an uncertain journey for months
18. see how you like it

C. Writing Sentences Correctly   Write each sentence correctly. Then write *declarative*, *imperative*, *interrogative*, or *exclamatory* to tell its type.

19. read more about the Pilgrims
   MODEL ▷ Read more about the Pilgrims.—imperative
20. what interesting people the Pilgrims were
21. aren't you glad they thought of Thanksgiving Day
22. theirs was the first permanent settlement in New England
23. let's always respect their place in history
24. the Pilgrims brought ideas of freedom to our country

EXTRA PRACTICE

2 Commas Within Sentences *pages 386–387*

A. Identifying Correct Usage of Commas Write *correct* for each sentence in which commas are used correctly. Write *incorrect* for each sentence in which commas are not used correctly.

1. Many Americans have come from Ireland, Germany, and Poland.
MODEL▷ correct
2. Yes Americans have come from many places.
3. Where did your ancestors come from, Kyoko?
4. Well, some of them came from Japan.
5. Some Americans came from Africa Haiti and Jamaica.
6. Others have come from Vietnam, Korea, and Thailand.
7. Many people came in the nineteenth century, but many others have come here more recently.
8. Carol tell us where your grandparents came from.
9. One set came from Russia and one set came from Poland.

B. Correcting Commas in Sentences Write each sentence. Add commas where they are needed. Then write why commas are needed.

10. The journey was often long lonely and difficult.
MODEL▷ The journey was often long, lonely, and difficult.
      commas in a series
11. Ships were crowded and conditions were often bad.
12. No immigrants didn't have an easy time.
13. They came with hopes dreams and ideals.
14. People came to America and they made a new life.
15. Bob how many of your relatives are in England?

C. Writing Sentences with Commas Write each sentence correctly. Add commas where they are needed.

16. Ralph tell me about the Statue of Liberty.
MODEL▷ Ralph, tell me about the Statue of Liberty.
17. It is fascinating and it is inspiring.
18. Yes I climbed the steps all the way to the top.
19. The stairs are narrow winding and crowded.
20. Have you been there before Susan?
21. Well I was there when I was a child.
22. It is a landmark and you should visit it.

3 Capitalization of Proper Nouns and the Pronoun *I* *pages 388–389*

A. Identifying Proper Nouns   Write the word in each pair that is written correctly.

1. independence day, Thanksgiving

[MODEL] Thanksgiving

2. thursday, Monday
3. New Year's Day, fourth of july
4. united states, West Germany
5. Pennsylvania, alaska
6. john adams, George Washington
7. Hoover Dam, columbia river
8. San Francisco, chicago
9. june, October

B. Correcting Proper Nouns and *I*   Write each sentence correctly. Use capital letters where they are needed.

10. We celebrate flag day on june 14.

[MODEL] We celebrate Flag Day on June 14.

11. The last monday in may is memorial day.
12. A holiday i really like is mother's day.
13. The third sunday in june is father's day.
14. In january we celebrate martin luther king day.
15. The first of april is known as april fool's day.
16. President Abraham lincoln was born in february.
17. In august i do not celebrate any holidays.
18. labor day is the first monday in september.

C. Writing Sentences with Proper Nouns   Complete each sentence with the kind of proper noun in parentheses ( ). Write each sentence correctly.

19. We visited the museum on _____.   (day of the week)

[MODEL] We visited the museum on Thursday.

20. It is located in _____.   (name of city)
21. It is an important museum in _____.   (name of state)
22. There I saw a painting of _____ .   (President)
23. I was in this museum last _____.   (month)
24. I went with my cousin _____.   (girl's name)
25. We admired the view of the _____.   (name of river)

4 Abbreviations *pages 390–391*

A. Identifying Abbreviations Write the abbreviation in each group of words. Then write the word the abbreviation stands for.

1. 1600 Pennsylvania Ave.

MODEL> Ave.—Avenue

2. Lincoln Hwy.

3. Revere St.

4. Baltimore Blvd.

5. Constitution Rd.

6. Memorial Dr.

7. New York Ave.

B. Choosing Abbreviations Write the abbreviation in parentheses ( ) that is written correctly.

8. I read about (Gen., gen) Lee.

MODEL> Gen.

9. (mr., Mr.) Carl Sandburg wrote about Lincoln.

10. The book *Profiles in Courage* was written by (Sen., sen) John F. Kennedy.

11. Here is a book about (gov, Gov.) William Bradford of the Plymouth Colony.

12. Many authors have written about (Mrs., mrs) Eleanor Roosevelt.

13. Read a biography about (dr, Dr.) Martin Luther King, Jr.

14. *The Story of My Life*, by (Ms., ms) Helen Keller, is a very inspiring book.

C. Writing Abbreviations Rewrite each item, using an abbreviation.

15. Mister Ben Franklin

MODEL> Mr. Ben Franklin

16. Doctor Elizabeth Blackwell

17. Governor Mario Cuomo

18. Senator William Proxmire

19. Captain John Smith

20. General Dwight Eisenhower

21. Roosevelt Boulevard

22. Independence Avenue

23. Williamsburg Road

24. Dixie Highway

25. Wall Street

26. Madison Drive

EXTRA PRACTICE

5 Letters *pages 392–393*

A. Identifying Correct Parts of a Letter Write the letter part in each pair that is written correctly.

1. dear claire   Dear Harry,

MODEL ▷ Dear Harry,

2. Your Friend,   Your friend,
3. Dear stu   Dear Wendy,
4. Albany New York   Houston, Texas 77092
5. Your pal,   Your Pal
6. February 8 1990   December 6, 1990
7. 125 Carson Avenue   324 pinetree road
8. best Regards,   Best regards,

B. Capitalizing and Punctuating Parts of Letters Write each letter part correctly.

9. your friend

MODEL ▷ Your friend,

10. dear rochelle
11. Boston massachusetts 02107
12. June 27 1990
13. 168 elm street
14. dear aunt margaret
15. September 2 1990
16. your loving niece
17. San diego California 92101

C. Writing Parts of Letters Add capital letters and commas to write each letter part correctly.

18. may 11 1991

MODEL ▷ May 11, 1991

19. your loving granddaughter
20. dear uncle steve
21. your best chum
22. october 22 1991
23. 612 east grove street
24. yours truly
25. dear grandfather
26. 3424 ocean avenue
27. tampa florida
28. love
29. 16 mountainview court

6 Envelopes *pages 394–395*

A. Identifying Correct Parts of Addresses   Write the item in each pair that is correct.

1. mrs. anna simms
   MODEL> Dr. Tom Dooley
2. boston massachusetts
3. Ms. Dolores Johnson
4. Newport News, VA 23630
5. Mrs. karen feinberg
6. 18 west elm street
7. Boulder, CO 80302
8. 3413 North Fremont Ave.

Dr. Tom Dooley

Washington, DC 20036
mr paul Smith
yonkers, new york 10710
Dr. Sandra Simmons
37 Jupiter Lane
cleveland, ohio
141 edgar Street

B. Writing Addresses   Write each address in correct order.

9. Chicago, IL 60614
   Ms. Ann Taylor
   1440 Oak Street
   MODEL> Ms. Ann Taylor
   1440 Oak Street
   Chicago, IL 60614

10. 12 Congress Street
    Mr. Edward Duncan
    Boston, MA 02210
11. Ms. Sheila Sloane
    Chaska, MN 55318
    111 Connors Boulevard
12. Flushing, NY 11358
    98 Eastern Boulevard
    Ms. Sonia Gomez

13. Weston, CT 06883
    Dr. Tom Barnes
    9 Silver Avenue
14. 48 Riverview Street
    Vershire, VT 05079
    Ms. Ann Strong
15. 6 S. Main Street
    Mr. Timothy Phillips
    Yardley, PA 19067

C. Using Postal Abbreviations in Addresses   Abbreviate the underlined word. Write each item correctly.

16. Milwaukee, <u>Wisconsin</u> 53233
    MODEL> Milwaukee, WI 53233
17. Casselberry, <u>Florida</u> 32707
18. Plymouth, <u>Michigan</u> 48170
19. Elizabeth, <u>New Jersey</u> 07458
20. Birmingham, <u>Alabama</u> 35203

21. Midlothian, <u>Virginia</u> 23113
22. Cortez, <u>Colorado</u> 81321
23. Rockport, <u>Maine</u> 04856
24. Los Angeles, <u>California</u> 90024

EXTRA PRACTICE

7 Outlines *pages 396–397*

A. Building Outlines Write the items for each outline section in the correct order. Indent and add capital letters as needed.

1. B. yellowstone
    A. grand canyon
    I. national parks
    C. yosemite

> MODEL I. National parks
>   A. Grand Canyon
>   B. Yellowstone
>   C. Yosemite

2. C. colorado
    II. american rivers
    A. mississippi
    B. missouri

3. B. mt. whitney
    A. mt. mckinley
    III. american mountains
    C. mt. rainier

4. B. painted
    IV. american deserts
    C. great salt lake
    A. mojave

5. A. golden gate
    C. sunshine skyway
    V. american bridges
    B. george washington

B. Forming Outlines Write the information on each line in the correct form for the outline part shown in parentheses ( ).

6. 1. famous landmarks   (main topic)

> MODEL I. Famous landmarks

7. 2. famous buildings   (main topic)
8. b. mt rushmore   (subtopic)
9. a. statue of liberty   (subtopic)
10. 3. american forests   (main topic)

C. Writing Outlines Change the information in each group of notes into correct outline form for the first main topic of a report.

11. Important American women, Betsy Ross, Amelia
    Earhart, Sally Ride

> MODEL I. Important American women
>   A. Betsy Ross
>   B. Amelia Earhart
>   C. Sally Ride

12. Important inventions, telephone, radio, camera
13. Famous writers, Mark Twain, Washington Irving,
    Nathaniel Hawthorne

EXTRA PRACTICE

UNIT 9 **8 Titles** *pages 398–399*

A. Identifying Titles   Write the title that is correct in each pair.

    1. Johnny Tremain   jungle book   (book)

MODEL > Johnny Tremain

    2. <u>Dixie</u>   "Yankee Doodle"   (song)

    3. <u>owl</u>   <u>American Heritage</u>   (magazine)

    4. Mexicali Soup   "An Eskimo Birthday"   (story)

    5. "boston globe"   <u>New York Times</u>   (newspaper)

    6. the old chisholm trail   "The Erie Canal"   (song)

    7. benjamin franklin   "Daniel Boone"   (poem)

B. Correcting Titles   Write each title correctly.

    8. america the beautiful   (song)

MODEL > "America the Beautiful"

    9. abe lincoln grows up   (book)

  10. chicago   (poem)

  11. paul bunyan   (story)

  12. home on the range   (song)

  13. american health   (magazine)

  14. san francisco chronicle   (newspaper)

  15. i've been working on the railroad   (song)

  16. eleanor roosevelt, woman of courage   (book)

  17. newsweek   (magazine)

C. Writing Titles Correctly in Sentences   Capitalize and punctuate each title. Write each sentence correctly.

  18. I read the poem paul revere's ride.

MODEL > I read the poem "Paul Revere's Ride."

  19. I like the story called john henry and his hammer.

  20. Read this article in the newspaper, the <u>boston globe</u>.

  21. A famous cowboy song is goodbye, old paint.

  22. A wonderful book is <u>little house on the prairie</u>.

  23. The magazine <u>national geographic</u> has great photos.

  24. Walt Whitman wrote the poem i hear america singing.

  25. Here is a book entitled <u>meet george washington</u>.

  26. Please sing streets of laredo for me.

9 Direct Quotations and Dialogue *pages 400–401*

A. Identifying Direct Quotations   Write each sentence. Underline the direct quotation.

1. Mary exclaimed, "Look at this old letter!"
   MODEL ▷ Mary exclaimed, "<u>Look at this old letter!</u>"
2. "I can't believe it was written so long ago," she said.
3. Lee said, "The paper is so yellowed with age."
4. The guide told them, "It was written in this room."
5. "Thomas Jefferson sat at that desk?" Mary asked.
6. "Yes, and he used that quill pen," said the guide.
7. "History is alive in this room!" Lee exclaimed.

B. Forming Direct Quotations   Use capitalization and punctuation correctly to write each direct quotation.

8. Dave asked have you ever been to Boston
   MODEL ▷ Dave asked, "Have you ever been to Boston?"
9. Kim answered my family and I have been there once
10. it's a very historic city added José.
11. Dave said i walked the Freedom Trail
12. José said we saw Paul Revere's house
13. don't forget the Old North Church laughed Kim.
14. one if by land and two if by sea explained Dave.
15. Dave asked have you been to Minuteman National Historic Park
16. this is the place where the Revolution began he continued
17. what a thrilling place to visit exclaimed Kim

C. Completing Direct Quotations   Complete each direct quotation with a word that tells how the speaker talks. Add punctuation and capitalization where needed. Write each sentence correctly.

18. Ann _____ the Liberty Bell is in Philadelphia.
    MODEL ▷ Ann declared, "The Liberty Bell is in Philadelphia."
19. She _____ that's where Independence Hall is.
20. Her friend Toni _____ the Declaration of Independence was written and signed there in 1776.
21. I wish I could have met those men _____ Ann.
22. How exciting it must have been to know Ben Franklin _____ Toni.

WRITER'S HANDBOOK

Contents

Sentences

sentence • A **sentence** is a group of words that expresses a complete thought. The words in a sentence should be in an order that makes sense. Every sentence begins with a capital letter and ends with an end mark.

Mr. Worley is a good basketball player.

• There are four kinds of sentences: *declarative, interrogative, imperative,* and *exclamatory.*

declarative • A **declarative sentence** makes a statement. It ends with a period (.).

I asked for a second helping.

interrogative • An **interrogative sentence** asks a question. It ends with a question mark (?).

Did you ever taste such delicious soup?

imperative • An **imperative sentence** gives a command or makes a request. It ends with a period (.).

Please pass the corn.

exclamatory • An **exclamatory sentence** expresses strong feeling. It ends with an exclamation point (!).

What a beautiful day for a party!

simple sentence • A sentence that expresses one complete thought is called a **simple sentence.**

Albert wants to have a party.

compound sentence • A **compound sentence** is made up of two simple sentences joined by *and, or,* or *but.* A comma (,) is used before the word that joins the two sentences.

simple sentence   simple sentence

Soon it was evening, and we had to leave.

We didn't want to go, but it was late.

We'll have another party soon, or we'll all go on a trip.

- Each sentence is made up of two parts, the *subject* and the *predicate*.

subject   predicate

| My sister | will wear her new dress to the party. |

- The **subject** is the part that tells whom or what the sentence is about.

Everyone in our family came to the party.

- All the words in the subject are called the **complete subject**.

My cousins from California called us on the phone.

- The **simple subject** is the main word in the complete subject of a sentence.

My baby sister got a lot of attention.

- A **compound subject** is made up of two or more simple subjects joined by *and*.

My aunt and my uncle took photographs of us all.

- The **predicate** is the part of a sentence that tells what the subject is or does.

All of us had a very good time.

- All the words in the predicate are called the **complete predicate**.

The first course was a delicious chicken soup.

- The **simple predicate** is the main word in the complete predicate of a sentence.

My grandparents prepared the meal.

- A **compound predicate** is made up of two or more predicates joined by *and*.

A few of us washed the dishes and dried them.

Nouns

noun
- A **noun** is a word that names a person, a place, or a thing.

  My brother is in Texas drilling for oil .

singular noun
- A **singular noun** names one person, place, or thing.

  teacher   city   bicycle

plural noun
- A **plural noun** names more than one person, place, or thing. For help with the spelling of plural nouns, see the *Spelling* section of this **Writer's Handbook.**

  job—jobs   boy—boys   class—classes
  fox—foxes   match—matches   dish—dishes
  city—cities   turkey—turkeys   mouse—mice

common noun
- A **common noun** names any person, place, or thing.

  musician   state   planet

proper noun
- A **proper noun** names a particular person, place, or thing. It begins with a capital letter.

  B eethoven   V irginia   M ars   T uesday
  O ctober   H alloween   T empe, A rizona

possessive noun
- A **possessive noun** shows ownership.

  one boy's notebook   each tree's shadow

singular possessive noun
- A **singular possessive noun** shows ownership by one person or thing. To form a singular possessive noun, add an apostrophe and *s* (**'s**) to a singular noun.

  every mayor's speech   in James's room

plural possessive noun
- A **plural possessive noun** shows ownership by more than one person or thing. To form the possessive of a plural noun ending in *s* or *es*, add only an apostrophe.

  the planets' orbits   the ladies' dresses

- To form the possessive of a plural noun that does not end in *s*, add an apostrophe and *s*.

  the children's teacher   the sheep's owners

Pronouns

- A **pronoun** is a word that takes the place of a noun or nouns.

  pronoun

  > Mark plays the violin. He plays very well.

- A **subject pronoun** takes the place of a noun or nouns in the subject of a sentence. The words *I, you, he, she, we, they,* and *it* are subject pronouns.

  subject pronoun

  > I enjoy listening to music.

- An **object pronoun** follows an action verb or words like *at, for, to,* and *with.* The object pronouns are *me, you, him, her, it, us,* and *them.*

  object pronoun

  > Deborah showed him the stage.
  > You can share with me .

- *I* and *we* are subject pronouns. They are used in the subject of a sentence.

  I, me, we, us

  > Danny and I went to a concert. We really liked it.

- *Me* and *us* are object pronouns. They are used after action verbs or after words like *at, for, to,* and *with.*

  > Kim taught me a song. Jan will stay with us .

- The words *I* and *me* appear last when they are used with another noun or pronoun.

  > Mother and I brought a camera.
  > Everyone thanked her and me .

- The words *we* and *us* may be used before nouns in a sentence.

  > We Joneses love the city.
  > Many kinds of music appeal to us students .

- A **possessive pronoun** shows ownership and takes the place of a possessive noun. The possessive pronouns are *my, your, her, his, its, our,* and *their.*

  possessive pronoun

  > This is Meg's book. This is her book.

pronoun contraction
- A **contraction** can sometimes be formed by joining a pronoun and a verb. An apostrophe takes the place of missing letters.

I + am = I'm   you + have = you've
you + are = you're   they + will = they'll

Verbs

action verb
- An **action verb** is a word that tells what the subject does or did. It is the main word in the complete predicate.

Jonathan throws the baseball.

linking verb
- A **linking verb** connects the subject to a word or words in the predicate. The most common linking verbs are forms of *be*.

Margaret is an excellent swimmer.

main verb
- Sometimes the simple predicate is made up of two verbs. The **main verb** is the most important verb in the predicate. It comes last in a group of verbs.

Juanita has passed the junior lifesaving test.

helping verb
- A **helping verb** works with the main verb to tell about action. The helping verb always comes before the main verb.

helping main
verb   verb

Andrew had completed the 100-meter dash in 15 seconds.

tense
- The **tense** of a verb tells the time of an action.

present tense
- A **present-tense** verb shows action that happens now.

The ball bounces twice before it reaches him.

past tense
- A **past-tense** verb shows action that happened in the past. Many past-tense verbs end in *ed*.

She jumped higher than anyone else.

future tense
- A **future-tense** verb shows action that will happen in the future. The future tense uses the helping verb *will*.

We will win the game tomorrow.

subject-verb agreement
- A subject and its verb should agree.

- A present-tense verb changes spelling to agree with the subject. If the subject is singular, add *s* or *es* to the verb. The pronouns *I* and *you* are followed by plural verbs.

> The gym teacher shows us how to dive properly.
> You showed the teacher what you learned.

- Usually if the subject is plural, do not add an ending to the verb.

> All of the runners wait at the starting line.

- When the main verb ends in *ing,* the helping verb should be *am, is, are, was,* or *were.*

> I am practicing for the school olympics.

- When the main verb ends in *ed,* the helping verb should be *has, have,* or *had.*

> We had practiced our routine for many hours.

- Some verbs change spelling when *ed* or *es* is added. If a verb ends in *e,* drop the *e* before adding *ed* or *es.*

spelling verbs correctly

> like—liked   please—pleases

- Some one-syllable verbs end with a short vowel sound and a consonant. Double the final consonant before adding *ed.*

> skip—skipped   pat—patted

- If a verb ends in a consonant + *y,* change the *y* to *i* before adding *ed.*

> carry—carried

- An **irregular verb** does not end in *ed* in the past tense.

irregular verb

> He sees.   He saw.   He has seen.

- There are two forms of past-tense verbs. One form is used with the helping verbs *have, has,* or *had.* For some irregular verbs the two forms are the same, but for many of them the two forms are different.

Present	Past	Past with *have, has,* or *had*
bring	brought	brought
go	went	gone

- For some irregular verbs, the past-tense form used with helping verbs ends in *n* or *en*.

Present	Past	Past with *have, has,* or *had*
grow	grew	grown
write	wrote	written

verb contraction

- A **contraction** can sometimes be formed by joining a verb and *not*. *Not* is shortened to *n't*.

is + not = isn't   does + not = doesn't   will + not = won't

Adjectives

adjective

- An **adjective** is a word that describes a noun or a pronoun.

Our neighbors have a large dog.

- Most adjectives tell *what kind*. Some adjectives tell *how many*.

There are some stray cats on our block.

The adjective *some* tells *how many*. The adjective *stray* tells *what kind*.

articles

- The adjectives *a, an,* and *the* are **articles.** An article is a special kind of adjective.

- Use *a* with singular nouns when the noun or the word before the noun begins with a consonant sound.

a bird   a common sparrow

- Use *an* with singular nouns when the noun or the word before the noun begins with a vowel sound.

an ostrich   an orange parrot

- Use *the* before a specific noun or nouns.

the zoo   the cages

adjective that follows a linking verb

- An adjective that follows a linking verb describes the subject.

linking verb

The elephants are friendly.

- An adjective that follows a linking verb can describe either a noun or a pronoun.

  The panther is black . It is graceful .

- Adjectives can describe by comparing people, places, or things.

  adjectives
  that compare

- Add *er* to most adjectives to compare two things.

  er

  Bill's dog is older than our dog.

- Add *est* to most adjectives to compare more than two things.

  est

  The whale is the largest animal of all.

- When you add *er* or *est* to an adjective that ends in *e*, drop the *e*.

  blue   bluer   bluest

- When a one-syllable adjective ends in a short vowel sound and a consonant, double the last letter.

  big   bigger   biggest

- When an adjective ends in a consonant plus *y*, change the *y* to *i*, and add *er* or *est*.

  silly   sillier   silliest

- *More* or *most* is used with some adjectives to make comparisons. Use *more* to compare two things.

  more, most

  The dolphin is more intelligent than the whale.

- Use *most* to compare more than two things.

  The shark is the most dangerous animal in the sea.

- Remember that some two-syllable adjectives use *er* and *est* to make comparisons. Others use *more* and *most*. Check in a dictionary when you are not sure.

- Some adjectives that compare have special forms.

  special forms

  good—better—best   bad—worse—worst
  many—more—most   little—less—least
  much—more—most

Adverbs

adverb • An **adverb** is a word that describes a verb. An adverb may come before or after a verb that it tells about.

He carefully parked the car.
She drove slowly .

adverbs that tell *how* • Some adverbs tell *how*. These verbs usually end in *ly*.

He honked the horn loudly .

• A few adjectives that tell *how* do not end in *ly*.

The car runs well in cold weather.

adverbs that tell *when* • Some adverbs tell *when* an action happens.

I will take the driving test tomorrow .

• Adverbs that tell *when* sometimes end in *ly*.

The test is given weekly .

adverbs that tell *where* • Some adverbs tell *where* an action happens.

Patty drove downtown .

adverbs that compare • Adverbs can be used to compare two or more actions. When you compare two actions, add *er*. When you compare more than two actions, add *est*.

Tim climbed high into the tree.

Maria climbed higher than Tim.

Carl climbed the highest of all.

• Use the words *more* and *most* to make comparisons with adverbs ending in *ly*. Use *more* when comparing two actions. Use *most* when comparing more than two actions.

Sally's dog learns tricks quickly .

Her cat learns tricks more quickly .

Her pony learns tricks most quickly .

- A word that means *no* is called a **negative.** Negatives include no, *not, nobody, nothing, nowhere, none,* and *never.*

  negative

- The adverb *not* and contractions made with *not* are negatives.

  Elaine isn't in this class.

- Do not use two negatives in the same sentence.

  correct: He doesn't know anything.

  He knows nothing .

  incorrect: He doesn't know nothing.

Capitalization

sentence • A **sentence** begins with a capital letter.

> **D**oes Maria like to write?
> **W**hat a wonderful novel this is!

proper noun • A **proper noun** names a particular person, place, or thing. Every proper noun begins with a capital letter.

> **M**aria Grant   **B**razil   **S**unday

• Each word in a person's name begins with a capital letter.

> **S**cott **C**arpenter   **C**arl **L**ewis   **T**revor

• A person's title begins with a capital letter, whether the title is fully written out or abbreviated. An initial that is used as part of a name is capitalized.

> **D**r. Mary **S**. Owens   **P**rofessor **D**. **J**. Marcos

• The first word and every important word in the name of a place begins with a capital letter.

> **S**alt **L**ake **C**ity   **E**urope   **U**nited **S**tates of **A**merica

• The days of the week and the months of the year begin with capital letters, whether they are fully written out or abbreviated.

> **T**uesday, **J**anuary 2   **S**at., **F**eb. 3

• The first word and every important word in the name of a holiday begins with a capital letter.

> **N**ew **Y**ear's **D**ay   **F**ourth of **J**uly

I • The word *I* is always written with a capital letter, and contractions that begin with *I* begin with capital letters.

> I   I'm   I'll   I'd

abbreviations • Many **abbreviations** begin with a capital letter and are followed by a period.

> Doctor—**D**r.   Street—**S**t.
> January—**J**an.   Mister—**M**r.

WRITER'S HANDBOOK • Mechanics

- Capital letters are used in the heading, the greeting, and the closing of a letter.

heading	237 East Main Street
	Hartford, Connecticut 06110
	November 3, 1990
greeting	Dear Martha,
closing	Your friend,

- The first word, the last word, and other important words in the titles of books and stories begin with capital letters.

<u>The Adventures of Peter Rabbit</u>

" Jan's Day at the Zoo"

- A **direct quotation** is the exact words that someone has said or written. The first word of a quoted sentence is always capitalized.

The teacher said, "Today we will work on grammar."
The story begins, "Once upon a time there was a king."

- Capitalize the first word in each main topic and subtopic of an outline.

I. Natural fibers
   A. Silk
   B. Cotton
   C. Wool

Punctuation

- A **sentence** ends with a punctuation mark.

- A **declarative sentence** and an **imperative sentence** each end with a period.

The train is late.
Give me a ticket to El Paso.

- An **interrogative sentence** ends with a question mark.

Where is the station?

- An **exclamatory sentence** ends with an exclamation point.

What a wonderful trip this has been!

- Use a period (.) after an initial.

  P.T. Barnum   Booker T. Washington

- Place a period after an abbreviation.

  August—Aug.   Avenue—Ave.
  Friday—Fri.   Road—Rd.

- Use a period at the end of a direct quotation if the quotation is a statement or a command and no words follow it.

  Jerry said, "I enjoy traveling by plane."

- Use a period after every Roman numeral in a main topic and after every capital letter before a subtopic.

  I. Disasters
    A. Earthquakes

comma

- Use a comma (,) before the word *and, or,* or *but* when it joins the two simple sentences in a compound sentence.

  The team went by bus, and we traveled by car.

- Use a comma to separate the words in a series.

  We will visit Boston, New York, and Philadelphia.

- Use a comma to set off the word *yes, no,* or *well* at the beginning of a sentence.

  No, we won't have time to see Baltimore.

- Use a comma to set off the name of someone directly addressed.

  Don't forget to pack your raincoat, Polly.

- In the heading of a friendly letter, use commas between the city and the state and between the day and the year.

  567 Willow Drive
  San Ramon, California 94583
  December 10, 1990

- In the greeting of a friendly letter, use a comma after the last word.

  Dear Uncle Charlie,

- In the closing of a friendly letter, use a comma after the last word.

  Your nephew**,**

- Use a comma to separate a speaker's words from the rest of the sentence in a direct quotation.

  The conductor called out **,** "All aboard!"
  "Let's go to the dining car **,** " said Father.

- Use an apostrophe (') to replace a letter or letters that have been left out in a contraction.

  apostrophe

  I + am = I **'** m   he + would = he **'** d
  did + not = didn **'** t

- Add an apostrophe and *s* to most singular nouns to show possession.

  the **bus's** engine   the **flight attendant's** uniform

  To form the possessive of a plural noun that ends in *s* or *es*, add only an apostrophe.

  the **passengers'** tickets   the **buses'** drivers

  To form the possessive of a plural noun that does not end in *s*, add an apostrophe and *s*.

  the **children's** baggage

- Use quotation marks (" ") to show the exact words a speaker says. Put quotation marks before and after the direct quotation. The end punctuation comes just before the ending quotation marks.

  quotation marks

  Billy said, **"** I'd love to be a pilot. **"**
  " Are you sure? **"** asked his sister.

- Use quotation marks around the titles of stories, poems, and songs.

  " Jack and the Beanstalk **"**   **"** Homework Machine **"**
  " Oh, Susannah! **"**

- Underline the titles of books, magazines, and newspapers.

  underline

  <u>The Secret Garden</u>   <u>Time</u>   <u>Washington Post</u>

WRITER'S HANDBOOK • Mechanics

Troublesome Words

its, it's • Use *its* when you mean "belonging to it."
Use *it's* as a contraction for *it is.*

The snake sheds its skin.

It's a perfect day for a picnic. (it + is)

It's been a very dry summer. (it + has)

your, you're • Use *your* when you mean "belonging to you."
Use *you're* as a contraction for *you are.*

Is this your coat?

You're the fastest runner in the class.

I, me • *I* is a subject pronoun. It is used in the subject of a sentence.
Me is an object pronoun. It follows an action verb.

Deborah and I are first cousins.

The librarian showed me where to find the book.

She checked it out for me .

their, they're, there • Use *their* when you mean "belonging to them."
Use *they're* as a contraction for *they are.*
Use *there* when you mean "in or at that place."

The band members were carrying their instruments.

We eat lots of peaches when they're in season.

Please put the package over there .

to, too, two • *To, too,* and *two* sound alike but have different meanings.
Use *to* when you mean "in the direction of."
Use *too* when you mean "also."
Use *two* when you mean the number.

Let's walk to town this morning.

"I want some milk too ," said his sister.

There are two pints in a quart.

good, well • *Good* is an adjective. It describes a noun. *Well* is an adverb. It describes a verb.

Olga is a good swimmer.

Bert swims well , too.

Negatives

- A word that means *no* is called a **negative.**

no	nothing
not	nobody
none	nowhere
never	

- Contractions made with the adverb *not* are negatives.

can't	wouldn't
don't	shouldn't
won't	couldn't

- Two negatives usually are not used in the same sentence.

correct: There wasn't anybody in the store.

There was nobody in the store.

incorrect: There wasn't nobody in the store.

Agreement

subject-verb
agreement

- A present-tense verb should agree with its subject.

- If the subject is a singular noun or pronoun, use a singular verb form. Most singular verb forms end with *s* or *es*. The singular pronouns *I* and *you* are not followed by verbs ending in *s* or *es*.

The teacher explains things to us.

He wants our attention.

- If the subject is a plural noun or pronoun, use a plural verb form.

The actors learn their lines.

They want fish for dinner.

WRITER'S HANDBOOK • Usage

Paragraph

paragraph
- A **paragraph** is a group of sentences that tells about one main idea. A paragraph often begins with a **topic sentence.** The topic sentence expresses the main idea of the paragraph. It tells what all the other sentences in the paragraph are about. The other sentences in a paragraph are called **detail sentences.** Detail sentences add information about the topic. They help the audience understand the main idea.

Writer's Guide: Paragraph
1. Write a topic sentence that clearly tells the main idea of your paragraph.
2. Indent the first line.
3. Write detail sentences that tell about the main idea.

topic sentence —

detail sentences —

Dogs have helped people in many ways. Long ago, when people hunted wild animals for food, dogs helped with the hunt. They also helped people take care of their farm animals. In some parts of the world, they pulled people and their loads. Besides all the help they gave to people in their work, dogs have always given people friendship and protection.

How-to Paragraph

- In a **how-to paragraph,** a writer gives directions that explain how to do something. Steps are given in time order.

how-to paragraph

Writer's Guide: How-to Paragraph
1. Write a topic sentence that tells what you are going to explain.
2. Write a detail sentence that lists all materials needed.
3. Write more detail sentences to tell the steps in order.
4. Use time-order words such as *first, next, then, last,* and *finally* to show correct order.

How to Play Fishing in the Dark

    Fishing in the Dark is fun for people of all ages. You will need a blindfold and a fishing pole made from a wooden spoon, string, and a magnet. You will also need twenty paper fish with paper clips. Here's how to play. First, scatter the fish on the floor. Then, blindfold the first player. The player holds the pole over the fish and drags the magnet across the floor. The magnet picks up fish. The other players take off the fish the magnet picks up. Everyone takes a turn for one minute. The players who catch the most fish are the winners.

topic sentence

materials

time–order words in steps

Paragraph of Information

paragraph of information

- In a **paragraph of information,** a writer gives facts about one topic.

Writer's Guide: Paragraph of Information
1. Write a topic sentence that tells the main idea.
2. Add detail sentences that give facts about the main idea.
3. Write an interesting title that tells about your paragraph.

title

The Amazing Electrical Music Box

topic sentence

When Americans wanted to listen to music, they often used the phonograph. This electrical machine had three main parts. The turntable was a round spinning platform on a small, flat box. It was for spinning records. These records were thin, black discs as big as dinner plates. A moving turntable arm read the soundtracks in the grooves of the records. Another part of the phonograph was a box called a receiver. It turned the signals from the turntable into music. Knobs on the receiver were used to adjust the sound. The third part was made up of two boxes called speakers. They were connected by long wires to the receiver. They carried music to diffrent parts of the room.

facts

Paragraph of Comparison

- In a **paragraph of comparison,** a writer shows how two people, places, or things are alike.

paragraph of comparison

Writer's Guide: Paragraph of Comparison
1. Think of three ways your subjects are alike.
2. Write a topic sentence that tells what you are going to compare and that your subjects are alike.
3. In the detail sentences, give examples that clearly show the likenesses.
4. Write about the likenesses in the same order you introduced them in the topic sentence.

The Old Wharf and Pier 9 are alike in a few ways. Both were built in the early 1900's. For a long time they were used as docks for fishing boats. Today, both long, wooden wharves still stretch out into the green harbor.

— topic sentence

— likenesses

Paragraph of Contrast

paragraph of
contrast

- In a **paragraph of contrast,** a writer shows how two people, places, or things are different.

Writer's Guide: Paragraph of Contrast
1. Think of at least two ways your subjects are different.
2. Write a topic sentence that tells what you are going to contrast and that your subjects are different.
3. In the detail sentences, give examples that clearly explain the differences between your subjects.
4. Write about the differences in the same order in which you introduced them in the topic sentence.

topic sentence ——

differences ——

However, the Old Wharf and Pier 9 do not look very much alike. The Old Wharf is still used by the fishing fleet. At dawn it is a lively place as the fishers put their boats to sea. By late morning it is deserted, except for a few lazy gulls. Pier 9, on the other hand, has changed greatly. Only the harbor cruise boat docks there now. In the morning it is as still as a ghost town. By noon its souvenir shops and fish restaurants are crowded with chattering tourists. It is a bustling place then.

WRITER'S HANDBOOK • Composition

Persuasive Paragraph

- In a **persuasive paragraph,** a writer tells his or her opinion on a topic. The writer tries to convince the audience to agree with his or her opinion and to take some action.

Writer's Guide: Persuasive Paragraph
1. Write a topic sentence that tells your opinion.
2. In the detail sentences, give at least three reasons that will convince your audience to agree with your opinion.
3. Save your strongest reason for last.
4. Give examples to explain your reasons.
5. At the end of the paragraph, state your opinion again. Then urge your audience to agree with you.

Our world is a lot noisier and unhealthier than it needs to be. Some noises can't be helped. We have to put up with the sounds of buses, trucks, drills, and saws. After all, people have to go places and build things. We all add unnecessary noises to this uproar, however. Families in the parks and teenagers on the streets play their radios loudly. Some people shout when they could talk quietly. Yesterday someone was shouting in the library and I couldn't study. Scientists have found that loud noise may damage hearing. It also creates the stress that makes people cross or sick. We'd all feel better and healthier in a quieter world. That's why we should do our part to cut down on the racket.

— opinion

— reason/example

— restated opinion and request for action

Descriptive Paragraph

descriptive
paragraph

- In a **descriptive paragraph,** a writer describes a person, a place, a thing, or an event. A writer should include details that let the reader see, feel, hear, and sometimes taste and smell what is being described.

Writer's Guide: Descriptive Paragraph
1. Write a topic sentence that tells what you will describe.
2. Write detail sentences. Use colorful and lively words to describe your topic.
3. Choose words that will help your audience picture what you are describing.

topic sentence —

    The path through the woods was like a dark tunnel. He knew he was still on the path because the ground was _hard_ and _bumpy_ under his bare feet. At last, he came out from under the trees. He saw a _broad_ field lit with moonlight. He smelled freshly cut alfalfa. An owl _hooted_. Small creatures _rustled_ in the grass. Beyond the field was another grove of trees like a _low_ _black_ cloud. The path carried him near this grove.

colorful
words in
detail
sentences —

WRITER'S HANDBOOK • Composition

Dialogue

- In a **dialogue** a writer tells the exact words that people say to each other.

dialogue

Writer's Guide: Dialogue
1. Place quotation marks before and after the exact words of a speaker.
2. Use a comma to separate a quotation from the rest of the sentence unless a question mark or an exclamation point is needed.
3. Begin a new paragraph each time the speaker changes.
4. Be sure the dialogue sounds like real people talking.
5. Use words such as *said, called, answered,* and *shouted* to show how the speaker says the words.

"I'm going to the library." said Kenny. "Do you want to go with me?" — **exact words**

"Sure." answered Paul. "I have some books to return." — **new speaker**

Kenny suggested. "Maybe we can do our homework there. also." — **new speaker**

"That's a good idea." said Paul. "I could use some help with the math problems."

"Okay." said Kenny. "Let's go!"

Journal Entry

- In a **journal** a writer keeps a record of daily events. Writers often include ideas and feelings in their journals. Each daily record is called an **entry**.

Writer's Guide: Journal Entry
1. Write the date of the entry.
2. Write one or two important things that happened on that day.
3. Explain why the events are important to you.

date of entry

what happened

why it is important

November 19, 1990

Today I went to the hospital to see my new baby sister. She was born last night. Dad took me after school. I bought a stuffed animal for my sister and flowers for Mom. Mom let me hold the baby. She is so tiny. It's hard to believe that I was once that small. I wonder what it is going to be like to have a baby around the house. It will probably be very strange because I was the only child in our family until yesterday.

Personal Narrative

- In a **personal narrative,** a writer tells a story about an experience in his or her life.

Writer's Guide: Personal Narrative
1. Write a strong beginning to capture your reader's interest.
2. Write detail sentences in the middle that describe events in time order.
3. Write an ending that tells what happened as a result of the events.

There was no way I was going to be in the 4-H Club show. Just the thought of being on stage gave me goose bumps. My friend Amy said that I would have fun if I gave it a chance. I just made a face at her. I told her I would help make the costumes. That was enough fun for me!

Then one day the girl playing Queen Iris got sick. My group needed someone to say her lines at rehearsals. They talked me into doing it until she got well. On opening night she was still in bed. Amy told me not to be a coward and to help save the show. The next thing I knew, I was on stage. To my surprise, my goose bumps vanished. The applause at the end was thrilling. Now I have decided to be an actress.

strong beginning

middle

ending

Story

story • In a **story** a writer tells about one main idea. A story has *characters*, a *plot*, and a *setting*. It has a *beginning*, a *middle*, and an *ending*.

Writer's Guide: Story
1. Write an interesting beginning to present the main characters and the setting.
2. Write the middle of the story. Tell about a problem that the characters have to solve in the plot. Tell about what happens in order.
3. Write an ending. Tell how the characters solve the problem.
4. Write a title for your story.

title —

beginning
(characters
and setting) —

middle —

ending —

The Lost Keys

Rico was going to a baseball game with his mother. When Mrs. Perez looked into her purse, she couldn't find her car keys. Rico and his mother searched everywhere. They looked in the kitchen drawers. They checked all the shelves. Then Rico saw something dangling from his dog's mouth. Muff had found the keys! After giving Muff a big hug, Rico ran out to the car.

Fable

- In a **fable** a writer tells a story that has a *moral*. A moral is a lesson that the audience learns by reading the fable. A fable has a *beginning,* a *middle,* and an *ending.*

fable

Writer's Guide: Fable
1. Write a beginning in which you present the characters and the setting.
2. Write a middle that tells the events of the plot in order.
3. Write an ending that tells how the events turn out.
4. Sum up the fable in a moral.
5. Add a title.

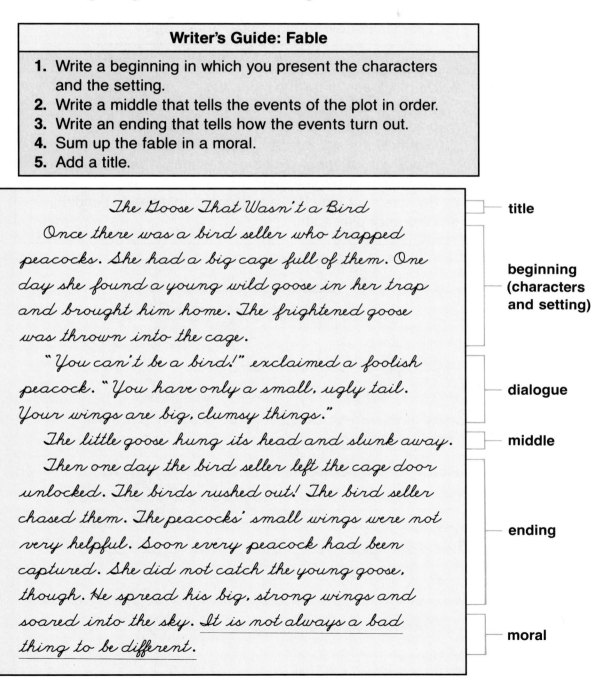

The Goose That Wasn't a Bird — title

Once there was a bird seller who trapped peacocks. She had a big cage full of them. One day she found a young wild goose in her trap and brought him home. The frightened goose was thrown into the cage. — beginning (characters and setting)

"You can't be a bird!" exclaimed a foolish peacock. "You have only a small, ugly tail. Your wings are big, clumsy things." — dialogue

The little goose hung its head and slunk away. — middle

Then one day the bird seller left the cage door unlocked. The birds rushed out! The bird seller chased them. The peacocks' small wings were not very helpful. Soon every peacock had been captured. She did not catch the young goose, though. He spread his big, strong wings and soared into the sky. — ending

It is not always a bad thing to be different. — moral

Play

play ● In a **play** a writer tells a story that is meant to be acted out by performers. A play has characters, one or more settings, and a plot. The conversation between characters in a play is called **dialogue**. The writer includes **stage directions** that tell the characters how to move, act, and speak.

Writer's Guide: Play

1. Use dialogue to tell the story. Let the characters' conversations explain the action. In a play, do not use quotation marks to show what the characters say.
2. Write clear stage directions that tell the characters how to move, act, or speak. Put the directions in parentheses.
3. Underline all stage directions.
4. Be sure your play has a beginning, middle, and ending.
5. Give your play a title.

---

title —

dialogue —

stage directions —

> Saturday Fair
>
> Narrator: It is a lovely Saturday morning in May. Everyone in the village is getting ready for the fair, including the Johnson family.
>
> Mrs. Johnson (calling loudly): James! Morgan! Breakfast is ready!
>
> James (knocking on and opening the door to his brother's room): Aren't you ready yet? We have to leave in a little while.
>
> Morgan (yawning as if just waking up): No, I'm not.
>
> James: Come on, Morgan. Mom, Dad, and Allison are downstairs already. Let's go, slowpoke!

Poem

- In a **poem** a writer paints a picture or expresses a feeling with words. Some poems have several words that begin with the same sound. Many poems have **rhymes.** The words in a poem often have a definite **rhythm,** or beat.

Writer's Guide: Poem
1. Use colorful words to paint a clear picture or to express a feeling.
2. Use rhyme and rhythm to help express feeling.
3. Make comparisons between two things that do not seem alike.
4. Give your poem a title.

The Sun ← title

The sun
Is a piece of gold
That shines high in the sky.
It's a pity
That each night
It must say good-bye.

← words that rhyme

News Story

news story

- In a **news story,** a writer gives information to the audience. A news story answers the questions *who, what, when, where,* and sometimes *why.* The title of a news story is called a **headline.** Headlines often contain a strong verb.

Writer's Guide: News Story
1. Write a short paragraph that introduces the story. Write details that tell *who, what, when, where,* and *why.*   2. Write detail sentences that give more information about the event.   3. Write a short, interesting headline. Use a strong verb.   4. Begin each important word in the headline with a capital letter.

headline

This paragraph tells *who, what, when, where,* and *why.*

These detail sentences give more information about the event.

Senior Citizens Thank Student

Greg Adams was honored by the Verona Senior Citizens Center on March 10 for starting a visiting service. He is a fourth-grade student.

Greg started the service about six months ago. While visiting his grandmother, a resident at the Center, he realized that many people there never have visitors. Greg began spending time talking with the residents. Then he decided to organize a group of students to go to the Center. With the permission of the director, the students visit with the senior citizens. The residents and the students have enjoyed getting to know one another.

Book Report

- In a **book report,** a writer tells about the important events in a book. The writer also gives his or her opinion of the book.

Writer's Guide: Book Report

1. In your first sentence, give the title of the book and the name of the author. Remember to underline the title of the book.
2. Tell about the important events. Tell about the characters and the main idea of the book. Give some interesting details, but do not tell the ending.
3. Give your opinion of the book. Tell why a person might or might not like the book.

Encyclopedia Brown Saves the Day was written by Donald J. Sobol. Encyclopedia Brown is the greatest detective in Idaville, and he is only ten years old. In this book Encyclopedia solves ten cases, including one about some kidnapped pigs. Encyclopedia cleverly proves that an adult did not steal the pigs. The thief was one of the children who came to him for help in the first place. Who stole the pigs? Was it Carl or Lucy?

I liked this book because I got a chance to solve each of the cases too. The solutions are at the end of the book.

title
author
summary
opinion

Research Report

research report

- To write a **research report,** a writer gathers information from several sources, takes notes, and makes an outline. Then he or she uses the notes and the outline to tell about the topic.

Writer's Guide: Research Report
1. Use your notes and outline to write your research report.
2. Write one paragraph for each subtopic in your outline.
3. Follow your outline to write details about your topic.
4. Give your research report a title.

title —

main idea —

detail sentences —

subtopic —

detail sentences —

The Scary and Shy Octopus

Have you ever seen a giant octopus in an old horror movie? Its snaky arms would come out of the sea to crush a tiny boat. No wonder most people think of an octopus as a fierce creature. Nothing could be less true.

An octopus can't help being ugly and looking dangerous. It is made up of a fat, soft body and eight long arms called tentacles. It has two huge, bright eyes that see everything and a hard beak that can easily crack a crab shell. Most octopuses are about as big as your hand, but the biggest on record was 28 feet long.

However, an octopus will not usually attack humans or sea creatures. When frightened, it jets away from its enemies by drawing in water and forcing it out in a stream behind it. It will also squeeze its boneless body into very narrow hiding places. Its only idea is to protect itself.

An octopus changes color easily when it's excited. A relaxed octopus will shimmer like a pale rainbow, and a frightened octopus will turn dark purple when it sees an eel. These color changes are just one more thing that make an octopus the scary, shy, and very interesting creature that it is.

Friendly Letter

- In a **friendly letter,** a person writes to someone he or she knows. The five parts of a friendly letter are the *heading,* the *greeting,* the *body,* the *closing,* and the *signature.*

Writer's Guide: Friendly Letter
1. Write the heading. It contains your address and the date. **2.** Write the greeting. Capitalize the first letter of each word. **3.** Write a message in the body of the letter. Remember to indent the first line of each paragraph in the body. **4.** Use a closing to end your letter. **5.** Sign your name below the closing.

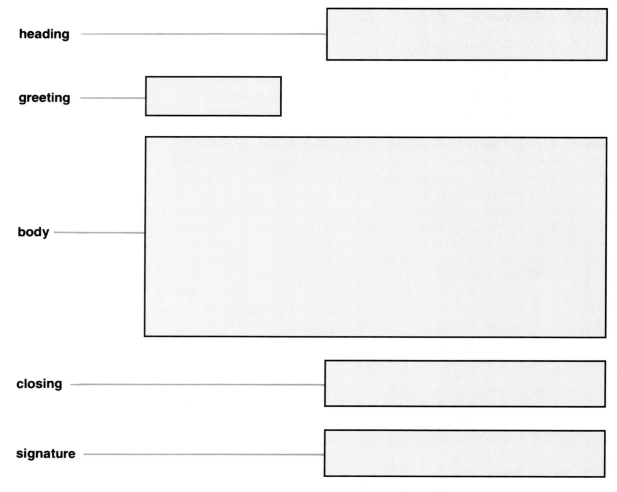

heading

greeting

body

closing

signature

937 Shawnee Court
Augusta, Georgia 30907
July 18, 1990

Dear Rachel,

I have been having a great time in day camp this summer. I have a swimming class at the lake almost every day.

I have to tell you about something funny that happened last week. An important program director named Mr. Goldberg came to visit the camp. The counselors showed him around. One of the counselors took him for a canoe ride. Julia paddled him past our swimming class. I was floating on my back. Just then my little brother Luis yelled because he had felt a fish brush his leg. Then he lost his head and grabbed the canoe. When he tried to climb on board, it tipped over. Julia and Mr. Goldberg were dunked. We were all worried then. Mr. Goldberg's head popped up, and he laughed. What a relief.

There are only three more weeks of day camp left. The summer is going by quickly. I don't have enough time for everything I want to do. I hope that you are enjoying yourself this summer. Let me hear from you soon.

Your friend,
Carminda

Invitation

invitation • In an **invitation** a writer invites someone to come to a party or another event or to do something. An invitation has the same five parts as a friendly letter.

Writer's Guide: Invitation
1. Be sure to include a heading, a greeting, a body, a closing, and a signature.
2. In the body, tell *who* is invited and *what* the invitation is for.
3. Tell *when* and *where* the event or activity will take place and any other information your guest needs to know.

heading

704 East Third Avenue
Roselle, New Jersey 07203
February 5, 1990

greeting

Dear Grandma,

body

I hope you will come and spend next weekend with us. I am going to be performing in my first piano recital in the Fine Arts Center that Friday night at 8 o'clock. I would like you to be there. I will be playing a piece by Mozart. I am really excited about it. Please try to come.

closing

Love,

signature

Judy

WRITER'S HANDBOOK • Composition

Thank-You Note

• In a **thank-you note,** a writer thanks someone for doing something. A thank-you note has the same five parts as a friendly letter.

Writer's Guide: Thank-You Note

1. Be sure to include a heading, a greeting, a body, a closing, and a signature.
2. In the body, tell why you are thanking the person.
3. If you have been a visitor somewhere, tell why you enjoyed yourself.
4. If you received a gift, tell how you are using it.

1563 Circle Drive
Nashville, Tennessee 37211
May 15, 1990 — **heading**

Dear Uncle Charles and Aunt Ann, — **greeting**
 Thank you for taking us to the marine park. We had a terrific time. I liked the killer whales most of all. The trainers have done an amazing job. It must be exciting to work with the whales.
 Mom took my film to be developed. I hope my shots of the whales turn out. I will send you copies if they do. — **body**

 Love, — **closing**
 Andy — **signature**

Envelope

An **envelope** is used to send a letter or a note. The **receiver's address** is the address of the person who will receive the letter. It is written near the center of the envelope. The **return address** is the address of the person who writes the letter. It is written in the upper left corner. A **postal abbreviation** is used for each state name. The **ZIP code** is written after the state abbreviation.

stamp

return address

Bobbi Jacobs
2833 Bay Village Road
West Fork, AR 72774

receiver's address

Ms. Velma Massey
1623 Knox Lane
Warren, OH 44485

Postal Abbreviations

Alabama	AL	Kentucky	KY	North Dakota	ND
Alaska	AK	Louisiana	LA	Ohio	OH
Arizona	AZ	Maine	ME	Oklahoma	OK
Arkansas	AR	Maryland	MD	Oregon	OR
California	CA	Massachusetts	MA	Pennsylvania	PA
Colorado	CO	Michigan	MI	Rhode Island	RI
Connecticut	CT	Minnesota	MN	South Carolina	SC
Delaware	DE	Mississippi	MS	South Dakota	SD
District of Columbia	DC	Missouri	MO	Tennessee	TN
		Montana	MT	Texas	TX
Florida	FL	Nebraska	NE	Utah	UT
Georgia	GA	Nevada	NV	Vermont	VT
Hawaii	HI			Virginia	VA
Idaho	ID	New Hampshire	NH	Washington	WA
Illinois	IL	New Jersey	NJ	West Virginia	WV
Indiana	IN	New Mexico	NM	Wisconsin	WI
Iowa	IA	New York	NY	Wyoming	WY
Kansas	KS	North Carolina	NC		

Vocabulary

base word • A **base word** is a word to which other parts may be added.

> *Fair* is the base word of *unfair*.
>
> *Build* is the base word of *builder*.

prefix • A **prefix** is a group of letters added to the beginning of a word. It changes the meaning of the base word.

Prefix	Meaning	Example	Meaning
un	not	unlucky	not lucky
re	again	rebuild	build again
dis	not	dislike	not like

The unlucky team lost the game.

We will rebuild the shed after the storm.

Do you dislike corn on the cob?

suffix • A **suffix** is a group of letters added to the end of a word. It changes the meaning of the base word.

Suffix	Meaning	Example	Meaning
er	one who	painter	one who paints
or	one who	visitor	one who visits
ful	full of	beautiful	full of beauty
less	without	fearless	without fear
able	able to be	wearable	able to be worn

The painter stood on a ladder.
The class was polite to the visitor.
We enjoyed the beautiful sunset.
The lion seemed fearless.
Rick's torn coat was not wearable.

- A **synonym** is a word that has almost the same meaning as another word. Often a word has more than one synonym.

  Odor is a synonym of *smell*.

  Fast, rapid, and *quick* are synonyms.

synonym

- An **antonym** is a word that has the opposite meaning from another word. Sometimes a word has more than one antonym.

  Up is an antonym of *down*.

  Soft and *quiet* are antonyms of *loud*.

antonym

- **Homographs** are words that are spelled the same, but have different meanings.

  The dogs bark loudly.

  The canoe is made of birch bark .

homographs

- **Homophones** are words that sound alike but are spelled differently and have different meanings.

  Have you read the story?

  Carmen is wearing a red dress.

homophones

- A **compound word** is made up of two smaller words. When combined they are usually written as one word.

  cowboy   something   rattlesnake

compound word

WRITER'S HANDBOOK • *Vocabulary*

Study Steps to Learn a Word

1 **Say** the word. Recall when you have heard the word used. Think about what it means.

2 **Look** at the word. Find any prefixes, suffixes, or other word parts you know. Think about other words that are related in meaning and spelling. Try to picture the word in your mind.

3 **Spell** the word to yourself. Think about the way each sound is spelled. Notice any unusual spelling.

4 **Write** the word while looking at it. Check the way you have formed your letters. If you have not written the word clearly or correctly, write it again.

5 **Check** your learning. Cover the word and write it. If you did not spell the word correctly, practice these steps until the word becomes your own.

Guidelines for Creating a Spelling Word List

You may want to keep your own spelling word list in a notebook. You can organize your spelling word list alphabetically, by subject areas, by parts of speech, or in other categories. Follow these guidelines.

1. Check your writing for words you have misspelled. Circle each misspelled word.

marched in the (perade)

2. Find out how to spell the word correctly.
- Look up the word in a dictionary or a thesaurus.
- Ask a teacher or a classmate.

marched in the (perade) — *parade*

3. Write the word in your notebook.
- Spell the word correctly.
- Write a definition, a synonym, or an antonym to help you understand the meaning of the word.
- Use the word in a sentence.

parade—a group of people marching together
The school band marched in the parade.

4. When you write, look at your spelling word list to check your spelling.

Frequently Misspelled Words

against	couple	knew	sign
already	course	knocked	slept
another	describe	laid	sometimes
anymore	different	laughing	stopped
anything	does	maybe	straight
anyway	dollars	minute	struck
attention	dropped	months	surprise
awhile	either	myself	telephone
backyard	everybody	onto	their
beautiful	everywhere	orange	through
believe	except	outside	throw
bicycle	excited	pair	throwing
biggest	favorite	passed	tired
birthday	field	piece	tomorrow
board	finally	poison	toward
bottom	finish	practicing	trouble
break	guess	probably	until
brought	happened	problem	unusual
caught	happening	putting	wants
cheek	happily	quiet	wear
circle	hear	really	where
climb	heard	remember	which
climbed	herself	remembered	woman
climbing	himself	scared	worried
clothes	instead	scream	
	kitchen	screamed	

Vowel Sounds

- The **short vowel sounds** are usually spelled with one letter. short vowel sounds

  /a/ is spelled **a,** as in *bad*
  /e/ is spelled **e,** as in *met,* or **ea,** as in *instead*
  /i/ is spelled **i,** as in *fit*
  /o/ is spelled **o,** as in *stop*
  /u/ is spelled **u,** as in *but,* or **o,** as in *son*

- **Long vowel sounds** are usually spelled with more than one letter. long vowel sounds

- Here are five ways to spell the /ā/ sound. /ā/

  a-consonant-e, as in *bake*
  ai, as in *mail*
  ay, as in *say*
  ey, as in *grey*
  eigh, as in *eight*

- Here are seven ways to spell the /ē/ sound. /ē/

  e-consonant-e, as in *stampede*
  e, as in *me*
  ee, as in *free*
  ea, as in *each*
  ei, as in *receive*
  ie, as in *field*
  y, as in *story*

- Here are five ways to spell the /ī/ sound. /ī/

  i-consonant-e, as in *five*
  i, as in *lion*
  ie, as in *pie*
  igh, as in *right*
  y, as in *sky*

- Here are five ways to spell the /ō/ sound. /ō/

  o-consonant-e, as in *bone*
  o, as in *no*
  oe, as in *toe*
  oa, as in *toast*
  ow, as in *flow*

/o͞o/ • Here are six ways to spell the /o͞o/ sound.

oo, as in *food*
ou, as in *group*
u, as in *flu*
u-consonant-e, as in *rude*
ue, as in *true*
ew, as in *blew*

Letter Combinations

ie, ei • The /ē/ sound is often spelled *ie,* but if the /ē/ sound follows the letter *c,* it is spelled *ei.* If the letters make the /ā/ sound, they are written *ei.*

niece   receive   weigh

final /ər/ • There are three ways to spell the final /ər/ sound.

ar, as in *dollar*
er, as in *mother*
or, as in *sailor*

final /əl/ • There are four ways to spell the final /əl/ sound.

al, as in *local*
el, as in *bushel*
le, as in *title*
il, as in *pencil*

Syllable Division

compound words • Follow these rules for dividing words into syllables. Divide compound words into syllables between the two words.

handbag—hand·bag   haircut—hair·cut

• When a word has two consonant letters between two vowels, divide the word between the two consonants.

mistake—mis·take   hello—hel·lo

- When a two-syllable word has a long vowel sound in the first syllable, divide the word before the middle consonant.

  baby—ba·by   meter—me·ter

- When a two-syllable word has a short vowel sound in the first syllable, divide the word after the middle consonant.

  edit—ed·it   robin—rob·in

Verbs

- The past tense of many verbs is formed by adding *ed*.

  past tense

  walk—walked   fill—filled

- If the verb ends in *e*, drop the final *e* and add *ed* to form the past tense.

  love—loved   dine—dined

- If the verb ends in a consonant, a short vowel, and a consonant, double the final consonant before adding *ed*.

  dip—dipped   knot—knotted

- If the verb ends in a consonant plus *y*, change the *y* to *i* before adding *ed*.

  cry—cried   marry—married

Nouns

- To form the plural of most nouns, add *s* to the singular noun.

  plurals

  cat—cats   lake—lakes

- If a noun ends in *s*, *ss*, *x*, *ch*, or *sh*, add *es* to form the plural.

  pass—passes   fox—foxes
  lunch—lunches   dish—dishes

- If a noun ends in a vowel plus *y*, add *s* to form the plural.

  day—days   boy—boys

- If a noun ends in a consonant plus *y*, change the *y* to *i* and add *es* to form the plural.

fly—flies   lady—ladies

- If a noun ends in *f*, change the *f* to *v* and add *es*. If a noun ends in *fe*, change the *f* to *v*, drop the final *e*, and add *es*.

wolf—wolves   life—lives

- The plurals of some nouns are formed by changing the spelling of the singular noun.

woman—women   child—children

- Some nouns have the same singular and plural forms.

sheep—sheep   moose—moose

Contractions

- A **contraction** is a shortened form of two words. An apostrophe (') takes the place of the missing letters in each contraction.

pronoun contractions

- Pronouns can be joined with some helping verbs and linking verbs to form contractions.

you + are = you're   she + has = she's
we + would = we'd   they + will = they'll

verb contractions

- Some helping verbs and linking verbs can be joined with the word *not* to form contractions. The word *not* is shortened to *n't*.

is + not = isn't   have + not = haven't
should + not = shouldn't   could + not = couldn't

The verb *will* forms a contraction in a special way.

will + not = won't

Possessive Nouns

- To form the possessive of a singular noun, add an apostrophe and *s*.

    the tree's shadow   Max's book

- To form the possessive of a plural noun ending in *s* or *es*, add only an apostrophe.

    the players' uniforms   the axes' handles

- To form the possessive of a plural noun that does not end in *s*, add an apostrophe and *s*.

    the men's names   the deer's faces

singular noun

plural noun

Abbreviations

- An **abbreviation** is a short way to write a word. Nearly every abbreviation ends with a period. The abbreviation of a proper noun begins with a capital letter.

    Mister— Mr.   August— Aug.   Tuesday— Tues.

- Words such as *Street, Avenue, Boulevard, North, South, East,* and *West* are often abbreviated.

    62 E. Lake Rd.   5861 Tate Ave.

- Postal abbreviations of state names are written with two capital letters. They do not end with a period.

    Kansas— KS   Texas— TX

proper noun

Adjectives That Compare

er • To compare two things, add *er* to most one-syllable adjectives.

loud—louder   soft—softer

est • To compare more than two things, add *est* to most one-syllable adjectives.

bright—brightest   soon—soonest

final e • If the adjective ends in *e*, drop the *e* before adding *er* or *est*.

large—larger—largest   blue—bluer—bluest

short vowel + consonant • If a one-syllable adjective ends in a short vowel sound plus a consonant, double the last letter before adding *er* or *est*.

fat—fatter—fattest   big—bigger—biggest

consonant + y • If the adjective ends in a consonant plus *y*, change the *y* to *i* before adding *er* or *est*.

happy—happier—happiest   funny—funnier—funniest

Adverbs That Compare

er, est • To some one-syllable adverbs, add *er* to compare two actions and *est* to compare more than two actions.

Bill works hard .
Alyssa works harder than Bill.
Kathy works the hardest of them all.

WRITER'S HANDBOOK • Spelling

GLOSSARY

Contents

Composition Terms

AUDIENCE *the reader or readers for whom a composition is written* This opening sentence from a review of a school play shows that the audience is the students of Plessecy School.

> *No student of Plessecy School should miss the fourth-grade class play. No Time for Puppies.*

DRAFTING *the actual writing of a composition, beginning with a first version that will be revised later* This boy is using a diagram to write his first draft.

EDITOR'S MARKS *marks used to revise or proofread written work* Use these marks when you revise.

∧	Add something.	↻	Move something.
✗	Cut something.	�	Replace something.

Use these marks when you proofread.

≡	Capitalize.	ᕦᕤ	Add quotation marks.	∼	Transpose.
⊙	Add a period.			◯	Spell correctly.
∧	Add something.	✗	Cut something.	⊓	Indent paragraph.
⋏	Add a comma.	⌃	Replace something.	/	Make a lowercase letter.

FINAL DRAFT *the final copy of a composition, ready to be published* This example shows the final draft of the revising example on page 7 of this Glossary.

> My family took a trip to California. We went down into a big cave. Some rocks in the cave looked like frozen waterfalls.

FIRST DRAFT   *the first version of a composition, in which the writer tries to get his or her thoughts on paper*   Notice that this first draft is somewhat choppy.

> *I have a friend. My friend's name is Jim. My friend lives next door. His house is red.*

PREWRITING   *the part of the writing process in which the writer thinks of ideas and tries to organize them*   This prewriting chart is used to organize ideas about animals.

Animals You Can See		
Marsh	Forest	Beach
wading birds	owls	gulls
crayfish	squirrels	crabs
raccoons	deer	starfish

PREWRITING STRATEGIES   *ways to help writers think of and organize ideas for compositions*   These are some examples of prewriting strategies.

- **brainstorming**   *an activity in which an individual or a group tries to give all possible ideas about a topic*

How can you go somewhere?   walk   ride in a car   ride a bike

GLOSSARY

- **charting** *a way of writing and organizing facts or ideas in groups*

Hobby	Supplies	Type
stamp collecting	album, hinges	quiet
swimming	bathing suit	active

- **diagramming** *a way of showing how ideas are related*

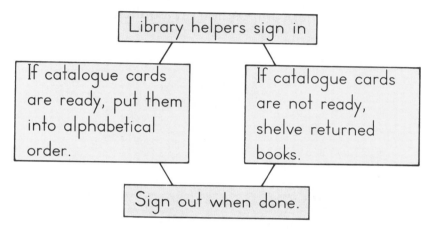

- **list making** *a way of writing ideas brainstormed by one or many people*

Things to Take on a Trip

suitcase	money	clothes
maps	tickets	first-aid kit

- **mapping** *a way of organizing ideas on paper or on the chalkboard*

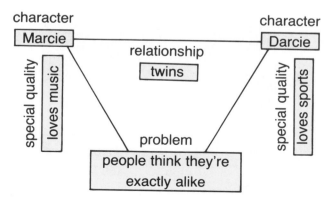

PROOFREADING *checking a composition to correct mistakes in capitalization, punctuation, usage, grammar, and spelling* Notice the punctuation change in this example.

> My brother came home. And we played ball.

PUBLISHING *sharing a final draft of a composition with others* This girl is putting her composition on a bulletin board.

PURPOSE *the reason for writing a composition* The purpose of writing directions, for example, is to tell people how to do something.

RESPONDING *answering questions asked by yourself or by another person about a composition* This girl is responding to her own question.

What words besides *fly* could I use to say what a bird does?

Maybe I could write *soar* or *swoop* or *dart* . . .

RESPONSE GROUP *a group of students who help revise each other's work by asking and answering questions about it* These students are responding to a question about the plot of a story.

| Does my character sound like a real person? | I think you should have him fight harder to solve his problem! | Maybe you can have him fail once or twice first. |

REVISING *the process of rethinking ideas, looking for ways to improve organization and language* Notice these changes in a revised draft.

> We went down into a big cave. ~~This was when~~ my family took a trip to California. Some rocks in the cave looked like frozen waterfalls.

TASK *a writing assignment* It was Gloria's task to write a how-to paragraph.

> To make cookies you will need flour, milk, two large eggs, chocolate chips, and brown sugar. First, beat the eggs.

WRITING PROCESS *a process with stages of prewriting, drafting, responding and revising, proofreading, and publishing*

Literary Terms

CHARACTERS *the people or animals in a story, poem, or play* Sometimes authors are concerned mainly with bringing their story characters to life. The story's main action, or **plot,** is not as important as how the characters think, feel, and act. For example, in *The Secret Garden*, author Frances Hodgson Burnett tells us about the thoughts and feelings of her main character, Mary. We learn how Mary's feelings are changed by the things that happen to her and by the people she meets in her new home in England. The story is *about Mary*, not just about the events in her life. Other stories, such as "The Hen and the Apple Tree" by Arnold Lobel, are concerned mainly with action.

FICTION *a story invented by the writer* A work of fiction may be based on true events, but it always includes made-up characters and experiences. A work of fiction may be short, like "The Hen and the Apple Tree," or long. There are many kinds of fiction.

Historical fiction is based on true events but includes made-up characters and happenings. **Fantasy** may be set in a real or a make-believe world, but its characters do impossible things and travel to impossible places. In **science fiction,** the action is usually set in a future world, which characters often reach through time or space travel.

Fiction is written in many forms. A **novel** is a book-length story. A **fable** is a story that teaches a lesson. A **short story** is a tale told in just a few pages.

FIGURATIVE LANGUAGE *words used in unusual rather than usual ways* Figurative language is often used to compare things that at first seem very different. One kind of figurative language is a **simile,** which says that something is *like* something else. For example, in "Memories," Kimberly Freeman says that the foam on ocean waves looked like party hats. Another kind of figurative language, called a **metaphor,** compares two things by saying that one thing *is* another. For example, someone might write, "The fog was a soft gray blanket."

NONFICTION *a true story; any writing that describes things as they actually happened, or that presents information or opinions about something* "Show-offs of the Sea" by Gerry Bishop, for example, is a science article that tells us facts about sea slugs. *Benjamin Franklin, Amazing American* is the written history of a person's life, or **biography.** Other common forms of nonfiction include editorials, news stories, personal diaries and journals, and travel stories.

GLOSSARY

PLOT *the action in a story*   When you tell what happens in a story, you are talking about the plot. The plot is the writer's plan of the action. It tells *how, when,* and *why* things happen. For instance, in "The Hen and the Apple Tree," the plot involves a hen who recognizes and fools a wolf.

The most important part of a plot is **conflict,** a character's struggle with opposing forces. The character may struggle with nature, with another character, or with ideas in his or her own mind. In the novel *Tuck Everlasting* by Natalie Babbitt, for example, Winnie must struggle with her own wishes and feelings as she decides whether or not to share the Tuck family's special life.

PUN *a joke that depends on two words that sound alike but have different meanings, or on two different meanings of the same word*   This riddle, for example, has a pun in it.

Q. Why did the window go to the doctor?
A. Because it had a pane.

The pun depends on the meanings of *pane,* which is part of a window, and *pain,* which is something that might make a person go to the doctor.

RHYME *two lines of poetry that end in words that have the same ending sounds*   *Beard* and *weird* are the rhyming words in these lines from the poem "Dirty Dinky."

O what's the weather in a Beard?
It's windy there, and rather weird.

RHYTHM *the repeating pattern of loud and soft syllables in a poem*   The syllables can be marked with ´ over each loud or stressed syllable and ˘ over each soft or unstressed syllable, as in this example from Robert Frost's poem "A Minor Bird."

Ĭ hăve wished ă bírd wŏuld flý ăwáy
Ănd nŏt síng bў mў hóuse aĬl dáy.

SETTING *when and where a story takes place*   A sentence such as *It was a dark and stormy night* gives information about the setting of a story. Writers can choose any time or place as a setting. Sometimes they describe it directly. For example, these sentences from Lee Pennock Huntington's *The Arctic and the Antarctic* could have been used to describe the setting of a story that takes place during winter in the Arctic.

During the Arctic winter, from November to February, the sun does not appear at all. The tundra is a vast expanse of snow.

In other stories, we must guess the setting from hints given in the story.

STANZA *lines of a poem that are separated from other lines by extra space* Some poems have stanzas that are all the same length, while others have stanzas of different lengths. "I'm Nobody!" by Emily Dickinson has two stanzas.

I'm Nobody! Who are you?
Are you — Nobody — Too?
Then there's a pair of us!
Don't tell! They'd banish us — you know!

How dreary — to be — Somebody!
How public — like a Frog —
To tell your name — the livelong June —
To an admiring Bog!

WORD PICTURE *a way of using language that helps readers see exactly what something in a story or poem looks like* Word pictures also tell what things sound like, smell like, and so on. They may include figurative language. Kimberly Freeman gives this word picture of a stormy ocean in "Memories."

Soon the green water turned into a choppy, dark-blue. The waves were bigger and foam that looked like party hats was on top of them. I loved watching the purple waves towering above everything and then riding in and breaking at the shore.

GLOSSARY

WRITER'S THESAURUS

Contents

What Is a Thesaurus?

A **thesaurus** lists words and their synonyms. Like a dictionary, a thesaurus lists words in alphabetical order. Each of these words is called an **entry word**. A list of synonyms follows the entry word. Sometimes a thesaurus lists antonyms.

Look at the parts of this thesaurus entry for the word brave.

The **entry word** is in color. It is followed by the part of speech and a definition. An **example sentence** shows how the word can be used.

▶

> **brave** *adj.* Not afraid. You were **brave** to run so quickly for help.

Synonyms for the entry word are in italics. Each synonym is followed by a definition and an example sentence.

▶

> *adventurous* Liking or seeking adventure. My *adventurous* family is always traveling to new places.
>
> *bold* Having or showing courage. Christopher Columbus was a *bold* explorer sailing into the unknown.
>
> *courageous* Having or showing bravery. The *courageous* firefighter entered the burning house.
>
> *daring* Bold and adventurous. Training lions is a *daring* job.
>
> *fearless* Without fear. Chen is *fearless* when he flies on the trapeze.

If an **antonym** is given, it is printed in dark letters.

▶

> **ANTONYMS:** afraid, fearful, frightened, scared

How to Use Your Writer's Thesaurus

Suppose you are writing a story about astronauts traveling to Mars. When you read your first draft, you realize that you have overused the word brave. You open your **Writer's Thesaurus** to find some synonyms. Here are the steps you should follow.

1. Look for the word in the Index to the Thesaurus. The Index lists every word in the **Writer's Thesaurus.**

2. Find the word in the Index. Here is an example.

    brave *adj.*

    Because brave is printed in color, you know it is an entry word.

3. Turn to the page in your **Writer's Thesaurus** on which brave is printed in color. Read the entry carefully. Not every synonym may express exactly what you want to say. Choose the synonym that makes the most sense in your story.

Remember: Not every synonym will have the exact meaning you want. Look at the entry for brave on page 8. You must decide which synonyms fit your work best.

◆ Sometimes a word is listed in the Index like this:

    courageous brave *adj.*

This means you will find *courageous* listed as a synonym under the entry word **brave.** Since *courageous* is not printed in color, you know it is not an entry word.

◆ You will also see some lines in the Index that look like this:

    afraid brave *adj.*

This means that **afraid** is listed as an antonym under the entry word brave.

WRITER'S THESAURUS

A

accompanied lonely *adj.*
acquire **buy** *v.*
actually **really** *adv.*
additional more *adj.*
adventurous brave *adj.*
afraid brave *adj.*
after *adv.*
after before *adv.*
aged **old** *adj.*
ages *n.*
aid hurt *v.*
alike different *adj.*
alike **same** *adj.*
alone **lonely** *adj.*
a lot of **most** *adj.*
always **often** *adv.*
always seldom *adv.*
a majority of **most** *adj.*
amuse entertain *v.*
amusing funny *adj.*
angry *adj.*
appear fade *v.*
approach **come** *v.*
arid **dry** *adj.*
arrive **come** *v.*
ascend **rise** *v.*
ashamed proud *adj.*
assist hurt *v.*
attractive **pretty** *adj.*
awful good *adj.*

B

bad good *adj.*
beautiful **pretty** *adj.*
beautiful ugly *adj.*
before *adv.*
before after *adv.*
begin *v.*
begin end *v.*
behind **after** *adv.*
big **huge** *adj.*
bland tangy *adj.*

blushing **red** *adj.*
bold **brave** *adj.*
bore entertain *v.*
boring exciting *adj.*
brave *adj.*
brief **short** *adj.*
bright *adj.*
burning **hot** *adj.*
buy *v.*

C

calm **peaceful** *adj.*
careless **foolish** *adj.*
cheer *n.*
cheerful **happy** *adj.*
chilly hot *adj.*
clean *adj.*
clever **wise** *adj.*
climb **rise** *v.*
close **end** *v.*
cold hot *adj.*
collect **combine** *v.*
combine *v.*
come *v.*
come go *v.*
complete **end** *v.*
confusing easy *adj.*
continue **remain** *v.*
cool hot *adj.*
courageous **brave** *adj.*
crawl fly *v.*

D

damage hurt *v.*
damp dry *adj.*
daring brave *adj.*
dark bright *adj.*
dark **sad** *adj.*
deafening **loud** *adj.*
delicious **good** *adj.*
delight **cheer** *n.*
delightful **happy** *adj.*
depart **go** *v.*
depart remain *v.*

descend **rise** *v.*
different *adj.*
different same *adj.*
difficult easy *adj.*
difficult **hard** *adj.*
dim bright *adj.*
dirty clean *adj.*
disappear **fade** *v.*
disappointed proud *adj.*
dislike like *v.*
disorganized clean *adj.*
distant **long** *adj.*
divert **entertain** *v.*
divide combine *v.*
dodge **move** *v.*
doubtfully really *adv.*
drag fly *v.*
drop rise *v.*
dry *adj.*
dull bright *adj.*

E

earlier **before** *adv.*
easy *adj.*
easy hard *adj.*
eat **taste** *v.*
elementary **easy** *adj.*
end *v.*
end begin *v.*
enjoy **like** *v.*
enormous **huge** *adj.*
entertain *v.*
entertaining **funny** *adj.*
equal **same** *adj.*
escape **slip** *v.*
excellent **good** *adj.*
exciting *adj.*
extend **go** *v.*

F

fade *v.*
fall rise *v.*

fall slip *v.*
far long *adj.*
fast slow *adj.*
fat thin *adj.*
fearful brave *adj.*
fearless brave *adj.*
finish begin *v.*
finish end *v.*
float fly *v.*
flow move *v.*
flushed red *adj.*
fly v.
following before *adv.*
foolish adj.
foolish wise *adj.*
forever ages *n.*
former old *adj.*
fragrance smell *n.*
frequently often *adv.*
frightened brave *adj.*
funny adj.
furious angry *adj.*
further more *adj.*

G

gallop run *v.*
gather combine *v.*
giant huge *adj.*
gigantic huge *adj.*
give take *v.*
glad angry *adj.*
glad happy *adj.*
glad sad *adj.*
glide fly *v.*
glisten v.
glitter glisten *v.*
gloomy bright *adj.*
gloomy sad *adj.*
glowing bright *adj.*
go v.
go come *v.*
good adj.
gorgeous pretty *adj.*
grab take *v.*
grasp take *v.*
gray bright *adj.*
gray sad *adj.*

great good *adj.*
greater more *adj.*
greatly really *adv.*

H

handsome pretty *adj.*
happiness cheer *n.*
happy adj.
happy sad *adj.*
hard adj.
harm hurt *v.*
hate like *v.*
help hurt *v.*
high adj.
hike walk *v.*
homesick lonely *adj.*
host entertain *v.*
hot adj.
hover fly *v.*
huge adj.
humble proud *adj.*
humorous funny *adj.*
hurt v.
husky mighty *adj.*

I

identical same *adj.*
ignore see *v.*
immense huge *adj.*
important adj.
inactive slow *adj.*
indeed really *adv.*
injure hurt *v.*
instant ages *n.*
intelligent foolish *adj.*
intelligent wise *adj.*
interesting exciting *adj.*

J

join combine *v.*
joy cheer *n.*
joyful sad *adj.*

L

large huge *adj.*
last remain *v.*
later after *adv.*
least most *adj.*
least seldom *adv.*
leave go *v.*
leave remain *v.*
less more *adj.*
less seldom *adv.*
like v.
little huge *adj.*
lively exciting *adj.*
lofty high *adj.*
lonely adj.
lonesome lonely *adj.*
long adj.
long short *adj.*
long ago ages *n.*
loud adj.
loud peaceful *adj.*
love like *v.*
lovely pretty *adj.*
low high *adj.*
low short *adj.*

M

many most *adj.*
march walk *v.*
meaningful important *adj.*
merry happy *adj.*
messy clean *adj.*
mighty adj.
mild tangy *adj.*
miniature huge *adj.*
miserable sad *adj.*
moist dry *adj.*
moment ages *n.*
more adj.
most adj.
move v.
much most *adj.*

N

never often *adv.*
never seldom *adv.*
new old *adj.*
nice good *adj.*
noisy loud *adj.*
noisy peaceful *adj.*
notice see *v.*

O

obtain take *v.*
odor smell *n.*
offensive ugly *adj.*
often adv.
often seldom *adv.*
okay good *adj.*
old adj.
open begin *v.*
orderly clean *adj.*

P

pay buy *v.*
peaceful adj.
plain pretty *adj.*
pleasant ugly *adj.*
pleased angry *adj.*
pleased proud *adj.*
pleasure cheer *n.*
powerful mighty *adj.*
powerless mighty *adj.*
prefer like *v.*
pretty adj.
previously before *adv.*
proud adj.
purchase buy *v.*

Q

quick slow *adj.*
quiet loud *adj.*
quiet peaceful *adj.*

R

race run *v.*
rarely seldom *adv.*
reach come *v.*
really adv.
red adj.
remain v.
remain go *v.*
repeatedly often *adv.*
restful peaceful *adj.*
rise v.
ruby red *adj.*
ruddy red *adj.*
run v.
run walk *v.*
rush run *v.*

S

sad adj.
sad happy *adj.*
sadness cheer *n.*
sail fly *v.*
same adj.
same different *adj.*
sample taste *v.*
savor taste *v.*
scalding hot *adj.*
scared brave *adj.*
scarlet red *adj.*
scent smell *n.*
see v.
seldom adv.
seldom often *adv.*
sell buy *v.*
senseless foolish *adj.*
sensible foolish *adj.*
separate combine *v.*
serious funny *adj.*
sharp tangy *adj.*
shine fade *v.*
shine glisten *v.*
shiny bright *adj.*
short adj.
short long *adj.*
significant important *adj.*

silent loud *adj.*
silly foolish *adj.*
simple easy *adj.*
simple hard *adj.*
slender thin *adj.*
slide slip *v.*
slight thin *adj.*
slip v.
slow adj.
slow exciting *adj.*
sluggish slow *adj.*
small huge *adj.*
small short *adj.*
smart wise *adj.*
smell n.
soar fly *v.*
sorrow cheer *n.*
sparkle glisten *v.*
sparkling bright *adj.*
sparse thin *adj.*
special different *adj.*
spicy tangy *adj.*
spirited exciting *adj.*
stampede run *v.*
stand rise *v.*
start begin *v.*
start end *v.*
stay move *v.*
stay remain *v.*
step walk *v.*
still loud *adj.*
stir combine *v.*
stop go *v.*
stop move *v.*
stroll walk *v.*
strong mighty *adj.*
sunny bright *adj.*

T

take v.
tall high *adj.*
tangy adj.
taste v.
terrible good *adj.*
thick thin *adj.*
thin adj.
thirsty dry *adj.*

thrilling exciting *adj.*
thunderous loud *adj.*
tidy clean *adj.*
tiny huge *adj.*
tiresome exciting *adj.*
tough hard *adj.*
towering high *adj.*
travel move *v.*
truly really *adv.*

U

ugly adj.
ugly pretty *adj.*
unchanged same *adj.*
understand see *v.*
unhappy happy *adj.*

unhappy sad *adj.*
unimportant
    important *adj.*
unite combine *v.*
unsightly ugly *adj.*
unusual different *adj.*
unwise wise *adj.*
upset angry *adj.*

V

vain proud *adj.*

W

waken rise *v.*

walk v.
walk run *v.*
warm hot *adj.*
watch see *v.*
weak mighty *adj.*
wet dry *adj.*
wise adj.
wise foolish *adj.*
wither fade *v.*
witty funny *adj.*
worn old *adj.*

Y

years ages *n.*
young old *adj.*

A

after *adv.* Coming next. We arrived first and John came **after**.

behind In back. The tired hikers lagged *behind*.

later Following in time. The play will begin *later* than usual.

ANTONYM: before

ages *n.* A long time. Dinosaurs lived **ages** ago.

forever For all time. It seems to be taking *forever* for the package to arrive.

long ago At a far-distant time. George Washington lived *long ago*.

years Multiples of twelve months. Grandpa has not seen his sister for *years*.

ANTONYMS: instant, moment

angry *adj.* Feeling or showing anger. Carl was **angry** about losing his book.

furious Full of wild anger. I was *furious* about the broken vase.

upset Disturbed. Jackie was *upset* about her test score.

ANTONYMS: glad, pleased

B

before *adv.* In the past. I have seen this movie **before**.

earlier At or nearer to the beginning. The hero is described *earlier* in the book than the villain.

previously Happening before. She had collected the money from the students *previously*.

ANTONYMS: after, following

begin *v.* To start. Laura will **begin** reading the story.

open To make ready to use. You can *open* a savings account at the bank.

start To set out to do. We *start* basketball practice tomorrow.

ANTONYMS: end, finish

brave *adj.* Not afraid. You were **brave** to run so quickly for help.

adventurous Liking or seeking adventure. My *adventurous* family is always traveling to new places.

bold Having or showing courage. Christopher Columbus was a *bold* explorer sailing into the unknown.

courageous Having or showing bravery. The *courageous* firefighter entered the burning house.

daring Bold and adventurous. Training lions is a *daring* job.

fearless Without fear. Chen is *fearless* when he flies on the trapeze.

ANTONYMS: afraid, fearful, frightened, scared

bright *adj.* Giving off a lot of light. The room is too **bright** without shades.

glowing Showing a warm color. The July sun was *glowing*.

shiny Able to reflect light. The *shiny* gold ring fit Maria perfectly.

sparkling Giving off sparks or flashes of light. The lake's *sparkling* waters were lovely.

sunny Filled with sunlight. The Fourth of July is usually a *sunny* day.

ANTONYMS: dark, dim, dull, gloomy, gray

buy *v.* To obtain by paying money. Students can **buy** books on Mondays.

acquire To get or obtain. Where do doctors *acquire* medicine?

pay To give money for goods or services. Customers *pay* for their groceries at the checkout counter.

purchase To get in exchange for money. Bakers *purchase* blueberries for muffins.

ANTONYM: sell

cheer *n.* Gladness; happiness. The gift brought **cheer** to the sick child.

delight Great pleasure. The baby laughed with *delight* at the rattle.

happiness A feeling of gladness. Everyone shared Grandpa's *happiness* at his surprise party.

joy A strong feeling of gladness. With great *joy* the team accepted its award.

pleasure A feeling of enjoyment. A beautiful garden gives me great *pleasure*.

ANTONYMS: sadness, sorrow

clean *adj.* Free from dirt. I swept the kitchen floor **clean**.

orderly Precisely arranged. The rows of desks in our classroom are *orderly*.

tidy Orderly. The *tidy* little house was freshly painted.

ANTONYMS: dirty, disorganized, messy

combine *v.* To put together. **Combine** flour and water for an inexpensive paste.

collect To gather. Peter will *collect* your homework papers.

gather To come to the same place. After the show, everyone will *gather* in the lobby.

join To connect. Please *join* hands in a circle.

stir To move with a circular motion; to mix. I *stir* pancake batter before breakfast.

unite To bring or come together to make one. The two clubs *unite* for a fund-raiser every year.

ANTONYMS: divide, separate

come *v.* To arrive. We **come** to this beach every July.

approach To move toward. They will not *approach* a frightened animal.

arrive To reach a place. The flight will *arrive* on time.

reach To extend. The snow may *reach* the front doorknob.

ANTONYM: go

different *adj.* Not alike. Chinese food is quite **different** from Mexican food.

special Out of the ordinary. This holiday dinner is a *special* treat.

unusual Not like most others. The log cabin was the most *unusual* house on the street.

ANTONYMS: alike, same

dry *adj.* Not wet. Angela watered the **dry** plants.

arid Not having enough water. The desert is an *arid* place.

thirsty Wanting a drink. Eating salty food makes you *thirsty*.

ANTONYMS: damp, moist, wet

easy *adj.* Not difficult. I got an A on the **easy** test.

elementary Simple. Some books in our public library are *elementary*.

simple Easy to understand or do. These directions look *simple*.

ANTONYMS: confusing, difficult

end *v.* To come to a conclusion. What time will the movie **end**?

close To bring to a finish. The play will *close* Friday.

complete To conclude. The students always *complete* their stories before lunch.

finish To consume completely. I *finish* breakfast before going to school.

ANTONYMS: begin, start

entertain *v.* To keep interested and give enjoyment to. Singers will **entertain** the audience.

amuse To hold the attention of others in a pleasant, funny way. Singing silly songs will *amuse* children.

divert To distract. The game will *divert* the guests until dinner is ready.

host To have guests. The Coles will *host* a dinner party in their home tonight.

ANTONYM: bore

exciting *adj.* Causing lively feelings. Grandmother told **exciting** stories about her travels.

interesting Holding attention. The movie had an *interesting* ending.

lively Full of life or energy. The *lively* puppy jumped into my lap.

spirited Full of spirit. The *spirited* campers clapped and sang songs.

thrilling Tingling with strong feeling. Riding in a hot-air balloon must be *thrilling*.

ANTONYMS: boring, slow, tiresome

F

fade *v.* To lose or take away color or brightness. Sunlight may **fade** your rug.

disappear To vanish. The setting sun will *disappear* suddenly beyond the horizon.

wither To become less fresh or strong. Rose petals *wither* after a frost.

ANTONYMS: appear, shine

fly *v.* To move through the air. Many birds **fly** south for the winter.

float To rest on water or in the air. Festival balloons *float* across the sky.

glide To move slowly and without effort. The toy plane can *glide* through the air.

hover To remain in or near one place in the air. The butterflies *hover* over the daisies.

sail To move on water or in the air. Little boats *sail* on the lake.

soar To fly or rise high into the air. Jets *soar* above the clouds.

foolish *adj.* Showing a lack of good sense. Walking barefoot in the street is **foolish**.

careless Reckless; done without care or effort. Leaving a new bicycle out in the rain is *careless*.

senseless Foolish; without purpose. Eating too much is *senseless*.

silly Unwise or funny. His *silly* remarks caused laughter.

ANTONYMS: intelligent, sensible, wise

funny *adj.* Able to cause laughter. The **funny** clowns danced with a seal.

amusing Giving enjoyment. Dad tells *amusing* stories about his childhood.

entertaining Holding attention in a pleasant way. The clowns at the circus are *entertaining* jugglers.

humorous Amusing. The comics in our newspaper are *humorous.*

witty Clever. A *witty* comic makes us laugh and think.

ANTONYM: serious

G

glisten *v.* To sparkle or shine. Icicles **glisten** in the sunlight.

glitter To reflect light. Victoria's new earrings *glitter* like stars.

shine To give off or reflect light. The sun does not *shine* through clouds.

sparkle To give off sparks of light. The metal canoes *sparkle* on the lake.

go *v.* To pass along. Drivers **go** slowly during rush hour.

depart To go away. They will *depart* for vacation in June.

extend To reach. The new highway will *extend* from Boston to Concord.

leave To move from a place. We *leave* the house for school at 8:00 A.M.

ANTONYMS: come, remain, stop

good *adj.* Having positive qualities. There are many **good** students in class.

delicious Pleasing to the taste. Bran muffins are *delicious* for breakfast.

excellent Very good. José gets *excellent* grades in spelling.

great Wonderful. The crowd thought the show was *great.*

nice Enjoyable. We had a *nice* afternoon visiting the zoo.

okay All right. Wearing boots to class on snowy days is *okay.*

ANTONYMS: awful, bad, terrible

happy *adj.* Full of joy; glad. I like books with **happy** endings.

cheerful Joyous. The colorful flowers make a *cheerful* room.

delightful Giving joy or pleasure. This is a *delightful* book about growing up.

glad Pleased or happy. The puppy was *glad* with the new bone.

merry Full of fun and laughter. The elf in the story did a *merry* little dance.

ANTONYMS: sad, unhappy

hard *adj.* Difficult to do or understand. The test was **hard** for a few students.

difficult Not easy. Elena is having a *difficult* time learning Chinese.

tough Very difficult. Moving the piano downstairs was a *tough* job.

ANTONYMS: easy, simple

high *adj.* Reaching a long distance up. The Rocky Mountains are **high** mountains.

lofty Very high. Their goal was to climb to the top of that *lofty* peak.

tall Of more than average height. My brother is *tall* for his age.

towering Very high. The Empire State Building is a *towering* skyscraper.

ANTONYM: low

hot *adj.* Having a high temperature. The room is **hot** in the afternoon.

burning On fire; hot. *Burning* leaves make my eyes water.

scalding Heated until almost boiling. Ice will melt quickly in *scalding* water.

warm Having or feeling a little heat. Jessie read a book by the *warm* fire.

ANTONYMS: chilly, cold, cool

WRITER'S THESAURUS

huge *adj.* Very big. The **huge** jet carried hundreds of passengers.

big Of great size. Texas is a *big* state.

enormous Much larger than usual. Some elephants have *enormous* ears.

giant Very large. A *giant* rock blocked the entrance to the cave.

gigantic Incredibly large. The trunk of a redwood tree is *gigantic.*

immense Extremely large, but still normal. We could not see the top of the *immense* building.

large Not small. Our *large* van can seat twelve people.

ANTONYMS: little, miniature, small, tiny

hurt *v.* To cause pain, injury, or damage. Hot, spicy foods **hurt** my mouth.

damage To cause injury to. Fires *damage* forests every year.

harm To destroy. Hot, dry summers can *harm* grass.

injure To harm or damage. Jenny did not *injure* herself when she fell.

ANTONYMS: aid, assist, help

I

important *adj.* Having great worth or meaning. This story is **important** to me.

meaningful Full of meaning. She wrote a *meaningful* news story for the school newspaper.

significant Having a special meaning. The score of the last game is *significant* to the team.

ANTONYM: unimportant

L

like *v.* To enjoy. I **like** to walk in the rain.

enjoy To get pleasure from. Puppies *enjoy* playing with toys.

love To enjoy very much. Parents *love* their children.

prefer To like better. I *prefer* corn to spinach.

ANTONYMS: dislike, hate

lonely *adj.* Feeling alone. Thoughts of my lost pet make me **lonely**.

alone Without anyone near. Mrs. Long lives *alone* in that big house.

homesick Unhappy because of longing for home. Lindsey was so busy at her grandparents' house that she was not *homesick* at all.

lonesome Feeling alone. Playing by myself makes me *lonesome.*

ANTONYM: accompanied

long *adj.* Stretching a great distance between two points. We traveled on a **long** highway.

distant Far off in space or time. Grandmother's house is in a *distant* town.

far Very distant. They came by boat from a *far* country.

ANTONYM: short

loud *adj.* Not quiet. My alarm clock is **loud**.

deafening Very loud. Construction noises are *deafening.*

noisy Making a loud sound. Students are *noisy* at recess.

thunderous Shaking with loud noise. The planes at the airport make a *thunderous* noise.

ANTONYMS: quiet, silent, still

M

mighty *adj.* Extremely strong; powerful. The mighty storm caused trees to fall.

husky Big and strong. The *husky* boxer practiced with a punching bag.

powerful Strong. The fence blew down during a *powerful* windstorm.

strong Having great power. Only a *strong* person can move a piano.

ANTONYMS: powerless, weak

more *adj.* Larger in quantity. I have more homework than my brother and sister.

additional Extra. Put two *additional* chairs at the table for our company.

further Added. There will be *further* news about the snowstorm later.

greater More in number. That tree has a *greater* number of branches this season.

ANTONYM: less

most *adj.* Almost all. Most birds fly.

a lot of A large number of. *A lot of* students ride the bus to school.

a majority of More than half. *A majority of* the students voted for our class president.

many Not few. *Many* skiers enjoy this mountain.

much Great amount. We wished him *much* happiness.

ANTONYM: least

move *v.* To go. All day long, visitors move past the new monument.

dodge To get out of the way. People *dodge* raindrops by walking under the eaves of buildings.

flow To move in a stream like water. Frozen water cannot *flow* through pipes.

travel To go from one place to another. We will *travel* to the city.

ANTONYMS: stay, stop

O

often *adv.* Many times. We often visit shut-ins.

always At all times. Sergio *always* uses an umbrella on rainy days.

frequently Happening time after time. That old car *frequently* backfires.

repeatedly Done again and again. Our teacher praises us *repeatedly*.

ANTONYMS: never, seldom

old *adj.* Lived or existed for a long while. The old house was built in 1910.

aged Old. Their *aged* dog will be 10 years old in October.

former From an earlier time. My *former* teacher was from Atlanta.

worn Aged or used. The *worn* leather shoes had holes.

ANTONYMS: new, young

P

peaceful *adj.* Not fighting. The leaders of the peaceful nations met last month.

calm Still. The sea looks very *calm* today.

quiet Free from noise. It is *quiet* in the library.

restful Relaxing. The sick child spent a *restful* morning reading in bed.

ANTONYMS: loud, noisy

pretty *adj.* Nice-looking; pleasant. We painted the bedroom a pretty shade of blue.

attractive Causing interest. Grandmother wore an *attractive* yellow dress.

beautiful Lovely. The *beautiful* lake was blue and clear.

gorgeous Very good-looking. Florists fill vases with *gorgeous* roses.

handsome Pleasing in appearance. Cinderella married the *handsome* prince.

lovely Very attractive. Our *lovely* new house is made of brick.

ANTONYMS: plain, ugly

proud *adj.* Thinking well of. I am **proud** of my good report card.

pleased Happy. Everyone was *pleased* with the potluck dinner.

vain Thinking too highly of oneself. Staring into a mirror may be a sign of a *vain* attitude.

ANTONYMS: ashamed, disappointed, humble

R

really *adv.* In fact. Is Wichita **really** the largest city in Kansas?

actually As a matter of fact. Those zookeepers *actually* train lions.

greatly Very much. Uncle Bob *greatly* appreciates our visits.

indeed Truly. Winter in Alaska is cold *indeed*.

truly Really. Niagara Falls is *truly* beautiful.

ANTONYM: doubtfully

red *adj.* Having the color of ripe tomatoes. Beth's cheeks were as **red** as a rose.

blushing Red in the face from shyness or embarassment. The *blushing* stranger picked up the groceries he had dropped.

flushed Red in the face. Daniel was *flushed* from running home.

ruby Deep red. In *The Wizard of Oz*, Dorothy wore *ruby* slippers.

ruddy Healthy-looking. The little boy had a round face and a *ruddy* complexion.

scarlet Very bright red. Little Red Riding Hood wore a *scarlet* cape.

remain *v.* To stay. I will **remain** at the office for an hour.

continue To go on with. The girls will *continue* the game after time-out.

last To go on. The show will *last* for two hours.

stay To remain in a certain place. We *stay* at school all day.

ANTONYMS: depart, go, leave

rise *v.* To get up after sleeping; waken. I **rise** each day by 7:00 A.M.

ascend To go up. The cars slowly *ascend* the icy hill.

climb To move up. They *climb* stairs quickly.

stand To get up after sitting or lying down. We *stand* to recite our poems.

waken To get up after sleeping. We *waken* the other campers at dawn.

ANTONYMS: descend, drop, fall

run *v.* To move quickly. We often **run** during recess.

gallop To go at a fast pace. Horses *gallop* with all four feet off the ground.

race To move very quickly. My brother and I *race* to the ringing phone.

rush To hurry. The players *rush* to the field for the game.

stampede To rush in a group. Cattle will *stampede* if frightened.

ANTONYM: walk

S

sad *adj.* Unhappy. This is a sad movie.

dark Without light. Shades make the room *dark*.

gloomy Not happy. Dark clouds make the day seem *gloomy*.

gray Gloomy. *Gray* clouds are often a sign of rain.

miserable Very unhappy. The team was *miserable* after losing.

unhappy Not joyful. The puppy in the pet store cage looks *unhappy*.

ANTONYMS: glad, happy, joyful

same *adj.* Not different. Pancakes and waffles are sometimes made from the same batter.

alike Similar. Twins sometimes look *alike*.

equal Having the same measure or amount. Mrs. Chuen and Mr. Silver have an *equal* number of students in their classes.

identical Exactly alike. Jessica and Jamie are *identical* twins.

unchanged Not any different. The old house has remained *unchanged* for years.

ANTONYM: different

see *v.* To be aware of or to look at things. Dad can see better with his glasses.

notice To pay attention to. Did you *notice* the rainbow?

understand To get the meaning of. Now I *understand* what you mean.

watch To look at. Fans *watch* the weekend games.

ANTONYM: ignore

seldom *adv.* Not often. We seldom eat at a restaurant.

least Almost never. The most serious people joke the *least*.

less Not as often. Third-graders write *less* than fifth-graders.

never Not ever. I have *never* seen a blue moon.

rarely Hardly ever. We *rarely* miss the school bus.

ANTONYMS: always, often

short *adj.* Not long. *The Giving Tree* is a short but meaningful book.

brief Not long from beginning to end. Marta will give a *brief* speech.

low Not tall. Landscapers plant *low* bushes in front of windows.

small Little. The *small* child could not reach the light switch.

ANTONYM: long

slip *v.* To shift or move accidentally. Careful skaters do not slip on the ice.

escape To get away from. Birds *escape* cold weather by flying south.

fall To shift or drop. Leaves *fall* from trees on windy days.

slide To fall by accident. An unsecured wagon may *slide* down a steep hill.

slow *adj.* Not fast. The runners got off to a slow start.

inactive Not energetic. Watching television is an *inactive* pastime.

sluggish Lazy. Coming into a warm room from outdoors makes me feel *sluggish*.

ANTONYMS: exciting, fast, quick

smell *n.* An odor. Do skunks have a strong smell?

fragrance A pleasant, sweet smell. The *fragrance* of the roses filled the room.

odor Any smell, pleasant or unpleasant. I love the *odor* of freshly cut hay.

scent A faint smell. The cooking turkey gave the kitchen a wonderful *scent*.

T

take *v.* To get hold of. Please **take** my hand when crossing the street.

grab To seize suddenly. Baby birds *grab* food from their parents' beaks.

grasp To hold firmly with the hand. Kim could not *grasp* the big snowball with her mittens.

obtain To get. Students must *obtain* library passes.

ANTONYM: give

tangy *adj.* Having a sharp, strong taste or flavor. The salad dressing is **tangy**.

sharp Strong in taste or odor. Some cheddar cheese has a *sharp* taste.

spicy Peppery or flavorful. Grandfather prefers *spicy* foods to bland ones.

ANTONYMS: bland, mild

taste *v.* To experience the flavor of something. Wait until you **taste** the barbecue sauce!

eat To chew and swallow. Did you *eat* fruit with lunch?

sample To test by trying. Customers may *sample* the new cheese spread at our display.

savor To taste with pleasure. Diners can *savor* Greek food at the new restaurant.

thin *adj.* Not thick. Spaghetti is a **thin** pasta.

slender Not fat or plump. Although Josh was a plump baby, he is now very *slender*.

slight Small. Race horses have *slight* builds compared to plow horses.

sparse Not growing close together. The man's hat covered his *sparse* hair.

ANTONYMS: fat, thick

U

ugly *adj.* Not pleasing to look at. Mounds of **ugly** garbage spoiled the view.

offensive Disagreeable. The *offensive* odor finally disappeared.

unsightly Displeasing. My room is an *unsightly* mess.

ANTONYMS: beautiful, pleasant, pretty

W

walk *v.* To go on foot at a normal speed. In case of fire, **walk** to the nearest exit.

hike To take a long walk. Some campers *hike* on steep paths.

march To walk with even steps. All students may *march* in the parade.

step To walk a short distance. Careful people *step* around puddles.

stroll To walk slowly. Mother and Father *stroll* in the park after dinner.

ANTONYM: run

wise *adj.* Not foolish. **Wise** people enjoy learning new things.

clever Very smart. A *clever* fox will avoid a trap.

intelligent Having great ability to understand and learn. *Intelligent* cats are easily trained.

smart Bright or intelligent. A *smart* dog learns quickly.

ANTONYMS: foolish, unwise

INDEX

INDEX

F

G

H

I

J

L

O

P

period, 32–35, 48, 80–81, 84–85, 96, 97, 98, 176–177, 185, 384–385, 390–391, 394–395, 396–397, 405, 408, EP4, EP5, EP13, EP15, EP52, WH2, WH13–14, WH51

    question mark, 32–33, 48, 98, 384–385, 400–401, 405, EP4, EP52, WH2, WH13

    quotation marks, 176–177, 185, 398–399, 400–401, 405, 409, EP28, EP59, EP60, WH25

Purpose for reading, 10, 52, 104, 150, 192, 236, 280, 326, 366

Purpose for writing, 21, 63, 111, 116, 144, 159, 201, 249, 291, 337, 375, G6

    to entertain, 149–151, 191–193, 202

    to express, 9–12, 235–239

    to inform, 51–57, 71, 103–107, 149–151, 325–328, 337, 365–368, 376

    to persuade, 279–283, 291, 298, 299, WH23

Q

Question mark, 32–33, 48, 384–385, 400–401, 405, EP4, EP52, WH2, WH13

Quotation marks, 176–177, 185, 398–399, 400–401, 405, 409, EP28, EP59, EP60, WH25

Quotations, direct, 176–177, 184, 400–401, 409, EP28, EP60, WH25

R

Reader's interest, capturing the, 332, 361

Reading model, 9–12, 51–55, 103–107, 149–151, 191–193, 235–239, 279–283, 325–328, 365–368

Reference books, 334, 347, 349, 353, 429–431. *See also* Dictionary; Encyclopedia.

Reports

    analyzing a, 329–330, 360

    book, 436–437, WH33

    research, 325–343, 344, 345, 360–362, WH34–35

Responding and revising, 6, 22–23, 64–65, 117–118, 160–161, 203–204, 250–251, 292–293, 338–339, 377–378, G6–7

Responding to literature, 12, 55, 107, 151, 193, 239, 283, 328, 368

Response group, 67, G7

Revising. *See also* Responding and revising.

    workshops, 24, 66, 119, 162, 205, 252, 294, 340, 379

Rhymes and rhyming words, 245–246, G9. *See also* Literary skills; Poem; Writing.

Rhythm, 245–246, G9. *See also* Literary Skills; Poem; Writing.

S

Sachs, Marilyn, 149–151

Science, 28, 70, 124, 166, 210, 256, 330, 382

Sentences, 29, 30–41, 44, 45, 48–49, 345, 358, 359, 386–387, EP3–5,WH2–3

    agreement in, 168–169, EP24, WH17

    compound, 162, 340, 350–351, 354–355, 358, 362–363, 386–387, EP49, WH2

    declarative, 32–33, 48, 98, 318, 384–385, EP4, WH2

    exclamatory, 34–35, 48, 98, 384–385, EP5, WH2

    fragments, 354–355, 363, EP51

    imperative, 34–35, 48, 98, 318, 384–385, EP5, WH2

    interrogative, 32–33, 48, 98, 318, 384–385, EP4, WH2

    joining with *and,* 119, 160–161, 294, 340

    predicate of, 36–37, 40–41, 49, 99, 126–127, 128–129, 130–131, 186, 294, 348–349, 362, 410, 415, EP8, EP48, WH3

    punctuation of, 32–35, 48, 98, 352–353, 354–355, 363, 384–385, 407–408, EP4, EP5, EP52, WH12, WH13–14

    run-on, 252, 354–355, 363, EP51

    series in, 119, 352–353, 363, 386–387, EP50, EP53

    subject of, 36–37, 38–39, 49, 98–99, 186, 294, 346–347, 362, 410, 415, EP6, EP7, EP47, WH3, WH17

    topic, 109, 330

Series. *See* Comma; Punctuation, comma.

Simile, 240–241, 244, 245–246, 275

Singular nouns, 74–75, 92, 95–96, 100, 186–187, 318–319, 410–411, EP10, WH4

    possessive, 86–87, 97, 101, 186–187, 318–319, 411, EP16, WH4

Social studies, 70, 166, 210, 256, 298, 344

INDEX

Y

4
5
6
I 7
J 8

continued from page IV

Production and Layout: Tom Vroman Associates

Photo Acknowledgments

PHOTOGRAPHS: Pages 3, HBJ Photo/Rob Downey; 6(t), HBJ Photo/Rob Downey; (b), HBJ Photo/Rob Downey; 7(t), HBJ Photo/Rob Downey; (b), HBJ Photo/Rob Downey.

UNIT 1: 8, HBJ Photo/Charlie Burton; 17, HBJ Photo; 20, Lew Merrim/Monkmeyer Press; 26(t), HBJ Photo; (1), HBJ Photo; (r), HBJ Photo; 27, HBJ Photo

UNIT 2: 50, HBJ Photo/David Phillips; 60, HBJ Photo; 67, HBJ Photo; 69, HBJ Photo

UNIT 3: 102, HBJ/Photo/Rodney Jones; 113, HBJ Photo; 121(1), HBJ Photo; (r) HBJ Photo; 122, HBJ Photo

UNIT 4: 148, HBJ Photo/Rodney Jones; 149, Morris Sachs; 156, HBJ Photo/Mark Cunningham; 164, HBJ Photo/Mark Cunningham; 165, HBJ Photo/Mark Cunningham; 179, HBJ Photo/Mark Cunningham.

UNIT 5: 190, HBJ Photo/Charlie Burton; 191, Van Williams/Harper & Row; 198, HBJ Photo/Mark Cunningham; 207, HBJ Photo; 208, HBJ Photo; 209, HBJ Photo/Mark Cunningham.

UNIT 6: 234, HBJ Photo/Rodney Jones; 247, HBJ Photo/Mark Cunningham; 254(t), HBJ Photo/Mark Cunningham; (1), HBJ Photo/Mark Cunningham; (r), HBJ Photo/Mark Cunningham; 255(1), HBJ Photo/Mark Cunningham; (r), HBJ Photo; 258, Suzie Bleeden/Globe Photos; 260, George Lange/Outline Press.

UNIT 7: 278, HBJ Photo; 279, Jill Krementz; 288, HBJ Photo; 296(1), HBJ Photo; (r), HBJ Photo; 300, AP/Wide World Photos.

UNIT 8: 324, HBJ Photo/Charlie Burton; 333, HBJ Photo; 335, HBJ Photo; 352(t), J. W. Mowbray/Photo Researchers; (c), Alese & Mort Pechter/The Stock Market; (b), Donna McLaughlin/The Stock Market.

UNIT 9: 364, HBJ Photo/Charlie Burton; 373, HBJ Photo/Mark Cunningham; 381, HBJ Photo/Mark Cunningham.